Ralph Wardlaw, J. S Wardlaw

Lectures on the Epistle to the Romans

Ralph Wardlaw, J. S Wardlaw

Lectures on the Epistle to the Romans

ISBN/EAN: 9783744679305

Printed in Europe, USA, Canada, Australia, Japan

Cover: Foto ©ninafisch / pixelio.de

More available books at **www.hansebooks.com**

POSTHUMOUS WORKS

OF THE

REV. RALPH WARDLAW, D.D.

EDITED BY HIS SON,

THE REV. J. S. WARDLAW, A.M.

VOL. VI.

A. FULLARTON & CO.:
44 SOUTH BRIDGE, EDINBURGH·
AND 115 NEWGATE STREET, LONDON.

MDCCCLXI.

ON THE

EPISTLE TO THE ROMANS,

BY THE

REV. RALPH WARDLAW, D D.

EDITED BY HIS SON,

THE REV. J. S. WARDLAW, A.M.

VOL. III.

A. FULLARTON & CO.:
44, SOUTH BRIDGE, EDINBURGH;
AND 115 NEWGATE STREET, LONDON.

MDCCCLXI.

LECTURE XLIX.

ROMANS XI. 7—32.

"What then? Israel hath not obtained that which he seeketh for; but the election hath obtained it, and the rest were blinded (according as it is written, God hath given them the spirit of slumber, eyes that they should not see, and ears that they should not hear) unto this day. And David saith, Let their table be made a snare, and a trap, and a stumblingblock, and a recompense unto them, let their eyes be darkened that they may not see, and bow down their back alway. I say then, Have they stumbled that they should fall? God forbid: but rather through their fall salvation is come unto the Gentiles, for to provoke them to jealousy. Now, if the fall of them be the riches of the world, and the diminishing of them the riches of the Gentiles; how much more their fulness? For I speak to you Gentiles, inasmuch as I am the apostle of the Gentiles, I magnify mine office; if by any means I may provoke to emulation them which are my flesh, and might save some of them. For if the casting away of them be the reconciling of the world, what shall the receiving of them be, but life from the dead? For if the first-fruit be holy, the lump is also holy; and if the root be holy, so are the branches. And if some of the branches be broken off, and thou, being a wild olive-tree, wert graffed in among them, and with them partakest of the root and fatness of the olive-tree; boast not against the branches: but if thou boast, thou bearest not the root, but the root thee. Thou wilt say then, The branches were broken off, that I might be graffed in. Well; because of unbelief they were broken off, and thou standest by faith. Be not high-minded, but fear: for if God spared not the natural branches, take heed lest he also spare not thee. Behold therefore the goodness and severity of God: on them which fell, severity; but toward thee, goodness, if thou continue in his goodness; otherwise thou also shalt be cut off. And they also, if they abide not still in unbelief, shall be graffed in: for God is able to graff them in again. For if thou wert cut out of the olive-tree, which is wild by nature, and wert graffed contrary to nature into a good olive-tree; how much more shall these, which be the natural branches, be graffed into their own olive-tree? For I would not, brethren, that ye should be ignorant of this mystery, (lest ye should be wise in your own conceits,) that blindness in part is happened to Israel, until the fulness of the Gentiles be come in. And so all Israel shall be saved; as it is written, There shall come out of Sion the Deliverer, and shall turn away ungodliness from Jacob. For this is my covenant unto them, when I shall take away their sins. As concerning the gospel, they are enemies for your sakes: but as touching the election, they are beloved for the fathers' sakes. For the gifts and calling of God are without repentance. For as ye in times past have not believed God, yet have now obtained mercy through their unbelief; even so have these also now not believed, that through your mercy they also may obtain mercy. For God hath concluded them all in unbelief, that he might have mercy upon all."

WE take this passage as a whole, for the sake of dividing it into its parts, and treating each of its topics in order; by which means needless repetition will be avoided, and a clearer view given of the contents and objects of the chapter.

There are *four* points to which it calls our attention; bearing, however, a very intimate relation to each other. They are, the rejection of the Jews, and the calling of the Gentiles; the restoration of the Jews and the fulness of the Gentiles;—with the connexion between the first and second, and between the second and third.

We shall notice each of these points distinctly:—verse 7. "What then? Israel hath not obtained that which he seeketh for; but the election hath obtained it, and the rest were blinded." What means the Apostle by "*that which he seeketh for.*"—The thing "sought for" was justification before God;—acceptance in His sight and eternal life.* By "*Israel*" is meant Israel *as a body*—the large majority: just as the people in Elijah's time who worshipped Baal might be called Israel, in distinction from the "seven thousand" who had not given way to that defection from Jehovah, and who were His *reserve*,—His *chosen remnant.* They did not attain the object of their desire, because they did not seek it in the right way.† They would have it *by works* when the God with whom they had to do had declared that it could be attained only *by grace:* and so the pride of their hearts proved *their* ruin, as it has proved the ruin of multitudes besides.

"But *the election* hath obtained it." The distinction previously made by the Apostle‡ is thus carried forward through

---

* Comp. chap. ix. 30—33.   † Chap. x. 2, 3.   ‡ Chap. ix. 6.

all his statements and reasonings: "the election" being a designation marking out a certain proportion of Israel from the rest—Jew from Jew—not Jews nationally from Gentiles nationally. That which they "sought after and did not attain to" was not *privilege*—for privilege they *did* obtain and enjoy. That which "the election" *did* obtain, therefore, was not privilege; for in *this* they were not distinguished from the rest. It was something more,—something spiritual and permanent. It was justification before God; eternal life. And there can be no reasonable doubt, surely, that what "the election," in distinction from others, actually obtained, was that *to which they were chosen*. Their election, therefore, was not national election to privilege, but personal election to salvation. To this they were "chosen through sanctification of the Spirit and belief of the truth;" and their "obtaining" it was the result and fulfilment of the divine purpose in their election.

"The rest were *blinded:*"—or *hardened.** It is the same thing whether we regard them as left to the self-induced hardness of their hearts, or to the blindness which naturally results from that hardness. All that, in either case, is meant, is, their being judicially left to the influence of their wilful and criminal prejudices and enmity "against the Lord and against his Christ."—And that they should thus harden themselves in unbelief and sin, was matter of prediction by the prophets:—verse 8. "According as it is written, God hath given them the spirit of slumber, eyes that they should not see, and ears that they should not hear unto this day."†

The figurative expression, "having eyes and not seeing, and having ears and not hearing," seems to describe strongly the ignorance arising from the state of the disposition; not from want of means and opportunities of knowledge, but from want of *heart* to knowledge, as the wise man expresses it. There is a wilful shutting of the mind to knowledge, as

---

* ἐπωρώθησαν.   † See Isa. xxix. 10; vi. 9, 10.

there is a wilful shutting of the eyes to light.* This is the ignorance that is criminal. In ignorance arising from *natural incapacity* of understanding, there can be no degree of blameworthiness—unless the incapacity has been the result of moral causes. Then there *is* sin. But the sin lies not in the ignorance arising from the incapacity, but in the moral causes from which the incapacity has arisen. As criminal ignorance springs from aversion of heart to the truth, it implies some kind of discernment of the truth; inasmuch as there can be no aversion manifested to that which is not at all discerned. The discernment is simply an intellectual apprehension of the meaning of certain propositions, without any perception of their excellence and divinity. There would be no wilful shutting of the eyes against the light, unless there were some perception of it, and some feeling of its painfulness. The difference between what light is to the eye of the body and what truth is to the eye of the mind lies here:—in the sensibility of a diseased eye which makes the light painful, there is nothing morally wrong: but the distemper which makes truth painful to the mind's eye, is a moral distemper; the alienation of the heart from God. It is this that produces the shutting out of the truth: this that constitutes the real cause of unbelief.†

When God is spoken of as "*giving* them eyes that they should not see, and ears that they should not hear," the terms are to be explained on the principle before laid down‡—as meaning no more than His giving them up to the influence of a perverse heart and will, by which the eyes of the understanding are shut and blinded.—These sentiments are in accordance with the simple statements of the word of God;§ and the justness of the views thus given will appear further from the next quotation:—verses 9, 10. "And David saith, Let their table be made a snare, and a trap, and a stumblingblock, and a recompense unto them: let their

---

* Compare Jer. v. 21, 23; Ezek. xii. 2; John viii. 43; Rom. i. 28.
† See John iii. 18—21.   ‡ Comp. chap. ix. 17, 18.
§ See John ix. 39—41; xii. 35—41; Matth. xiii. 10—15, and Isa. xxix. 10, in connexion with verses 13, 14.

eyes be darkened, that they may not see, and bow down their back alway."*

The Psalm from which these words are cited relates to "the sufferings of Christ and the glory that should follow."† "*Their table*" may be taken as meaning their prosperity and the abundance of good things enjoyed by them in Canaan. This deceived them. They drew from their enjoyments false inferences about the favour of God toward them, and their own consequent security. The abundance which God bestowed thus proved a snare. It should have drawn them to Him; it alienated them from Him. They forgot the Giver in His gifts; or rested in the gifts as a false and delusive pledge, independent of their faith and character, that it should always be well with them. Thus—"the prosperity of fools destroys them."‡—The same language of the 69th Psalm might be applied to the Gospel, considered, as it often is, under the image of *a feast.*§ This was a "*table*" spread for them. It was designed "for their welfare," even for their soul's life and nourishment and salvation. But the provision suited not their taste. And so it proved "a snare and a trap." They stumbled at it; and brought on themselves a threatened and merited "recompense." ||

The phrase in verse tenth, "*Bow down their back alway*," corresponds to the expression in the Psalm, "make their loins continually to shake." ¶ The meaning is obviously the same. The reference is to the burden and yoke of slavery and oppression—under which they should bow down and their limbs tremble.** It represents, however, in general, a state of sorrow and depression of spirit. "The Lord raiseth up them that be bowed down."††

The psalm is *prophetic*. And the terms of seeming imprecation may be rendered, as in many other places, by terms

---

* Ps. lxix. 22, 23.
† Comp. verse 4 with John xv. 25: verse 9 with John ii. 17; Rom. xv. 2: verse 21 with Matth. xxvii. 34, 48, &c. In Acts i. 20, verse 25 is applied to Judas the traitor.
‡ Prov. i. 29—33. § Isa. xxv. 6; Matth. xxii. 1—6.
|| Isa. viii. 14, 15. ¶ It is so in the Hebrew.—ED.
** Comp. Lev. xxvi. 13. †† Ps. cxlvi. 8.

of simple prediction, "Their table *shall be* made a snare, and a trap, and a stumblingblock, and a recompense unto them." At the same time, taking our translation as it stands, it may be regarded, when considered as uttered by the inspiration of God's Spirit, as expressive of *a holy acquiescence* in the righteous judgments of God upon His obstinate enemies. It is like saying—as the Israelites were commanded to say, when they struck their tents and began their marches—" Let God arise, let his enemies be scattered: let them also that hate him flee before him."*

The rejection of the Jews, and the principal and proximate cause of it, had been long ago predicted by Moses.† That cause was *their* rejection of the Messiah :—" Who both killed the Lord Jesus, and their own prophets, and have persecuted us; and they please not God, and are contrary to all men: forbidding us to speak to the Gentiles that they might be saved, to fill up their sin alway: for the wrath is come upon them to the uttermost."‡ "*The wrath*" is the wrath predicted against them for their rebellion; and is here connected with their rejection of Christ and the persecution of his followers.

We have seen before, that this rejection was not to be *total.*§ Was it then to be *final*—"Have they stumbled that they should fall?" (v. 11.) that is, so as to fall *irrecoverably?* The reply is a strong negative. But the subject of their restoration must be considered hereafter. We have *now* further to notice the connexion of their being rejected with the calling of the Gentiles, and *their* introduction to the privileges of the church—"I say then, Have they stumbled that they should fall? God forbid: but rather through their fall salvation is come unto the Gentiles, for to provoke them to jealousy. Now if the fall of them be the riches of the world, and the diminishing of them the riches of the Gen-

---

* Psal. lxviii. 1.
† Deut. xviii. 15—19. with Acts iii. 22, 23. and Deut. xxviii. 47. 48. 58, 59, 62, &c.; and particularly verse 49, &c., and 63. &c.; with Luke xix. 41—44, &c.
‡ 1 Thess. ii. 15, 16. § Verses 1 and 5.

tiles; how much more their fulness? For if the casting away of them be the reconciling of the world, what shall the receiving of them be, but life from the dead? As concerning the gospel, they are enemies for your sakes: but as touching the election, they are beloved for the fathers' sakes. Ye in times past have not believed God, yet have now obtained mercy through their unbelief." *

The Jews, the seed of Abraham, Isaac, and Jacob, were long, by the sovereign choice of Jehovah, his peculiar people. There were various intimations directly and indirectly given that His purpose in choosing them was not confined to their own benefit, but was connected with his designs of mercy to the whole world. There were Gentiles in Abraham's own family, which was the infant church of Israel; there were laws for the admission into that church afterwards, of Gentile proselytes; and God's house was called the "house of prayer for all nations." There were many prophecies of the calling of the Gentiles into the church in "the fulness of time;" although, like most other predictions relating to the kingdom of Messiah, they were much misunderstood even by good men: nor were the minds of the Apostles and followers of Jesus cleared of their darkness on the subject, till, by special revelation, the Lord intimated in vision *His* mind to Peter.

Not a few of the predictions concerning the calling of the Gentiles, are connected in the prophets with the accompanying intimation of the rejection of the Jews.† The one of these events is in the New Testament always represented as associated with the other; not properly as *an effect;* for there is no principle on which the one can be considered as *causing* the other—but as a designed attendant or consequence. It was God's revealed intention, that in case of the obstinate unbelief and pertinacious rebellion of the Jews, He would in righteous judgment, cast them off, and substitute the Gentiles in their room. It was only in this way that the

---

* Verses 11, 12, 15, 28, 30.
† See for example, Isa. xlix. 18—23.

calling of the Gentiles *arose out of* the rejection of the Jews. There was nothing in the latter that directly operated in the production of the former. It is otherwise, as we shall see, with the other branch of our subject. The restoration of the Jews will have, in various ways, a direct and powerful influence in bringing about "the fulness of the Gentiles." But as to the rejection of the Jews it only *made way* for the introduction of the Gentiles according to the intimated purpose of God.*

There are two ways indeed, in which the hostility of the Jews, and the divine judgments consequent upon it, *might* be considered as somewhat more closely connected with the benefit to the Gentiles—*First*, the effect of their hostility and persecution was to produce the more rapid and extensive diffusion of the Gospel among the Gentiles. By it the disciples and the teachers of Christianity were driven from Jerusalem and Judea, to scatter the seed of the word of the Lord among the surrounding peoples, and in the instances quoted from the Acts it appears, that the very refusal of the Jews was the occasion of *turning to the Gentiles*. —And *Secondly*, it is possible that in some instances, the judicial retribution sent on the Jews, being a fulfilment of prophecy, might contribute to the conviction, and so to the further bringing in, of the Gentiles. This, however, would only be in a very limited extent indeed.

The explanation of the different phrases—"if the fall of them be the riches of the world," (ver. 12.) "if the casting away of them be the reconciling of the world," (ver. 15.) is to be sought in the purpose of God, who had connected the one event with the other, and made the one to depend on the other, although both were, to His omniscient mind, alike certain. It was His purpose that "the unsearchable riches of Christ" should, by the Gospel, be communicated to the Gentile world, in consequence of their being refused by the worldly-minded Jews. It was His purpose, that the "word of reconciliation" should be proclaimed to the antecedently out-

---

* See Matth. xxi. 43; Acts xiii. 44—47; xviii. 5, 6; xxviii. 28, &c.

cast and alienated nations, and should be the means of bringing multitudes back from their wanderings and "reconciling" them to himself, in consequence of the stubborn refusal of His offers and entreaties as the God of salvation by the proud and infatuated seed of Abraham. It was simply *thus* that "the fall of them" was "the enriching," and the "casting away of them the reconciling, of the world." It was just as if a father should determine, and declare his determination, that if the presumptive heir to his estate should prove profligate and unworthy, the inheritance should descend to his younger son. It might then be said that the fall of the one was the enriching of the other. It was in the same way that the inheritance was taken from the Jews, and given to a nation that should "render the fruits" thereof to the divine proprietor.

The Apostle uses, in illustration of this, a natural and appropriate figure:*—verse 17. "And if some of the branches be broken off, and thou, being a wild olive-tree, wert graffed in among them, and with them partakest of the root and fatness of the olive-tree." The Church might be considered as planted, when Abraham was called. He was "*the root.*" This renders the reasoning of the Apostle clear and consistent. To make *Christ* the root, introduces perplexity and confusion into it.

Now observe. This church, which commenced with the calling of Abraham, is not represented as *annihilated* at the beginning of the New Testament dispensation, and another church as formed in its room. The "olive-tree" is not, in the figure, rooted up, and a fresh one planted. I can imagine nothing clearer than that, in this representation, the Church remains the same. Branches are broken off: other branches are grafted in: and, as we shall afterwards see, the restoration of the Jews is described by the "grafting in again," into the same tree, of the exscinded branches. The root and stock remain the same from first to last. If this does not represent the Church under the Old and New Testament dispen-

---

* Comp. Jer. xi. 16, 17.

sation as *radically* one and the same, I am at a loss to imagine in what way this sentiment could be more clearly conveyed.

In harmony with the figure, the Gentiles are represented as previously to their junction to the church, having been branches of a " wild olive " uncultivated, unpruned, unwatered, bearing no fruit unto God. This figurative representation of their natural state is illustrated by the plainer descriptions —" At that time ye were without Christ, being aliens from the commonwealth of Israel, and strangers from the covenants of promise, having no hope, and without God in the world:"—" Who in times past suffered all nations to walk in their own ways."*

The branches of "the wild olive " were "grafted in amongst them "—i. e., amongst the remaining branches of the "good olive." Does it not then follow that the Jews who believed continued in the church to which they already belonged? and that the New Testament church is therefore the same with the Old, only under a new form—more pure, select, and spiritual?—It is evident that the branches broken off were not broken off from the New Testament church; inasmuch as they never belonged to it: and yet those who are introduced into the New Testament church are not introduced into a church entirely distinct from the former,—and when they are restored, it is to the same church with that from which they had been ejected. Thus the Church, although changed and modified under various dispensations, continues substantially the same. There is no possibility, in my apprehension, of making anything like consistency of the Apostle's representations on any other principle than this.

The branches of the "wild olive" tree are "*cut out of it.*" This finely represents the deliverance of the Gentiles from their natural state by their conversion to God:—and, when transferred from their connexion with the "wild olive," in which they luxuriated only in the production of evil, they were grafted by the influence of the Spirit of God into the "good

---

* Eph. ii. 12; Acts xiv. 16.

olive," they partook with the remaining branches in its *root* and *fatness:*—in its *root;* that is, in the blessing of Abraham:* and of its *fatness,* that is, all the privileges and enjoyments of the church of God—and especially those divine communications from which all fruitfulness arises. The blessing was put into "the root" by Him who said to Abraham, "*In thee* shall all the families of the earth be blessed;" and it is partaken by being connected with the root: "For ye are all the children of God by faith in Christ Jesus."† Divine communications, privileges, and blessings were possessed before, but now more largely and freely. These are partaken by the Gentiles "*with them,*" that is, with the remaining branches —the believing Jews.‡

Such is the light in which we are taught to regard the casting off of the Jews and the bringing in of the Gentiles, and the connexion between the one and the other. Leaving, for the present, the other part of the subject, let us now attend to the practical improvement made by the Apostle of that part of it to which we have been attending. It is contained in verses 18—22: "Boast not against the branches: but if thou boast, thou bearest not the root, but the root thee. Thou wilt say then, The branches were broken off, that I might be graffed in. Well: because of unbelief they were broken off, and thou standest by faith. Be not high-minded, but fear: for if God spared not the natural branches, take heed lest he also spare not thee. Behold therefore the goodness and severity of God: on them which fell, severity; but towards thee, goodness, if thou continue in his goodness; otherwise thou also shalt be cut off."

Here are important lessons for us:—

1. *Humility.* All personal boasting being excluded by the grace of the Gospel, so is all glorying over others. Contempt and disdain are the effect of self-righteous pride and confidence. It is he who "trusts in himself that he is righteous," that "despises others." God might, in sovereignty,

---

* Eph. iii. 13, 14. † Gal. iii. 26.
‡ See Eph. ii. 11—22; iii. 6.

have spared and saved the natural branches, and ejected us, and allowed us to perish—" For he saith to Moses, I will have mercy on whom I will have mercy, and I will have compassion on whom I will have compassion."* It is " by grace that we are what we are:" and whenever we are duly convinced of this, and made to feel it, all contempt will be banished, and tender concern and pity will become our sentiment towards sinners generally, and equally our temper of mind towards those who have been by profession God's people, and have fallen away, and given evidence that they are "none of His." With right views of ourselves, we can despise no man; we must pity all. Only the pity must not imply approbation, or even any deficiency in the decidedness with which we condemn.

What more fitted to check the risings of pride in those whom the Apostle addressed, and to keep them humble, than the declaration, "Thou bearest not the root, but the root thee." It was in virtue of their being brought into connexion with Abraham "the root," that they enjoyed their privileges and blessings. The spirit of the words is, that the Jews have received *nothing* from the Gentiles, but the Gentiles *all* from the Jews.†

He supposes a ground that might be taken for boasting—verse 19. "Thou wilt say then, the branches were broken off, that I might be graffed in." When one supersedes another, he is apt to think he has some reason to be vain of it. The Jews were vain of their being preferred to other peoples as the chosen of God—yet God says to them, to humble them and check every such feeling of ungodly scorn—" Speak not thou in thine heart, after that the Lord thy God hath cast them out from before thee, saying, For my righteousness the Lord hath brought me in to possess this land: but for the wickedness of these nations the Lord doth drive them out from before thee." The same language might, in the full spirit of it, be applied to the Gentiles when taken in their room. They had no ground for glorying; the cause of the distinction

---

* Chap. ix. 15. † Comp. chap. xv. 7.

not lying at all in themselves. This leads to a further lesson—

2. *Vigilance.* He grants it to be as stated in verse nineteenth, in a certain sense; but it was not that the Gentiles were more worthy. He reminds them of the true cause of rejection, and the only way of standing, or of remaining in possession of the blessing—" Well: because of unbelief they were broken off, and thou standest *by faith.*" It was by faith that they had been brought into connexion with Abraham and with the church of God; and that faith was " not of themselves," but His gift. It is a humble principle. With all its confidence in God it associates diffidence of self. "Thou standest by faith; be not high-minded." "*High-mindedness*" is self-estimation and self-confidence; or professed confidence in God, but grounded on the notion of something in ourselves entitling us to trust as the reason of His favour. But this high-mindedness is perilous.* It is displeasing to God, and provokes the withdrawment of His countenance: "The proud he knoweth afar off."— "Be not high-minded, but *fear.*" "Blessed is the man that feareth." Had Peter *feared himself* as he *loved his Master* he had never fallen. The example they had before them of the rejection of the Jews was fitted to inspire this fear.† In this very case there was a salutary warning. *They* fell through unbelief.—"*Take heed, therefore,*" signifies, in this connexion—Beware of this example of unbelief; "hold fast the faith;" "cleave to the Lord." Think not that you stand, but "take heed lest you fall." Your standing is in the Lord, not in yourselves; look to Him for support. When the Apostle speaks of God's "*severity,*" he means not that it was beyond what was *due.* It was righteous—all righteous—even to the very utmost of it. His goodness to them had been wonderful—and characterized by long-tried patience and forbearance;—but the Gentiles are warned by the issue to beware of similar abuse of God's goodness to *them.* The Jews did not "continue in his goodness;" they forfeited it by their un-

---

* Prov. xvi. 18; xviii. 12. † Verses 21, 22.

belief and rebellion, in the face of all His multiplied and gracious admonitions and acts and gifts of kindness. The Gentiles were admitted to the enjoyment of His special goodness; but if they did not "continue in his goodness" they too might look for the same righteous severity, to cut them off in their turn.*

3. *Gratitude.* This will ever be proportioned to humility,—to a due sense of unworthiness. There can be no true gratitude where there is fancied *merit*. Just in as far as we feel the "goodness of God" to be undeserved, will we be thankful for it. How great has been His goodness to us Gentiles! Surely our hearts may well glow with deep and fervent gratitude in the view of "the riches of his grace" towards us! Let us manifest the sincerity and fervour of that gratitude by songs of praise, and by the more substantial evidence of practical godliness in all our walk and conversation, and by active zeal to advance the knowledge of God, and subjection to the sceptre of His grace, amongst Jews and Gentiles—looking in faith for the restoration of the one, and the fulness of the other.

Finally, let all who are living in the enjoyment of abundant and precious privilege, lay their responsibility to heart. O think of the just "severity" with which you must in the end be dealt with. The thread of life is slender and brittle:—yet you are trifling with your eternal interests,—trifling with a kind and gracious God, and with the concerns of your souls, while by this slender and brittle thread the sword of divine justice hangs trembling over your heads. Avail yourselves of God's present goodness, that you be not made to feel His future severity. Resist no longer the voice of an inviting and beseeching God. His voice is to you, even to you. It is the voice of love. It calls you to life and to happiness. But O sit not down in the listless

---

* It is remarkable how similar is the spirit of the admonitions addressed by God to Israel of old, and those addressed still to his professing people. Comp. Deut. viii. 11—20; x. 12—17; xxx. 15—20; with Heb. xii. 28, 29; Heb. iii. 19 with iv. 1; John xv. 2, 9, 10; Heb. x. 38; Rev. ii. 6, 10, 16, 26; iii. 3, 11, 15, 16, &c.

expectation that there will never be a change—that the goodness will last always, and be the same hereafter that it is now. He now smiles and invites you to Himself:—but be assured, if you will not comply with His invitation, there *is* a time coming—a time at hand, when He will frown you away from His presence. Flatter not yourselves with the weak and wicked sentimentalism that there can never be severity with God. Is not the very use you are making of this sentiment fearfully criminal—flattering yourselves in sin because you know that He is good! It will be the severity of just retribution that shall say to you—" Because I have called, and ye refused; I have stretched out my hand, and no man regarded; but ye have set at nought all my counsel, and would none of my reproof: I also will laugh at your calamity; I will mock when your fear cometh."

LECTURE L.

ROMANS XI. 7—32.

(SECOND DISCOURSE.)

THE present state of the Jewish people is without a parallel in the history of the world. Many kingdoms and empires, some of them of vast extent, and of high renown, have been invaded and subdued by others, and have either been entirely annihilated, or have been incorporated with their conquerors, and have lost their name and their separate existence. But here was a comparatively small people;—assailed by the victorious arms of imperial Rome;—the miserable victims of unheard of massacre and destruction; of tribulation, "such as had not been from the beginning of the world till that time, nor has been since, nor shall be hereafter;" driven from the land of their fathers, and dispersed through "every kindred, and tongue, and people, and nation." Wherever they have come, they have been an abject, despised, proscribed, and outcast race; "a proverb, and a by-word, and a hissing among all nations:" and amidst universal degradation, on the one hand, and some solitary but unsuccessful attempts to naturalize them, on the other, they have, to this day, scattered as they are, remained a distinct people, objects of marked separation, and, as far as their situation in different countries has admitted, with their own customs, their own synagogues, and the wretched remnants, the corrupted and pitiful mockery, of their own ancient worship. In this unprecedented and anomalous condition, have they continued, for the long period of more than seventeen successive centuries.—The facts of their history, compared with the predictions of Moses and the prophets in the Old, and of Christ himself in the New Testament, are most eminently fitted to establish our faith. The remote date of the former class of predictions is ascertained by the clearest and most unexceptionable evidence. The predictions themselves are the more remarkable, from the singularity and unlikelihood of the case: and, in despite of the vain attempts of deistical and political speculators to account for it on ordinary principles, the condition of this singular people has presented a kind of permanent miracle in attestation of the truth of God.

It is in a religious point of view, that their situation is especially interesting to the Christian mind.

The context represents them, as in a state of spiritual infatuation, or judicial blindness. For the "blindness which has happened to Israel," is a fulfilment of the prophetic imprecation, "Let their eyes be darkened, that they may not see:"—and never indeed to any people could the expression with greater truth be applied, that "God had sent them strong delusion, that they should believe a lie."—When Jesus was on earth, he thus warned them: "Yet a little while is the light with you: walk while ye have the light, lest darkness come upon you; for he that walketh in darkness knoweth not whither he goeth. While ye have light, believe in the light, that ye may be the children of light:"* and, condemning their obstinate incredulity as to *His* claims, and anticipating their credulous admission of the claims of others, "I am come in my Father's name, and ye receive me not; if another shall come in his own name, him ye will receive:"†—a declaration which was soon after affectingly verified, in the eagerness with which they listened to the pretensions, and embraced the offers, and followed the delusive counsels, of every miserable impostor, who, amidst their threatened and accumulated distresses, gave himself out as the deliverer and restorer of their nation,—the promised

* John xii. 35, 36.   † John v. 43.

Messiah. And, oh! how thick the veil of prejudice and enmity which "even unto this day remains upon their minds!" How clear, how minute, how full, is the accomplishment of the predictions relative to the Messiah, in Jesus of Nazareth! They themselves are perplexed and confounded,—reduced to the most wretched shifts, or put entirely to a stand, in their attempts to explain them otherwise. Yet with the most infatuated pertinacity, they persist in rejecting His claims: and, with the exception of such as have fallen into total infidelity (of whom the number, it is to be feared, is not small,) both those amongst them who think, and those who do not think, are vainly looking for another.

When we contemplate this people in their present state, we feel it difficult to persuade ourselves, that they are the same nation, whose wonderful history forms so large a portion of the records of inspiration. We behold them "scattered and peeled;"—outcasts of earth and heaven; treated as the "filth of the world, and the offscouring of all things." And is this the people who, in far remote times, were redeemed from Egyptian bondage, by the signs and wonders of Omnipotence?—before whom "the waters of the great deep were dried up, and the depths of the sea made a way for the ransomed of the Lord to pass over?"—who received their laws by the voice of the living God from the fires of Sinai?—who were conducted through the wilderness by the symbol of the Divine presence?—whose wants heaven and earth combined to supply?—"five of whom chased a hundred, and a hundred put ten thousand to flight?"—to whom the God of the whole earth, having driven out their enemies before them, assigned their promised inheritance; separating them from the nations, and choosing them as a special people to himself; dwelling amongst them as their Judge, their Lawgiver, their King, and their God; and maintaining the honour of His name amongst them by a continued course of inspiration, and prophecy, and miracle?—Are these the descendants of those venerable patriarchs, on whom God has conferred the highest honour ever bestowed on mortal man—the honour of having their names associated with His own, in

His favourite designation of himself, to the very close of time: " I am the God of Abraham, the God of Isaac, and the God of Jacob; this is my name for ever, and this is my memorial unto all generations?" Is this, in a word, the people, " to whom pertained the adoption, and the glory, and the covenants, and the giving of the law, and the service of God, and the promises; whose are the fathers, and of whom, as concerning the flesh, the Christ came, who is over all, God blessed for ever?"*—Oh, my brethren, can we look even on the scattered remnants of such a people, without the liveliest interest? Can we contemplate their present degradation and wretchedness, without a sigh of deep commiseration, mingling with our assent to the righteous retribution of offended Deity? Can we recollect the blessing they have been to the world, and to ourselves, as the chosen depositaries of the oracles of God, and the appointed communicators of His " saving health " to all nations, without shedding over them the tears of grateful sensibility, and sending up to heaven on their behalf, our united, and fervent, and importunate supplications?

And, blessed be God! our supplications are not those of hopeless despondency. The present state of this interesting people is not their last. A cheering ray darts across the gloom. The blessed light of prophecy, streaming through the opening clouds, settles on the distant prospect, and brings to view a scene, on which the eye of benevolence and piety rests with delighted anticipation.

To the prospects which are thus held out to us respecting the seed of Abraham—the grounds on which we are taught to rest our expectation of their fulfilment—and the connexion between their fulfilment and the fulness of the Gentiles—our attention is now to be directed.

Before proceeding to unfold the anticipations which the Spirit by which the Apostle spake gave him to indulge himself and to exhibit to others,—he devoutly utters his present feelings and anxious desires to be the means of spiritual

* Rom. ix. 4, 5.

benefit to individuals of the rebellious house. He does not allow his mind to be so carried away into distant time, and absorbed in the contemplation of the visions of futurity, as to produce forgetfulness of his perishing brethren around him, and the duty to which their situation, and his own connexion with them, powerfully called him:—verses 13, 14. "For I speak to you Gentiles, inasmuch as I am the apostle of the Gentiles, I magnify mine office: if by any means I may provoke to emulation them which are my flesh, and might save some of them."

In speaking to the Gentiles he was fulfilling his own special commission; for he was "the apostle of the Gentiles;" —"he who had wrought effectually in Peter to the apostleship of the circumcision, the same being mighty in him toward the heathen;" and, in what he here says, he "*magnified*," or put honour upon, "his office." His language indicates its importance and extent, as having *two objects:*— the carrying out, in the first place, by *his* ministry, the purpose of God,—in bringing the Gentiles, the whole world, to the knowledge of Himself;—the practical manifestation of the extensive and impartial benevolence of God in the filling up of His church from every kindred of the earth, as a consequence of the rejection of the Jews for their unbelief:—and then, secondly, the reflex effect of the success of this extensive ministry upon his own people, the unbelieving Israelites,—as *designed* by the calling of the Gentiles. The calling of the Gentiles—the success of the Gospel amongst them, he himself expected, and he gives *us* to expect, would in future time be a means of stirring up the Jews "to jealousy:" then the restoration of the Jews would, in its turn, be as "life from the dead to the Gentiles:"—and these two means would contribute to produce "the fulness" of both, to the glory of the divine faithfulness, and grace, and power. Viewed in these lights, how full of honour the office with which he had been invested!—its results how full of good to mankind, and of glory to God!—But, while contemplating what was future and distant, he feels his spirit glow with the intense desire of being useful to his countrymen *at the time;* of exciting, as far as might be, their "emulation" even *then,* and "saving some."

"*Emulation*" is the same word as "*jealousy*" in the nineteenth verse of the preceding chapter. But jealousy is of two kinds:—the one, from pride and hatred, incites to rage and to the persecution of its object: the other stimulates us to desire and seek after a participation in the same honour, and the same happiness as its object. This is what usually goes by the name of *emulation*. It is clear that the "jealousy" which is "cruel as the grave," cannot be the principle intended here. It is the emulation that stirs up desire after the good enjoyed that is meant. There was already enough, and far more than enough of the other. The jealousy and envy of the unbelieving Jews on all occasions when the Gospel was preached to the Gentiles, and the blessings of the Messiah's kingdom held out to their acceptance, was unbounded, and its fury most destructive. The Apostle was earnestly desirous that in "*some*" at least of his countrymen's minds there might, by the grace of God, be wrought a better principle, a more salutary feeling. They were "*his flesh,*"—dear to his very heart; and he longed and prayed that they might be induced to cast in their lot, in greater numbers, with those who had "received the love of the truth that they might be saved:"—"if by *any* means I might save some of them!"—Other means failing, *this* may, by the blessing of God, prove effectual. Earnest, however, as was his "heart's desire," few, comparatively, appeared as the fruits of his efforts. The great mass of the nation remained then, remain still, "blinded."

Let us now look forward, with him, beyond his own times, and, as now appears, beyond even ours, and contemplate the PROSPECTS held out by the Apostle.

In regard to these, I may first remark, in general, that we are taught to look for their *restoration to the church of God, and to all the fulness of its blessings.*

In their present state, they are represented as *fallen, diminished, cast away, broken off, blinded,* excluded from *mercy,* and perishing: and all this on account of their *unbelief,* their rejection of God and of his Christ. And the general idea of their restoration is set before us, under a variety of phraseology corresponding to these diversified views of the condition from which they are to be restored.—It is their "*fulness;*" their "*reception,*" or *recovery;* their being "*grafted in again;*" their "*obtaining mercy;*" "their *salvation.*"

We must satisfy ourselves with a very brief notice of what is implied in these different expressions.

Their "*fulness,*" is opposed to their "*diminishing.*"* The expression cannot surely mean less than a very general and extensive restoration,—*approaching* at least to universality. As the great body of them have been cast off, the great body of them will be restored,—brought back into the church of God, and to the possession of a "*fulness*" of privilege, even greater than before, as far as the present New Testament state of the church excels in true glory that of the church under the ancient economy. The same word is applied to the *Gentiles*, in verse twenty-fifth, in reference to the coming glory of the latter days. The Apostle elsewhere† denominates the church "the fulness of him who filleth all in all." When the Jewish people are restored, they shall form a part of this fulness of Christ; and Christ will be *their* fulness, by bestowing upon them the abundant blessings of his grace.

Their "*reception,*"‡ is opposed to their "*casting away.*"§ The word signifies accordingly their being *resumed*, or *taken back*. It refers to their previous state. They *had been* the church and people of God, enjoying His presence and favour, and in the exclusive possession of His word and worship. Into this state they shall be taken back; not indeed, as before, to constitute His church *alone*, and to enjoy exclusive spiritual immunities,—but to constitute a part of the Church, in a much more enlarged, and refined, and blessed state, than when they alone formed it.

This idea is still more clearly intimated, by their being

---

* Ver. 12. † Eph. i. 23.
‡ πρόσληψις. § ἀποβολή, ver. 15.

"*grafted in again.*"* The whole of this figure, on which the Apostle dwells through several verses, evidently teaches us that the Gentiles, on their receiving the Gospel, and being introduced into the Christian church, were grafted into *the same stock* from which the unbelieving Jews were *cut off*,—and that, when the latter shall be restored, it will be *grafting them again* into the same stock to which they before belonged. There is no interpreting the figure, as I have before said, with any consistency, except on the principle, that the Church of God has been all along the same; one Church, under various modifications of external constitution, corresponding to the gradual development of the purposes of God, which has been "like the shining light, that shineth more and more unto the perfect day." Their case resembles that of a family emigrating from their native country, and, after the lapse of centuries of privation and suffering in foreign lands, returning to *the same nation*, but in a state of such advanced improvement, as hardly to retain the marks of its identity.

The *salvation*, in verse twenty-sixth, evidently means something vastly superior to any mere temporal deliverance. That verse and the one following explain its nature as consisting in the two great blessings of *justification* from the guilt, and *sanctification* from the pollution of sin. "And so all Israel shall be saved: as it is written, There shall come out of Sion the Deliverer, and shall *turn away ungodliness from Jacob*. For this is my covenant unto them, when I shall *take away their sin*." They shall thus be "saved in the Lord with an everlasting salvation." As "saved" they shall be "added by the Lord to the church;"† and there, in the diligent use of the means of spiritual improvement, they will "work out their own salvation with fear and trembling, God working in them to will and to do of his good pleasure."

They are further described as *obtaining mercy*.‡—The *wrath* threatened has come upon them "to the uttermost:" and when the Lord returns to them *in mercy*, he will blot

---

* Ver. 23.   † See Acts ii. 47 in the Greek.   ‡ Vers. 30, 31.

out their sins, and remove their punishment. The expression may be illustrated from the language of the Psalmist:—" Lord, thou hast been favourable unto thy land: thou hast brought back the captivity of Jacob. Thou hast forgiven the iniquity of thy people; thou hast covered all their sins. Thou hast taken away all thy wrath: thou hast turned thyself from the fierceness of thine anger. Turn us, O God of our salvation, and cause thine anger toward us to cease. Wilt thou be angry with us for ever? wilt thou draw out thine anger to all generations? Wilt thou not revive us again, that thy people may rejoice in thee? Show us thy mercy, O Lord, and grant us thy salvation."* But the mercy of the latter days will not be mere restoration to temporal blessings. They are to obtain *the same mercy that has come to the Gentiles*. This these verses clearly intimate. And they suggest also the observation, that this mercy will consist in its being "given to them on the behalf of Christ to believe in his name."— " You in time past *did not believe*, yet have now *obtained mercy* through their unbelief; even so have these also now *not believed*, that through your mercy they also may *obtain mercy*."—" Obtaining mercy " is thus contrasted with " unbelief," and must consist, in the first instance, in its removal. It shall be *through faith* that they shall be brought back into the Church of God: verses 20th and 23d. " Because of unbelief they were broken off, and thou standest by faith. Be not high-minded, but fear." " And they also, if they abide not still in unbelief, shall be grafted in: for God is able to graft them in again."—They were cut off *for unbelief:* the Gentiles stood in their place *through faith:* and when they are restored to the Church, it shall be by their *embracing the Gospel*. This is the bond of union in the church of God. It is by the cross that Jew and Gentile are made one: " For he is our peace, who hath made both one, and hath broken down the middle wall of partition between us; having abolished in his flesh the enmity, even the law of commandments contained in ordinances; to make in himself, of two, one new man, so making peace; and that

---

* Psa. lxxxv. 1—7.

he might reconcile both unto God in one body by the cross, having slain the enmity thereby."*—The vail shall be taken from their minds. They shall see the glory of Him whom their fathers crucified; shall "look on Him whom they pierced, and mourn for him" with the bitterness of contrition; shall embrace him as "the Christ, the Son of the living God;" own him, with gladness and gratitude, as all their salvation; and unite in the song of the millennial church: "Thou wast slain, and hast redeemed us to God by thy blood, out of every kindred, and tongue, and people, and nation; and hast made us unto our God kings and priests: and we shall reign on the earth."†

That this conversion to God will be *very general*, appears, as I have already hinted, from the scope of the whole passage; and particularly, as I am disposed to understand it, from verse 26th:—"And so all Israel shall be saved: as it is written, There shall come out of Sion the Deliverer, and shall turn away ungodliness from Jacob."

By many, I am aware, the expression "all Israel" is applied to the *spiritual Israel*,—the whole *elect of God*. The following considerations induce me to think it ought to be understood of "Israel after the flesh:"‡

1. It is of *them*,—of *their* restoration, the Apostle is all along speaking. This is his subject; and the salvation of the spiritual Israel, consisting of Jews and Gentiles, would not, unless in a very indirect manner, be to his purpose. "Israel," in his reasoning, seems to be used *in one sense*. Compare especially with verse twenty-sixth, that which immediately precedes: "For I would not, brethren, that ye should be ignorant of this mystery, (lest ye should be wise in your own conceits,) that blindness in part is happened to Israel, until the fulness of the Gentiles be come in. And

---

* Eph. ii. 14—16. † Rev. v. 9, 10.
‡ "Calovius, Bengel, and Olshausen interpret 'all Israel' of *the elect believers of Israel;*—Beza, Estius, Koppe, Reiche, Köllner, Meyer, Tholuck, De Wette, al. hold that the words refer, as I have explained them above, to a national restoration of Israel to God's favour." *Alford.*—Ed.

so all Israel shall be saved." Surely the continuity of the Apostle's statement requires us to understand the appellation in the latter occurrence in the same sense as in the former.

2. The Apostle, you perceive, speaks of this as a "*mystery*," not merely the casting off of the Jews, but their casting off, connected with their temporary blindness, and future conversion. The mystery is very much akin in nature to that respecting the Gentiles; of which the Apostle speaks, in writing to the Ephesians, as the "mystery of Christ, which in other ages was not made known unto the sons of men, as it is now revealed unto his holy apostles and prophets by the Spirit; that the Gentiles should be fellow-heirs, and of the same body, and partakers of his promise in Christ by the Gospel."* It was a mystery,—that is, *a secret not before fully made known*,—that the Gentiles, having remained so long in darkness, were to be enlightened and brought directly into the church, without the medium of Judaism. So here is a parallel mystery: "blindness in part," that is, to a part of the nation, and for a season, "is happened" in divine judgment, "to Israel," *until a certain time:* "and so," when that time comes, "*Israel*," now cast off and blinded, shall obtain mercy, and be restored, and saved.

3. The Apostle speaks of this salvation of Israel, as the fulfilment of a divine prediction or declaration, which seems evidently to refer to the recalling of the rejected seed of Jacob into the church of God: "So all Israel shall be saved: as it is written, There shall come out of Sion the Deliverer, and shall turn away ungodliness from Jacob. For this is my covenant unto them, when I shall take away their sins."

4. "*All Israel*," is a general expression, not necessarily including *every soul*. It appears to signify, *Israel now cast off and dispersed* under Divine rebuke, *as well as* those of the same people, who had through grace believed. Similar is the language in Ezekiel†—"Then he said unto me, Son of man, these bones are *the whole house of Israel:* behold, they say, Our bones are dried, and our hope is lost; we are cut off for

---

* Eph. iii. 4—6. † Chap. xxxvii. 11.

our parts." If the passage, which promises the resurrection of these bones, is considered as having a primary reference to the restoration from Babylon, "the whole house of Israel" *must* be understood as a *general* expression; because that was far from being a universal return. If it has an ultimate reference, as seems very clear from the subsequent part of the chapter, to a remoter deliverance, to be effected in the latter days, then it is exactly parallel to the one before us, and on the same subject.

On the question respecting the return of the Jews to their own land, your time will by no means permit me to enter; and I feel it the less necessary, because, whatever may be the view of that question we are disposed to entertain, it is not of a temporal, but of a spiritual restoration that the Apostle treats in the passage before us. I must confess myself, however, strongly inclined to think, that, making all allowance for figurative language, by which spiritual blessings are so often represented under allusions to the ancient prosperity of the Israelitish people,—there are some passages which will hardly bear such an explanation; especially when it is considered, that the figurative language, of a similar kind, on the other side, derived from the former *sufferings* of Israel, evidently signifies not merely *spiritual* desertion, and depression, and curse, but temporal calamity, degradation, and distress;—and that the language which expresses temporal blessings, but which some understand spiritually, occurs at times in connection with the plainest predictions and promises of spiritual blessings; by which connection the two seem intended to be distinguished, as being both included in the divine purposes of mercy;—and further, that a good deal of straining seems, in some instances, necessary, to make out the application of the language in a spiritual sense.

Allow me a single additional remark or two, of a general kind, upon this point:

1. There can be no valid objection to the event from the *numbers* of the Jews: for, in the first place, though the calculations, or rather guesses, of different persons have varied so much as to extend from five or six millions, to twenty or

even thirty;—I am persuaded that the former is much nearer the truth, and that there are not at this moment more Jews in the world, than there were in the days of David or Solomon:—and, secondly, as a *partial* return to Judea fulfilled the predictions relative to the earlier captivity; so may it also in the present case.

2. Nor can there be any just objection on the ground of the distinction between Jew and Gentile being done away under the Gospel. The supposed fact is not at all, as far as I see, inconsistent with this. When the Jews acknowledge Jesus, they shall be one, as a church, with the Gentiles; and their return to their own land does not at all imply their becoming, as before, a distinct and exclusive ecclesiastical community; nor the continuance of the former separation in their intercourse and worship; nor even, indeed, the nationalizing of Christianity at all.

3. Nor can any such objection rest on the foundation, that *no good end* is to be answered by the event. The same end, it may surely be replied, will be served, and that in a very eminent degree, which is served by the accomplishment of prophecy in general. It will, if it take place, be a very striking event; especially when connected with the fulfilled predictions of their dispersion. Infidels ridicule the idea of such a thing. The event may silence their ridicule, and contribute, under the teaching of the Spirit, to advance the reception of the truth.—Predictions of *outward events*, it may further be observed, which are notorious, and strike the senses of men, are those by which God has usually been pleased to confirm His testimony.—With difficulties and improbabilities, whether arising from the inclinations of the Jews themselves, or from any other source, we have nothing to do. The sole question is, "What saith the Scripture?" He who has in His hand the hearts of all men, and all the resources of nature and of nations, can never be at a loss for means to accomplish His own purposes.

But I must proceed to a brief statement of the GROUNDS on which these prospects of restoration rest.

I confine myself entirely to those which are suggested by

the statements and reasonings of the Apostle in this chapter: and on this principle I notice

First,—*The connection of this dispersed and afflicted people with their holy fathers, the objects of God's original choice and peculiar love.* For this I refer you to the sixteenth verse: "For if the first fruit be holy, the lump is also holy; and if the root be holy, so are the branches."

The "*first-fruits,*" and the "*root,*" in these two similitudes, the one of which is taken from a well-known practice in the Jewish institutes, and the other from the correspondence in nature between the root and the branches, represent the same thing—the ancient Jewish fathers, Abraham, Isaac, and Jacob.—The principle of the argument here appears to me to be, the *primary respect* which, in the promises of the covenant with Abraham, Isaac, and Jacob, God had to *their natural offspring;*—that they should be holy, or separated unto Him as his church; and that there should be amongst them "a seed to serve the Lord."* The Apostle, I think, represents this principle as still operating; and the descendants of Abraham, Isaac, and Jacob, as now kept in a state of separation, that the operation of it may yet appear. Their present long dispersion, and subjection to Divine rebuke, are as consistent with this, as their former sufferings in Egypt and in Babylon were. God "remembered his covenant" with their fathers in former deliverances: so will He, in that which still awaits them. They are still the descendants of the same progenitors, with whom the covenant was made; and *by Divine constitution and appointment*, the "*first-fruits* being holy," the "*lump* is also holy," and "the *root* being holy, so are the *branches.*" The same view of this relation is brought forward again, in connection with the *immutability of the Divine purposes*, in verses 28th and 29th: "As concerning the gospel, they are enemies for your sakes: but as touching the election, they are beloved for the fathers' sakes. For the gifts and calling of God are without repentance."

* See Gen. xvii. 7.

"*Enemies for your sakes:*" their ejection having made room, as it were, for the introduction of the Gentiles.—"The election" seems, in this place, to signify, not the chosen remnant, but God's *choice* of their fathers, with their seed, to be " His peculiar people ;"—a choice expressed in former passages, to which many more might be added. Now, " God is not a man, that he should lie; neither the son of man, that he should repent: hath he said, and shall he not do it? or hath he spoken, and shall he not make it good? Behold," said Balaam, " I have received commandment to bless: and he hath blessed: and I cannot reverse it."*—The Jewish people, the seed of Abraham, God's friend, are still " beloved for their fathers' sakes." When God establishes His purpose, it shall stand. The promise of the covenant, in its *primary regard to the natural offspring*, was without limitation as to *time*. This primary regard has not ceased. He has not repented of His choice;—of His "gifts" to His people;—of His "calling" of them. I notice—

Secondly,—The *power of God*. This is adduced in verse twenty-third, "And they also, if they abide not still in unbelief, shall be grafted in: for God is able to graft them in again."

Their state might to us appear *desperate:*—so scattered are they and disunited:—so deplorably sunk and degraded:—so full of deep-rooted prejudice against Jesus of Nazareth, and of too well-grounded dislike to those who bear his name: and they have now continued so long, so very long, in this state; and have become so dead and seared, so callous to every spiritual impression, so given up to worldliness, or to infidelity. They are like branches cut off; withered; rotten; "twice dead." We are ready to exclaim, in contemplating the prospects exhibited by prophecy, " How can these things be?" The satisfactory and silencing answer is, " God is able "—" is able to graft them in again:" able to impart life to these sapless and withered boughs, and to make them fruitful to His praise.

* Numb. xxiii. 19, 20.

They and we both are taught to derive encouragement from former manifestations of God's power. Thus the prophet encourages the church of old, by reminding her of her origin, in circumstances so extremely hopeless. "Hearken to me, ye that follow after righteousness, ye that seek the Lord: look unto the rock whence ye are hewn, and to the hole of the pit whence ye are digged. Look unto Abraham your father, and unto Sarah that bare you; for I called him alone, and blessed him, and increased him. For the Lord will comfort Sion: he will comfort all her waste places; and he will make her wilderness like Eden, and her desert like the garden of the Lord; joy and gladness shall be found therein, thanksgiving, and the voice of melody."* Their redemption from Egypt, and all the subsequent wonders of God's power on their behalf, are frequently appealed to for the same purpose. —And *we*, my friends, may be reminded, for our encouragement, of the wonders of *Pentecost*. Their minds were then as utterly hostile as they are now: and He who effected the conversion of those "sinners against their own souls," who had just exclaimed, "His blood be on us and on our children," is able, by the energy of the same renewing grace, to turn to himself the hearts of their hardened children.— And the very grafting in of the *Gentiles*, who were as dead as the Jews are now, forbids all despondency. The question, indeed, addressed by Paul to Agrippa, is one which instantly solves all doubts, and removes all difficulties: "Why should it be thought a thing incredible with you, that GOD should raise the dead?"†—The bones in the Valley of Vision were separate, and scattered, and dry, and long bleached by the sun and the storm. Yet when the question is put, "Can these bones live?" the answer is given by Omnipotence;— "Behold, *I* will cause breath to enter into you, and ye shall live:—*I* will lay sinews upon you, and cover you with flesh, and put breath in you, and ye shall live."—"With God all things are possible." Notice

Thirdly,—The *reasonableness of the expectation:* "And if

---

* Isa. li. 1—3. † Acts xxvi. 8.

some of the branches be broken off, and thou, being a wild olive-tree, were grafted in among them, and with them partakest of the root and fatness of the olive-tree; boast not against the branches: but if thou boast, thou bearest not the root, but the root thee. For if thou wert cut out of the olive-tree, which is wild by nature, and wert grafted, contrary to nature, into a good olive-tree; how much more shall these, which be the natural branches, be grafted into their own natural olive-tree?"*

"*How much more*"—does not imply, that the power necessary for the one effect, is less than that required for the other: it expresses the idea of *reasonableness*. It is as the descendants of Abraham, Isaac, and Jacob, that they are called "the natural branches:" which is another distinct evidence of a *primary respect* in the covenant to the *natural offspring:* upon which, I repeat, the whole argument appears to rest. *Gentiles*, as well as Jews, were included in the promise, and partakers of the blessing: so that unless a reference of primary and special regard to the natural offspring be admitted, one is at a loss to conceive on what principle the question,—the *a fortiori* question, can be founded, "How much more shall these, which be the natural branches, be grafted into their own olive tree?"

The Gentiles held, as it were, a secondary place in the promise. The Jewish people, even in their present dispersion, are still the "*natural branches.*" The Gentiles had no original connexion with the stock: yet they were "grafted, *contrary to nature*, into the good olive-tree:" "*how much more*" then, may we not expect, the "children of the stock of Abraham," connected with the root, first in the promise, and the objects of special and primary regard, to be grafted in again?— "grafted into *their own* olive-tree"—that tree with which they have a *natural connexion.*—How insurmountable the objection arising from this, to the idea of the entire distinction of the Old and New Testament churches! Their *grafting* into *their own tree*, is their *restoration* to *their own church*. Notice

* Verses 17, 18, 24.

In the fourth place—*Prophecy.* This is a wide field; I dare not enter upon it. I must confine myself at present to a single remark or two on the prediction which is selected by the Apostle, (verses 26, 27) "And so all Israel shall be saved: as it is written, There shall come out of Sion the Deliverer, and shall turn away ungodliness from Jacob. For this is my covenant unto them, when I shall take away their sins."* The quotation is from Isaiah lix. 20, 21; which is given by the Apostle, nearly as in the Septuagint version, and probably according to the original reading of the Hebrew. The general import, however, of the Apostle's translation and our own authorized version of the passage in the prophet, is much the same.† Their *deliverance* was to be connected with their *turning from ungodliness;* and *both* were to be the effect of the power and grace of the same Deliverer. He turns them from their ungodliness; and to them thus turning from ungodliness, he comes with deliverance from its judicial and penal effects;—comes with returning favour and blessing. This was uniformly the tenor of God's covenant and dealings with Israel.‡ And the conditionality of the promise,—the dependence of His turning to them on their turning to Him, is not at all inconsistent with His agency in turning them to himself. Hence the prayer:—"Turn us, O God of our salvation, and cause thine anger toward us to cease." "Turn us again, O God, and cause thy face to shine; and we shall be saved." "Let thy hand be upon the man of thy right hand, upon the Son of man whom thou madest strong for thyself. So will not we go back from thee: quicken us, and we will call upon thy name."§

I only add, that every great deliverance of the church is represented *as coming out of Zion,* because it comes from

---

* Whence are these words, "*when I shall take away their sins,*" supplied by the Apostle? Probably Jer. xxxi. 34. [So Stuart. Alford says from Is. xxvii. 9.—ED.]

† "It may be that the whole citation is intended to express the sense of prophecy rather than the wording of any particular passage."—*Alford.*—[ED.]

‡ See Lev. xxvi. 39—45; Deut. xxx. 1—10, &c.

§ Ps. lxxxv. 4; lxxx. 3, 8, 17, 19.

Jehovah, whose residence was there. "Oh that the salvation of Israel were come out of Zion! When the Lord bringeth back the captivity of his people, Jacob shall rejoice, and Israel shall be glad." " Thy people shall be willing in the day of thy power; in the beauties of holiness from the womb of the morning: thou hast the dew of thy youth."†

* Ps. xiv. 7; cx. 3.

LECTURE LI.

Romans xi. 7—32.

(THIRD DISCOURSE.)

We called your attention, in last lecture, to the views held out in this chapter of the restoration of the Jews; and to the grounds on which the Apostle teaches us to rest the expectation of that event.

Before proceeding briefly to notice the promised "fulness of the Gentiles," and the connexion of the restoration of Israel with it as a means of its accomplishment, it was my intention to have taken a view of some of the prophecies relative to the event which we have already had before us, and to have compared them with the contents of this chapter. But the field is too extensive and complicated. It involves a number of questions; and on some of them every inch of ground is ground of debate. I relinquish, therefore, the intention for the present. I only observe in general, that almost all the prophets, and some of them largely and with particularity of detail, assure us of the coming event—the restoration of the people of Israel from their present scattered, degraded, and outcast condition:—and it should seem that this restoration is to comprehend, not only the Jews properly so called, or the descendants of the two tribes that adhered to the House of David after the death of Solomon, and of any of the ten revolted tribes who united with them at the return from the Babylonish captivity, but the remnant of these ten tribes themselves, respecting which there has been so much conjecture and so much inquiry and search; which I have no doubt are to be found in some part or parts of the world, whether any who have conceived they have discovered them be in the right or not, and which that God who knows His own "hidden ones," however long and however secret their concealment, will in His own way, and at His own time, bring to light, and to the enjoyment of all that He has promised to re-united Israel.—I have formerly expressed my conviction that the prophecies indicate their return to their own land; and I may now add that they seem to place this *before* the general spiritual conversion of the people to Christianity; such, at least, is the order in several of the largest and most express predictions.—With regard to the calculations of the prophetic seasons, of which some have been proved fallacious by the time having already gone by, and of which others, that fix it at a very near day, appear likely to have the same result, I can say nothing— unless it be, merely in general terms, that I am much inclined to suspect that the estimates of those who place the commencement of the millennial glory of the Church still at a considerable distance,—even so far off perhaps as the year 2000, are nearer to the truth. I would affirm nothing. The day will declare it; if it comes sooner, His people will hail its earlier arrival; and whensoever it comes, the facts of the fulfilment will bring fully to light and clear conviction the principle of calculation. And with regard to the personal advent of the Son of God, to lead the hosts of Israel against their enemies, and to take his seat, literally, on the throne of David at Jerusalem, I am confident there is no sufficient ground in the Scriptures for such an expectation; although this is by many conceived to be the very event by which the restoration and conversion of Israel is to be, like the redemption from Egypt, suddenly and miraculously effected.—I must, however, pass by these and some other topics connected with the present subject, but not brought before us in the Apostle's discussion of it; and shall proceed to a few brief remarks on the connexion between the restoration of the Jews and the fulness of the Gentiles.

There are two things spoken of by the Apostle in the chapter, in reference to the Gentiles;—their "*riches*," and their "*fulness*." The former, (verse 12th) refers to the first calling of the Gentiles into the church, in the room and upon the rejection of the Jews, to the participation of "the unsearchable riches of Christ."—The latter (verse 25th) relates to a remoter period;—an era of a vastly more extensive evangelization and conversion of the world to the faith and obedience of the Gospel, than has yet appeared. The *fulness* is the *completion of the riches.*

When the Redeemer had finished his work, and was risen from the dead, Jehovah said unto him, "Ask of me, and I shall give thee the heathen for thine inheritance, and the uttermost parts of the earth for thy possession."* The "*fulness* of the Gentiles" is the bringing in of all the "*desolate heritages*" included in this Divine grant and promise. The predictions respecting that period have been progressively, and are now most rapidly, receiving their fulfilment. "The kingdom of heaven," said Jesus in his parabolical instructions, (and the parables involved a prophecy) "is like unto a grain of mustard seed, which a man took and sowed in his field: which indeed is the least of all seeds; but when it is grown, it is the greatest among herbs, and becometh a tree, so that the birds of the air come and lodge in the branches thereof:" —"The kingdom of heaven is like unto leaven, which a woman took and hid in three measures of meal, till the whole was leavened."† The stone which, in the visions of the Babylonian monarch, was "cut out of the mountain without hands," and which "smote the image, and brake in pieces the

---

* Ps. li. 8.
† Matth. xiii. 31—33. The attempt to show, that these parables were not intended to convey to our minds the idea of *gradual progress*, but that the process of growth in the one case, and the process of fermentation in the other, are to be left entirely out of the account, and nothing regarded but the two extremes,—the little seed and the full-grown tree,—the insertion of the leaven, and the mass of dough,—is an attempt which, to every man of common sense, can only serve as an indication of the extreme exigency of the cause which requires such criticism for its support.

iron, the brass, the clay, the silver, and the gold," "became a great mountain, and filled the whole earth:" intimating, according to the prophetic interpretation, that 'the God of heaven was to set up a kingdom, which should never be destroyed; which should not be left to other people, but should break in pieces and consume the kingdoms signified in the vision, and itself stand for ever.'* "And the seventh angel sounded; and there were great voices in heaven, saying, The kingdoms of this world are become the kingdoms of our Lord, and of his Christ; and he shall reign for ever and ever."† "All the ends of the world shall remember, and turn unto the Lord; and all the kindreds of the nations shall worship before thee."‡ "His name shall endure for ever; his name shall be continued as long as the sun; and men shall be blessed in him: all nations shall call him blessed." "Blessed be his glorious name for ever: and let the whole earth be filled with his glory. Amen, and amen."§

The precise extent of the influence of true religion in the glorious and happy period thus predicted, we shall not attempt to decide. It is enough that the figures used to describe it, represent the change on the state of the world to be so great, as to resemble the creation of "a new heavens and a new earth, so that the former should not be remembered, nor come into mind."‖

Let us now attend a little to the reciprocal connexion of the two great events, the fulness of the Gentiles, and the restoration of the Jews, and their influence on each other. This is brought before us in verses 30, 31 :—" For as ye in times past have not believed God, yet have now obtained mercy through their unbelief; even so have these also now not believed, that through your mercy they also may obtain mercy."

The Apostle had spoken of the calling of the Gentiles, as a kind of consequence of the rejection of the Jews. It was the "casting away of them" that was the "reconciling of

---

* Dan. ii. 35, 44. † Rev. xi. 15. ‡ Ps. xxii. 27.
§ Ps. lxxii. 19. ‖ Isa. lxv. 17.

the world;"—the "fall of them the riches of the Gentiles;" and here—the Gentiles are said to have "obtained mercy *through their unbelief.*" When, therefore, Paul speaks of the *restoration* of the Jews, a startling inquiry might naturally suggest itself to the minds of the Gentiles:—'As *our acceptance* has been by *their rejection,* is *their recovery* to be in like manner by *our rejection?* Are *we,* in our turn, to be cast out, in order to *their* re-admission? Are we to be cut off, when they are grafted in again? Their exclusion made room for us: is our exclusion to make room for them?' —No: blessed be God! the cases in this respect are entirely different. "Ye have obtained mercy *through their unbelief;*" but it is not through your unbelief that *they* are to obtain mercy:—no; but it is "*through your mercy!*" This is an interesting and delightful difference indeed!

In the twelfth and fifteenth verses, the restoration of the Jews is evidently represented as *preceding* and *bringing about* "the fulness of the Gentiles." "Now, if the fall of them be the riches of the world, and the diminishing of them the riches of the Gentiles; how much more their fulness?" "For if the casting away of them be the reconciling of the world, what shall the receiving of them be, but life from the dead?" The expression in verse thirty-first, connected with verse twenty-fifth, looks like *the reverse* of this order. "Even so have these also now not believed, that through your mercy they also may obtain mercy." "For I would not, brethren, that ye should be ignorant of this mystery, (lest ye should be wise in your own conceits,) that blindness in part has happened to Israel, until the fulness of the Gentiles be come in. And so all Israel shall be saved." From this circumstance it appears reasonable to consider the two events as at once synchronous, (that is, happening together at the same time,) and as having a reciprocal influence in bringing about each other.—The "fulness of the Gentiles," we suppose, according to this view of the matter, begins to come in, and makes rapid and cheering progress towards its consummation; then the Jews, (the time being come for the removal of the vail from their minds) are, by the blessing of God, "provoked to emulation."—Having Jesus preached to them, and the New Testament scriptures put into their hands by the Gentiles, their attention is awakened; they inquire; they believe; they turn to the Lord: and their "reconciliation" hastens forward to its glorious completion, "the fulness of the Gentiles."

The Gentile church, possessing the gospel of God, and the divine oracles of new covenant truth, is the depository of future mercy to the Jews; as the Jewish church of old was the depository of future mercy to the Gentiles.—The calling of the Gentiles was the divine purpose, to be fulfilled upon the rejection of the Jews;—the restoration of the Jews is the divine purpose, to be effected through the mercy bestowed on the Gentiles. The knowledge of the Saviour was formerly imparted by the Jews to the Gentiles; it shall then be imparted by the Gentiles to the Jews. In this way, when the period in question arrives, they will feel reciprocally indebted to each other. "Salvation was of the Jews" to the Gentiles; it shall then be of the Gentiles to the Jews: and this will serve the more effectually to knit their hearts together in the blessed bonds of amity and love. For whatever may have been the wrongs (and alas! they have been multiplied and grievous,) which the Jews have suffered at the hands of the Gentiles, and in whatever way, and to whatever extent, it may please God, as of old, to avenge these wrongs; yet in the enlarged and purified Church of the living God, composed of Gentiles and Jews together, all wrongs, and grudges, and jealousies shall be buried in everlasting oblivion:—and "the wolf shall dwell with the lamb, and the leopard shall lie down with the kid; and the calf, and the young lion, and the fatling together; and a little child shall lead them. And the cow and the bear shall feed; their young ones shall lie down together: and the lion shall eat straw like the ox. And the sucking child shall play on the hole of the asp, and the weaned child shall put his hand on the cockatrice' den. They shall not hurt nor destroy in all my holy mountain: for the earth shall be full of the knowledge of the Lord, as the waters cover the sea."*

The bringing in of the Jews will contribute to hasten the fulness of the Gentiles, in such ways, it may be presumed, as the following:

1. *By the zeal which they themselves will naturally feel, and put forth in effort, for the glory of the Redeemer.*

Their recovery will be owned by them as "the doing of the Lord," and it will be "marvellous in their eyes." The riches of divine mercy and loving-kindness will animate their hearts with glowing gratitude; and will lead them most fervently to desire, and with all their powers to seek, the glory of their Benefactor and Redeemer;—to seek it, with an interest and a zeal proportioned to the virulence of their former hatred and opposition. Thus it was with Saul of Tarsus, when he became "a preacher of the faith which before he destroyed:" and if they shall be animated, as we may confidently presume, with a similar spirit,—what noble preachers, and missionaries, and heralds of the cross in all nations, may we not expect to arise from amongst them!—and what extensive good, through the Divine blessing, to follow their labours!

2. *By the mighty revival which this event will produce in the Gentile church.*

How will it stimulate them to emulation in active zeal! In this respect, as well as in others, it will be like "life from the dead." It will confirm their faith, enliven their joy, animate their gratitude, inflame their love, and inspire new confidence into their prayers and their exertions: and, in answer to these prayers, the Spirit of the Lord being copiously effused, "the word of the Lord shall have free course and be glorified."—" The people shall praise him, all the people shall praise him."

3. *By the influence of the event itself, as an accompanying evidence of the truth, and means of conviction and conversion to God.*

---

* Isa. xi. 6—9.

Such evidences were the signs and wonders and mighty deeds,—the various miracles wrought of old by prophets and apostles. When God "granted signs and wonders to be done by their hands," He is said to have "given testimony to the word of his grace;"—to have "confirmed the word by signs following;"—to have "borne witness, by signs and wonders, and divers miracles, and gifts of the Holy Ghost, according to his will."* The accompanying influence of the Spirit of God rendered these evidences of the truth effectual to the conversion of many. Similar may we suppose the effect to be, of this striking fulfilment of divine predictions,—arresting the attention, exciting the inquiry, silencing the infidelity, and, by the gracious influence of Heaven, subduing the hearts of multitudes to the Redeemer, "as the heart of one man."

I conclude with two or three practical reflections:

1st. In anticipating the prospects which this passage, and the prophetic scriptures in general, open to our view,—it is our duty not merely *to wait* and *to pray*, but *to act* and *to give*.

It will not do to sit down and enjoy our delight in contemplating the lovely visions of future times, and leave the God who has foretold them to accomplish them in His own way. God works by means. He who of old was wont to "give his people favour in the sight of their enemies," and thus to bring about to them the fulfilment of the purposes of His mercy, has long fulfilled His threatenings against them, by leaving them exposed to the operation of all the evil passions of men; even Christians too often joining in the general neglect, and persecution, and scorn. And He who, at the close of their former captivity, stirred up the spirit of Cyrus, king of Persia, to proclaim their liberty, and restore them to the land of their fathers, will stir up in the bosoms of His own people the sentiments of compassion, and gratitude, and zeal, and bring about, by their active instrumentality, the accomplishment of His promised mercy. They are already,

---

* Acts xiv. 3: Mark xvi. 20: Heb. ii. 4.

after a long period of guilty supineness, feeling and yielding to the sacred impulse. Let us, my brethren, seek to feel it more deeply ourselves, and to communicate it to the bosoms of others:—that the prayers of the whole Christian church may ascend to God, and the liberality and the exertions of the whole Christian church may be combined, in His name and under His blessing, for the illumination and conversion of the seed of Abraham, His friend.—It is not for us to be regulated in our conduct by calculations of times and seasons; though even upon such as may fancy it their duty to suspend their efforts till God's time shall arrive, we might make the intimations of prophecy, and the signs of the present period, to bear with irresistible force:—but it is ours to seize the present moment; not to say "the time is not come, the time that the Lord's house should be built;" but at once to obey the command of God, "Consider your ways. Go up to the mountain, and bring wood, and build the house, and I will take pleasure in it, and I will be glorified, saith the Lord."* Were the time ever so far distant, let us not forget that there must be a commencement,—that remote efforts are often preparatory to future results;—the breaking up of the ground;—the first streak of the dawn.

2*dly.* Let me remind you of the *obligations under which, as Gentiles, believing Gentiles, possessors of the blessings of salvation, you lie to the Jewish people.*

You admit the principle, that, whilst, both for temporal and spiritual blessings, your offerings of praise should ascend to "the Father of lights, from whom cometh down every good and perfect gift," you ought at the same time to acknowledge and to bless the *instrument* of His kindness. And, if the feeling of obligation should bear proportion to the magnitude of the good conferred, O how shall we estimate the amount of your debt of gratitude, when it is a return for "all spiritual blessings in heavenly places, in Christ Jesus!" Yes, my brethren, you owe all to *them.* The prophets, and apostles, and evangelists, were Jews; and to them

* Hag. i. 2, 8.

you are indebted for the living oracles of God, and for all the joys and all the hopes inspired by the knowledge of "the only true God and Jesus Christ whom he hath sent." There is not one in the entire catalogue of the blessings that belong to you, as members of the "fellowship of God's dear Son," (who himself also was "made of the seed of David according to the flesh,") which may not be traced to the same source. They were Jews who evangelized the Gentile world of old, by the zealous, and disinterested, and persevering efforts of Gospel love. And you are now enjoying the blessed fruits of these efforts. And how has the debt been paid? With a few exceptions, the only answer, alas! that truth can give to the question, is,—by insults, and proscriptions, and cruelties; by curses, and bonds, and blood:—by a treatment, in which Mahometans and Pagans have joined with professing Christians, and which has itself eminently contributed to produce, and deepen, and maintain, the very degradation and want of principle which are universally assigned as its cause. O feel for that people, to whom, though thus so long treated as outcasts from the family of man, the world, and yourselves, are under such obligations. There is more to be paid them now than a debt of gratitude; there is a reparation of injury. And you cannot more effectually cancel the claims which, in both respects, they have upon you, than by giving them back the very blessings which they have been the instruments of bestowing.

3*dly. Present appearances are encouraging.*

It is given as one of the signs when the time to favour Zion is come, that "her saints take pleasure in her stones, and favour the dust thereof." There is an interest now excited, and rapidly on the increase, and producing practical efforts, in behalf of the long-neglected subjects of our present pleading. The attention of Christians, and even of mankind at large, is drawn powerfully towards them. The persecutions, on the one hand, which in some quarters they have been suffering; the regard, on the other hand, shown them by some of the crowned potentates of Europe, and the Christian exertions made on their behalf in this country;—

are all contributing to this effect. And there are, besides, pleasing and promising symptoms appearing amongst themselves. A spirit of thoughtfulness, investigation, and inquisitiveness, has gone forth to a considerable extent amongst them. There is an obvious diminution of the virulence of prejudice, and animosity, and scornful aversion. They receive, in many instances, the Christian tracts; and, above all, the *Christian Scriptures*, translated for their use into their own ancient and revered tongue. They read, they converse, they discuss; they hold meetings for conference with Christian ministers; and, as of old, they have "great reasonings among themselves." Multitudes are said to be under powerful convictions of the truth of Christianity, and apparently on the very eve of publicly avowing these convictions, and embracing Jesus as the Christ. These are all tokens for good. Let them have their full animating effect on our minds. Let Christians be of one heart and one soul, in this great and good cause; and "Jehovah will arise, and build up Zion."

4*thly*. Let all remember, that *salvation is in every instance the fruit of free and sovereign mercy*.

The former awfully disobedient, and alienated, and hardened state of the Gentiles, made it manifest, that *their* salvation was of mercy,—free mercy;—the fulfilment of a sovereign purpose of mercy. The present no less hardened state of the Jews will, in like manner, make it manifest, that *their* salvation also is of the *same mercy;*—of mercy equally free, and rich, and sovereign. The salvation, indeed, of every sinner, without a single exception, Jew or Gentile, must be "to the praise of the glory of God's grace." I dare not, as I value the approbation of my Master, and the safety of my own soul, flatter any one of my hearers with the possibility of obtaining salvation in any other way, than as the free "gift of God, through Jesus Christ our Lord:" "in whom we have redemption through his blood, the forgiveness of sins, according to the riches of his grace."

Finally:—*Let us mark and imitate the example of the Apostle, in minding present duty while anticipating future prospects.* Even *we* may never see the blessed scenes predicted in this chapter and the concurrent prophecies of the Word of God:—but like Paul we have a present duty to perform, altogether independent of prophetic "times and seasons, which the Father hath put in his own power." It belongs to us, not only to use means for hastening on the glory of the latter days, but to seek with all earnestness the salvation of our own contemporaries, at home and abroad, who are hourly dying and perishing. Our success may be small; even as nothing, compared with the distant scenes which the visions of prophecy unfold. But let us not so dazzle our eyes by gazing on the bright effulgence of the glory to come, as to make them dim to the vision of objects that are near at hand and have an immediate demand on our notice. We are never sure by what particular means it may please God to bring about his purposes; and how far present exertion may be a commencement to the great events that are in prophecy. We may be beginning the scaffolding for the future temple. But at all events, let us never lose sight of the inestimable preciousness of a single soul. He who has been the instrument of saving even one soul has not lived in vain:—he has effected more than if he had been the deliverer of an empire from temporal calamity—although history should never know his name in the one case, while it would have been blazoned to future generations in the other. In bringing one sinner to Christ, you not only secure an eternity of happiness to the individual,—you at the same time fix a new centre of pious influence from which the power of the truth may diffuse itself around;—and this may be the occasion of provoking others also to jealousy. Abundant matter-of-fact evidence, I am aware, shows that the tendency of the truth and of the display of its holy influence is to stir up the enmity of the natural mind. Yet it is at the same time one of the means by which the Spirit operates in producing conviction, and even exciting to emulation. Its *holy* influence may be the means of producing the former, and its *happy* influence the latter. When it appears, according to its true nature and tendency, producing peace and joy, removing anxious fears, calming the turbulent passions, bestowing comfort in trouble, and hope and confidence in death;—such a manifestation of its character may excite some to emulation: it may lead to think—to desire that which produces effects so precious—to feel the vanity of the world—to seek Christ, the favour of God, and the hope of glory, as the only substantial and durable blessings.*

* The views presented in this and the preceding Lecture were given to the world very many years ago, in a Sermon preached in behalf of "The Society for the Promotion of Christianity among the Jews," and afterwards published.

LECTURE LII.*

ROMANS XI. 33—36.

"O the depth of the riches both of the wisdom and knowledge of God! how unsearchable are his judgments, and his ways past finding out! For who hath known the mind of the Lord? or who hath been his counsellor? Or who hath first given to him, and it shall be recompensed unto him again? For of him, and through him, and to him, are all things: to whom be glory for ever. Amen."

THE works and ways of God are not revealed to us as subjects of mere barren speculation. It is our duty, and ought to be our delight, to see God in them all. The contemplation of them is designed to increase our acquaintance with His character, and to animate our feelings of admiring and thankful devotion. Thus it was with Paul. Having expatiated on the mystery of the divine procedure in the dispensation of His grace to mankind;—and more especially, on that alternation of righteous judgment and abounding mercy, apparent in His conduct toward the Jews and the Gentiles; the unbelief and rebellion of the former, while it brought vengeance and rejection upon themselves becoming the occasion of favour and blessing to the latter;—and then the mercy shown to the latter, being, in its turn, the means of "restoring the joy of God's salvation" to the former;—God thus making each, reciprocally, the source of benefit and blessing to the other,—"concluding all in unbelief, that He might have mercy upon all,"—"mercy rejoicing against judg-

---

* This Lecture was, it appears, delivered in its present form "at the Ordination of Mr. Weiss, Jewish Missionary." It seemed best to insert it without alteration.—ED.

ment:"—the Apostle's heart is full. The survey has filled it with "wonder, love, and praise." He breaks out into the utterance of devout astonishment, and of lowly yet lofty adoration:—"O the depth of the riches both of the wisdom and knowledge of God! how unsearchable are his judgments, and his ways past finding out! For who hath known the mind of the Lord? or who hath been his counsellor? Or who hath first given to him, and it shall be recompensed unto him again? For of him, and through him, and to him, are all things: to whom be glory for ever. Amen."

The first of these verses ought, I am more than inclined to think, to be somewhat differently translated. As it stands, it is only the "wisdom" and the "knowledge" of God that are the objects of adoring wonder; as each containing an unsearchable "depth of riches,"—each an inexhaustible mine. But with no less at least, if not more of literal fidelity, the verse might be rendered—"O the depth of the riches, and wisdom, and knowledge of God!"—There are thus *three* things, instead of two only, that excite the Apostle's admiration, and draw from his utmost soul the sublime ascription of praise;—the "*riches*" of God—(that is, the riches of his mercy)—his "*knowledge*,"—and his "*wisdom*."*

In support of this, the following considerations may be noticed:

1. The term "*riches*" is frequently used by this Apostle in the sense thus affixed to it,—with special reference, that is, to the goodness and grace of God. "The same Lord over all is *rich* unto all that call upon Him:"—"Despisest thou the *riches* of his goodness, and long-suffering, not knowing that the goodness of God leadeth thee to repentance?"—"In whom we have redemption through his blood, the forgiveness of sins, according to the *riches* of his grace:"—"God who is *rich* in mercy:"—"That in the ages to come he might show the exceeding *riches* of his grace, in his kindness toward us, through Christ Jesus:"—"Unto me, who am less than the least of all saints, is this grace given, that I

---

* So Bengel, Tholuck, Olshausen, and others.—ED.

should preach among the Gentiles the unsearchable *riches* of Christ:"—"I bow my knees unto the Father of our Lord Jesus Christ,—that He would grant you, according to the *riches* of his glory,"—or his *glorious riches*, "to be strengthened with might by his Spirit, in the inner man:" and, as the Apostle had just been speaking, in terms of admiration, of the extent and freeness of the divine *mercy*, this seems to be the sense which most naturally befits it here.—Then—

2. By this rendering, there is produced a correspondence between the three subjects of admiration, and the three questions which follow;—only—(which with the Apostle is no unusual thing) inverting their order. Thus the question, in the thirty-fifth verse—"Who hath first given to him, and it shall be recompensed to him again?" corresponds to the admiration of God's *riches*, as those in the thirty-fourth correspond to his *wisdom* and *knowledge;*—the question being intended to express the superabundance of His grace, as apparent in its unmerited freeness:—no one, when summoned to establish a claim upon Him, being able to respond to the challenge:—"Who hath first given to Him? and it shall be recompensed unto him again?" Let the claim be made good:—and "from the just God the compensation is sure."

We are called, then, by the language before us to consider two things:—The depth of the divine riches, wisdom, and knowledge;—and the influence which the contemplation of them should have on our sentiments and feelings.

I. Let us, in the *first* place, then, dwell a little on THE DEPTH OF THE DIVINE "RICHES, AND WISDOM, AND KNOWLEDGE."

1. "O the depth of the RICHES of God!"

"The *riches*" of God might be considered as having received illustration in the whole of the previous contents of the Epistle; which are, in truth, a development of the boundless amplitude of His love, in the redemption wrought by His Son. But the Apostle's devout reflection is evidently meant to be understood as having special reference to the theme of the present chapter;—the dealings of God's mercy with *Jews* and with *Gentiles*,—severally, and in union. The God of salvation

—the God of the everlasting covenant—proved himself "*rich in mercy*" toward "the seed of Abraham his friend." The largesses of His love to them were such as no other people enjoyed. But when they refused His grace, displayed in the very greatest of His gifts—"despising and rejecting" the divine Messiah;—then, in righteousness and sovereignty,—the mercy, proffered and proudly scorned, is transferred to the Gentiles. But not to the final exclusion of the chosen people. By the Gentiles—while it is enjoyed for themselves, it is, at the same time, to be, as it were, kept in store,—so that, when God's time of returning favour shall come, it may be again shared by them with the Jews,—and that in more glorious profusion than ever,—the very "fulness of the blessing."—As the Jews had been depositaries of it for the Gentiles, the Gentiles, in their turn, were to be depositaries of it for the Jews. And one of the effects of the temporary "casting away" of Israel will be—the more strikingly glorious manifestation of the "depth of the riches," and the munificent freeness, of divine mercy.—For many ages, the stream that flowed from this unfathomable depth appeared taking its course through Judea alone,—winding through the length and breadth of the land of promise. At "the fulness of time,"—in consequence and in punishment of the infidelity and rebellion of the people whom Jehovah had thus peculiarly and highly favoured,—its course was changed. It found a new channel. Diverted from Palestine, its pure and swelling waters overflowed with blessing to those nations, which had before been dwelling in "the shadow of death"—in "dry and thirsty lands where there was no water." And now, "the wilderness and the solitary place have been glad for them; and the desert has rejoiced and blossomed as the rose:"—the "glory of Lebanon, and the excellency of Carmel and Sharon," are transferred to the wastes of the heathen. For eighteen centuries, the hallowed stream has been wending its refreshing and fructifying course, in all directions, through this wide wilderness; and it is destined, in process of time, to make the whole extent of it "like Eden, the entire desert like the garden of the Lord." But the land of Israel is not to be left for ever in destitution of its cheering and fertilizing influence. It is yet again to reach that once fruitful, but now desolate and blighted region; and to bless it with new and perennial verdure. "Judgment shall then dwell in the wilderness, and righteousness remain in the fruitful field. And the work of righteousness shall be peace; and the effect of righteousness quietness and assurance for ever."

Thus Jehovah manifests his "delight in mercy." And rich mercy it is, both to Jew and to Gentile; conferred, free of all obligation on the part of the Giver, and in opposition to all desert on the part of the receivers. This is the sentiment so strongly and truly expressed in the thirty-fifth verse —"*Who hath first given unto him?—and it shall be recompensed unto him again?*"—God is just. Justice consists in giving every one his due. If, then, any being in existence can show that from him Jehovah has been a receiver; if he can thus make it good that He owes him a debt,—can substantiate a claim upon Him for its payment;—the payment will be made—instantly made,—the recompense not one moment withheld. If any *human* being can establish such a claim, let him advance it:—and the moment it is proved, it will be met. But there is blasphemous presumption in the very thought. To no creature whatever can the infinite God ever be under obligation. He is the universal Giver. He receives nothing. The boundless ocean of His love is not kept full by the influx of tributary rivers. It is an ocean which sends forth its streams of blessing over the universe; and which, although receiving no supplies, never sinks from its fulness. It is self-supplied, from the secret and everlasting springs of infinitude. To the question, "Who hath first given to Him?" there never has been, and there never can be, any other answer than one—*No created being.* The highest seraph before the throne regards not his glory and bliss in the light of *recompense*. He owes, and feels that he owes, all that he enjoys to infinite goodness alone; owning himself an "unprofitable servant, who has done that which was his duty to do;" but who has conferred nothing that can merit any return.—To *man*, when in innocence, the blessed God lay under no obligation beyond what arose from His own benevolent and holy nature, by which we are necessarily led to expect that happiness should accompany sinless obedience;—or from His own free and spontaneous promise, in harmony with that moral nature, giving the assurance that it should.—And when man had "fallen by his iniquity," the God against whom he had sinned was under no obligation to make any provision for his recovery. The rebel—the sinner—could have no claim whatever for anything of the kind. He *has* made it:—but it has been in mercy. The provision has come from the depth of His riches,—from the inexhaustible mine of His grace. The entire scheme of salvation, in its invention, its revelation, its preparation, its execution, its application, and in all its happy results to men, in time and in eternity,—is the product and the manifestation of sovereign mercy. Jesus Christ is God's gift—His "unspeakable gift:"—He "spared not his own Son, but freely gave him up for us all." And all the blessings of eternal life are equally gifts,—gifts of grace, bestowed on his account:— "how shall He not, *with him*, also freely give us all things?" "O the depth of his riches!"

Ye who have "tasted that the Lord is gracious,"—you are every one of you sensible, that all your happiness, in possession and in hope, is the gift of the "unsearchable riches" of God's mercy:—that you never had,—that you have not now,—and that you never can have—any claim, even the least and most distant, upon Him:—no—not so much as for one moment's existence in any condition less miserable than the "second death." You ask no *recompense:*—you ask a *gift;* a gift "without money and without price,"— "the gift of God, through Jesus Christ our Lord." And, in receiving it, you gratefully adore the mercy that confers it with such munificent freeness. "O the depth!" you exclaim, "of the riches of God! Who hath first given to Him? and it shall be recompensed unto him again."

It is a wonderful expression in the thirty-second verse— "For God hath concluded all in unbelief, that He might have mercy upon all!"—The sentiment—or general principle

—is closely analogous to that in Gal. iii. 22, "But the Scripture hath concluded all under sin, that the promise by faith of Jesus Christ might be given to them that believe." What marvellous grace is this! Were we for the first time hearing the words, "God hath concluded all under sin"—or, "God hath concluded all in unbelief,"—without having been previously aware of the constitution of mercy made known in the Gospel,—what should we naturally have expected to be the sequence? Should it not have been—"that he might visit all with righteous vengeance?"—"that wrath might come upon all to the uttermost?" But what in reality is it? "The Scripture hath concluded *all under sin,—that the promise, by faith in Jesus Christ, might be given to them that believe!*"—"God hath concluded them all *in unbelief—that he might have mercy upon all!*" Surely, well might Jehovah say, "My thoughts are not your thoughts, neither are your ways my ways:—for, as the heaven is higher than the earth, so are my ways higher than your ways, and my thoughts than your thoughts!"—"*O the depth of the divine riches!*"

Let us gladly and gratefully accept the mercy in its unfettered freeness and rejoice in its unbounded fulness. But for the riches of mercy, through the cross of the divine Mediator,—the Saviour of the world,—of Jew and Gentile alike,—we perish. But Jews may say as to Gentiles, and Gentiles as to Jews—"We believe, that through the grace of the Lord Jesus Christ, *we* shall be saved even as *they!*"— But I must pass to another part of my subject:—

2. "O the depth of the WISDOM AND KNOWLEDGE of God!" —And, as the exercise and manifestation of His "wisdom and knowledge"—"How unsearchable are his JUDGMENTS, and his WAYS past finding out!"

God's "*knowledge*" is His perfect acquaintance with all *existences* and all *events, past, present, and future;* and, along with this, with the entire range too of *possibilities;*—with the very minutest circumstances and occurrences in all worlds, all intuitively discerned, and never forgotten;—and with the most secret sentiments, affections, and desires, and the most passing and evanescent thoughts and the most deeply concealed and cherished alike, of all His intelligent creatures. And it is knowledge that reaches, not only through all time, but from eternity to eternity!

The *wisdom* of God is the attribute that applies this infinite knowledge, in His boundless administration, to the attainment of the best possible ends;—wisdom being, in brief definition, *the right use of knowledge.* There may, in God's intelligent creatures, be *not* a little knowledge, where there is *very* little wisdom to guide it. But in God himself, the knowledge and the wisdom are equal and infinite:—the knowledge unbounded, the wisdom unerring.

God's "*judgments*" are evidently to be understood here as meaning His counsels,—determinations,—or decrees; whatever He purposes to do.

God's *ways* comprehend all the endlessly varied methods by which, in the government of the universe, He works out the accomplishment of these purposes of His mind.

And the lesson which, under the form of devout exclamation, we are here taught, is, that in "the wisdom and knowledge of God" there is a "*depth*" that should overwhelm our minds with amazement;—and that, as a native consequence of this, the "*judgments*" which are the result of this "wisdom and knowledge,"—which are drawn from its hidden and fathomless depths,—are themselves, by us His creatures, who "are but of yesterday and know nothing," "*unsearchable;*"—and the "*ways,*" by which these "judgments" are carried out to their ultimate completion, involve in them so many secret connexions and dependencies,—such an impenetrable complexity and intricacy of operation,—as to be, by our limited minds, "*past finding out,*"—or, according to the more literal meaning of the original word, "*untraceable:*"*—the term containing an allusion to *footprints,* by which we can trace out the course a man has followed. And of Jehovah, accordingly, in fine harmony with this idea, the inspired psalmist says:—"Thy way, O God, is in the sea,

---

* ἀνεξιχνίαστοι.

and thy path in the great waters, and thy footsteps are not known?"*

The infinite disparity between the divine mind and ours might seem quite a sufficient reason for our ignorance, and our inability to sound "the depths of the wisdom and knowledge of God," or clearly to comprehend His "judgments" and trace His ways. There is, however, another consideration suggested here. It is the entire INDEPENDENCE of the Godhead:—"*For who hath known the mind of the Lord? or who hath been his counsellor?*"—The words are cited from a most sublime passage in the prophecies of Isaiah, setting forth, in terms instinct with the dignity and glowing with the fire of inspiration, the greatness and the grace of Jehovah;—"Who hath directed the Spirit of the Lord, or, being his counsellor, hath taught him? With whom took he counsel?—and who instructed Him, and taught Him in the path of judgment, and taught Him knowledge, and showed to Him the way of understanding?"—Jehovah consults with none. He determines and acts alone. He follows, with unerring wisdom, the light of infinite knowledge. His purposes were all in His mind, ere any creature had existence; when there was no Being besides Himself;—when He had his own existence in the to us awful and incomprehensible solitudes of eternity. —O the grandeur of that nature!—

"Grand beyond a seraph's thought!"

—which then had its being alone; and, full in its own infinite resources, felt no want and no dreariness!—When we, the "creatures of yesterday, whose foundation is in the dust, and who are crushed before the moth," take upon us to examine the "judgments" and the "ways" of such a Being, what self-diffident humility becomes us! It may well be—nay it ought to be—our previous expectation that, in such investigation, we should find not a little beyond our depth,—not a little, of which the short line of our wisdom cannot take the soundings:—that we should find many an occasion for the

* Psa. lxxvii. 19.

lowly confession of the psalmist—" Such knowledge is too wonderful for me: it is high; I cannot attain unto it!" To come to such a subject in any other frame of spirit than that enjoined of old by Him who said—" Put off thy shoe from thy foot; for the place where thou standest is holy ground," —is to discard reason, and to place ourselves in the highway, not to infidelity alone, but to atheism. There are parts of the divine procedure toward our own world, which are full of inscrutable mystery.—I might illustrate this general statement, by a reference, first of all to that *mystery of mysteries* —the origin of evil in the universe of a holy and a benevolent God,—the God who " is Light" and " Love." Not that this mystery was first exemplified in our world. It originated earlier. How much earlier, we cannot tell; but the parents of our race had a tempter, who was the chief of a host of fallen spirits of light. This is a mystery that has baffled the wit of man from the beginning hitherto, and that will continue to baffle it to the end; which we shall never fully see through, till we come " to know even as we are known." It is of importance to bear in mind, that this mystery is not a mystery of *doctrine*, but a mystery of *fact*. It is not a Bible dogma; it is *a fact in providence*, which existed before revelation, and independently of it. To reject revelation, is not to get quit of the mystery. It remains. And it remains in an aggravated form; inasmuch as, while every other system, necessarily finding the mystery, leaves it as it found it, in all its inexplicable fearfulness,—revelation, while it records the fact, provides a remedy; and shows us divine holiness and divine justice, in harmonious operation with divine love, and divine mercy, rearing on the ruins of man's apostate nature a glorious temple to Jehovah's praise;—stamping on the very evil He had permitted to enter the deepest impress of His abhorrence;—and in the wonderful plan of salvation, setting His own character, and the principles of His moral administration, before the admiring universe, in lights in which they never otherwise could have been seen. And if the mystery is not thus fully solved, and divested of all perplexing questions,—it is, at all events, wonderfully mitigated in regard to the light in which it placed the divine character; our painful wonder in the contemplation of the mystery of the entrance of evil, being swallowed in our delighted admiration of the mystery of redeeming love,—the "great mystery of godliness!"—I might dwell too on the mystery involved in the length of the interval, and on the state of the world during that interval, between the fall and the fulness of time;—on the large extent of the unevangelized portions of our world, after the lapse of eighteen centuries of the Christian era;—on the extension and long continuance of such systems as Mahometanism and Popery;—on the extinction of the light of Christian truth in churches and lands in which it was once enjoyed;—and on other extraordinary facts of a similarly mysterious description,—pointing out, in each case, along with the mysterious character of the fact, its causes, such ends as we see to have been answered by it and its other explanatory or mitigating circumstances. But your time prohibits me from so much as touching any such topics.

I must say a few words on the particular *mystery* in the divine administration treated of in the chapter which our text concludes,—the mystery, by the contemplation of which the impassioned burst of adoration was drawn forth;—after which I shall briefly generalize the great principle of the text; in doing which the *second* head of our discourse will receive its concise illustration; namely, *the influence which the contemplation of the depth of the riches, and wisdom, and knowledge of God should exert on our sentiments and feelings.*

That the Apostle speaks of the dealings of God with His ancient people as a mystery, appears from the twenty-fifth verse:—" For I would not, brethren, that ye should be ignorant of this mystery, (lest ye should be wise in your own conceits,) that blindness in part is happened to Israel, until the fulness of the Gentiles be come in." The meaning of the term here, however, is not so much a thing in itself difficult of comprehension; although even in this acceptation of it, it might, to a certain extent, be justly applied to the case under review; there being something in the whole history of the

Jewish people, and of the divine dealings with them, which, while we can see the principles of the divine justice and the divine mercy, in all its successive stages, from the beginning till now, clearly apparent, and the divine character, in His treatment of them free from all possible impeachment, is yet full of the marvellous. They are, in their present state, an anomaly in the general history of the nations of the world,—a description, indeed, of standing miracle:—and the long continuance of their blindness, and their outcast and seemingly abandoned condition,—even although we see an adequate reason for its unwonted duration in the superior magnitude of the sins which have brought it upon them, is yet so unlike the longings and yearnings of Jehovah's ancient compassion for the people of His covenant,—so unlike the—" How shall I give thee up, Ephraim? how shall I deliver thee, Israel? how shall I make thee as Admah? how shall I set thee as Zeboim? My heart is turned within me; my repentings are kindled together: I will not execute the fierceness of mine anger;—I will not return to destroy Ephraim:—for I am God, and not man, the Holy One in the midst of thee,"—that we are ready to adopt the desponding questions of the sweet singer of Israel—and, heaving the sigh over the "perpetual desolations," to exclaim—" Will the Lord cast off for ever? and will he be favourable no more? Hath God forgotten to be gracious? hath he in anger shut up his tender mercies? Is his mercy clean gone for ever? doth his promise fail for evermore." "Seventy years" was the longest period of divine visitation for their sins in ancient times,—when they were dispossessed of the land that it might enjoy its Sabbaths, in freedom from heartless externalism and idolatrous profanation. But now that their period of desertion and dispersion is drawing on to two millenniums,—we are apt to wonder whether God is ever again to " remember his covenant:"—But, when we have asked our questions of sceptical astonishment, we must, like the psalmist, conclude with—" This is mine infirmity:"—and, like him, we must recover the tone of our faith and our hope, by " remembering," as he did, " the works of the Most High, and his wonders of old." The time is long; but it is not to be for ever. Even yet, they are "beloved for the Fathers' sakes." Jehovah has *not* "forgotten to be gracious." Times of mercy still await them. The promise has *not* "failed for evermore." "The night is far spent, the day is at hand." The "breath" is coming from the four winds, to quicken the dry and scattered bones in "the valley of vision." By the Spirit of the Lord, coming down upon them, in simultaneous and ample effusion, in all places throughout the wide world, whither the vengeance of a righteous God hath driven them,—"the vail shall be taken away" that has been so long and so darkly upon their hearts;—and they shall "turn to the Lord," accepting the punishment of their iniquity, "looking," with penitential mourning, on Him whom their fathers pierced, and whom they have ever since been piercing anew by consenting to the deed of their fathers. And then, as I firmly believe, though on grounds into which we cannot now enter,—they shall be gathered from all the countries of their wide dispersion,—by such instrumental agency as He who has "the hearts of all men in his hands, turning them as the rivers of water, whithersoever he will," can never be at a loss to find, and to employ, and to prosper; —and shall be settled again, nationally, in the land of their fathers;—not absorbed and lost, when converted to the faith of Christ, amongst the Christian population of the Gentile world; but holding forth to mankind, in their restoration, as a distinct people, but no longer distinct in their faith and worship,—a conspicuous and marvellous manifestation of Jehovah's faithfulness to His covenant. "They shall be his people, and He will be their God, in truth and in righteousness." "And Jerusalem shall be inhabited again, in her own place, even in Jerusalem:"—"for the gifts and calling of God are without repentance." All this the Apostle calls a "*mystery;*" in a sense very much akin to that in which he so denominates the calling of the Gentiles, and their union with the Jews in the spiritual kingdom of the Messiah; that is, in the sense of *a secret not before fully made known.* In his Epistle to the Ephesians, he speaks of "the mystery of Christ, which in other ages was not made known unto the sons of men, as it is now revealed unto his holy apostles and prophets by the Spirit; that the Gentiles should be fellow-heirs, and of the same body, and partakers of his promise in Christ, by the Gospel." It was a mystery, that the Gentiles, having remained so long in darkness, were to be enlightened, and brought directly into the church, without the medium of Judaism. So here is a parallel mystery. "Blindness in part"—that is, to a part of the nation, and for a season,—"is happened to Israel"—*until a certain time:* and *so,* when that time comes, *Israel*—the same Israel,—not, I apprehend, the spiritual Israel of all nations,—but the Israel to whom the blindness—the judicial blindness—had happened,—and that had been so long cast off—shall obtain mercy, be restored, and saved;—and that, in fulfilment of the prophetic promise—"There shall come out of Zion the Deliverer, and shall turn away ungodliness from Jacob."

And let us, in drawing to a close, generalize in its application a little the great principle and spirit of our text.—I might apply it to the endlessly diversified histories of individuals and families; in which there is a vast amount of inexplicable mystery. But I must confine myself to what is more of a public character; to what relates to the nations of the world, and the interests of the kingdom of Christ.—How pregnant with consolation and delight is the assurance, that the affairs of the universe are all under the presiding guidance of the wisdom of the Infinite Mind;—and, what to us is of most immediate concern, the affairs of our own world! How settling and tranquillizing to our spirits, to have the full conviction of this, even in seasons when we are specially constrained to own that God's "judgments are unsearchable, and his ways past finding out!" In surveying the complicated, strange, and seemingly contradictory events that are taking place among the nations,—how very differently are our minds affected, when we are enabled to view all in this light,—from what they could not fail to be, had we nothing on which to stay our distracted spirits, but a blind undesigning *Fate!* When at times, amidst "wars and rumours of wars,"—agitated and revolutionized nations,—some passing from despotism to freedom, and some from freedom to despotism, —overturned and overturning thrones,—distracted and divided churches,—the conflicting elements of truth and error,—of Christ and antichrist,—of heaven and hell,—giving rise to present perplexity and future apprehension;—when, in a word, the world presents the aspect of the ocean in a storm:—how cheering to feel assured, that "the Spirit of God moves upon the face of the waters;"—so that, boisterous and troubled as they are, no angry billow can lift its foaming crest, but under the control of Him who "stilleth the noise of the seas, the noise of their waves, and the tumult of the people!"

All the events that have taken place from the beginning till now, are parts of one stupendous whole. *We* cannot discern the various junctures and mutual dependencies,—the "wheels within wheels," and the intricate movements of the vast machine. But the eye of Him who constructed it, and who, without one moment's intermission, superintends all its turnings, sees, at one glance, with unerring precision, every one of them. All its parts are, in their respective places, indispensable. The removal of a single wheel, or pin, might disarrange or suspend the motion, and prevent or mar the result. Thus every event—the least as well as the greatest—in the scheme of Providence, is essential to the real harmony, and the final issue, of the whole. The absence of any one of them would spoil the plan. Some events in themselves are of immense importance; others of almost incalculably little. But these, little events are necessary for linking the greater ones; and are thus, many a time, of essential value. In a chain, composed of links of various sizes, it matters not, in regard to the effect, whether it be a larger or a smaller one, that gives way. In either case, the continuity is gone; the chain is broken. What the poet has said of "*nature's chain*" is not less true as to that of Providence:—

> " From nature's chain whatever link you strike,
> Tenth or ten-thousandth, breaks the chain alike."

—The man who accustoms himself to observe the ways of God, will not seldom have the suggestion forced upon his mind, of his arrangements being made as if for the purpose of contradicting all that to us might seem reasonable and likely; as if to show us, experimentally, that we must not presume to make our wisdom the standard of His,—and to impress the truth of His own declaration—"My thoughts are not your thoughts, neither are your ways my ways, saith Jehovah:—for, as the heavens are higher than the earth, so are my ways higher than your ways, and my thoughts than your thoughts!"—Our business, then, is—humbly to confess our ignorance and short-sightedness; to put our trust in that wisdom which "knows the end from the beginning;"—the wisdom of Him "whose mind none can know," further than He is himself pleased to reveal it, and who is His own only counsellor; and to rest in the full satisfaction that all is ordered wisely and well; that our fancied amendments upon His plans would very soon throw all into confusion; and, with one heart and one voice, to sing—

"Thy ways, great God, are little known
To my weak erring sight;
Yet shall my soul, believing, own
That all thy ways are right!"

We are further, by this text, taught the lesson, of viewing all things in their relation to God; and viewing them, in this highest of all relations, in the spirit of lowly yet lively devotion:—"*for of Him, and through Him, and to Him, are all things; to whom be glory for ever and ever. Amen.*"—The simplest interpretation of these words—the interpretation which most immediately and naturally presents itself to our minds, is, beyond comparison, the best. "All things are OF Him, as the great Originator and first Cause of all existence besides his own:—THROUGH Him, as the universal Preserver and Governor;—and TO Him, as the infinitely glorious End.

And here there opens a boundless and delightful field—on which it is impossible for us even to enter. We can but glance at the general meaning. All existence is OF Him;

all events are THROUGH Him; and of all His works of creation and all His ways of providence, it is true that they are TO Him:—the entire scheme eventually issuing in the fulfilment of His purposes and the glory of his name.

What an impressively sublime and interesting view it is, which revelation thus gives us of the blessed God!—how different, not only from the fooleries of the grosser idolatries of heathenism,—but from all the results of the unaided wisdom of man, even in its best estate. It teaches us to regard Him as possessed of eternal, independent, necessary existence,—alone having immortality; as bringing all things into being by the simple volition of His mind, uttered or unuttered—as, by His omnipotent, and unceasingly active and pervading energy, preserving and animating the whole system;—as directing, by His ever-present superintendence, the entire course of events,—so that His own glory, and the good of the universe, may be the sure and the finally glorious issue.—Many are the systems,—systems of human philosophy, in which He is hardly, if at all, to be found. But here—in this blessed Book—He is ALL IN ALL—first, last, and midst, —the Alpha and the Omega; the Author, the Upholder, and the Final Cause, of all created existence!—here He holds the place to which all His intelligent creatures must hold Him entitled. He is supreme. He is over all, God, blessed for ever. "OF HIM, THROUGH HIM, AND TO HIM ARE ALL THINGS."

Such is the sublime sentiment of this passage:—and it is in harmony with others which the pages of inspiration furnish,—both in its abstract truth, and in the spirit, or posture and emotion of mind, with which the sentiment is uttered. For in this Book, we many a time meet with sentiments, such as are in themselves noble and elevated,—but which are rendered still more lofty and impressive, by the form in which they are presented. Thus it is in the text. It is not the abstract sentiment of the divine supremacy merely that is didactically brought before us. We have it in union with the devotion which it is fitted to inspire. We see the effect of the contemplation of it on the mind of the writer.

We see that mind expanding itself to its utmost enlargement, to take in the vast conception:—his heart, at the same time, swelling with rapturous emotion;—his soul, sinking under an abasing sense of its own nothingness,—and yet rising to conscious elevation, in feeling itself capable, even how inadequately soever, of contemplating the grandeur of Godhead: —his eye lifted to heaven, filled with the tear—the trembling tear—of holy transport! The effect thus produced upon our minds is unspeakably more impressive. We catch the spirit by which the devout worshipper is animated. Our spiritual sympathies are awakened. We not only apprehend abstract truth; we feel the impulse of piety;—we kindle at his ardour;—we cease to speculate;—we adore;—with kindred fervour, we join in his devout exclamation—" O the depth of the riches, and wisdom, and knowledge of God! how unsearchable are his judgments, and his ways past finding out! For who hath known the mind of the Lord? or who hath been his counsellor? or who hath first given to him, and it shall be recompensed to him again? For of him, and through him, and to him, are all things: to whom be glory for ever. Amen."

And when we thus say—"To whom be glory for ever and ever! Amen!"—we utter a *conviction;* we breathe a *desire;* and we bring ourselves under a sacred *pledge.*—We utter a *conviction;*—the conviction that thus it *must,* that thus it *shall* be; the very supposition of the contrary,—the supposition that by the conduct of any of his creatures the glory of "the Lord of all" should, in even the slightest degree, be ultimately tarnished, involving the most presumptuous blasphemy. We breathe a *desire;* the desire that so it *may* be; that the issue of the entire system of the divine administration, in our world and in all worlds, from first to last, and in all its departments, may, by the display, in the eyes of the intelligent universe, of the harmony of all his infinite excellences, be "glory to God in the highest:"—and let us not forget, that the very expression of such a conviction and such a desire brings us under a *pledge*—a sacred pledge:— What is it?—that throughout life, each of us in our several spheres, we make God's glory our highest aim, and strive, by every means in our power, to promote it. O let us feel, deeply feel, what unworthy hypocrisy there would be, in thus honouring Him with our *lips*, while we are not glorifying Him in our *lives*. Words are light and easily uttered. Any man may say with the mouth—"*To* whom be glory for ever and ever!"—But to say it with the mouth, while we do not seek to realize the prayer by the service of our consecrated persons, in all their powers, is but to utter a lie.—Let us not have the guilt of it upon our consciences. If you are in earnest, my friends, in uttering the sentiment, you cannot fail to seek the advancement of God's glory, by using every endeavour to diffuse the knowledge of his Name, and of that Gospel which is the grand manifestation of the purity and the benevolence, the justice and the mercy, the light and the love, of His character and His government, amongst both Jews and Gentiles; thus to aid in the reclaiming of the one from their unbelief and apostasy, and of the other from their ignorance and idolatry. The former may, in the divine administration, be one of the most efficient means of accomplishing the latter:—for "if the fall of them be the riches of the world, and the diminishing of them the riches of the Gentiles, how much more their fulness!"—"if the casting away of them be the reconciling of the world, what shall the receiving of them be, but life from the dead?"—Let us *redeem the pledge*, then, my fellow-Christians. We may not live to witness the realization of the glorious prospects that are opened to the eye of our faith and hope by the visions of prophecy. But we may assist in preparing the way; and we cannot be wrong in making the aim of this Apostle ours—"that we may by all means save some!" And should we not survive to see the final triumph on earth, in the restoration of Israel, and the coming in of "the fulness of the Gentiles,"—we shall hear of it in heaven, when voices shall be heard there, "loud as from numbers without number," saying—"The kingdoms of this world are become the kingdom of our Lord and of his Christ; and he shall reign for ever and ever!"

LECTURE LIII.

ROMANS XII. 1, 2.

"I beseech you, therefore, brethren, by the mercies of God, that ye present your bodies a living sacrifice, holy, acceptable unto God, which is your reasonable service. And be not conformed to this world; but be ye transformed by the renewing of your mind, that ye may prove what is that good, and acceptable, and perfect will of God."

THE preceding part of the Epistle has been principally, although not by any means exclusively, doctrinal and argumentative. Not, I say, exclusively. In the sixth chapter the writer enlarges on the general holy tendency of the truth,—as leading from the service of sin to the service of God, and furnishing the most powerfully persuasive motives to a life of practical holiness: and in the latter part of the seventh, the experience is delineated of every true child of God, in regard to the opposition in his mind between the two contending principles of "the flesh" and "the spirit"—the remaining propensities of corruption, and the affections and desires of "the new man," or the spiritual life in the soul.— In the eighth chapter also the practical influence of the Gospel is directly and forcibly urged.

The Apostle now proceeds to the more particular and detailed practical improvement of the doctrines so fully illustrated in the former chapters. This is his ordinary manner. There is an inseparable connexion—a connexion that pervades the word of God, and is only dissolved in the ravings of heresy—between doctrinal and practical religion; between truth enlightening the understanding, and truth affecting the heart and regulating the conduct.* There are persons to be found who can talk abundantly and talk well, and who can even "reason high" upon the doctrines of Christian theology. They can detect and expose the fallacies of Socinian, Arian, Arminian, and Antinomian heresies; and perhaps of the minute branches and subdivisions of each. They have all the terms of scholastic and controversial divinity by rote and ready at command. Yet with all this speculative knowledge, they are practical Antinomians,—with "a name to live while they are dead." They call the Calvinistic doctrines their creed: but they make it manifest that whatever tenets they profess are held by them as mere opinions. They have been taught them as a system in their early days, and have thus grown up in "the form of godliness," while they have continued destitute of its power. Their views have all been general; never taken home to themselves with serious self-application. They have learned the Gospel as *scholars;* not as *sinners.* They have never seen and felt their own true condition,—their destitute and hopeless wretchedness; nor experienced in themselves the subduing power of gratitude for redeeming mercy. They can *talk,* but they do not *feel.* Their religion consists rather in arguing for truth than in living humbly and consistently under its holy influence. Now, the revelation of God is not given us merely for our information—to impart a speculative acquaintance with truth to the understanding. However important the discoveries made in the Book of God, they fail of their purpose if they stop at the intellect; if they pass only from the book to the head, and do not reach the heart. The grand end of *truth* is to produce *character*—to "form a people for the Lord," who shall "show forth his praise." The Sun of righteousness is in the spiritual world what the sun in the firmament is in the world of nature—the source at once of light, and heat, and gladness, and fruitfulness.

The Apostle introduces this part of his Epistle with the lan-

---

* Jam. i. 14—18; 1 John i. 5—7.

guage of affectionate entreaty:—"*I beseech you, therefore, brethren.*" They were his brethren, as fellow-believers in Christ, children of God, members of His spiritual family, and heirs of His glory. They were his brethren, without distinction of Jew or Gentile; for he now "knew no man after the flesh." He "beseeches" them with tender and earnest solicitude. His entreaty, relating to a matter in which the glory of Christ and their own eternal well-being were alike involved, was dictated at once by love to *Him* and by love to *them.*

Mark the motive he employs:—"*By the mercies of God.*" You are aware, that in ordinary language the word "*mercies*" often signifies favours or gifts conferred upon us. We thank God for all his daily *mercies.* The word in the original has not at all this sense. It means the mercies or *compassions* of the divine character; the fulness of tender love that there is in God.*

This, however, comes in effect to much the same thing; for the mercies of the divine character appear in *their practical manifestations to us.* The infinite fulness of His love is displayed in the gift of that love to men—His "unspeakable gift," the gift of His own Son—and with Him all the blessings of salvation in time and in eternity.†

The appeal in these words is to *gratitude.* This is one of the mainsprings of Christian activity in the ways of God. It is appealed to on all occasions. It is like the great wheel that keeps all the connected machinery in motion; while faith, maintained in exercise by the Spirit of God, by keeping this love in vigorous exercise, is like the power of water or of steam, that gives its motion to the wheel.

The faith of "the mercies of God," as made known in the Gospel, is a faith that "worketh by love;" and this love incites to active, cheerful, and constant obedience to the will of Him who is the "Father of mercies." This generous principle at once restrains from evil, and stimulates to good. The remembrance of "the mercies of God" checks in the be-

---

* It is the same word—2 Cor. i. 3; Phil. ii. 1; Col. iii. 12—*οἰκτιρμοί.*
† His mercy is thus associated, Psalm cxxxvi. 23; Luke i. 76—79; Eph. ii. 4—7; 1 Pet. i. 3—5.

liever's bosom the indulgence of sinful desires. It closes and seals the lips when the heart is tempted to the utterance of perverse things. It arrests the hand when it is stretched out to the perpetration of evil. Its language is—" How shall I do this wickedness, and sin against God"—the God of my life, the author of all my joys, the rock of my salvation? Shall I thus repay the riches of eternal mercy? shall I dishonour that Saviour who "loved me, and gave himself for me?" shall I grieve that Holy Spirit, by whom I am sealed unto the day of redemption? Perish the perfidious thought! The believer feels in all its persuasive power the appeal here addressed to him. It touches every spring of spiritual sensibility within him. He is indignant at the imputation thrown upon the Gospel as of loose and licentious tendency, feeling as he does that the only principle that has wrought in himself with efficient energy has been the love which the belief of that Gospel engenders. Nothing won his heart to God till he saw with the eye of spiritual discernment the "mercies of God" as discovered in Jesus Christ. When the character of Jehovah as seen in the cross has been by the enlightening Spirit brought before his mind, the enmity of his heart has been slain:—his affections have been won to the God of salvation, and all the energies of a willing mind inscribed with "holiness to the Lord."

The Apostle first inculcates the consecration of the whole person to God—for active, continued, spiritual, self-devoting service;—a service, in every view that can be taken of it, infinitely reasonable:—"I beseech you, therefore, brethren, by the mercies of God, that ye present your bodies a living sacrifice, holy, acceptable unto God, which is your reasonable service." This figurative language comprehends the entire sum of active obedience. It expresses the duty of complete personal consecration to God.

The "*body*"—it is hardly necessary to remark—*must* here signify *the person:* not the mere corporeal frame, even although with all its complement of members; but the body considered as animated by the intelligent soul. The one cannot be presented without the other. The one indeed must be presented *by* the other. How can the body be presented but by the voluntary agency of the presiding spirit within? and when the body is presented by the act of the willing soul, nothing can be more absurd than the idea of its being presented apart from itself. In presenting the body, we might consider the soul as the officiating priest,—but we rather regard the whole man as the priest, and the whole man as the victim. We present OURSELVES.*

And in this phrase, "*present* your bodies" or persons, there is an obvious reference to what was done to the victims that were devoted to the altar.† They were presented to be slain; and all the preparatory rites duly performed. They were given up, or devoted to God; and the general idea, therefore, is that of self-dedication to Him, in all our powers of body and of soul.

And it is called "*a living sacrifice.*" In this expression there is a happy and beautiful allusion, in the way of contrast, to the ancient sacrifices. These were presented *to be slain*—victims devoted to death. They were killed. Part of them was consumed on the altar; part was eaten; and the rest burned with fire without the camp: and there was thus an end of them—they were no more.—In contrast with these slaughtered and dead victims, we are called upon to present ourselves as a "living sacrifice;" not devoting ourselves *to death*, like the human sacrifices whose blood was spilt in the sanguinary rites of heathen idolatry; but devoting ourselves to a *life* of consecration to God. The expression may include—

1. *Active service.* The victims slain—*dead*—could do no further service of any kind. But the sacrifice spoken of here is that of a living, conscious, intelligent, voluntary agent; presented, not by others, but by himself,—and presented *for life* in all his powers.

* Olshausen and De Wette consider that σῶμα is used to "indicate that the sanctification of the Christian life is to extend to that part of man's nature which is most completely under the bondage of sin."—ED.

† παραστῆσαι—the word generally *used for bringing to offer in sacrifice.*—ED.

2. *Continued devotedness.* The victims at the altar could be offered but once. One act presented them; one act slew and consumed them. They were gone; and could never appear at the altar of God again. But the "living sacrifice" is one which *continues* in a state of active consecration to God—presented anew every day and every hour, in the habitual exercise of the mind and heart, and the unremitting homage of the life.

3. As the Apostle is addressing himself to believers, we ought, perhaps, to include the idea of the *new life* as distinguishing them from the world and from their former selves, when they were in a state of spiritual death:—the "living sacrifice" being that not merely of a living, active, intelligent creature,—but of a sinner brought under the influence of the vivifying Spirit of God. The sacrifice must not possess mere animal life, but must be instinct with spiritual life—the new life of holy sensibilities and holy principles to which the soul is "born again by the incorruptible seed of God's word," and the omnipotence of the Spirit. And

4. Although it is a living sacrifice, it is a sacrifice *ready for death,* should the cause of God require it. The life is to be *so* devoted to God, as to be at all times and entirely at His service, and, if need be, cheerfully surrendered for His glory. It includes, in a word, willingness to *be,* to *do,* or to *suffer* whatever He may see fit to appoint.*

The sacrifice must be "*holy.*" The body, considered in itself, is capable of no more than outward and ceremonial cleansing. The proper original idea of *holiness* is that of consecration or setting apart to God. Of holiness in this sense, irrational creatures, and even inanimate things, were capable. But in a rational being, holiness necessarily includes something more. It includes *moral purification*—the spiritual cleansing of the heart. No intelligent creature can be fit without this for the service of a holy God. The ancient victims were ordained to be free from blemish. In

* Luke xiv. 26 expresses the general principle: and we have exemplifications of it in Acts xx. 22—24; Phil. ii. 17.

this they were types of Him who, in his one offering, is described as the "*Lamb of God*, who taketh away the sin of the world." In this moral purity his people resemble him.

And in proportion as they *are* thus holy, the sacrifice will prove "*acceptable unto God.*"—No sacrifice of a sinner, whatever it be, can be acceptable to God except through a mediator.* For a sinner to think of presenting anything to God otherwise is unwarrantable and fearful presumption:— and it must be especially so, when the sacrifice presented is the very person of the guilty creature!—At the same time, the offering itself must be *holy*—purified from the pollutions of sin—not willingly defiling itself by contact with the world, but "separated unto God."

Of this presentation of our persons to God "a living sacrifice, holy, acceptable," the Apostle says, "*which is your reasonable service.*" Different ideas have been attached to the original word.† That adopted and expressed by our translators has the best claims, I think, to our approbation.—What is here required is a "reasonable service," in opposition to the foolish, irrational services of the heathen to their gods:—it is a "reasonable service," even in opposition to the external rites of Judaism, when these were performed, as they too often were, without a spiritual understanding of their import and design, and without a believing respect, in the mind of the worshipper, to the typified atonement. These rites were far from unreasonable, when viewed in their spiritual import, and typical relations: they derived from these a true dignity, and were worthy of the infinitely wise God by whom they were instituted. They were a most "reasonable service" when performed according to His intention. He never appointed them as *in themselves* an acceptable service and mode of worship; and when considered in the light in which He appointed them, they were worthy of himself:— but it was the *spirit* of them that made them a reasonable service. And now that they are set aside, the "reasonable

---

* 1 Pet. ii. 4, 5; Heb. xiii. 15, 16; Col. iii. 17.
† τὴν λογικὴν λατρείαν.

service" is, under the influence of faith in Him whom they typified, to present ourselves in holy dedication to God. This was from the beginning required, as well as now:—and it has been from the beginning, is now, and ever must be, a "reasonable service." It should need no argument, surely, to prove it reasonable for an intelligent creature to worship and serve his Creator—to love and fear and obey Him. And the *kind* of service—the personal, spiritual, holy service, with body and spirit which are His, is in harmony with the true character of God, and with the obligations of His creatures to Him for all His mercies and loving-kindnesses. Both the inward principles of religion and their outward expression are "reasonable." The man who can question whether it be "reasonable" to love and to fear God, or to give expression, both verbal and practical, to these devout affections of heart, must be far gone indeed, through the influence of a deceived heart, from the exercise of sound reason. Every conscience assents to the truth of the Apostle's sentiment. If it be "reasonable" to slight what is infinitely venerable; to hate what is infinitely lovely; to refuse obedience to the highest authority, and the expression and manifestation of gratitude to the greatest benefactor; to scorn the favour of one on whose favour our happiness for the entire extent of our existence depends; to live without prayer to Him from whom alone we can obtain any good, and without thanksgiving to Him from whom comes, without exception, all the good that we enjoy;—if this be "reasonable," then is irreligion "reasonable:"—but in proportion as these things are what every rational being should instinctively feel that he has cause to be ashamed of, in that proportion is irreligion, both in principle and in practice, the most *un*reasonable thing in existence or in imagination.

The next exhortation, "Be not conformed to this world," is in harmony with this, and inseparably connected with it. The presenting of the person as a living sacrifice to God is utterly inconsistent with *conformity to the world*.

The precept is one of very comprehensive import. But it

is one of which the terms are general, and capable, consequently, of having a considerable variety of shades of meaning affixed to them. Perhaps our best way of ascertaining their true spirit, will be to begin with the consideration of that to which they are here opposed—"but be ye transformed by the renewing of your minds, that ye may prove what is that good, and acceptable, and perfect will of God."

"*The mind*" means here either the understanding by "the renewing" of which in the spiritual discernment of the truth, the heart is "renewed," and the character "transformed;" or the "transformation" enjoined *identifies* with "the renewing of the mind;" in which case the "mind" will be taken, as it often is, in its more comprehensive sense of "the inward parts" in general, the whole soul, considered as the seat both of the intellect and of the passions. We are naturally, in principle and in practice, in heart and in life, "conformed to this world." In one or more of its various forms of allurement, it has our desires, and engrosses our attention and pursuit. When conversion to God takes place, a change appears. God takes that place in the heart which the world occupied. New principles of character are introduced, which exert a transforming influence upon the whole man. The general name for the whole set of new principles and affections is *godliness*. This was what was wanting; and the introduction of this is the essence of the change:—"If any man be in Christ, he is a new creature: old things are passed away; behold, all things are become new."* The change is not perfect at first. The *principles* are introduced; and their influence is progressive. Believers are often admonished to grow and advance in newness of mind and character:— "That ye put off, concerning the former conversation, the old man, which is corrupt according to the deceitful lusts; and be renewed in the spirit of your mind; and that ye put on the new man, which after God is created in righteousness and true holiness."† "*Be ye transformed by the renewing of your mind*," means then—growing in this conformity to

* 2 Cor. v. 17. † Eph. iv. 22—24.

the image of God—in the beauty of holiness—in spirituality, and purity, and heavenliness of affection and desire.

This leads us to observe, that where the renewal and transformation have really taken place, and the holy and blessed principle of them continues in due operation; where the inward holy energy of the truth of God prevails; where there is a sincere and earnest desire to increase in likeness to God and in "meetness for the inheritance of the saints in light," as the one thing needful to our happiness,—there will not be much necessity for drawing with jealous precision the boundaries of propriety and duty on this subject. Why? Because *the principle*, in sincere and influential operation, will be the best director of the life. The man who is under its power will discern, with a spiritual *tact*, what is consistent or inconsistent with his principles, and with the one end which he has in view. Such a one will not be ever desirous to know how far he may go with the world, and yet retain his Christian profession. It is a most melancholy symptom of a man's spiritual state, when he discovers a disposition to urge such inquiries. Mark the character given of Christians—"If ye were of the world, the world would love his own: but because ye are not of the world, but I have chosen you out of the world, therefore the world hateth you:" "I have given them thy word; and the world hath hated them, because they are not of the world, even as I am not of the world."* And on the ground of their separation from the world, how very strong are the expressions of Scripture— "Love not the world, neither the things that are in the world. If any man love the world, the love of the Father is not in him. For all that is in the world, the lust of the flesh, and the lust of the eyes, and the pride of life, is not of the Father, but is of the world:" "Ye adulterers and adulteresses, know ye not that the friendship of the world is enmity with God? whosoever therefore will be a friend of the world is the enemy of God."†

It is very difficult, on a subject like this, to draw bound-

---

* John xv. 1 ; xvii. 14, 16. † 1 John ii. 15, 16; Jam. iv. 4.

ing lines, especially when there is not time for minute specification. We may notice in general, however,—

1. That there must be no "conformity to the world" in what is *sinful*, whether in principle or in practice. This is manifest. It requires no proof. There are "worldly lusts," respecting the indulgence of which our maxim must be—"Touch not, taste not, handle not."* This general principle will leave no hesitation as to those worldly amusements, and places of public exhibition and entertainment, that are directly or indirectly licentious in their character and tendency; such as are constructed on the principle of adaptation to the likings of the worldly mind, and are calculated, instead of cherishing, to dissipate all serious and spiritual feeling, and to induce an earthly, sensual, and ungodly state of heart. What other state of heart than this is to be cherished in the theatre or in the ball-room and card-party? The question, according to the verse before us, ought to be—Whether the tendency of these is to "transform us by the renewing of our mind," or to "conform" our hearts and characters to "this world." Tried by this Bible test, no child of God will find room for hesitation.

2. There are many things, of which it cannot perhaps be distinctly affirmed that they are in their own nature sinful, which may yet, when indulged in, mark a worldliness of disposition at variance with the admonition before us—at variance with the character of the Christian, as one who is not of this world.—There is such a thing as preaching the Gospel by *the conduct*.† Now, in order to the influence of the Gospel being apparent, there must be a marked and visible distinction between believers and the world. It ought to be apparent that believers are under the influence of different and peculiar principles. The sum of this is, that the operation should appear in them, not only of sobriety and righteousness, which the men of the world might so far approve—but of *godliness*. This is their special distinction. It is the

* Comp. Eph. ii. 2, 3; with iv. 17—19; v. 7—11; 1 Pet. iv. 1—4.
† See Matt. v. 16.

first and highest principle in their character; and it ought not to be, and it must not be, concealed. There should not, in this differential quality (as logicians would call it) between the believer and the world, be any difficulty in distinguishing him. There are some professing Christians who go such lengths with the world, in mixing with them, if not in their gross sins, yet in their time-killing vanities; that, while they may be distinguished from the openly wicked, it is almost, if not altogether, impossible to discern between them and that part of the world that are esteemed the more decent and sober. But is this enough? Is this letting our light shine with sufficient distinctness before men? Should not the proper operation of the principle of godliness produce a sufficiently marked difference between the man of God and even these? And how can this be, but by their living more above the world—by their letting it appear that they have treasures and enjoyments of a higher order?—If a man appears deriving his daily enjoyment from those very sources to which the people of the world have recourse, in order, as they say, to drive away care, to beguile the way, to make their time pass lightly—which amounts to banishing the irksomeness of serious reflection and anticipation; we may not, perhaps, reasoning abstractly, be able to fasten the charge of direct criminality upon each of the occupations and amusements in itself,—yet we cannot be at a loss to perceive that the state of his heart is not spiritual but worldly. In this view, I should apprehend, there are practices which ought to be shunned, even although, on abstract grounds, we may be able to make it out to the satisfaction of our own conscience, that in their own nature they are not directly evil—provided they are practices which have come to be considered as *marking a worldly character*. When the world are disposed to praise a professor of the Gospel for his liberality and freedom from strait-laced bigotry in such things, he who is the subject of such commendation has good reason more than to suspect that he is going too far. Such commendation does not arise from any real approbation of these things as done by the so-called saint (for there is generally an abundantly shrewd discernment of his inconsistency), but from a fondness of having the example and sanction of such a character, to keep themselves in countenance.—My fellow Christians, a steady consistency is best, not only for our own sakes, but for the sake of the world. It may indeed gall them; but be assured it will command their secret respect:—whereas the contrary, by hiding from their view the true points of difference, serves to confirm them in their delusions; and, while it may draw flattery from the lips, will be contemned in their hearts. The character of the Christian should be like a polished mirror, clear and unsullied by inconsistencies. It should reflect the glory of God:—it should exhibit His likeness. But the breath of the world mars its lustre, dims it, and destroys the clearness and distinctness of the reflection: thus at once injuring the glory of God, and depriving the world of the benefit that would accrue from the consistent exhibition of His character and the influence of His truth.

3. Let Christians, on this subject, judge by the effect which "conformity to the world," even in its vanities, must have on their own best interests. If they are sensible that they have and *can* have no tendency to promote them, but on the contrary that they tend to hinder their advancement in the divine life—dissipating the mind—deadening spiritual sensibilities and desires—interrupting the communion of the soul with God—laying a weight on the wings of faith and hope, and repressing their buoyancy and their tendency heavenward;—let them be on their guard,—let their self-vigilance take the alarm; for they are in imminent danger. He who is for ever disposed to ask—What harm is there in this? What evil is there in that?—is, I should fear, one who is desirous to have as large a measure of this world at least as the utmost stretch of a sufficiently elastic conscience will allow him to take. He has too much in him of the wish to "serve two Masters." How far this desire to have as much of the world as he can is in harmony with such admonitions as the following, I leave you to judge:—"If ye then be risen with Christ, seek those things which are above, where Christ sit-

teth on the right hand of God. Set your affection on things above, not on things on the earth. For ye are dead, and your life is hid with Christ in God."*

I am at a loss to imagine to myself the satisfaction a Christian can enjoy in seeing the world kill their time. It is, methinks, one of the most pitiable sights on earth, to behold a man or woman running the giddy round of gaiety, thoughtless of eternity, and concerned only to shorten by present amusement the time given to prepare for eternity, and of which the shortness is at the same time the subject of universal complaint. And an assembly of such! convened for the purpose of helping each other to pass their time so as most effectually to exclude from their thoughts the very things which ought most of all to occupy them!—What a heart-melting sight! I should think a man of spiritual mind, present at such a scene, must needs feel his spirits sink as theirs rise;—his grief increase as their mirth increases; and the bursting sigh should come from his inmost soul—" O that they were wise!"

This consideration, of the influence of *example*, is one of no little weight. By every Christian, duly alive to the importance of the spiritual and eternal interests of others around him, and solicitous to have his hands clear of the blood of souls, it will be felt as involving a most serious responsibility. I would not push it to an unreasonable length. I am well aware that there is hardly a thing, how harmless soever, in the conduct of the people of God, which the men of the world are not ready to pervert or to aggravate, so as to derive from it encouragement in one or other of their own vain or sinful courses. Still, the well-known fact of the proneness of the world to take such encouragement from whatever they can construe favourably to themselves in the behaviour of Christians,—to laugh in their sleeve at their inconsistencies, as *they* very well see them to be,—and to represent them as, after all, much like themselves, only making a compromise with their consciences, and purchasing this and that

* Col. iii. 1—3.

worldly indulgence by a more than ordinary sanctimoniousness on other occasions:—this well-known fact, I say, should make Christians very jealous of themselves. Even the *little* of worldly conformity at times discovered, is pleaded to an immensely greater extent than it may justly warrant. Still —granting this to be *unreasonable*, it *is* so pleaded. If, therefore, the thing itself is not one which *duty requires*, it should surely be no light matter to the believer, that such practical results *do* arise from his conduct. Let him call it an abuse of his example; probably it is. Still, if it be the means of doing serious harm, even by its perversion, to the souls of others—ought it to be lightly practised?—ought it to be persisted in?—And this the more especially when the general tendency on their own spiritual sensibilities and growth in grace is taken into the account.

Let this then be the test. Let all "conformity to the world" be shunned, that manifestly tends, and is felt as tending to impede the spiritual "transforming" and "renewing of the mind." Whatever hinders *that*, robs the Christian of his "chief good." They who ran in the Olympic course took care to be free of all weight and of all encumbrance, and to allow nothing to turn them aside or to draw away their ardent eye from the goal and the prize—" Wherefore, seeing we also are compassed about with so great a cloud of witnesses, let us lay aside every weight, and the sin which doth so easily beset us, and let us run with patience the race that is set before us, looking unto Jesus."*

There is a further consideration by which the twofold admonition is enforced—"*that ye may prove what is that good, and acceptable, and perfect will of God.*"† The more they were "transformed by the renewing of their mind," the more of course would they *do* the will of God. The state of the heart would appear in the state of the conduct. Inward pro-

---

* Heb. xii. 1.
† Many eminent critics render—" *that ye may prove, or discern what is the will of God*, (namely) *what is good and acceptable and perfect.*" This is perhaps the more correct rendering, but the structure of the sentence does not demand it. The other is good. Alford's objections seem but slender.—ED.

gress in holiness would manifest itself in outward progress in practical godliness. The two must ever be proportionals. And the more this is the case, the more does the believer "prove"* the excellence himself, and manifest the excellence to others, of the "good, and acceptable, and perfect will of God." He proves it "*good*"—obedience to it forming the happiness of its willing subject—every command and every prohibition of God being calculated to do good to those who obey them.† His words "do good to them that walk uprightly." It is "*acceptable*"—that is, well-pleasing to God. So every part of the divine will necessarily must be. And on this ground believers are frequently urged to obedience—it being understood that their obedience is dictated by right principles—the principles of the Gospel.‡ Our communion with God and our experience of His love will be proportioned to the unreservedness with which we "keep his commandments, and do those things that are pleasing in his sight."§—It is "*perfect.*"‖ The people of God are made to experience its humbling perfection in its still leaving them behind. Perfect conformity to God's perfect will is the constant desire and aim of the renewed man. He can be satisfied with nothing short of this. He proves the perfection of the divine will in progressive advances in holiness—its perfection as a rule, and its perfection as a means of happiness. The holier he becomes, he becomes the happier. And when sin is no more,—when the soul is brought into full conformity to the will of God—the happiness will be complete. He shall "prove," in everlasting experience, the blessed results of such conformity.¶

I can only at present, in the way of practical improvement of a practical subject, press upon my hearers the importance of bringing their Christian profession to a Scriptural test. What avails—and what will avail in the end, any profession that will not abide this touchstone! There are three points here, then, to which all who "name the name

---

* i. e. *experimentally*—δοκιμάζειν.—Ed.   † Psal. xix. 11 : Prov. iii. 17.
‡ Comp. Heb. xiii. 20, 21; 1 Thess. iv. 1, 2: Col. i. 10.
§ John xv. 10; xiv. 21.   ‖ Psal. cxix. 96.   ¶ 1 John iii. 1—3.

of Christ"—that is all who call themselves Christians—do well to take heed, that they may be found possessors of more than a mere external and national Christianity—of a Christianity whose principles and character are in harmony with the Bible description. The first is—that you feel, in an humble heart, a deep sense of your obligation for the "mercies of God" as manifested in Christ to sinners, guilty, helpless, hopeless, and miserable:—that you evince in practice a consequent earnest desire to "glorify God," as the God of your salvation,—and that you be decided on the part of God in opposition to the world;—that God have your heart and tongue and hand—that with the heart you love him, with the mouth confess him, and with the hand serve him, keeping in mind the words of the Saviour himself—" No man can serve two masters: for either he will hate the one, and love the other; or else he will hold to the one, and despise the other. Ye cannot serve God and mammon:"*— "Whosoever shall be ashamed of me, and of my words, of him shall the Son of man be ashamed, when he shall come in his own glory, and in his Father's, and of the holy angels."†

* Matt. vi. 24.   † Luke ix. 26.

LECTURE LIV.

ROMANS XII. 3—8.

"For I say, through the grace given unto me, to every man that is among you, not to think of himself more highly than he ought to think; but to think soberly, according as God hath dealt to every man the measure of faith. For as we have many members in one body, and all members have not the same office; so we, being many, are one body in Christ, and every one members one of another. Having then gifts differing according to the grace that is given to us, whether prophecy, let us prophesy according to the proportion of faith; or ministry, let us wait on our ministering; or he that teacheth, on teaching; or he that exhorteth, on exhortation: he that giveth, let him do it with simplicity; he that ruleth, with diligence; he that showeth mercy, with cheerfulness."

THE duty inculcated in the first verse, of "presenting our persons a living sacrifice, holy and acceptable unto God," includes in it our considering all we are and all we have as bestowed by Him, to be employed in his service and to his glory. This, moreover, is the very spirit of the disconformity to the world inculcated in the preceding verse; the idol of the world—the idol of unregenerate human nature, being SELF; which, under one or other of its forms and claims, is worshipped, in opposition to God, by "high and low, rich and poor together."

In order to our serving God aright, in entire self-consecration, there is no feature of character so essential as *humility*. Pride and vanity, engendered by the possession of any thing in which we have, in the providence of God, been made to differ from others, is, in as far as it operates, the very spirit of the world. They lead us to pervert the design of the gifts and talents bestowed on us,—to alienate them from the glory of the Giver, and to apply them to the acquisition of honour and applause to ourselves.

This seems the natural connexion of the third verse:— "For I say, through the grace given unto me, to every man that is among you, not to think of himself more highly than he ought to think; but to think soberly, according as God hath dealt to every man the measure of faith."

By "*the grace given to him,*" the Apostle seems here to mean, not merely the grace by which he, in common with others, had been "turned from darkness unto light, and from the power of Satan unto God," but the favour which had superadded to this the more peculiar honour of "putting him into the ministry," as an Apostle or inspired ambassador of Christ.*

Here, then, he speaks with *apostolic authority*. Having declared the doctrines of God by commission from Himself, he proceeds, by the same authority, to communicate His will. —And while he communicates, he exemplifies. In the very use of this phrase, he exhibits a pattern of the humility and self-exclusion he enjoins. He had, as an Apostle, an exalted position. But he here shows us the view he ever took of his office; regarding it as a favour conferred upon him for a divine purpose which he was solicitous it should answer. This is in harmony with his language elsewhere:—"For I am the least of the Apostles, that am not meet to be called an apostle, because I persecuted the church of God. But by the grace of God I am what I am: and his grace which was bestowed upon me was not in vain; but I laboured more abundantly than they all: yet not I, but the grace of God which was with me."†—Now this was the very light in which he wished the believers whom he addresses to consider their own gifts and privileges: —and he teaches them by both precept and example.

Do we desire that our counsel or our command should come home to those whom we address with persuasive in-

---

* In this sense he uses the same phraseology in other places. Rom. xv. 15, 16; Eph. iii. 2, 3; vii. 8.

† 1 Cor. xv. 9, 10.

fluence? then let us see that we ourselves exemplify that which we advise or enjoin. How powerless the admonitions of him who inculcates on another that which he neglects himself; who "binds burdens for other shoulders," which he himself refuses to "touch with one of his fingers!" How worthless and inefficient the exhortations of a proud man to humility, of a passionate man to meekness, of the hard-hearted to tenderness and sympathy, of the miser to liberality, of the spendthrift to economy! *Be* yourselves, my brethren, what you exhort others to be; and your exhortations will have an hundred-fold more power and efficacy.*

"I say *to every man among you*." The command is universal—all being in danger of the fault; the tendency to pride and the excess of self-estimation being naturally strong in every bosom; prone to catch at every thing by which it can obtain any gratification to itself; magnifying any good qualities the subject of it may actually possess, and imagining others of which he is destitute.

When an admonition against any particular fault is publicly delivered, nothing is more common than for persons to *hear for others*. They think immediately of some one whom they conceive to stand in special need of the admonition; they wish he may be present; they hope he is; they look about and they stretch their necks to see. The feeling from which this arises may at times be good. But it is very dangerous; and he who indulges it is apt to lose a great deal of benefit to himself. Remember, then, the admonition here is "to *every one* that is among you,"—to every person, man, woman, and child,—to each individually. The language of every divine counsel is, in the first instance,—"Consider thyself." Self-consideration and self-correction is the only way in which we can be qualified for considering the characters and correcting the faults of our neighbours; for fulfilling in a right spirit the apostolic injunction—"Look not every man on his own things, but every man also on the

---

* Matth. vii. 3—5.

things of others;"* and that very injunction is accordingly preceded by the recommendation of the same temper of mind as that now before us—"Let nothing be done through strife or vain-glory; but in lowliness of mind let each esteem other better than themselves."†

But what is the spirit and amount of the injunction?— The language does not at all imply that we are to *undervalue* our gifts, whatever they may be; but that we must not be proud and vain of them; that we must use them, in the spirit of dependent humility, for the glory of God and for the good of others.—The words in the original literally mean, "*think so as to be sober*,"‡ entertain, that is, such thoughts of yourselves as that you may both *feel* and *act* soberly. This implies moderation in the estimate of our powers, and a sense of our insufficiency to make any right use of them to their proper ends, without aid from above; and, with regard to conduct, that, in the practical use of our powers, we act not from the wish to shine, to make a figure, and to bring ourselves forward; but rather, keeping ourselves out of view, to apply whatever of mental or spiritual endowment the Dispenser of all good may have been pleased to confer upon us with a single eye to His glory; and in such a way that others may be led not to think of *us*, but to "admire the grace of God *in* us."

We have an exemplification of the opposite state of mind in the use made of their spiritual gifts by many in the church of Corinth. They coveted such gifts as were showy, attractive, and calculated to excite surprise, rather than such as were more immediately profitable although less splendid. On this account the Apostle reproves them; and inculcates the desire not for self-display but for the edification of the church.§ To seek gifts for *show* rather than for *use*, was to

---

* Phil. ii. 4. † See Phil. ii. 3.

‡ Rather, perhaps, "Be minded so as to be sober-minded"—φρονεῖν εἰς τὸ σωφρονεῖν. The whole clause presents a play on words which can hardly be given in English—μὴ ὑπερφρονεῖν, παρ᾽ ὃ δεῖ φρονεῖν· ἀλλὰ φρονεῖν εἰς τὸ σωφρονεῖν. Alford gives it, 'not to be high-minded above that which he ought to be minded; but to be so minded as to be sober-minded.'—ED. § See 1 Cor. xiv. 12, 18—20.

be "children in understanding;" vanity being an indication in general of a weak mind, and in weak minds usually most predominant. On the other hand, to seek the gifts in question, with the denial of the spirit of vanity and ostentation, and for the humbler but more substantial end of profiting others—this was "in understanding to be men." He who is above being vain of the possession of gifts in himself, will be without malicious envy at the possession of them by others.

The admonition may be applied, with the strictest propriety, to gifts of every kind—to all our faculties and endowments. There is no command to underrate them. Evils result from underrating as well as from overrating them. He who forms too low an estimate of his powers and capacities, will be prevented by it from bringing them into exercise in their full amount and vigour, for the ends for which they have been conferred. He who fancies he has no talent will unavoidably fail to improve to good purpose what he has. The *effect* will be the same, although the principle may be very different, as when the slothful servant, under the pretext of the fear of his master, "wrapt his talent in a napkin" and "hid it in the earth." To the right use of what we have, a right estimate, both of its nature and of its measure, is indispensable:—and it is thus our duty to consider and ascertain, with all possible accuracy, the kind and amount of whatever talents we possess, that we may both put them to use in their *full amount*, and put them to use in a *right direction*.

The motive to humility follows:—"*According as God hath dealt to every man the measure of faith.*" Spiritual gifts were possessed and exercised *by faith.** How this description of faith could exist apart from saving faith, it is not easy for us to conceive. Yet that either it, or at least the supernatural gifts connected in such passages with it, might be possessed without "the true grace of God," we can hardly doubt when we consider the case of Judas; and such language

---

* Mark xi. 22, 23; 1 Cor. xiii. 2.

as that of our Lord when he says—" Many will say to me in that day, Lord, Lord, have we not prophesied in thy name? and in thy name have cast out devils? and in thy name done many wonderful works."* And that of the Apostle when he exclaims—" Though I speak with the tongues of men and of angels, and have not charity, I am become as sounding brass, or a tinkling cymbal. And though I have the gift of prophecy, and understand all mysteries, and all knowledge; and though I have all faith, so that I could remove mountains, and have not charity, I am nothing."† This much we may say, that such gifts were not bestowed as attestations of personal character, but in connexion with the advancement of the cause of truth: so that we can conceive of their being bestowed, in particular cases, in evidence of the truth declared, even although the declaration of it was made by one who was not himself a genuine spiritual subject of its power. I am not aware of any explanation of this seeming anomaly—that of miraculous gifts unassociated with grace —that is more satisfactory than that between the attestation of personal character and the attestation of the testimony delivered. The "*measure of faith*" appears here to mean the measure of the gifts possessed by faith. As for those who in modern times have affirmed that nothing hinders our working miracles now, but the want of faith, and who have recently begun to fancy that they have found it,— the best way to treat their pretensions is to ask *Where is the proof?* In no one instance has the pretension been fairly and distinctly authenticated. Unquestionably, if supernatural gifts are again to be bestowed on the church of God, it will be in some less equivocal way than aught that has yet appeared among our modern pretenders; the whole of whose procedure has hitherto had no other effect than that of exposing the cause of truth to scorn and ridicule, bringing down the power of Deity from its sublime grandeur and consistency of operation, and associating it with all the raving and drivelling of fanaticism.‡

* Matt. vii. 22. † 1 Cor. xiii. 1, 2.
‡ The allusion here is manifestly to the followers of Irving.—ED.

The motive in the passage before us is the same as that employed by the Apostle in his Epistle to the Corinthians— "For who maketh thee to differ from another? and what hast thou that thou didst not receive? now if thou didst receive it, why dost thou glory, as if thou hadst not received it?"* The question, "Why dost thou glory, as if thou hadst not received it?" can receive no answer in harmony with the claims of vanity or pride. He who is rich only by the bounty of another has nothing surely on which to plume himself. Let Christians view all they owe and have as from God; and this will check the risings both of pride on the one hand and of envy on the other. And since faith in its ordinary sense, as connected with salvation, is "the gift of God," in its origin and increase, and in the virtues and spiritual attainments that spring from it —to all of these the motive may be extended. It applies, indeed, in the full spirit of it, to everything we have that can be turned to account in God's service—to whatever may, by the perversion of it, be the occasion of inordinate self-esteem.

The Apostle *illustrates* his point in the next verses: "For as we have many members in one body, and all members have not the same office; so we, being many, are one body in Christ, and every one members one of another." The comparison expresses the union of believers with Christ as their common Head;—and their union among themselves, as joint members of his body. The two leading ideas intended by the use of it here, are the *unity* of the body though composed of many members, and the *variety of functions* which these members are fitted and designed to fulfil:— and the absurdity of supposing pride and boasting among the members of the animal frame, with their concomitants contempt and disdain, affords an apt illustration of the equal folly of such tempers among the members of the spiritual body.† The bond of union amongst the members

* 1 Cor. iv. 7; also xii. 4—11.
† This idea is amplified in all its force and beauty—1 Cor. xii. 12—21, 26, 27.

of this body is love to Christ the Head, and to one another for his sake—a principle, with which the indulgence of pride and vanity, of self-conceit and scorn, is altogether incompatible.

Having stated the general idea of union and of corresponding duty, he proceeds to greater particularity—verses 6—8. "Having then gifts differing according to the grace that is given to us, whether prophecy, let us prophesy according to the proportion of faith; or ministry, let us wait on our ministering; or he that teacheth, on teaching; or he that exhorteth, on exhortation: he that giveth, let him do it with simplicity; he that ruleth, with diligence; he that showeth mercy, with cheerfulness."

It is by no means necessary to consider all the particulars in this enumeration as including the exercise of miraculous gifts; nor to assume that the writer intends to specify the different *official* situations in the Church. The very term *office*, I believe, misleads not a few into this idea. But it is obvious that *all the brethren* were members of the body; and the Apostle is speaking of the several functions of all the members. As each member in the natural body, however little and insignificant it may seem, has its own place and its appropriate use; so in the body of Christ, every individual member has some function which it may usefully discharge:—and it is a great misfortune when the members of a church of Christ get into the habit of interpreting passages such as this as if they had regard only to those who bear office in the Christian community. All have their places, and all their functions. The whole church is addressed; and the duty inculcated is, that all should use the peculiar gifts possessed by them for the general good.

It is impossible to enter into the discussions which some of the particulars of this enumeration have occasioned. It would be tedious, and in some respects not very profitable; especially as in most of them, we could have to do with little more than conjectures, each having its own degree of probability. It is one of the passages which have been pressed into the service of certain forms of church government:—

but a single glance at it ought to satisfy any candid and judicious person that it is quite too general for such a purpose.

"*Whether prophecy, let us prophesy according to the proportion of faith.*" In the ordinary use of the term "*prophecy*" in the New Testament it signifies the "declaration either of future events, or simply of truth, under the immediate supernatural impulse of the Spirit of God." It is one of the miraculous gifts:* and the prophets are distinguished from the ordinary pastors and teachers.† There is a full account of the gift, with directions for its proper exercise in the church, in the fourteenth chapter of the first Epistle to the Corinthians: from which two things are clear—that it was not confined to such as bore office otherwise in the church; and that it is as different from what has been called brotherly exhortation as the dictates of immediate inspiration are from those of the ordinary exercise of the human judgment—or the direct intimations of God from the private sentiments or uninspired interpretations of men.‡

The original phrase rendered "according to the *proportion of faith*"§—is one which has given rise to an expression common in books of theology and in Christian conversation—"the *analogy of faith.*" We hear it said of particular sentiments, that they are consistent with the analogy of faith—by which is meant the harmony of the entire scheme of divine truth. Now there is such a thing as this harmony; and it is our duty, and should be our pleasure to trace it out, and to give to every truth its proper place and its proportional weight in the system. The great danger is in framing for ourselves, or too hastily adopting a system, and then interpreting texts according to it. In this way, different sects have their respective analogies of faith; and when an interpretation is put upon a text that accords not with their peculiar creed or confession, it is apt to be at once rejected as not in agreement with such a supposed analogy. This principle of interpretation is hazardous; and has led to a great deal of

---

* 1 Cor. xii. 10. † 1 Cor. xii. 28: Eph. iv. 11.
‡ See 1 Cor. xiv. 1, 3, 29—32.
§ κατὰ τὴν ἀναλογίαν τῆς πίστεως.

forcing and torturing of the word of God—tempting men to think at least, if not even to say respecting particular texts, when interpreted in a sense which, however obvious, does not precisely square with their system—"That wont do; we *must* make something else of it than that." But the admission that there is such a thing as the analogy of faith, or the harmony of divine truth, is one thing; and admitting this to be the sense of the term here, is quite another. It evidently is not. If prophecy means speaking by the Spirit of God, that which was spoken could not be otherwise than in agreement with the scheme of divine truth. Here the expression is of the same import with "the *measure* of faith"* in verse third. The meaning is, that every man who prophesied should prophesy *according to the extent of his gift.* The Spirit's communications to the prophets were such as to be perfectly known to those who were the subjects of the inspiration. They were to beware of *exceeding His impulse*— of adding to his dictates anything of their own. This corresponds with the spirit of the general admonition; inasmuch as a vain conceit of the gift might tempt them thus to exceed, that they might appear to possess it in the greater extent.

"*Or ministry, let us wait on our ministering.*"—Here is a word of very wide import. It is used of the apostleship;† of the office of evangelist;‡ of the pastoral office;§ and of the deacon's office.‖ The word being thus general, there have of course been diverse applications of it. Some understand it of deacons and ruling elders; some of deacons only; some of evangelists; some of bishops or pastors. From the very nature of the word, it is of course impossible to determine with certainty which is right, or whether all are not wrong. May it not apply generally to every description of

---

* The rendering, *analogy of faith*, is common with Romish expositors, and is that also of Calvin and Beza and some other Protestants. "But," says Alford, justly, "the comparison of $\mu\acute{\epsilon}\tau\rho o \nu$ $\pi\acute{\iota}\sigma\tau\epsilon\omega\varsigma$ above, and the whole context determine it to be—the measure of *his* faith." Compare also Tholuck.—ED.

† Acts i. 17, 25.   ‡ 2 Tim. iv. 5.   § Col. iv. 17.
‖ Acts vi: 1 Tim. iii. 8.

official ministry or service in the Church? The spirit of the rule is certainly applicable to this extent:—"Let us wait on our ministry"—that is, let us use the gifts fitting us for this ministry with humility, with faithfulness, with assiduous and persevering constancy.

"*Or he that teacheth, on teaching.*" Here too interpreters differ. Some explain the words of such as were employed in the religious tuition of the young and the ignorant who desired instruction—and who in early times got the title of catechumens. Others conceive the reference to be to the stated official public teachers in the church; and of the teacher's office there is abundant evidence.*

There is no such evidence, however, of a separate class of official brethren under any such designation as *exhorters*. There is nowhere else the slightest intimation or hint of such a thing. When therefore it is added, "*he that exhorteth, on exhortation,*"—we may either consider it as only expressing another part of the teacher's duty,—or the general duty of the brethren to "exhort one another," implying a peculiar obligation to be assiduous in the duty, lying on those on whom God had bestowed peculiarly suitable qualifications for it. Every member being called upon duly to fulfil his peculiar function, all who had gifts for exhortation were to use them diligently and faithfully, so as to promote the general improvement of the church—the health and vigour of the spiritual body. This leaves the question to be determined by other passages, whether the exhortation to which the brethren are in other places called be of a public and official or of a private and voluntary nature.†

The same uncertainty of signification and variety of explanation attends the remaining clauses. "*He that giveth*" is understood by some as meaning the distributor of the alms of the church — the *deacon*. By others again it is understood of the brethren who by their contributions supply to the deacons the funds for the poor; while "he that

---

* Eph. iv. 11: 1 Tim. ii. 2: Gal. vi. 6.
† Heb. iii. 13; x. 25: 1 Thes. v. 11.

ruleth"* is translated "he that *presides*," and is understood of presiding in the distribution of the charities so collected, that is also of the deacon. In fact this is one of several passages, in which the terms employed would, I doubt not, be definitely and distinctively understood at the time, but which it is now difficult for us with certainty to appropriate to their respective owners.† *This* we can say, however; that respecting the standing offices and order of the church we have sufficiently clear intimations, both by precept and example, in other places; while in passages like that before us, whatever be the functions or departments of duty we understand by the different phrases, whether public or private, personal or official, —the admonition is, in every view, equally applicable and equally obligatory, and consequently equally useful and necessary:—the general idea being, that every function which the Head of the church qualifies any member of the body to fulfil, that function he should see that he *does* fulfil in his proper place, in the right spirit, and with becoming zeal.

"*He that giveth*," may be taken literally of all the acts of Christian liberality. He who possesses the means of supplying the wants of others is a steward for God, and a debtor to his brethren, and to the cause of Christ. The duty of giving is often inculcated‡—and the fulfilment of the duty was delightfully exemplified in the first church at Jerusalem, "when the multitude of them that believed were of one heart and of one soul: neither said any of them that ought of the things which he possessed was his own; but they had all things common. Neither was there any among them that lacked: for as many as were possessors of lands or houses sold them, and brought the prices of the things that were sold, and laid them down at the apostles' feet: and distribu-

---

* ὁ προϊστάμενος.
† The passage is in a similar predicament in this respect with 1 Cor xii. 28, where the various terms, however definitively they might be understood at the time, are now susceptible of various conjectural senses according to the previous views of the expounder. Questions of the order of the churches must be determined from parts of Scripture of a more plain and pointed description than these, or not at all.
‡ As in Heb. xiii. 16; 1 Tim. vi. 16—18.

tion was made unto every man according as he had need."*
The *ability* to give was itself a gift, to be used for the benefit of the Church:—this was the function of those who possessed it. And we have here the manner or state of mind in which it was to be done—"*with simplicity.*" Not from any false unworthy principle of ostentation or self-righteousness; but with a single-hearted desire to glorify Christ, and to do good to his people.† But the word is often rendered *liberality*.‡ This, from the connexion, may be its meaning here. And we may justly observe that the two are closely allied. The believer who *has* this world's substance, and is under the influence of simplicity of principle in the use he makes of it, *will* give with liberality. Simplicity of principle will lead him to think solely of the use to which the Giver of all good, the Master whom he serves, intended he should apply his bounty; and under the influence of this principle, his sole question will be, What does that Master require of me? What do His poor need—what does His cause need— which I have it in my power to give? He who thus regulates his giving will be such a "cheerful giver" as the Lord loveth.§

"*He that ruleth, with diligence.*" It is rule *in the church* that is evidently meant; as the context speaks of the functions to be performed by different members *in the body.* It is not at all necessary to infer that "ruling" is a *distinct office* from that of "teaching." If it were, the same inference that finds a *ruler* distinct from the "pastor and teacher," must find that the "pastor and teacher" has nothing to do with ruling. It is the duty of *diligence* in ruling that is inculcated, by whomsoever the duty is discharged. Ruling and teaching are united in the same office.‖ A bishop and an elder are in the New Testament identical; and it is a part of the qualifications of the bishop that he be "apt to teach;" and while he "waits on his teaching," he must at the same time be diligent in the rule or presidency of the church; to see that the

* Acts iv. 32, 34, 35. † Matt. vi. 3.
‡ ἁπλότης: compare 2 Cor. viii. 2; ix. 11, 13; Jam. i. 5.
§ 2 Cor. ix. 8—10. ‖ Heb. xiii. 7, 17; 1 Thes. v. 12, 13.

laws of Christ are regularly administered—nothing which they prohibit done, nothing which they enjoin neglected, and nothing done "by partiality."

"*He who showeth mercy, with cheerfulness.*" Here, too, the deacon's office has been understood; it being one of the distinguishing duties of the deacon to perform the offices of mercy and compassion to the poor and suffering; visiting the sick—the widow and orphan—the prisoners for Christ—the stranger. But it appears to be more general. These were the duties of all.* But some might have more leisure, better opportunity, and greater ability and qualifications both of body and mind for such interesting functions—for looking after, and comforting, and relieving the various distresses and wants of others. And while they "put on bowels of mercies," they are here enjoined to fulfil the claims of mercy "*with cheerfulness;*" not "by constraint, but willingly;" not as a mere duty, required by conscience, but a delightful occupation, which their hearts dictated and enjoyed. Besides this there is a cheerful alacrity in the manner of expressing our sympathy and administering the kindnesses of compassion, which has the happiest effect on the object of mercy. It cheers his spirits; it doubles the value of the sympathy; it inspires grateful love; it thus promotes cordial union with all its blessed effects. He who has been made a partaker of the "mercies of God"—will cherish "bowels of mercies" himself, and "show mercy with cheerfulness."

How lovely are the practical principles of the Gospel! The Apostle lays the foundation of all in a grateful regard to God who has revealed his "mercies" in Christ Jesus. With this he associates spirituality of mind—elevation of affection and desire above the present sinful and vain world—and to these he adds humility and lowliness of spirit; and then the disinterested consecration of all our powers and capacities of usefulness to the good of others, according to our spheres of action and influence in the Church. "IF YE KNOW THESE THINGS, HAPPY ARE YE IF YE DO THEM."

* Matt. xxv. 35, 36.

LECTURE LV.

Romans xii. 9—11.

"Let love be without dissimulation. Abhor that which is evil; cleave to that which is good. Be kindly affectioned one to another with brotherly love; in honour preferring one another; not slothful in business; fervent in spirit; serving the Lord."

You will at once be sensible that the series of practical precepts on which we now enter, is of such a nature that, were we to go into the enlarged consideration of each particular, we might be detained by it, and detained with both pleasure and profit, for many successive Sabbaths. Every one of the duties inculcated might afford ample materials for a separate discourse. But in expounding, we must treat them with greater brevity.

The first injunction is to *unfeigned love*. And from the very circumstances of its thus taking the precedence in such an enumeration, can we fail to draw the inference of its first-rate importance? "God is love;" and love is the law of the universe. Everything that discovers itself amongst mankind that is opposite to love is an evidence of their fallen state. The essence of their apostacy lies in the absence of the love of God; and of this, all the hatred that appears between creature and creature is one of the many results and indications. Were God loved as the common Father of the universe, all His creatures would be loved for His sake. The terms employed by the apostle John in application to the members of His spiritual family in Christ Jesus might then be applied with a more extensive range: "Every one that loveth him that begat, loveth him also that is begotten of him."*

But the love *here* enjoined is love to one another as *fellow-christians*,—a love different from that general benevolence which is due to fellow-men. It is love for God's sake as their common Father in Christ; for Christ's sake, their one Lord and Redeemer; for the truth's sake, of which the common faith and the hope thence arising are their bond of union. And the connexion of the admonition to love with the counsels immediately preceding is intimate and obvious. What is the uniting principle among the many members of the one body of which Paul had spoken, but "love unfeigned?" —how could the various gifts bestowed on the members of that one body be mutually exercised,—how could their various reciprocal functions be discharged so as to promote edification,—without love? Unless their gifts were used in love, they would be the occasion of evil rather than the source of benefit; engendering jealousies and strifes, and marring spiritual prosperity, both personal and social. How strikingly is this lesson conveyed by the connexion of the closing words of the twelfth chapter of the first Epistle to the Corinthians, with the thirteenth chapter! The "more excellent way"—better than all their gifts even in the richest abundance, is the cultivation of *love;* of which the Apostle first affirms in the strongest terms the indispensable necessity,† and then proceeds to enumerate the excellencies and sound the praises, as the permanent virtue of earth and heaven.‡ The very frequency with which love is inculcated is designed to impress its necessity in the churches of Christ, which cannot prosper, which cannot indeed *subsist* without it. Surely if it be true that without love the individual is "nothing," it must be equally true that without love a church is "nothing." If there can be no Christianity without love, there can be no Christian church without love. And Christian love must be "*without dissimulation.*" With the God who "searches the heart," sincerity is the first virtue; or rather it is the quality

---

* 1 John v. 1.   † Verses 1—3.   ‡ Verses 4—14.

indispensably requisite to any virtue in the whole catalogue being acceptable in His sight. It is the character of the "Israelite indeed" that he is "without guile." This is true of his feelings and conduct both towards God and towards men. How odious the character given by God himself of some of His ancient worshippers! "They come unto thee as the people cometh, and they sit before thee as my people, and they hear thy words, but they will not do them: for with their mouth they show much love, but their heart goeth after their covetousness."* And of the generation that came out of Egypt by Moses—"Nevertheless they did flatter him with their mouth, and they lied unto him with their tongues. For their heart was not right with him, neither were they steadfast in his covenant."† Hypocrisy in everything is bad;—in professions of friendship and love, it is peculiarly detestable. Treachery is infamous; but treachery under the immediate guise of affection is doubly infamous. Who does not hold in abhorrence the man "whose words are smoother than oil, while they are drawn swords?" who says, "Art thou in health, my brother?" and smites him under the fifth rib?—who approaches with the "Hail, Master!" of wonted cordiality, and betrays that Master with a kiss into the power of his murderers?—The only proof of love being "undissembled" must be found in the conduct.‡ Dissembled love indeed is no love; it is the absence of love; it is the opposite of love; it is the worst description of hatred. It is so when there is not only a negation of affection,—lurking indifference towards the person who is the object of fawning profession, but when under the mask of love there are concealed the features of envy, malice, resentment, or disdain. This, alas! is more than possible. Yet is there nothing more difficult than hypocrisy—the continued simulation of a state of mind opposite to the really existing one. When there is such a lurking principle, counteracting the kindly impulse of love—a feeling in the heart belying the words and the

---

* Ezek. xxxiii. 31. † Psa. lxxviii. 36, 37.
‡ 1 John iii. 18; James ii. 15, 16.

looks, there will generally, to an eye of any discernment, be a something that bewrays the latent treachery. Haman durst not refuse to obey the royal mandate, and to proclaim before Mordecai, "Thus shall it be done to the man whom the king delighteth to honour;"—yet were the words in his lips like wormwood and gall; and you can readily conceive how unlike would be his manner to the hearty acclamations of one who proclaimed the honours of a friend. And although the case may be somewhat different with the man who of his own accord assumes a profession of friendship, feigning its manner and uttering its words to serve some selfish purpose of his own; yet even then it requires an experienced and practised dissembler to prevent some part of the true expression of the countenance from discovering itself through the mask.

Let us not forget that in everything we have to do with a God who "searches the heart and tries the reins;" and let us search *our own* hearts, and try our own reins, and see to it that in no part of our professions either to God or man there be any guile.*

"*Abhor that which is evil; cleave to that which is good.*" Were we to take this in close connexion with what goes before, we might be led very naturally to observe, that the manifestation of our abhorrence of evil and approbation of good *in others* is in perfect harmony with the sincerest love. It is our duty to "cleave to that which is good in others," in the way of showing how it draws and fixes our peculiar attachment, of commending and encouraging and imitating it; and to testify our "abhorrence of evil" in the way of faithful warning and reproof, and shunning in every form and degree the obnoxious fault. The contrary is not love. It was a precept of the law of Moses, "Thou shalt not hate thy brother in thine heart: thou shalt in any wise rebuke thy neighbour, and not suffer sin upon him,"† and assuredly this precept, as part of the law of "love without dissimulation," has lost no part of its obligation under

* John xiii. 34, 35; 1 Pet. i. 22. † Lev. xix. 17.

the Gospel. Paul exemplified this operation of love when he "withstood Peter to the face, because he was to be blamed;" and dissimulation was the very evil of which the Apostle of the Gentiles then testified his abhorrence. Flattery, opposed to faithfulness, is dissimulation.*

But the precept must be understood more generally. It implies of course an earnest desire to have a clear and discriminating "*knowledge* of good and of evil." There is a woe denounced in the divine volume against such as confound them.† In the acquisition of this knowledge, the word of the Lord must be our rule;—this word being the discovery of His will; and "evil" consisting in all that is adverse to that will; while "good" consists in all that is in agreement with it. And why is evil to be avoided, and avoided *with abhorrence?* Not merely on account of the destruction it brings on those who practise it; but for what it is in itself, and in its tendencies as regards God;—all moral evil including in it opposition to the divine holiness, to the divine authority, to the divine glory, and to the divine love. It is to God himself infinitely hateful.‡ And the corresponding duty of His people is, to cherish the same abhorrence.§

And how is abhorrence of evil to be *shown?* It is no mere latent feeling, existing in the heart without any appropriate manifestation in the life. The precept is a practical one. He who "abhors evil" in his heart will shun it in every form and in every degree. From what we *hate* we turn away; we cannot bear its presence; we cannot look upon it. He then who feels this will not tamper with temptation, but flee from it as from a noxious and deadly serpent. He will not be disposed to sport on the confines of the regions of evil and good,— the boundaries that separate the land of light from the land of darkness. He will not venture to the very threshold of hell, satisfied if he can only keep himself out of that "place of torment." Having turned his back upon sin with a sincere aversion, he will "hate even the appear-

---

* Prov. xxix. 5; xxviii. 23.   † Isa. v. 20.
‡ Psa. v. 4, 5; Hab. i. 13.   § Psa. xcvii. 10; Prov. viii. 13.

ance of evil," not the central darkness only of the region of sin, but the very twilight that surrounds its borders. As a man would shrink from touching the raiment that had just covered the putrid loathsomeness of a malignant distemper, and hold his breath till he was out of the reach of its tainted effluvia, —so will the believer "hate the very garment spotted by the flesh."

And "abhorrence of evil" is necessarily connected with "*cleaving to good.*" The expression implies "full purpose of heart"—the ardent desire of the mind, and the habitual and persevering consistency of the life.—Whatever is according to the mind and will of God is "*good.*" It is never to be renounced. It must be firmly adhered to in defiance of the opinions and the commands of men; in the face of temptation and difficulty, of reproach and contumely, of disadvantage and loss. We must "set our faces as a flint," with resolute and steady perseverance.* "*Cleaving* to that which is good," implies not only a conscientious but a *hearty* attachment— an attachment not only from conviction, but from pleasure; "delight in the law of the Lord after the inward man," and a decided, constant resistance to all the tempting influences of "the law of sin in the members;"—the maintaining of a steady, uncompromising consistency of character, "not with fleshly wisdom but by the grace of God,"—not with worldly temporizing in the spirit of men-pleasers, but with the lofty principle which animated Paul when he said— "With me it is a very small thing that I should be judged of you, or of man's judgment; HE THAT JUDGETH ME IS THE LORD."†

Verse 10. "Be kindly affectioned one to another with brotherly love; in honour preferring one another." The original word rendered "*kindly-affectioned*" is a very strong one—being compounded of one which is used for the tenderest of nature's affections, and another which seems to import delight in its exercise.‡ To see any thing else than the tenderness of love among the disciples of Jesus,

* 1 Cor. xv. 58; Gal. vi. 9. † 1 Cor. iv. 3, 4. ‡ φιλόστοργοι.

it is thus intimated, is as *unnatural* as to see coldness and distance and enmity between the brothers and sisters of the same family.* It is not a mere negative regard that we owe to one another,—the absence of ill-will; it is a tender, powerful, melting love. It is a spiritual affection; the affection which unites the members of God's spiritual family;— the natural affection of "the new man," by which he feels himself drawn to his fellow-believers as to *kindred* in Christ, sons and daughters of the same heavenly Father. Were we more "spiritually-minded" we should be more feelingly alive to the sympathies of this love. When Christians feel toward each other as they ought, there is a sacred delight in the mutual interchange of its kindly offices and tender emotions, such as the "world knoweth not of."—How high the pattern and how strong the motive!—"Beloved, let us love one another: for love is of God; and every one that loveth is born of God, and knoweth God. He that loveth not, knoweth not God; for God is love. In this was manifested the love of God toward us, because that God sent his only begotten Son into the world, that we might live through him. Herein is love, not that we loved God, but that he loved us, and sent his Son to be the propitiation for our sins. Beloved, if God so loved us, we ought also to love one another."†

Genuine love and true humility are natural associates. Where, therefore, this love exists and operates in due measure, the following duty, which indeed is only one of the modes of its operation, will be spontaneous and easy:—"*in honour preferring one another;*" some translate the words—"with respect or esteem, bringing one another forward."‡ The *spirit* of both translations is much the same; and it forms a part of the practical exhibition of the temper of mind inculcated in verse third.§—A forward, ambitious, self-displaying, and self-recommending spirit,—a spirit that is ever obtruding itself upon notice, thrusting itself into every honour, advancing claims to every situation that brings with

---

* Ps. cxxxiii.   † 1 John iii. 12—17; iv. 7—11.
‡ τῇ τιμῇ ἀλλήλους προηγούμενοι.   § And Phil. ii. 3.

it any *eclat*, is a spirit altogether repugnant to the meekness and lowliness of Christ. How beautifully was this temper of mind checked and repressed by our Lord, and its opposite enforced by all the weight of his authority and example:— "The kings of the Gentiles exercise lordship over them; and they that exercise authority upon them are called benefactors. But ye shall not be so: but he that is greatest among you, let him be as the younger; and he that is chief, as he that doth serve. For whether is greater, he that sitteth at meat, or he that serveth? is not he that sitteth at meat? but I am among you as he that serveth."*—Ambition is envious. Its object and aim are, to be uppermost:—but instead of pursuing this aim by a generous emulation, it is gratified if others are kept down. But fellow-christians, in the exercise of predominant humility and love, should seek to bring one another forward; to draw out one another's gifts to the greatest advantage, without the littleness of jealousy or the fear of eclipse; and to advance one another to honour rather than to push themselves into prominence and distinction.—Don't mistake, however. The precept does not mean that we are to act with a blind indiscrimination. We are not to bring forward into any station those who really are not fit for it. This would be a false humility on our part; and at the same time it would be a highly improper sacrifice of the general good, and an act of unkindness and cruelty instead of real favour to the individual. For in fact, whatever semblance there may be in it of good-will, nothing can be a more real disadvantage and injury than for a person to be put into a station to the duties of which he is not competent; to be raised to an elevation which he cannot sustain; to be invested with honours that sit awkwardly and incongruously upon him, exposing him to a notoriety that brings with it the reverse of admiration—the ridicule of the unfeeling and the painful pity of those whose hearts are awake to the delicacies of sensibility.—In all our own desires to excel, the desire should be regulated by a regard to *the edifying of*

---

* Luke xxii. 25—27.

the church:—and if this be our end, we shall sincerely and earnestly seek, not to hide the excellences of others in order that our own may be the more conspicuous, but to secure for them due notice and profitable employment. How fine the spirit and example of Moses:—"And there ran a young man, and told Moses, and said, Eldad and Medad do prophesy in the camp. And Joshua the son of Nun, the servant of Moses, one of his young men, answered and said, My lord Moses, forbid them. And Moses said unto him, Enviest thou for my sake? Would God that all the Lord's people were prophets, and that the Lord would put his Spirit upon them!"* This was true greatness of mind —rising above the weakness of envy, and solicitous only for the glory of God and the good of Israel.

Verse 11. "Not slothful in business: fervent in spirit: serving the Lord."—The word rendered "*business*"† is one of very general import, and has been variously understood. It might be applied to whatever requires zeal or diligent application;—and thus the exhortation might be identified with that of Solomon:—"Whatsoever thy hand findeth to do, do it with thy might; for there is no work, nor device, nor knowledge, nor wisdom, in the grave, whither thou goest."‡ —It is usually interpreted, and, I am inclined to think, rightly, of a man's calling or occupation in life—his *business*. In many other parts of the divine word, diligence is enjoined in the most peremptory terms;§ and mark the motive by which it is especially recommended to Christians —a motive worthy of Him who said—"It is more blessed to give than to receive"—"Let him that stole steal no more: but rather let him labour, working with his hands the thing which is good, that he may have to give to him that needeth."‖ O that it were more deeply impressed upon all our minds, that neither self nor family must engross our minds in the application of diligence to our worldly calling—that one, and not the least, of the advantages attending the ac-

---

* Numb. xi. 27—29.   † σπουδὴ.   ‡ Eccles. ix. 10.
§ As in Prov. vi. 6—11; xxvii. 23—27.   ‖ Eph. iv. 28.

quisition of worldly substance is the opportunity afforded of helping the poor and aiding the cause of God.

With regard to the man of the world,—the business of the world engrosses his attention and pursuit; his desires and views, while he is urging on with all assiduity the prosecution of his earthly calling, are bounded by the limits of the present life, and unassociated with the sentiments and feelings and hopes and joys and exercises of godliness. It is far otherwise with the people of God. They, while "not slothful in business," are, at the same time, *"fervent in spirit, serving the Lord."* Fervour of spirit is the warmth of love and zeal. This should be infused into our service of the Lord in all its departments. The opposite is the temper of mind most strongly condemned by the Lord, as the object of his very loathing.* In the service of the Lord lukewarm indecision is worse than coldness and open hostility. We are in danger from the world's influence. Its various secular occupations are apt to have the effect of water thrown on fire. We stand in need of the constant supplies of the divine Spirit to maintain the affections in due fervency—to keep alive our love and zeal—to stir up the slumbering embers, while in the diligent improvement of privileges we supply the inward fire with fuel.— The "fervour of spirit" enjoined is not at all an ignorant enthusiasm. It springs from and is fed by knowledge—" Did not our heart burn within us, while he talked with us by the way, and while he opened to us the scriptures?"† It is by the believing contemplation of the blessed and glorious discoveries made in this Book, that the fire burns;—the fire being nothing else than the warm glow of devout and adoring admiration of the character of the Lord, and of lively gratitude for his goodness and his grace. Then, in what direction is this "fervency" to be exercised? In *"serving the Lord."*‡

The word used for *"serving"* is not the one which on

---

* Rev. iii. 14—16. † Luke xxiv. 32.
‡ Another reading, καιρῳ for κυρίῳ, is adopted by some eminent critics, but manuscript authority seems decidedly in favour of the ordinary reading, which is also much better suited to the passage.—ED.

various occasions is so translated, where it signifies properly worshipping or rendering homage. The word here is the one for acting the *part of a servant*.* It includes, therefore, *all duty*. The discharge of duty, in all its variety, constitutes the *service of the Lord:*—and it is to this that believers are called. This leads me, then, to remark, with the view of bringing the three requirements of the text into harmony with each other; and thus to show the due adjustment and proportions of all the parts of the Christian character—by which the doctrine of God our Saviour is adorned—1. We are to beware of being so engrossed with the occupations of the world as to allow them to interfere with the immediate and stated duties of religion,—to jostle out the service of God in the closet, in the family, or in the sanctuary—or to prevent the attention requisite to the advancement of our spiritual interests by the study of the Scriptures and other means of improvement.—2. While by "diligence in business" we are bound to provide in temporal things for our own, and especially for those of our own house,—it being the Scripture maxim that "the children should not lay up for the parents, but the parents for the children,"—yet we must beware of allowing our solicitude about making what we may deem a suitable provision of this world's good for them, to interfere with the duties of a higher solicitude, so as that we should neglect their best concerns, and leave no proper time for their spiritual instruction. The fervour of our spirit must not be expended in the acquisition for them of what perishes in the using, but rather in serving the Lord ourselves, and persuading *them* to serve Him.—3. There is, at the same time, a harmony in Christian duties; a just proportion in all the practical features of the believer's character. Christian converse, for example,—the intercourse of fellow-believers in communicating their sentiments and feelings on the things of God, is a most pleasing and profitable exercise; but if, in order to enjoy it, a Christian neglects his present duty, leaving un-

---

* δουλευοντες.

done in his worldly business things which ought to be done, —even his religion itself may become his sin. The great aim of the Christian ought to be, to give to every duty its proper time, and place, and due proportion; weighing and adjusting and keeping in regularity all the various parts and seasons of worldly and religious engagements; maintaining and exhibiting the beautiful harmony of business and devotion; of the respective claims of time and eternity. At this all should ever aim, so as to leave no room for censure on either side:—the men of the world having no fault to find as to neglect or inactivity in business; and the fellow-christian none in regard to personal, domestic, and public religious duties.—4. Religion should be carried into everything:— all our ordinary daily duties should be done under its influence —all performed "as to the Lord." The spirit of what Paul says to Christian servants may be transferred to all the worldly occupations of believers: "Obey in all things your masters according to the flesh: not with eye-service as menpleasers; but in singleness of heart, fearing God: and whatsoever ye do, do it heartily, as to the Lord, and not unto men.*

And, my beloved brethren, if we are impressed and influenced by the contemplation of these as we ought to be, there is a view of the service of the Lord which we shall never forget, but put into it all the active fervour of our spirits. We shall not be slothful in what I may call *the business of God*. We hold relations to this world; and on account of these *its* businesses must be industriously minded: for "if any man provide not for his own, and specially for those of his own house, he hath denied the faith, and is worse than an infidel." But, as believers in Christ and subjects of his kingdom, we have relations of a still higher description. We are bound to serve the Lord by the promotion of the knowledge of his name and the advancement of the interests of his cause and kingdom in the world. We do not serve the Lord if we neglect this. It is the first and most imperative duty of every believer. The application of all our in-

---

* Col. iii. 22, 23.

fluence and all our resources to the propagation of His Gospel, to the purification, independence, progress, and triumph of His kingdom, is a duty which ought to engage all the fervour of zeal. We must not allow the business of this world *so* to engross us, as that the business of the kingdom of Christ shall be excluded and left to others. Every believer should feel that "to him to live is Christ;"—that in whatever sphere it pleases Providence to place him, it should be, not an inquiry postponed to those which relate to his earthly and secular business, but an inquiry that takes precedence of all others—What have I in my power to do in the service of my divine Master? What can I do for Christ?—And, my brethren, when fellow-believers, fellow-servants of the same Lord, who have been exemplary for fervour of spirit in the service of Christ, and have manifested this fervour by activity and generosity, inscribing holiness to the Lord on all their powers and on all their worldly resources, deeply lamenting, as they advanced to the close of their earthly course, that they had not done more and given more for this highest and holiest and most benevolent object—when such fellow-servants are removed, is it not a call to us to seek earnestly that the fervour of our own spirits may be more than ever excited,—and that by this excitement, we may be roused to greater liberality and activity than ever in "serving the Lord," in making the advancement of Christ's kingdom one of the primary objects and most interesting and persevering occupations of our life?—Let this be our practical improvement of the death of beloved and valued brethren—that we question our consciences more closely, each one of us, as to what we can do, in our respective spheres, for Christ and for perishing souls,—so that, while we by no means neglect the temporal wants and woes of men, we be chiefly concerned about their everlasting interests. What can I do? Can I teach a Sabbath-school? Can I give Bibles, and distribute tracts? Can I assist, by counsel, by money, by active effort, the operations of Christian societies for the evangelization of our country and of the world? Can I visit and instruct the poor? Can I persuade any to devote themselves to missionary work? Can I go as a missionary myself? What am I doing? What am I giving? How am I praying? For what purpose am I seeking the acquisition of this world's good?—*is it that I may have wherewith to serve the Lord? Is this motive first or last?*—if last, is this consistent with the fervour of spirit which His service legitimately requires? O my brethren, we are admonished how short our remaining time of service may be. Let us take the warning. Let us act as those dear Christian friends who have left us would admonish us to act could they now address us. With special reference to the advancement of the glory of Christ and the salvation of souls, they would say—" Whatsoever thine hand findeth to do, do it with thy might; for there is no work, nor device, nor knowledge, nor wisdom, in the grave, whither thou goest."

I must for the present draw towards a close, by observing how prone men are to separate, when it suits their purpose, what " God has joined together." In this way, the Bible is many a time cited as authority in vindication of what it most distinctly condemns. Thus men who give themselves wholly to the world will readily refer to those passages of the word of God in which industry and application to the lawful callings of the present life is commended and enjoined. " We are told in Scripture, you know, that we ought to be diligent in business." Very true, we reply; but are we not equally told in Scripture that we ought to be " fervent in spirit, serving the Lord?" If, therefore, your fervour of spirit is given to your secular engagements—if you allow the world to exclude the Lord,—the service of Mammon to supplant the service of God;—your diligence in business is not at all obedience to the divine will; it is only a following out of the inclinations of a selfish and worldly heart. You are without God; and your quoting Scripture in your behalf is no better than an insult. Look at the verse before us. It commands us not to be slothful in business:—but why do you stop there? Why do you not equally feel the obligation of what follows? Why will you presume to adduce the authority of God as an excuse for refusing him your heart, and for giving it entirely to the world. The character which his Word sanctions and commends is the character of him who serves Him with fervour of spirit, from faith and love, and whose diligence in business is a part of that service, the world being sought in subordination to Him, and with the view of being used to His glory. A man may be an active, plodding, persevering man of business, chargeable with no crimes and misdemeanours in the conduct of his affairs such as subject him to human censure, nay, manifesting so large a measure of uprightness and honour in all his transactions as to draw forth the high commendations of all about him; while the will of God, and the glory of God, and the love of God, are not "in all his thoughts;" while his heart is an utter stranger to the hallowed fervour of devout feeling; and if the word of God is ever on his lips, it is only in the way of light and half-jocular allusion, in vindication perhaps of what he knows in his conscience it condemns. In short, a man may be all that could be wished as a man of business, and yet be living without God.

On the other hand, let those who profess to be "fervent in spirit, serving the Lord," beware of being guilty on *their* part of separating what God hath united. Let us see no idle, slothful professors; who neglect their business, do injustice by this means to those with whom they stand connected in it, and give occasion to the adversary to speak reproachfully. It is equally contrary to the divine word, and equally injurious to the cause of religion, to see a Christian, with all his professions, as entirely devoted to the world as his neighbours, giving no indication that there is anything which he places before it, and esteems more highly, and desires more fervently—no indications of the fervour of spirit which the service of the Lord requires;—and, on the other hand, to see one who bears the name of Christ and the profession of devotion, shamed by the men of the world in diligence and in the integrity and honour and generosity of business.

LECTURE LVI.

ROMANS XII. 12—14.

"Rejoicing in hope; patient in tribulation; continuing instant in prayer; distributing to the necessity of saints; given to hospitality. Bless them which persecute you: bless, and curse not."

"THE joy of the Lord," said Nehemiah to the Israelites, with a force of truth which all the children of God have ever experienced,—"The joy of the Lord is your strength." Dulness and depression of spirit utterly incapacitate a man for vigorous exertion. They relax the nerves and paralyze the limbs of the corporeal frame; and they deprive of their tone and energy all the active principles of the spiritual nature.

There is thus a close and natural connexion between the admonition in the eleventh verse, and that in the beginning of the twelfth; and there is at the same time an intimate relation between the different clauses of the twelfth verse itself.

"*Rejoicing in hope.*" The poet has said—and the saying is founded in the felt unsatisfactoriness of all earthly enjoyments,—their insufficiency to fill the mind and to impart true and permanent happiness; in the vanity of human wishes,—the restlessness of human desires—the incessant craving after something more—" Man never *is*, but always *to be* blest." True, however, as this may be amongst those whose constant cry is—" Who will show us any good?"—it is far from true of the people of God, the children of His family, the objects of His love, the heirs of His glory. *Their* blessedness is by no means all in reversion—

all future—all anticipated but never possessed. Even here, they have substantial joys—the joys of God's salvation—the joys that spring from a present sense of God's forgiving grace and fatherly love. These joys, to which all others are subordinate, give sweetness to every temporal blessing; and alleviation and comfort to every temporal affliction,—compensating losses—sustaining under the burdens of sorrow—remaining as a portion when all things else fail. But still, a large proportion of their bliss *is* future:—they "rejoice *in hope*."*

The believer's hope may be regarded as consisting of *three parts*. There is, *first*, the hope, resting on the many assurances of God's word, of such supplies of grace to the close of life as are necessary to his preservation from the many influences that combine against his spiritual security and progress—arising from the allurements and intimidations of the world, the wiles of the wicked one, and that which constitutes the source of special danger in all temptations, the deceitfulness and earthliness and evil tendencies of his own heart. There is, *secondly*, the hope, respecting the departing spirit at death, that when absent from the body, it shall be at home with the Lord, in the possession of all the blessedness which a spirit separated from the body is capable of enjoying. There is, *thirdly*, the hope, respecting the body, that though laid in the dust,—food for worms, a body of humiliation, it shall not remain there, but shall be raised up to new and glorious and incorruptible life, "at the revelation of Jesus Christ."—There is thus the hope *till* death, the hope *at* death, and the hope at the resurrection, stretching to eternity. And while each believer enjoys this hope as to himself—his hope has at the same time a *social* aspect. As a large proportion of his joy on earth is social, there is this element blended with all his anticipations. Did it relate exclusively to himself, the hope were comparatively dreary. It includes the glory of his Saviour, and the happiness of the "multitude which no man can number"—a

---

* See chap. v. 1, 2; also 1 Pet. i. 3—9.

glory and a happiness to be completed at "the great day." In the religion of Jesus there is no selfishness. The joy to which it introduces is social; and it is the consummation of this social joy that is the object of hope. The hope and the joy together date their origin from the resurrection of the Redeemer:* and the same is the source of joy to the end.†

Nothing can be more natural or immediate, than the connexion between "rejoicing in hope," and being "*patient in tribulation.*" Christian patience is accordingly represented under two aspects, which, however, are inseparably associated with each other—patience in the endurance of evil, and patience in the expectation of good; or, as systematic divines have designated them, a *suffering* patience, and a *waiting* patience. They are one principle. What indeed is the patient waiting for future good, but the patient submission to present evils in the anticipation of the good to follow? Hence it is called "*the patience of hope;*" ‡ and its association with hope is frequent.§

Of the varied tribulation to which believers are in this life subject, some are common to them with others, some peculiar to themselves. In all of them, whatever may be their kind or their measure, they are called to *patience*. And with regard to this Christian grace,—it implies, observe, more than suffering and waiting. It is not a mere indolent acquiescence in the will of God. While it submits, it *acts*. Its very submission is not mere submission to what is felt to be inevitable; but a submission arising from the full and satisfied conviction that all is right—the result of a wisdom, and faithfulness, and love, all alike infinite and unchanging. And this patience is to be a stimulus to effort—to unflinching determination and unrelaxing perseverance in the ways of the Lord:—even in the midst of trials, *waiting* and *working*.

When our "tribulations" arise from men, as God's instruments for our correction, patience will be manifested under *His* hand by meekness and forgiveness towards those whom

---

* John xvi. 20—22.   † Heb. iii. 6, 14.
‡ 1 Thes. i. 3.   § Heb. x. 32—37: Jam. v. 7, 8.

He employs in inflicting the chastisement. Thus it was with Him who "when he was reviled, reviled not again" —who was "led as a lamb to the slaughter," and who "as a sheep before her shearers is dumb, opened not his mouth." The Lord Jesus, in forewarning his disciples of suffering, animates them to "patience" under it by setting before them the good hope of His Gospel:—"Let not your heart be troubled: ye believe in God, believe also in me. In my Father's house are many mansions: if it were not so, I would have told you. I go to prepare a place for you. And if I go and prepare a place for you, I will come again, and receive you unto myself; that where I am, there ye may be also." "These things have I spoken unto you, that ye should not be offended. They shall put you out of the synagogues; yea, the time cometh, that whosoever killeth you will think that he doeth God service. And these things will they do unto you, because they have not known the Father, nor me. And ye now therefore have sorrow; but I will see you again, and your heart shall rejoice, and your joy no man taketh from you. These things I have spoken unto you, that in me ye might have peace. In the world ye shall have tribulation: but be of good cheer; I have overcome the world."*

Hope is the great sustainer and cheerer of the human mind. Even the men of the world comfort themselves in the midst of depressing circumstances with the hope of a favourable change:—

```
              ———————————— the darkest day,
Live till to-morrow, will have past away.
```

But with regard to the present life, to-morrow may be still darker. All is uncertainty. But the believer, while, in common with others, he enjoys the hope of a favourable change in the gloomy aspect of his earthly lot, has the surer and better hope, beyond all the fluctuations of time, of a final and everlasting repose from all the sins and sorrows of

---

* John xiv. 1—3; xvi. 1—3, 22, 33.

mortality; of the dawn of a day of unclouded serenity and brightness, to which no dark morrow shall ever succeed. This hope makes him "patient in tribulation;" because he knows, not only that the tribulation is to come to a close, and to be succeeded by this pure and everlasting felicity, but that it is intimately connected with it as part of the means employed by God to fit His people for its final and full enjoyment.*

If the joy of hope is thus connected with patience in trouble, no less intimate is the connexion between both and "*continuing instant in prayer.*" Taking the word of God as our rule, we can entertain no sceptical hesitation about the duty of PRAYER. It is inculcated by numberless precepts, and recommended by no fewer examples;—and by the very highest of all, the example of the Son of God himself.† Prayer, for ourselves and for one another, is one of the most efficient means of our establishment in *the faith*, and consequently in the exercise of all the graces and virtues connected with it.‡ The spiritual life comes from God. He produces it in the soul; and He sustains it in all its principles. The preceding clauses exhort us to "rejoice in hope," and to be "patient in tribulation:"—but to whom are we to look for the grace that is needful to our fulfilling the duties?—to whom but to Him who is designated the "God of hope." We are "patient in tribulation," because we "rejoice in hope;" but we can neither "rejoice in hope," nor be "patient in tribulation," but by "continuing instant in prayer." To have constant and free access to the throne of the divine grace is a precious privilege; and the character of the Father *to* whom we come, and that of the Mediator *by* whom we come, are alike pregnant with encouragement to avail ourselves of the privilege. The Father to whom we come is the "God of patience and consolation;" the "Father of mercies and the God of all comfort;" our Father who hath "loved us and given us everlasting consolation and good hope through grace;" the

---

* 2 Cor. iv. 16—18.
† Luke xviii. 1; xxi. 36: 1 Thess. v. 17: Eph. vi. 18: 1 Pet. iv. 7.
‡ Jude 20, 21.

"God of our salvation"—Light, and Love: and the divine greatness and indescribable tenderness and condescension of our blessed Mediator give us the delightful confidence that we can never fail of acceptance if we come in his name and plead his merits and intercession.* O let us make free though humble use of our privilege!—for "if we being evil, know how to give good gifts unto our children; how much more shall our heavenly Father give the Holy Spirit to them that ask him?"† "He is able to do exceeding abundantly above all that we ask or think"—and he *will* "supply all our need according to his riches in glory by Christ Jesus."—"He that spared not his own Son, but delivered him up for us all, how shall he not with him also freely give us all things?"

Verse 13. "Distributing to the necessity of saints; given to hospitality."—Both the admonitions in this verse may be regarded as expressions—practical expressions, of the love inculcated in verses ninth and tenth. All Christian love must be practical. The love of God—of the Father, the Son, and the Spirit, to us sinners, has been a practical love, and in this respect it is the pattern for the love enjoined on His people. He allows of no faith and no love that are unproductive.‡

The duty of "*distributing to the necessities of saints*" has various recorded exemplifications, approved of God, and held forth for our imitation. First, as to the needy in the same church: "All that believed were together, and had all things common; and sold their possessions and goods, and parted them to all men, as every man had need." "And the multitude of them that believed were of one heart and of one soul: neither said any of them that ought of the things which he possessed was his own; but they had all things common. And with great power gave the apostles witness of the resurrection of the Lord Jesus: and great grace was upon them all. Neither was there any among them that lacked: for as many as were possessors of lands or houses

---

* Heb. iv. 14—16. † Luke xi. 13.
‡ Jam. ii. 15, 16: 1 John iii. 17.

sold them, and brought the prices of the things that were sold, and laid them down at the apostles' feet: and distribution was made unto every man according as he had need."* It is the incumbent duty of all churches thus to make provision, liberal and effectual provision, for the wants of the poor. It was the saying of Jesus, "The poor ye have always with you:" and we learn, in a very indirect and incidental way, that it was his own custom, from the scanty stock of his own little company, to distribute a portion to the needy:—"For some of them thought, because Judas had the bag, that Jesus had said unto him, Buy those things that we have need of against the feast; or, that he should give something to the poor."† And, however unreasonable their murmurings against the woman that "poured upon his head" the "box of precious ointment," the very terms in which they expressed them, showed that he had inculcated the principle of kindness to the poor upon his disciples: "Now, when Jesus was in Bethany, in the house of Simon the leper, there came unto him a woman having an alabaster-box of very precious ointment, and poured it on his head, as he sat at meat. But when the disciples saw it, they had indignation, saying, To what purpose is this waste? For this ointment might have been sold for much, and given to the poor."‡ To the support and comfort of the poor, whom the God of grace has chosen rich in faith and heirs of His kingdom, *all* should contribute, regularly, liberally, cheerfully, as God hath prospered them. But the distribution is not to be confined to the particular Christian society with which believers happen in the providence of God to be connected. In the verse before us, it extends generally to "*the saints*"—to all that are Christ's, whom it is in our power to relieve or to benefit. And here too we have examples. "And there stood up one of them, named Agabus, and signified by the Spirit that there should be great dearth throughout all the world: which came to pass in the days of Claudius Cesar. Then the disciples,

* Acts ii. 44, 45; iv. 32—35.
† John xiii. 29. ‡ Matth. xxvi. 6—9.

every man according to his ability, determined to send relief unto the brethren which dwelt in Judea: which also they did, and sent it to the elders by the hands of Barnabas and Paul." "Upon the first day of the week, let every one of you lay by him in store, as God hath prospered him, that there be no gatherings when I come. And when I come, whomsoever ye shall approve by your letters, them will I send to bring your liberality unto Jerusalem."* This kindness we owe to the saints for Christ's sake; who has assured us, that whatever is done from this principle to *them*, He will regard and recompense as if done to himself. We have not now the opportunity which certain "holy women" so eagerly embraced when he was on earth in person, of "ministering to him of our substance." No. That was in his humiliation, when, bearing the sins of men he could say —"The foxes have holes, and birds of the air have nests; but the Son of man hath not where to lay his head." From all such need he is now far removed, never again to require the aid of his creatures. But in one sense we have him still with us. He is with us *in his members*. He that injures *them* injures *him;* he that does good to them does it to him. On this principle he said to the persecuting Saul, when he was "making havoc of the church," "Saul, Saul, why persecutest thou ME?"—and on the same principle he assures us, "Whosoever shall give you a cup of cold water to drink in my name, because ye belong to Christ, verily I say unto you, he shall not lose his reward." "Inasmuch as ye have done it unto one of the least of these my brethren, ye have done it unto ME."† What a motive to generous liberality!—a motive which cannot but verify in the experience of his disciples, his own divine maxim, "It is more blessed to give than to receive." When we recollect who *He* is, what is the love he hath shown to us, and what the affections of his heart are toward all for whom he died, and whom it is his purpose to save—how can we ever resist the

---

* Acts xi. 28—30: 1 Cor. xvi. 2, 3: Phil. iv. 14—18.
† Mark ix. 41. and Matth. xxv. 40.

appeal—and it was to excite to the duty before us, of "distributing to the necessity of saints" that it was originally made—"Ye know the grace of our Lord Jesus Christ, that, though he was rich, yet for your sakes he became poor, that ye through his poverty might be rich."

It should further be observed, that while there lies a peculiar obligation on the disciples of Christ to provide for the wants of their brethren; just as there lies on the members of one family circle to attend, in the first instance, to one another's necessities as having a prior claim to those of their fellow-men in general:—yet the liberality of Christians is by no means to be bounded even by the comprehensive designation of *Saints*. It ought to embrace mankind; first the saints, then the world.*

The other part of practical kindness is "*given to hospitality.*" And here, the first duty I have to do is to caution you against misconception. The words do not at all mean, that fellow-christians are to be for ever visiting;—going about in a ceaseless rotation of eating and drinking from house to house,—giving and paying back entertainments; far less vying with each other in the elegance and costliness of such entertainments.—While it is a duty and a pleasure to be social, sociality may be carried to a very injurious extent, both as to frequency and expense. By too great frequency time may be wasted, and becoming and necessary duties neglected; and, while there is an extreme of penurious stinginess that exposes religion to reflection as well as its opposite, yet the opposite is that to which, in times of luxurious refinement and emulous display, Christians are most in danger of being tempted; and there may be in this respect a needless profusion and finery which, not only on account of the spirit of worldliness which it indicates and cherishes, but also on account of throwing away money which might be much better employed, it would be for the honour of the Gospel to shun.

* Gal. vi. 10.

In those early times, believers were not seldom, by the cruelty and rapacity of persecution, deprived of their homes, and robbed of their substance and their means of life. These cases gave great scope for the duty here enjoined. They had a claim on hospitality which no Christian could possibly resist. Who that had an empty corner in his house wherein he might lay himself, however uncomfortably, would not open his door to the homeless and the destitute for the sake of that blessed Master in whose cause they suffered? Who that had one morsel of bread to eat would not have divided it with a poor brother in such circumstances?

There were *Christian strangers* also—on journeys, perhaps in the immediate service of the Gospel,—or visiting countries at a distance from their own, whether in that service or for other purposes. These were worthy objects of the hospitality enjoined. So are they still. Servants of God, travelling in the cause of Christ, should never be left at a loss for quarters, where there are brethren that have accommodation in their power. The greater strangers they are, so much the greater is their claim. Christianity itself (when they come duly recommended) ought to be quite enough to ensure amongst fellow-believers a kind reception. The rule in this matter is the same as in the case of liberality. Every one must suit his practice to those means with which providence has furnished him.—Hospitality, it is true, was still more necessary then and there than now and in such a country as ours. *Inns* for the accommodation of travellers were far from being so common as among us. But still, in many cases, the expense of inns, whether to the person's self, or to the cause for which he travels, is heavy; the company and publicity of an inn, especially on Sabbaths, may be irksome; and on all occasions the testimonies of Christian affection (the affection that unites the family of God over all the earth) are gratifying and delightful;—and it is right that the world should see how Christians love one another. It has a cold, heartless, unfriendly appearance when a Christian stranger has to do the best he can in an inn in the midst of those who have plenty of room for him in their houses. Such passages as the following show at once the imperativeness of the duty, the peculiar cases that have a claim upon its fulfilment, and the spirit in which it ought to be discharged: —"Use hospitality one to another without grudging;" "Beloved, thou doest faithfully whatsoever thou doest to the brethren, and to strangers; which have borne witness of thy charity before the church: whom if thou bring forward on their journey after a godly sort, thou shalt do well: because that for his name's sake they went forth, taking nothing of the Gentiles. We therefore ought to receive such, that we might be fellow-helpers to the truth;" "Be not forgetful to entertain strangers: for thereby some have entertained angels unawares."*—While such precepts have a special application to the people of God as the objects of attention and kindness, the spirit of them ought to be extended, as in the former case, to helpless strangers generally, to the friendless and shelterless, to all who need such attention, and whom obvious propriety does not on other grounds interdict our receiving, when we have the means, and are sure that there is no imposture. But all such general precepts necessarily call for the exercise of much discretion, prudence, and discrimination.

Verse 14. "Bless them which persecute you: bless, and curse not." Here is a different class of men, and a different feature of character. Christians had enemies as well as friends. Jesus had said to his disciples, "If ye were of the world, the world would love his own: but because ye are not of the world, but I have chosen you out of the world, therefore the world hateth you."† From the world they had to endure reproach and calumny—outward oppression and violence—bonds, imprisonments, and death. *Here* the Apostle refers especially to the persecution of the *tongue*. But the spirit of the precept is far more extensive, applying to all descriptions of injury they could be called to suffer for the name's sake of their Master. There were those who had not the fear that restrained Balaam when he said, "How shall I curse whom God hath not cursed? or how shall

---

* 1 Pet. iv. 9; 3 John 5—8; Heb. xiii. 2. † John xv. 19.

I defy, whom the Lord hath not defied?" There were those who uttered their malignant imprecations with all virulence and without restraint. When the Lord pronounces his blessing on those who are "evil spoken of," let not his disciples forget the qualifying word:—it must be "*falsely*, for his sake." If the charge be *true*, there is no blessing. But how provoking soever to the natural spirit of pride and resentment, to be falsely calumniated and reviled, here is the duty: "Bless them which persecute you:—bless and curse not." To "*bless*" is to speak mildly and kindly *to* them in return, and to seek God's blessing *upon* them,—especially His converting and saving mercy. It is opposed to "*cursing*," which is the wish and imprecation of evil in return for the evil done to us. The precepts of Jesus himself are the same as that of this Apostle by his Spirit.* So are those of other Apostles.† And the spirit and letter of the precept are beautifully and impressively exemplified—by Him especially who lays upon us the injunction, when for those who nailed him to the tree he breathed the prayer—"Father, forgive them, for they know not what they do."‡ And his general character was in uniform harmony with this remarkable illustration of it—"Who, when he was reviled, reviled not again; when he suffered, he threatened not; but committed himself to him that judgeth righteously."§—We have other examples, too, of a piece with his own. Stephen died in the same spirit with his Master, exclaiming, "Lord, lay not this sin to their charge."‖ Paul and his fellow-apostles maintained the same temper towards their persecutors—"Being reviled, we bless; being persecuted, we suffer it; being defamed, we entreat."¶

There is, in the verse before us, an emphatic repetition well worthy of notice. It implies that the duty is important, and at the same time that it is far from easy:—"Bless them which persecute you: *bless and curse not.*" The force of the language is—Let no provocation, however great and however

---

* Matth. v. 43, 44. † 1 Pet. iii. 9. ‡ Luke xxiii. 34.
§ 1 Pet. ii. 23. ‖ Acts vii. 60. ¶ 1 Cor. iv. 12—13.

long persisted in, prevail over you:—"*Bless;*" continue to bless; persist in blessing while your enemies persist in persecuting and cursing: bless on—and let nothing tempt you to curse. Should you be called even to "die for the name of Jesus,"—to "resist unto blood,"—let your latest breath be spent in blessing!—This is a temper of mind not among the principles and tendencies of corrupt nature: and because it is opposite to these, men have chosen to decry and vilify it as cringing servility, tameness, and mean-spiritedness. But it is in truth the *sublime* of principle. It is more; it is *divine.* God blesses while men curse; He is "kind to the evil and unthankful." He bestows His favours even on blasphemers of His name. He invites to himself and to life those who ungratefully disown and despise Him and say, "Thy gifts be to thyself, and thy rewards to another." All day long He "stretches out his hands to a disobedient and gainsaying people." O! if the Almighty were to act towards those who affect to hold in contempt the tameness, and to spurn at the unreasonableness of the spirit He here enjoins— if the Almighty were to act towards them on the principle on which they proudly claim the right and assert the propriety of their feeling and acting towards those who in word or in deed trespass against them,—if He were to apply the rule of equity, "with what measure ye mete, it shall be measured to you again,"—how sad would be their case!—the immediate withdrawment of every expression and indication of kindness; the drawing back of the sceptre of grace; the final closing of the lips of mercy; the fearful denunciation and awful execution of all the curses that are written in this Book. So little do men think of having their own principles applied to themselves.—The conduct recommended, I have said, is divine; and there can be nothing that raises human nature so high in true honour as what brings it into likeness to God. When God gives a man the means of doing good, He puts him into a capacity of resembling Himself in being the steward and almoner of His bounty. So when He places a man in circumstances of provocation,—circumstances that tempt him to feel resentment and to give utterance to the feeling, He puts him in a capacity of exercising the divine virtue of forbearance. O! who can calculate the amount of provocation which the divine Being has every day, every hour, every moment to bear! and if we had *nothing* to bear, we should never be in circumstances to resemble God—to be "merciful *as* our Father in heaven is merciful."

What, in conclusion, is the effect—what the sentiment, what the feeling, which persecution should engender in the bosom of the persecuted? Is it not lively compassion towards the infatuated man who, by the very spirit which he is indulging and manifesting, is giving evidence of being still "in the gall of bitterness, and in the bond of iniquity." And ought not this pity to prompt the fervent prayer for such, that they may be brought to know the excellence of what they are now despising, and the happiness of those whom they are cursing, and whose names they are casting out as evil. Nothing, as we shall see afterwards, is better fitted for disarming and subduing the rage of an enemy, and nothing, in spite of all that men can say, tends more to recommend our religion than the manifestation of "the meekness and gentleness of Christ" amidst the revilings and buffetings of the ungodly. And if enmity against the Gospel should fill even the hearts of friends and kindred with gall and wormwood, of which the bitterness should pass from the heart to the lips, and that tongue in which there ought to be "the law of kindness" should utter the words of cutting sarcasm, of contumelious reviling, of unmerited reproach, and angry imprecation; there is nothing for the Christian but to bear it patiently, to repay it with the smile and the tear of love, and with the persuasive eloquence of silent practical kindness.—"BLESS AND CURSE NOT."

LECTURE LVII.

ROMANS XII. 15, 16.

"Rejoice with them that do rejoice, and weep with them that weep. Be of the same mind one toward another. Mind not high things, but condescend to men of low estate. Be not wise in your own conceits."

PROCEEDING in his enumeration of the practical virtues of the Christian character, the Apostle, in the first of these verses, inculcates that of *sympathy*—of sympathy, understood in its most comprehensive acceptation, as signifying a fellow-feeling with both the joys and the sorrows of others.

In the preceding part of the chapter, the figure is used of the body with all its parts and organs, to represent the unity of the church in all its members, and the duty of each to fulfil its appropriate function. When using the same figure elsewhere, the Apostle beautifully applies it in illustration of the sympathy here enjoined—"That there should be no schism in the body; but that the members should have the same care one for another. And whether one member suffer, all the members suffer with it; or one member be honoured, all the members rejoice with it. Now ye are the body of Christ, and members in particular."* Every one feels the truth of this. A wound, or a disease, that affects directly any one part of the frame, affects the frame throughout. The foot cannot be injured, and the hand be indifferent to the hurt: a bone cannot be broken, and the muscles be insensible to the fracture: one eye cannot be lost without

* 1 Cor. xii. 25—27.

the other participating in the pain, and straining itself to supply the deficiency. Lacerate a nerve,—puncture the brain, and you may convulse the whole body. And, on the other hand, "Whether one member be honoured:"—that is, have special attention bestowed upon it—special favour shown it,—"all the members rejoice with it." There is the one description of sympathy as well as the others. When the hand is sound, it can follow steadily and accurately the tracings of the eye; and when the eye is sound, it guides the operations of the hand. When a pleasant sensation is produced in any one member or part of the body, the pleasure is not confined to that spot; the thrill goes through the entire frame. There is thus "no schism in the body:" all the members have the same care one for another:—for in truth they are all sensible that in caring for each other they are at the same time caring for themselves. And thus ought it to be among the members of the body of Christ. There must be no indifference to one another's circumstances. In no description of union should that generous sensibility and kindliness of spirit be more intensely experienced and cherished, which makes the joys and the woes of others its own. There are two parts of this sympathy—two departments, rather, of the operation of the same principle:—

"*Rejoice with them that rejoice.*" Perhaps the remark usually made has truth in it, that we are less inclined to this kind of sympathy than to the other; that it requires a greater degree of disinterestedness and self-control, there being certain powerful evil principles by which it is resisted. At the prosperity of others, the malignant principle of envy is ever in danger, in some form and in some degree, to get possession of our hearts, and if not entirely to suppress, at least to damp the ardour of generous and open-hearted fellow-feeling. It is true that the sympathy with joy or the sympathy with sorrow will predominate in individuals according to the respective constitutional tendencies or induced habits of their minds:—but still our self-love is more generally in danger of degenerating into selfishness, when we compare our circumstances with those of the more prosperous than when we compare them with those of the more unhappy. It may indeed be fairly questioned whether the naturally cheerful man will be less ready to sympathise with the sorrows of others than the man of plaintive and mournful cast of mind: for it will often be found that the latter has more of *self* in his character than the former:—and it is according to the degree in which self is absent and generous sensibility present that there will be the disposition to *both* descriptions of sympathy. And this is quite consistent with the fact, that we learn more tenderly to sympathise with the woes of others by being the subjects of suffering ourselves; and especially of suffering of the same or a similar kind;—the reason of which seems sufficiently simple, namely, that by having been in the same situation, we are able to enter more correctly and fully into the feelings of those who are placed in it,—this being only a recalling of our own experience. By such experience, too, we are enabled, in some degree, to regulate the feeling of sympathy;—for if, from our own knowledge of the situation, we see those who are brought into it discovering a distress that is evidently extravagant, and beyond due bounds, we cannot go along with it; and if this excess is very great, it will generate an opposite sentiment of disgust and contempt. If we wish, indeed, for the fellow-feeling of others either with our joy or our sorrow, we must beware of excess in the manifestation of either.

By the precept before us, envy and indifference are alike prohibited. How inconsistent with the spirit of love, when anything has occurred in a brother's history which is especially gratifying to him; when he relates it with the smile of satisfaction, in the expectation of its being received with a kindred pleasure—saying to us by his whole look and manner, "Rejoice with me!"—and we hear the tale with all the imperturbable quiescence of sullen apathy. How sadly fitted is this not merely to throw a damp on our friend's spirit, but to excite feelings incompatible with reciprocal affection—to stir up indignation, or to cool and alienate the heart! The generous spirit of true Christian friendship and love will answer with a smile of complacency every look of satisfaction in a brother's countenance, and add to his happiness the assurance of its being cordially participated. By cherishing this spirit we turn all the streams and rills of others' joy into the channel of our own:—we make them all tributary to the swelling river of our own pleasures.

And we must not be less inclined to sympathise with *sorrow* than with joy;—that is, we should feel with it and desire and seek to relieve it. We must "*weep with them that weep.*" This stands opposed to that cold-blooded selfishness, which is ever ready, when called to contemplate and pity the sorrows of others, to say—Have we not distresses enough of our own? why must we be perpetually troubling ourselves with those of other people? This spirit was among the earliest manifestations of human depravity. "Am I my brother's keeper?" was one of its first recorded utterances. Every one of us is his brother's keeper. We ought to have a heart tenderly susceptible of fellow-feeling with his every pang; and from this fountain of tenderness tears of no feigned sympathy should be ready to mingle with those of every weeping sufferer. Such sympathy, every one who has experienced what sorrow is, well knows, is a wonderful sweetener of its bitterness and lightener of its pressure. And, on the contrary, nothing can be more agonizing than the indifference and callousness of a friend from whom we have looked for the alleviating influence of tender condolence. The agony of this is often greater than that of the grief itself for which we have sought relief. Far from fellow-christians, members together of God's spiritual family, be this hard-heartedness— this listless disregard of each other's trials! Both in sympathy with joy and in sympathy with sorrow, we become assimilated to the blessed God:—we are of one mind with Him.* And these principles of the divine and human character appear in lovely exemplification in the blessed Master whose followers we call ourselves. How deep and how tender was the sympathy which wept at the grave of Lazarus; which was moved with compassion for the weeping widow of Nain;

---

* Psalm xxxv. 27; Isa. lxiii. 9; Zech. ii. 8.

which dissolved in pity over the coming woes of Jerusalem, and which, with a heavy-laden heart, forgetting for the moment his own unprecedented sorrows, turned to those who wailed after him on the way to Calvary, saying, "Daughters of Jerusalem, weep not for me, but weep for yourselves and for your children!" Let us cultivate resemblance to the tender-hearted Saviour. And let us, in this as in former instances, remember, that our sympathy is not to be confined to fellow-christians, though such have special and peculiar claims to its exercise:—we should feel a lively interest in all the concerns of our fellow-*men*,—in their joys and in their sorrows; and should seek to promote to the utmost of our power the former, when their nature and their sources are legitimate, and to alleviate and remove the latter. And in times of abounding distress, in our city or in our country, never let believers in Christ forget their duty. Let the world see the grace of God in its practical operation. Let the followers of Jesus redeem the pledge which they have given by the very profession of his name. Let them show their likeness to him by being forward to every good work of compassion and practical kindness.

Verse 16. "Be of the same mind one toward another." The original word* here used is of general import, sometimes referring to the understanding and sometimes to the dispositions. Most frequently, I think, in the New Testament, the reference is to the latter. Here it evidently is so—the words "one toward another" fix it to this sense. The meaning is, cherish towards each other the same reciprocal sentiments and feelings of esteem and regard,—the same good desires for one another's welfare,—the same kind purposes and resolutions.—Unity of sentiment in the great essential truths of the Gospel is indispensable to the peculiar unity of regard which must subsist amongst fellow-christians. This is self-evident. The truth as it is in Jesus is the very ground of the regard, which from its nature can have no subsistence apart from the "one faith."† But while there must be this

---

* τὸ αὐτὸ φρονοῦντες.   † 2 John 1, 2.

measure of unity—it is equally manifest, that perfect identity of views in every iota is not, and cannot be, necessary. If it were, we might bid farewell in despair to the very *possibility* of the affectionate regard which is inculcated. Every individual in that case must concentrate his regard upon himself, and be his own solitary object of interest; his own friend, his own brother, his own church; having exclusive fellowship with himself, and even that hardly always in the best bonds.

Unity of judgment, however, and unity of affection have a mutual influence in producing and promoting each other. Unity of affection tends to unity of judgment, by subduing prejudice, softening down opinionative perverseness, and leading to unbigoted and unbiassed candour of investigation;— all being disposed to pay a due measure of deference to the judgment of others, and all being ready to yield to the evidence of truth, and desirous to find it, that under its common influence they may "edify one another in love." O that there were more of such a spirit in us all, and in all that name the name of Jesus! The more unity of heart there is amongst Christians, the more may we expect to see the prevalence of unity of sentiment. And, on the other hand, the more there is of unity of sentiment, the more may we reasonably expect of the unity of affectionate regard.—It has indeed been alleged by some that the nearer Christians come to each other in sentiment, if they still differ, there is the greater likelihood of the bitterness of dissension. And there is some ground for the observation. When the difference between two bodies of professed believers, for example, is of such a nature that the necessity of distinct fellowships is at once apparent, so that the idea of coalescing is out of the question, and hardly if ever presents itself to their minds as a thing attainable, they may mingle with feelings of more easy cordiality, than when there is just one little point, it may be, that keeps them asunder, and either party is apt to be fretted because the other cannot be induced to yield it. But still, it must stand as a general maxim, though subject to occasional exceptions, that the greater the unity of sentiment, the greater the harmony of feeling; and this harmony of feeling, be it remembered, is necessary to unity in worship.* The exhortations to such unity as is here inculcated are frequent and earnest.†

From the nature of the Christian body, as composed of persons of all ranks and conditions in life, *humility* becomes especially needful to this unity of affectionate regard. Humility is always so represented.‡ Hence it follows here— "Mind not high things, but condescend to men of low estate."—"*Mind* not." It is the same word as in the preceding clause. The meaning is—*affect* not high things;—set not your hearts upon them. While "to the poor the gospel is preached," it is not to the exclusion of the rich; nor is the converting power of the divine Spirit confined to any one condition of life. There has always been a mixture of "high and low, rich and poor," in the spiritual kingdom of Christ. It is here, in a peculiar manner, the poor and rich meet together in equality before that Lord who is the Maker of them all. They are "all one in Christ Jesus." Here the prince must give the right hand of fellowship to his meanest dependant.§

"Mind not *high things*." Those who were higher than their brethren in secular condition were to beware of so setting their hearts on their elevation as to affect superiority, and to regard with feelings of haughtiness and disdain such as were in this respect their inferiors. Those, on the other hand, who were lower in station, were not to "seek great things for themselves," to set their desires on worldly elevation, disdaining their equals and courting the familiar intercourse of those above them. The feelings and the practical exemplification of humble affability and condescension on the one hand, and of a spirit that does not discontentedly aspire above its station on the other, are what the words evidently inculcate. "There is a generation—O how lofty are their eyes! and their eyelids are lifted up!" This is not the generation of God's children. A haughty spirit and lofty

---

* Rom. xv. 5, 6. † Phil. ii. 1—5; iii. 15—17. ‡ Eph. iv. 1—3.
§ Col. iii. 11.

eyes become not those who in their addresses to God daily own themselves "less than the least of all his mercies." True humility must not be confined to intercourse with God. It must appear in its influence on the entire tenor of our conduct and intercourse amongst our fellow-christians and our fellow-men. He who is truly humble when on his knees before the throne, will be humble in the family circle and in all the relations and transactions of life. He will not rise from his lowly prostration before his Maker, to erect his head and assume the post of haughtiness among his fellows in nature or in grace. If he has looked up to God through the tears of a truly lowly and broken-hearted penitence, he will not turn the same eye immediately down upon those beneath him with the expression of proud and careless superciliousness. He will "*condescend to men of low estate*"*— acting towards them in a spirit of kind consideration, and assuming no air of superiority. Christians are in the strongest terms warned against an aspiring worldliness—a spirit of secular self-promotion and stateliness and dignity—a spirit such as would lead them to count the meanest office of love to the meanest of the Lord's disciples a degradation. Let all who feel the risings of such a spirit come with me to the upper room where Jesus their Master held his last meeting with his chosen few:—let them look at Him; let them hear Him:—"Jesus knowing that the Father had given all things into his hands, and that he was come from God, and went to God; He riseth from supper, and laid aside his garments; and took a towel and girded himself. After that he poureth water into a bason, and began to wash the disciples' feet, and to wipe them with the towel wherewith he was girded." "So, after he had washed their feet, and had taken his garments, and was set down again, he said unto them, Know ye what I have done to you? Ye call me Mas-

---

* The margin of the English version has, "Be contented with mean things;" and others render "inclining to things that are lowly;" as the τοῖς ταπεινοῖς may be either neuter or masculine. Alford is decidedly in favour of the rendering in the text of the English version—and on good grounds. Dr. D. Brown prefers it also.—Ed.

ter and Lord: and ye say well; for so I am. If I then, your Lord and Master, have washed your feet, ye also ought to wash one another's feet. For I have given you an example, that ye should do as I have done to you."*

Let every one whose heart is inclined to any sentiment of haughty superiority—who from the pedestal of worldly elevation is disposed to look down on any of his fellow-believers, the brethren of his Master and Lord, contemplate this wonderful scene, and blush for shame. If he does not feel the power of Christ's words—where, O where is the spirit of Christ? Is he *sincere* in calling him Master and Lord? Does he not hear that Master saying to him in terms of mortifying expostulation—"Why call ye me, Lord, Lord, and do not the things which I say?" There is a peculiar beauty too, I would here remark, when those who themselves, in the providence of God, have risen from a low to a high condition, retain the same kindly affability towards those who are now beneath them which they displayed towards them when equals. This is the more striking and the more to be admired, because the contrary is common even to a proverb.

I must not, however, quit this exhortation without remarking that it ought not to be understood as meaning,—nor will the Christian in an inferior condition, who possesses good sense and true humility himself, think of so interpreting it—that the high and the low, the rich and the poor, are to be perfectly levelled in the ordinary intercourse of life; that, because believers are one in Christ Jesus, there ought to be the very same frequency and freedom and familiarity of intercourse between all stations. This would be a very foolish interpretation, requiring what never, in the nature of things, can be maintained,—what would make Christianity incompatible with the arrangements and distinctions of civil society, and expose it to strong objection, and severe animadversion and reproach. The poor who would insist on such an interpretation would do well to institute a process of self-examination to ascertain whether the spirit by which it is dic-

---

* John xiii. 3—5, 12—15.

tated be not the very spirit, under another form and modification of it, which the words prohibit. The interpretation would be most injurious to the poor; injurious to their contented habits and so to their temporal happiness and their spiritual prosperity. To encourage any such expectation in the poor would be as pernicious on the one side as to encourage a spirit of haughtiness in the rich would be on the other. He who looks down with disdain, and he who looks up with envy, are substantially influenced by the same spirit —they are "minding high things;" and, only changing places, they would exchange feelings:—envy in the inferior would become disdain in the superior, and disdain in the superior would become in the inferior envy.

"*Be not wise in your own conceits.*"—Self-dependence and self-sufficiency are sadly natural to fallen man. The believer of the Bible can be at no loss for their origin.* The consequence of drinking in the spirit of the too insinuating assurance of the first Tempters has been, that ever from that day men "professing themselves to be wise, have become fools." The result in regard to "the things of God" is brought fully out by this Apostle when he says, "Where is the wise? where is the scribe? where is the disputer of this world? hath not God made foolish the wisdom of this world? For after that, in the wisdom of God, the world by wisdom knew not God, it pleased God by the foolishness of preaching to save them that believe."† The wisdom of the world having thus been proved vain, the believer in Christ has learned to renounce it, and to submit his mind to the dictation of the word of God. This is the spirit of the apostolic admonition—"If any man among you seemeth to be wise in this world, let him become a fool, that he may be wise."‡

The temper of mind recommended may be viewed in relation to *God* and in relation to *men*. When viewed in relation to God, it may be considered as embracing the two departments of *truth* and *duty*,—including the subjection of the mind and of the conscience to the instructions and to

---

* Gen. iii. 4, 5.   † 1 Cor. i. 19—21.   ‡ 1 Cor. iii. 18.

the authority of God. Instead of spurning at His word, or at the offers of his enlightening Spirit which its promises contain, resolving, in the loftiness of self-sufficiency, to walk in our own light, to find truth and duty for ourselves, and to reject all that we cannot discover or cannot understand;—instead of setting up our wisdom as the test of God's, taking whatever in His word accords with our own preconceptions, and refusing the rest;—if we act up to the precept before us, we shall feel and own our need of divine guidance to lead us both to truth and duty; sitting down to his word as humble learners, our sole inquiry, "What saith the Lord?" —and looking up for his Spirit to illumine and enlarge our minds, and to give right convictions and becoming tenderness to our consciences.*

The same lowly temper of mind which renders a man distrustful of himself, and leads him to seek divine counsel, will dispose him also not to fancy himself above receiving counsel from his fellow-men. He who is sensible (as every one will be who is not "wise in his own conceit") of his own deficiency in knowledge, will be willing and happy to gain accessions to it from any quarter. It will be his delight to have new ideas imparted, and to have old ones corrected and enlarged, whosoever may be the instrument of effecting these ends. We very often miss a great deal of knowledge by the false shame of letting our ignorance appear. This is one form of the very spirit here condemned. It is a foolish because a pernicious pride; we are serious losers by it. To forfeit knowledge from the shame of ignorance is to starve our minds for the gratification of our vanity. And while we should be humbly ready to receive instruction, we should not be less so to listen to admonition and advice. This the self-conceited man is never inclined to do. He is always in the right; contemptuous and stubborn:—and even in cases where he suspects his judgment may be wrong, his pride will not allow him to confess his error or to alter his course;— he will rather proceed against his conviction, than appear to

* See Psal. xxv. 8, 9, 12; lxxiii. 24: Prov. iii. 5—8: Jer. x. 23, &c.

be indebted to the counsel of another. He is, moreover, always prone to form his judgments hastily, and to take his resolutions with a promptitude amounting to rashness, because slow deliberation might indicate weakness of capacity and deficiency in that intuitive discernment for which he is desirous to get the credit. And then, when he has taken his ground, however prematurely, he keeps it with a bigoted tenacity for the very same reason,—that change would involve a reflection on his own sagacity. When other men see difficulties, many perhaps and great, he can discover none, or at least they are but few and trivial:—and where others can discover none, he shakes his head, looks very wise and penetrating, and discerns obstacles that are insuperable:—the thing is far from being so simple or so easy as they imagine. He *must* have an opinion of his own. What everybody sees is not worth seeing: what he affects to value himself upon seeing is what no one else can see. And he must too have his own way. Of three ways, two long and crooked and one short and straight, he will prefer one or other of the crooked to the straight, if the straight happen to have been pointed out to him by another. Being thus full of himself, he is supercilious and petulant, or he is harsh, dogmatical and overbearing in his behaviour to others. This character is contrasted in Scripture with that of the *truly* wise—the humble self-diffident child of God.[*]

And let me also observe in reference to this temper of mind, that the same humility which disposes us to receive counsel, will direct us also in the manner of *giving it*. To give advice, especially in opposition to existing predilections, for a particular course, is one of the most delicate and difficult of duties. And there is nothing which, if we wish to discharge it successfully, is more especially necessary, than shunning every appearance of self-conceit. The self-conceited man can never be a good counsellor. If we would persuade and benefit our friend, we must *hide self*. It is the common complaint, on the part of the givers of advice, that it is very

---

[*] Prov. xii. 15; xv. 31—33.

seldom taken. It may be worth their while to inquire how far this, to the extent in which the complaint is well-founded, may not have for its cause the spirit and manner in which advice is given. If it be given in the spirit of self-sufficiency and dictatorial consequentiality, how can we expect it to be well received?—Let me not be mistaken. I am far from meaning to say, that *all* the aversion to receive counsel arises from the manner in which it is conveyed. The counselled may be "wise in their own conceits" as well as the counsellors:—and let the adviser be ever so self-diffident and gentle, there are those who from self-sufficiency will not be advised —" like the deaf adder that stoppeth her ear, which will not hearken to the voice of charmers, charming ever so wisely."
—Let us, then, both in giving and receiving counsel, attend to the admonition, "BE NOT WISE IN YOUR OWN CONCEITS:" —and in both, feeling our "lack of wisdom," let us "ask of God, who giveth to all men liberally, and upbraideth not; and it shall be given."

LECTURE LVIII.

ROMANS XII. 17—21.

"Recompense to no man evil for evil. Provide things honest in the sight of all men. If it be possible, as much as lieth in you, live peaceably with all men. Dearly beloved, avenge not yourselves, but rather give place unto wrath: for it is written, Vengeance is mine; I will repay, saith the Lord. Therefore, if thine enemy hunger, feed him; if he thirst, give him drink: for in so doing thou shalt heap coals of fire on his head. Be not overcome of evil, but overcome evil with good."

RESENTMENT is a modification of pride. By an injury done to us, we not only sustain a certain amount of pain or of loss, —we are at the same time *mortified*. He who has done us the wrong appears in our eyes as having acquired a certain superiority. Against this our pride rises, and urges us by retaliation to be *even* with him. This is a principle which the world too generally applaud. They call it *spirit*, and the contrary is in their vocabulary *mean-spiritedness*:—and some philosophers have concurred in the commendation of the principle, as a wise provision of nature. Let us see, then, how the Christian law stands:—"Ye have heard that it hath been said, An eye for an eye, and a tooth for a tooth: but I say unto you, That ye resist not evil: but whosoever shall smite thee on thy right cheek, turn to him the other also."* Our Lord's language has reference to a precept belonging to the criminal code of Israel,† of which the application was to be determined and the execution ordered by the judicial authorities; but which had been perverted, by the

* Matth. v. 38, 39.   † Exod. xxi. 24, 27; Lev. xxiv. 19, 20.

same principle that had produced the perversion of other statutes, into a permission of personal retaliation, or private revenge. But such never was its import, any more than the precept to "love our neighbour" implied a permission to "hate our enemy."

The expressions of our Lord, as they are here interpreted by his servant, are strongly descriptive and imperative of the *spirit* of his religion. They do not mean that there is never to be any remonstrating, however calm and gentle, against injurious treatment: for He of whom it is said, that He "gave his back to the smiters, and his cheeks to them that plucked off the hair," that "he was led as a lamb to the slaughter," that "when he was reviled, he reviled not again,"—did actually set the example of such remonstrance.* Nor do they mean that in no case are we ever to seek such redress of the wrong done to us as the circumstances of the case admit. For surely Paul was not acting in opposition to his own precept when he expostulated with the magistrates of Philippi, and insisted on such steps being taken as would serve to do away the effects of the injurious treatment which himself and his fellow-labourers had sustained.† Our Lord's expression— "If any man smite thee on thy right cheek, turn to him the other also," is a proverbial one for meek submission to affronts and injuries. The expression of the Apostle, "Recompense to no man evil for evil," means that we are not to inflict *injury for injury*—to retaliate for the sake of retaliation—to gratify resentment. It is precisely the spirit prohibited by the wise man,—" Say not, I will do to him as he hath done to me; I will render to the man according to his work."‡

There may be cases of wrong by which the interests of others are implicated as well as our own: and there may be cases in which, character being concerned, not comfort of mind only but usefulness is at stake;—cases in which an appeal to the law of our country, to establish our injured reputation, or to secure our endangered or recover our ab-

---

* John xviii. 22, 23.   † Acts xvi. 37.   ‡ Prov. xxiv. 29.

stracted property, may be an imperative duty—for our own sake, for our family's sake, for the church's sake, for the Lord's sake. But we are interdicted from prosecuting an offence for the sake of bringing our enemy to suffering; from gratifying our resentment even by legal means.—There may be cases which (although in as far as we are ourselves personally concerned, we might be desirous to pass all over) require us, however reluctantly, to call the defaulters to account, for the sake of the public good—for the protection of the injured laws and the safety of the community:— but in such cases, we would do well to take heed to our motives, lest, through the deceitfulness of our hearts, we should be found covering over a feeling of personal resentment and retaliation under the pretext of regard to the public benefit. We are often very fond of having some such specious covert for what is at bottom purely selfish, or has in it at least a large proportion of this unworthy principle.—Let Christians beware of their allowing the prevailing opinions and favourite maxims of the world to interfere in any degree with their firm adherence to the explicit laws of their divine Master, and the true spirit of his Gospel. It is *His* will, and *His* example they are ever to follow, not the inclinations of their own corrupt hearts, nor the course of an ungodly world.—I may just remark, before quitting this clause, of which the spirit is expanded afterwards, that, Christian country as it is called, Scotland bears on her national arms an emblem and a motto as thoroughly as possible *anti*-christian.*

The next admonition is a very important one—"*Provide things honest in the sight of all men.*" Things "*honest,*" or things *honourable,*† in the true acceptation of the term,— things in harmony with the dignity of the Christian character. The word does not mean merely things "*honest*" in the sense in which the word is now in general used among us—namely, for what is according to truth and integrity, in the mutual

---

* The thistle, and *Nemo me impune lacessit*—Touch me, and you shall smart for it.—Ed. † καλα.

transactions of business and of ordinary intercourse. And when we substitute the term *honourable,* I need not say that *it* is not to be understood in that false sense in which it is too often employed by worldly men, which identifies it with a quick, and jealous, and selfish pride,—but in the sense of high-toned moral principle,—principle that will stoop to nothing mean and sordid, and justly, even by the world, despised as well as condemned. And surely, amongst believers in Christ, followers of the Holy One and the Just, all should be invariably of this description. It is sad when it is otherwise, when in the conduct of any one of them there is to be seen what is beneath the standard of the conventional morality and reciprocal honour of the world; when, instead of the superior strictness and loftiness by which the conduct of such ought to be characterized, there is a laxity and a depression that provoke the leer and the sarcasm of the ungodly. "Let it not be so, brethren, among you."

"*Provide* things honest in the sight of all men." See to it—make it an object of your special and constant attention, that your conduct exhibit, in every part of it, the influence of sterling and steadily operating principle,—of undeviating rectitude,—resolute, unbending integrity;—that you discharge with faithful punctuality all the duties of your respective situations, and of whatever trust is committed to you; that in your intercourse with the world no allurement can induce you to come down from the lofty ground of uncompromising Christian morality, or to swerve one inch from the straightforward line of duty,—adhering amidst all temptations (which may at times be held out even for the very purpose of putting your principles to the test) to the stern dictates of truth and honesty; and to that generosity and liberality, and candour and simplicity, and unequivocal downrightness and openness of character which Christianity, wherever it is allowed its own proper influence, cannot fail to produce. Let the world see that in all your ways you act not from calculations of interest, but from decision of principle—not with the vacillating policy of fleshly wisdom, but by the grace of God, with your "eyes looking right on, and your eye-lids looking straight before you." Let them see, that those virtues which they prize, as the virtues that are most essential to the being and the well-being of society, and which they outwardly practise from motives of expediency, or at the best of mere earthly morality, are in *your* conduct refined and elevated by the influence of principles and motives of a higher order—nobler and purer in their nature and more efficient and constant in their operation, derived not from earth but from heaven.

The considerations by which this conduct might be enforced are various. Not to speak of the peace and comfort thence arising to our own mind, and a regard to our own interests and the general interests of society, there is a higher motive—the *credit of religion and the honour of Christ.* To this Paul points when in reference to his own conduct on a particular occasion he thus expresses himself:—" Avoiding this, that no man should blame us in this abundance which is administered by us: providing for honest things, not only in the sight of the Lord, but also in the sight of men."* He did not think it enough to provide for honest and honourable things in the sight of God—to have a conscience clear there, in regard to the calumnious insinuations of his enemies:—he felt it necessary, to his official usefulness and the honour of his Master and the prosperity of His cause, that all should, as far as possible, be so managed as to prevent and do away suspicion and reproach, however groundless and unreasonable they would have been, amongst men. It will not do for Christians to affect being independent of the opinion of the world. You see in the instance before you, that even the Apostle Paul was not. Nothing indeed must be said or done for the sake of the world's good opinion, inconsistent in the slightest degree with our principles as subjects of Christ; but if there be two courses, one of which may induce the suspicion of those who are seeking occasion against us, or give them even a pretext for insinuating evil, while

---

* 2 Cor. viii. 20, 21.

the other will make all clear, and deprive them of every such pretext, we are not warranted to set the world at defiance,—to say What's the world's opinion to me?—and to take the very course at which cavils may be raised and surmises insinuated, for the purpose of showing our independence and disdain. For the sake of Christianity, whose honour is involved in the character of its professors and supporters, let us follow the example of Paul and deal prudently, "cutting off occasion from them who desire occasion" against both ourselves and our principles: and let us remember that the good of the men of the world themselves is involved in this matter—their good both for time and for eternity.*

While by such motives the subjects of Jesus should be induced not only to live to God, but *so* to live to God as that amongst men "the adversary shall have no occasion to speak reproachfully,"—they must, I repeat, beware of all compromise of principle. No consideration of personal reputation, or personal ease and enjoyment and freedom from suffering, must ever induce them to a single step aside from the centre line of consistency. They must do what is right, be the consequence what it may. Hear the language of Peter:—" For he that will love life, and see good days, let him refrain his tongue from evil, and his lips that they speak no guile: let him eschew evil and do good; let him seek peace, and ensue it. For the eyes of the Lord are over the righteous, and his ears are open unto their prayers: but the face of the Lord is against them that do evil. And who is he that will harm you, if ye be followers of that which is good? But and if ye suffer for righteousness' sake, happy are ye: and be not afraid of their terror, neither be troubled; but sanctify the Lord God in your hearts: and be ready always to give an answer to every man that asketh you a reason of the hope that is in you with meekness and fear: having a good conscience; that whereas they speak evil of you, as of evil doers, they may be ashamed that falsely accuse your good conversation in Christ."†

---

* Matt. v. 14—16; 1 Pet. ii. 11, 12.   † 1 Pet. iii. 10—16.

On the other hand, it was far from their duty then, and is as far now, to *court* persecution, wilfully and needlessly to stir up the rage of the enemies of the cross:—they are admonished to the very opposite; to do all in their power consistently with a good conscience to prevent, assuage, and disarm it. Such seems the principle of our Lord's admonition:— "Behold, I send you forth as sheep in the midst of wolves: be ye therefore wise as serpents, and harmless as doves. But beware of men: for they will deliver you up to the councils, and they will scourge you in their synagogues;"* and such is the spirit of the admonition here in verse eighteenth:— "If it be possible, as much as lieth in you, live peaceably with all men." Fellow-christians, subjects together of the "Prince of peace," members together of the family of " the God of peace," are taught, in the first instance, to live in peace and harmony *with one another*. Nothing can be more delightful than the prophetic description of the pacific influence of the Gospel:—"The wolf also shall dwell with the lamb, and the leopard shall lie down with the kid; and the calf, and the young lion, and the fatling together; and a little child shall lead them. And the cow and the bear shall feed; their young ones shall lie down together: and the lion shall eat straw like the ox. And the sucking child shall play on the hole of the asp, and the weaned child shall put his hand on the cockatrice' den."† And frequent are the injunctions of their Lord and Master to the spirit and practice of peace:—"Salt is good: but if the salt have lost his saltness, wherewith will ye season it? Have salt in yourselves, and have peace one with another." "Be perfect, be of good comfort, be of one mind, live in peace; and the God of love and peace shall be with you."‡ All the commands to love and to humility are commands to peace; these being the principles by which peace is to be maintained.—But their duty extends further than to peace among themselves. The verse before us embraces in its injunction "*all men*."§

---

* Matt. x. 16, 17. † Isa. xi. 6—8.
‡ Mark ix. 50; 2 Cor. xiii. 11; also 1 Thes. v. 13; Eph. iv. 3.
§ Comp. Heb. xii. 14.

Of the spirit and conduct thus enjoined we have a fine exemplification in the psalmist—"My soul hath long dwelt with him that hateth peace. I am for peace: but when I speak, they are for war."* But of the spirit of peace, as indeed of every other excellence, the perfect pattern is to be seen and studied in the life of Christ. And in his life too we have the best commentary on the words before us—"*If it be possible, as much as lieth in you,* live peaceably with all men." If we are not in peace with all men, the fault must not be ours: it must be solely *because we cannot,*— because the terms required for peace are not such as can be granted consistently with "a good conscience." It is of much importance to have a proper view and impression of the meaning of the words. We are ever in danger of interpreting in harmony with the natural likings and tendencies of our minds. The meaning here is not, we apprehend, that we have permission to yield to strong provocation, and that we may bring our so yielding under the covert of the verse before us by saying, "We *could not*—it was not possible for us—to command our temper: *who* could, under such provocation?" Apologies such as this are common in the mouths of Christians; but they are not to be found in the New Testament. The language does not refer to the impossibility of keeping our own temper, but to the felt impossibility, after we have done all that lieth in us, of subduing the malevolent and angry passions of those who set themselves against us. It belongs to us to do everything in our power for peace, by exhibiting in our entire demeanour the "meekness and the gentleness of Christ," that courteous affability and engaging suavity of manner, that generous kindness of desire and beneficence of conduct, which are, in their proper tendency, fitted "to turn away wrath." The provocation must not come from our side. The aggression must be unprovoked. We must "suffer for righteousness' sake." And even when the attack is unjustly made, we must "keep our heart" with the firmness of self-control, and our lips "as with a bridle:"—not giving

* Psa. cxx. 6, 7.

way to the risings of resentment,—not "rendering evil for evil or railing for railing;" but still showing that our disposition and anxiety are for peace, and that we are ready to sacrifice everything for it but conscience.

There is, I allow, a great variety in the natural, and perhaps still more frequently in the educational tempers of men. But let me entreat my fellow-christians to be on their guard how they admit this as an apology for the indulgence of a hasty spirit, —for being "easily provoked." Nothing is more common than for Christians, when charged with excess of passion, to say— "I do confess it is wrong; *but* you know my temper,—how naturally quick and fiery it is;—and you cannot but admit too that I *had* provocation." This may be all true. But it is not a very good symptom when there is an eagerness to plead it. It ought to be the subject of deep concern, of humiliation, confession, prayer for forgiveness, and for grace to overcome the evil. Let it be laid down as a fixed principle, that there is no temper which the grace of God is unable to subdue. It is sufficient for everything. As there is no sin of which the guilt is so heinous as to be beyond the atoning virtue of the *blood* of Christ; so is there no evil propensity,—no lust, no passion, which is beyond the subduing power of the *Spirit* of Christ:—and it is remarkable, as I have already hinted, that we nowhere find any such apology, or even palliative suggested, for a flattering unction to the conscience, in the New Testament scriptures. But let me not be mistaken: for a mistake here might not only bear hard on the constitutionally irritable, but might prove soothingly detrimental to the naturally sweet-blooded and gentle. While the former are in danger of finding in natural constitution an apology for the deficiency of grace; the latter are in at least equal danger of placing in their books to the credit of grace what fairly belongs to mere constitutional temperament. And this is a twofold danger. There is the danger of complacent self-satisfaction, and confidence that has but a very dubious source: and there is the danger of excessive severity and harshness in the condemnation of others. Now it may happen—it often does happen, that in some, grace has in this particular little to do; while in some others, grace may actually have effected a great deal more in the way of correction and subjugation, even while yet there remains a good deal to subdue. In him who plumes himself on his gentleness there may be far less of the power of principle, than in him who has prayed and watched and striven, and who still mourns over much to conquer. Let us all be on our guard. Let us "look to ourselves," and beware of every kind and every degree of self-flattery and self-deception. It is true that some sins are more heinous in their nature than others; it is true that the same sin committed by another may be more aggravated in its moral turpitude than when committed by us;—yet surely it would be no very auspicious symptom of our character, or of the state of our hearts towards God, were we disposed, on this or on any other ground, to seek excuses and palliatives for our own transgressions.

The remaining verses of the chapter are an amplification of the same precept as that in verses fourteenth and seventeenth :—" Dearly beloved, avenge not yourselves, but rather give place unto wrath: for it is written, Vengeance is mine; I will repay, saith the Lord. Therefore if thine enemy hunger, feed him; if he thirst, give him drink: for in so doing thou shalt heap coals of fire on his head. Be not overcome of evil, but overcome evil with good."

There are duties—duties of imperative obligation and first-rate importance, which may be performed in the *letter*, while they are broken in the *spirit*. In carrying out, for example, the injunction of our Lord—" Moreover, if thy brother shall trespass against thee, go and tell him his fault between thee and him alone: if he shall hear thee, thou hast gained thy brother. But if he will not hear thee, then take with thee one or two more, that in the mouth of two or three witnesses every word may be established. And if he shall neglect to hear them, tell it unto the church: but if he neglect to hear the church, let him be unto thee as an heathen man and a publican."* It is quite possible, that every step of this pro-

* Matt. xviii. 15—17.

cess may be gone through with punctilious adherence to the letter, while in each successive step there may be felt and breathed the very spirit which is here condemned. And such is the deceitfulness of the heart, he who is following the rule may overlook the spirit of it in its letter, and flatter himself with his close adherence to the law of Christ, while in the sight of Christ, he is deeply and grievously sinning all the while; saying in his heart—I will show him what it is to injure *me!* and feeling in the end an unholy satisfaction in his triumph. The spirit by which he is influenced may not appear to others:—he may take good care of that. But I would have him to remember that if he is conscious that such is his temper of mind, he has in that consciousness what ought to convince him that he deserves as really to be counted as " a heathen man and a publican " as the pursued and excommunicated offender. The same observation applies to the rules of discipline in general in the churches of Christ. The principle is not punitive revenge but restorative love—hatred of the sin, but faithful affection to the sinning soul:—"the destruction of the flesh, that the spirit may be saved in the day of the Lord Jesus."*

As to men in general, we are to see that we never avenge our injuries with our own hand. We may, with the qualification formerly stated, remonstrate, and even apply for legal redress;—but when there is no prospect of any redress being obtained, we are not by the precept before us warranted in pursuing the offender merely for the sake of seeing him humbled and brought to suffering. When an injury cannot be repaired it is but a pitiful satisfaction to say it is *revenged*.

The reason assigned for the interdiction of personal revenge is very striking:—" *For it is written,*† *Vengeance is mine; I will repay, saith the Lord.*" Thus the divine Being claims "vengeance" or recompense as His own peculiar prerogative. Even if we could not see clearly the reasons for His will in particular cases, yet having once ascertained this Book to be from Him; we should yield implicit obe-

---

* 1 Cor. v. 5. † Deut. xxxii. 35.

dience to its dictates, believing that all is good, and that every alteration would be ultimately injurious. But it is pleasing when we can see the reasons of a command or prohibition, and see them to be worthy of God. The present prohibition is recommended by such considerations as—
1. The peace and happiness of our own bosoms. There is nothing so wretched as a bosom agitated by the harassing disquietudes of angry and revengeful passions,—restless with conflicting and turbulent emotions. The spirit of revenge is like the shelving rocks in the bottom of the deep, which cause the waters to boil in the foaming whirlpool:—the spirit of forgiveness and love keeps the soul, to use the poet's beautiful expression—

> "Calm and unruffled as a summer sea,
> When not a breath of wind flies o'er its surface."

2. Self-partiality unfits us for measuring correctly the amount of injuries done to ourselves, and consequently the amount of vengeance due. It is a maxim which universal experience has made proverbial, that no man is a proper judge in his own cause. We are always in danger, therefore, of forming an extravagant estimate; and so of exacting recompense or inflicting vengeance beyond what is due.—3. We are likewise very incompetent judges of the motives by which others are actuated. We cannot discern them with any certainty. So that, as we are apt to measure out our retaliation by the actual effects which we feel to be the result of an action, and that at the very time when we are smarting under these effects, by which the balance of our judgment is disturbed, we may not only exceed in "vengeance," but we may inflict "vengeance" where there ought, were we to judge the action by its motive and intention and not by its unintended and unfortunate result, to be approbation and grateful reward. —4. When we do exceed in our vengeance, what is the consequence? All such excess is injury. This injury calls for revenge in return. The same principles operate in producing excess in the return; and thus there is no prospect but of perpetuated wrong, and interminable hostility. Thus

there is wisdom in the interdiction—divine wisdom in Deity retaining the right to recompense in His own hands. He, and He alone, can accurately and infallibly appreciate the amount of culpability; and can alone, therefore, apportion the punishments. The passions indulged in revenge are such as the God of the Bible can never sanction. They are such as, if indulged universally, would fill the world with unutterable wretchedness and horror. Pride and revenge are principles in the world's morality:—they are sometimes misnamed *honour;* and under this specious title they challenge to the field of deadly contest the man who by word or look or act has offered or seemed to offer an insult, and will be satiated with nothing but blood. I need not surely say that this false and foolish honour is no Bible principle. It is saying the very least that can be said, that there is no conceivable case in which this practice can be lawfully followed by a Christian—either in the way of giving or of accepting the challenge—for if the one be wrong, the other cannot be right. There can hardly be an exception to the verdict that the blood of every duel is the blood of murder.

In this view of the motive presented to dissuade from revenge, we must beware of associating with the divine words anything like such a spirit in God's execution of merited punishment. This can have no place in the administration of the Most High. Punishment is with Him the act of a holy and righteous Ruler, who from His independence and self-sufficiency is infinitely above being moved by passion.* The punishments which He inflicts are the expression of an infinite disapprobation and hatred of sin, and a regard to the good of the universe, which sin tends to ruin. For we are ever apt to take too limited a view of the divine mercy. It may be, in the extensive government of God, as it is in the subordinate and more limited administrations of human rulers,—that mercy to the individual may be injustice and cruelty to the community.

Instead of revenge, the opposite conduct is enforced:—

* Job xxii. 2—4.

"Therefore, if thine enemy hunger, feed him; if he thirst, give him drink: for in so doing thou shalt heap coals of fire on his head."* The conduct enjoined needs no comment. It is that of doing good instead of evil to our enemy:—for the cases specified, of feeding when hungry and giving drink when thirsty, involve in them the general injunction of doing good *in every way in our power*. But there are different interpretations of the motive by which the conduct is recommended:—"*for in so doing thou shalt heap coals of fire on his head.*" By some this is understood of aggravating his guilt and condemnation, loading him with a heavier vengeance from that God "to whom vengeance belongeth." It is obvious, however, that, although this may express *a fact*, it *cannot* be a *motive*. The aggravation of our enemy's retribution from God is a thing which it is impossible for us to *desire*, without a fearful violation of the spirit of the passage. It would be a kind of refinement in revenge:—abstaining from it in person, but acting, in hypocritical kindness, so as to insure it with heavier accumulation in another quarter.

The other view is the more pleasing by many degrees. And the more pleasing it is, the more should we be gratified to find that it is the more natural and agreeable to the connexion. According to it the "heaping of coals of fire on his head," having in it an allusion to the smelting of ore or metal in the furnace, denotes subduing, or melting him down to conciliation and kindness. And while this view allows of our considering it as a *motive*, which is incomparably more natural than any interpretation which regards it only as a *fact*,—it is at the same time in harmony with the verse which follows, which, in truth, appears itself to be a literal explanation of the figure previously used—"*Be not overcome of evil, but overcome evil with good.*" We are "overcome of evil," when we allow our angry passions to get the better of us on our being wronged,—when we admit the spirit of revenge, and are tempted to retaliate the injury. We "overcome evil

* Comp. Prov. xxv. 21, 22.

with good" when we soften and disarm those passions in others by the practical exercise of the contrary; when we tame ferocity by gentleness; when we conciliate enmity by kindness; when by the pouring on of oil we smooth the surge which we should have lashed and rebuked in vain; when by the power of forbearance and of practical love we open the secret spring of tenderness, and quench the fire of the flashing eye in the tear of penitential affection. This is true heroism.* To "render evil for evil is human; to render evil for good is devilish; to render good for evil is divine."† The spirit inculcated in the passage before us is exemplified, and by the force of example recommended:—"And it came to pass, when the time was come that he should be received up, he stedfastly set his face to go to Jerusalem, and sent messengers before his face: and they went, and entered into a village of the Samaritans, to make ready for him. And they did not receive him, because his face was as though he would go to Jerusalem. And when his disciples James and John saw this, they said, Lord, wilt thou that we command fire to come down from heaven, and consume them, even as Elias did? But he turned, and rebuked them, and said, Ye know not what spirit ye are of. For the Son of man is not come to destroy men's lives, but to save them. And they went to another village."—"And while he yet spake, behold a multitude, and he that was called Judas, one of the twelve, went before them, and drew near unto Jesus to kiss him. But Jesus said unto him, Judas, betrayest thou the Son of man with a kiss? When they which were about him saw what would follow, they said unto him, Lord, shall we smite with the sword? And one of them smote a servant of the high priest, and cut off his right ear. And Jesus answered and said, Suffer ye thus far. And he touched his ear, and healed him."‡ These very instances show us, however, especially the latter, that the effect ascribed to kindness is not always to be counted on;—that there is a malignity which

---

* Prov. xvi. 32; xix. 11. † Matt. v. 43—48.
‡ Luke ix. 51—56; xxii. 47—51.

no means of conciliation may soften. When this *is* the case, the blame is not ours. We may suffer from the untamed fury of our inveterate enemy; but we have delivered our souls in the sight of the God with whom we have to do. Let the guilt be with our adversaries if all our kindness fail. God approves; and we shall have no regret when we stand before His tribunal at last.

Can we look back, my brethren, on the contents of this chapter, without exclaiming what a happy world would this be, were Christians what they ought to be, and all men Christians! What a lovely combination of principles and affections and practical virtues is here! How astonished would any impartial reader be, if, after having perused it, he were told by one of the enemies of the Gospel, how much mischief the religion of which these are the precepts, and of which "the mercies of God" constitute the moving spring, had produced in human society,—what desolations it had wrought in the earth,—how many streams of blood might be traced to it as their fountain! Would he not (I suppose the man to read this chapter for the first time and in ignorance of the doctrines of Christianity)— would he not instantly suspect or conclude that there must be some mistake? Would he not see and feel this to be the most unlikely thing in the world? Let the man who can impute such effects to Christianity read this description of its practical character, and blush for his ignorance or his enmity. Christianity in principle is the glorious manifestation of the light and love, the holiness and the grace of God in a scheme for the restoration of his fallen creatures to His own lost favour and image:—and as for Christianity in practice, *here it is*. When professing believers of the Gospel act (as, alas! they too often and too flagrantly have done to admit of concealment or palliation) inconsistently with any part of these divine admonitions, they so far act an *un*christian not a Christian part. They "lie against the truth." Let them by all means be condemned, as severely as the cases may deserve. What we wish of unbelievers is, that they would study the Gospel *here*—in the life of its Author and the writings of his Apostles. The various corruptions of Christianity and sad departures, under the profession even of its true principles, from its practical spirit and preceptive injunctions, are only so many native consequences from the truth of the view given in its records of the character and state of man as a fallen and depraved creature, subject to all the perverting influences of endlessly various lusts and temptations. But *here*, I repeat, is practical Christianity, and the man is a Christian just in proportion as he bears these features of character, and no further. Profession is not principle; and true principle will show itself in practice. Without this all is vain—"a sounding brass and a tinkling cymbal"—mere empty noise—unprofitable to the man himself and pernicious to others. Study, then, this chapter, ye who name the name of Christ. If you study it aright, it will humble you. You will be sensible of deficiencies that will "lay you low and keep you there." Let this consciousness render both the work of Christ and the work of the Spirit the more precious to you;—the former for taking away the guilt of all your conscious failures; and the latter for giving efficiency to your sincere desires (desires inspired too by himself) in "striving against sin." And keep in mind that *all the graces* here enumerated must be cultivated *together*. You must not think, if you find one in some measure of lively operation, that this is to be a cover for the want or the deficiency of others. You must have them all. You must cherish them all. And they must all appear in your daily character, in the family, in the church, and in the world. Thus you will "hold forth the word of life," and "glorify God in your body, and in your spirit, which are God's."*

---

* It may be mentioned, that besides these Lectures on the twelfth chapter of this Epistle, there is a series of twenty-five *Sermons* on its great practical lessons. They were written at an early period of the Author's ministry, and recomposed with much care within a few years of his death. Their introduction here would have been out of place, and would have extended the volume beyond due limits.—ED.

LECTURE LIX.

ROMANS XIII. 1—7.

" Let every soul be subject unto the higher powers. For there is no power but of God: the powers that be are ordained of God. Whosoever therefore resisteth the power, resisteth the ordinance of God; and they that resist shall receive to themselves damnation. For rulers are not a terror to good works, but to the evil. Wilt thou then not be afraid of the power? do that which is good, and thou shalt have praise of the same: for he is a minister of God to thee for good. But if thou do that which is evil, be afraid; for he beareth not the sword in vain: for he is the minister of God, a revenger to execute wrath upon him that doeth evil. Wherefore ye must needs be subject, not only for wrath, but also for conscience' sake. For, for this cause pay ye tribute also: for they are God's ministers, attending continually upon this very thing. Render therefore to all their dues: tribute to whom tribute is due; custom to whom custom; fear to whom fear; honour to whom honour."

*THE subject to which these verses demand our attention is the duty which Christians owe to the civil government of the country in which they live. And that we may have at once before us a full view of the Scripture requirements on this important subject, we shall take one or two other passages in

* This lecture was in substance delivered as early as the year 1820, and afterwards published. The author re-delivered it in 1832, prefacing it with the following remarks:—" Nearly twelve years ago, I had occasion to call your attention to this subject, at a time when our country was in a state of great political ferment, and in some parts of it especially, in which our own city and neighbourhood were included; of no small alarm. Subsequently to that period, divine providence was gracious to our land, in bringing about a greater degree of public satisfaction and harmony than had for a long time before existed. Recently there has been excitement of a somewhat different description, and in which the population of the country is more generally of one mind.

connexion with that which has just been read:—" Put them in mind to be subject to principalities and powers, to obey magistrates, to be ready to every good work." " Submit yourselves to every ordinance of man for the Lord's sake: whether it be to the king, as supreme; or unto governors, as unto them that are sent by him for the punishment of evil-doers, and for the praise of them that do well. For so is the will of God, that with with well-doing ye may put to silence the ignorance of foolish men." " I exhort therefore, that, first of all, supplications, prayers, intercessions, and giving of thanks, be made for all men; for kings, and for all that are in authority; that we may lead a quiet and peaceable life in all godliness and honesty. For this is good and acceptable in the sight of God our Saviour; who will have all men to be saved, and to come unto the knowledge of the truth."*

It is not my province, brethren, to address you as politicians, but as Christians;—as persons professing subjection to Jesus, as King in Zion, and Lord of the conscience.

The high spirit that is abroad, and which corresponds with the ardent tone of popular feeling which pervades Europe, needs not to be stimulated, but rather to be regulated and controlled: and it is well that Christians should be kept in remembrance, that, while they have a part to act as members of civil society—their Christian profession not destroying their earthly relations, nor obliterating the interests and the duties thence arising—that this part, as well as every other, must be acted on Christian principles, and in harmony with the paramount authority and claims of the King of Zion, and the kingdom which is 'not of this world.'

" The subject has come again in our way at a period when it may not be unseasonable for believers to be reminded of those principles and of those claims, that they may be enabled, while cherishing the feelings and desires of loyal and patriotic freemen, to keep these feelings and desires from leading them into any courses that are unbecoming their obligations as subjects of Jesus, and their condition and prospects as 'strangers and pilgrims on the earth.'

"It would be puerile affectation, and a useless and therefore unwarrantable waste of time and labour, to throw what was then delivered and afterwards given to the public in another form, into new arrangement and new expression:—and therefore what I am now to say must be substantially the same, only with such occasional alterations and additions as subsequent consideration may have suggested."

* See Titus iii. 1; 1 Tim. ii. 1—4; and 1 Pet. ii. 13—15.

It is not, therefore, to what political speculators, either on the general principles and theory of government, or on the different sides of party politics, may be pleased to represent as your duty, that I desire your attention:—it is to the plain and authoritative injunctions of your Divine Redeemer and Lord; even that Lord to whom you are constantly addressing the inquiry—" What wilt thou have me to do?"

I am well aware, how unfond we naturally are of all precepts that inculcate *subjection.* There is in our nature a proud repugnance to everything of the kind. Yes; even when the demand is made for the Eternal himself,—" the blessed and only Potentate, the King of kings, and the Lord of lords." Even of " Jehovah and his Anointed," our haughty spirits are ever prone to say, " Let us break their bands asunder, and cast away their cords from us."—But when the spirit of the high-minded sinner has been brought down by the Gospel, and he has bowed with " a broken and contrite heart" to the sceptre of the Saviour's grace;—the humble subjection of his conscience, which then takes place, to the authority of God, involves in it "a meek and quiet spirit" of submission to all the authority which that God has vested in any of His creatures. The obedience which he yields, as a child, as a servant, as a subject, being yielded from religious principle, becomes obedience to God; and " whatsoever he does," he thenceforward " does it heartily, as to the Lord, and not to men."

In interpreting the language in which our duty is enjoined upon us in the word of God, nothing is of greater consequence, along with a tender susceptibility of conscience, than a disposition to explain particular precepts agreeably to the general principles,—the *spirit,* the *genius,* of the Gospel. The language of the Bible is always weighty and decisive; but it is, at the same time, in many instances, general. With dignified authority of tone, it enjoins duties of very extensive import; not always descending to minute particularization; not starting and refuting every captious objection that might be imagined; but leaving the application of the general injunction, in the infinitely varying circumstances of human life, to be made with simplicity of heart, according to the evident spirit of all its discoveries. Upon this principle, we might connect the precepts now before us with those which immediately precede them. The whole of the twelfth chapter breathes the full spirit of humility and love. The following are its concluding admonitions:—"Recompense to no man evil for evil. Provide things honest in the sight of all men. If it be possible, as much as lieth in you, live peaceably with all men. Dearly beloved, avenge not yourselves, but rather give place unto wrath: for it is written, Vengeance is mine; I will repay, saith the Lord. Therefore, if thine enemy hunger, feed him; if he thirst, give him drink: for in so doing thou shalt heap coals of fire on his head. Be not overcome of evil, but overcome evil with good."—Such is the connexion in which are introduced the duties to "the powers that be:"—and that these duties are all comprised under the great Christian law of love, appears from its being immediately added to the statement of them, " Owe no man any thing, but to love one another; for he that loveth another hath fulfilled the law."—Surely this ought to lead us, in explaining the terms employed on the subject before us, to stretch their application to the *extreme of peace*, if such an extreme there be, rather than to try how far it is possible to extract from them a *license to resist*.—And let every Christian mark the pointed manner in which the command is addressed to each individual personally: "Let *every soul* be subject to the higher powers:—*whosoever* resisteth the power, resisteth the ordinance of God."—Instead of expounding the verses as they lie in order, it may leave a more distinct and clear impression to arrange their contents, along with those of the parallel passages, under separate heads.—Let me then call your attention, first to THE DUTIES ENJOINED, and then to THE CONSIDERATIONS ENFORCING THEM.

I. Of the DUTIES ENJOINED, I mention, *respect, support, obedience,* and *prayer.*

In the first place: we owe to all in authority, whether supreme or subordinate, *civil respect and honour*, corresponding to their different stations, both in our speech and our behaviour.

I am afraid that Christians in general are far from being sufficiently sensible of the obligation of this duty, or of the sin of its opposite; especially in regard to their language respecting their rulers.—The Apostles Peter and Jude, in describing the anomalous and fearful character of those false teachers that so early made their appearance in the Christian church, have both noted amongst its hideous features, their "self-willed presumption," their "despising dominion," and "not being afraid to speak evil of dignities."* Ought not this to make believers in Christ "*afraid*" of any approach to what is so severely condemned? There is a respect due to the *office* of magistracy, apart from the personal character of him by whom the office is filled; a respect of which, did your time permit, a variety of examples might be produced for your imitation, from the scripture history; and a respect which must be still more strongly obligatory, when excellence of character is associated with official dignity,—when the man honours the office, and not the office the man.

Words, be it remembered, are the signs of thought;—the expressions of sentiment and feeling. They are, therefore, far from being harmless in themselves; and they are very far from being harmless in their possible consequences:—" Behold, we put bits in the horses' mouths, that they may obey us; and we turn about their whole body. Behold also the ships, which, though they be so great, and are driven by fierce winds, yet are turned about with a very small helm, whithersoever the governor listeth. Even so the tongue is a little member, and boasteth great things. Behold what a pile of wood† a little fire kindleth! And the tongue is a fire, a world of iniquity; so is the tongue among our members, that it defileth the whole body, and setteth on fire the course of nature, and it is set on fire of hell."‡ The man who indulges his tongue in contumelious and reviling language against the authorities of the land, language fitted to bring

---

* 2 Pet. ii. 10; Jude ver. 8.　† ἡλίκην ὕλην.　‡ James iii. 3—6.

government itself into contempt and disrepute, is a dangerous enemy of his country's weal, as well as a direct and open violator of the express commands of God. His injunctions are, "*Render to all their dues,—fear to whom fear, honour to whom honour.*" "Fear God, honour the king." "Curse not the king, no, not in thy thought; and curse not the rich in thy bed-chamber; for a bird of the air will carry the voice, and that which hath wings will tell the matter."*

Let me not be understood as affirming that on any occasion we are so far to forget our character for sincerity and dignity, as, either in language or in behaviour, to demean ourselves to the use of fawning, servile, hypocritical adulation. We are not called to use the language or in any way indicate the sentiment of commendation, when the character and the conduct of the ruler, whether religiously, morally, or politically considered, is of a description which we cannot in conscience approve. But, whatever sentence we are called to pronounce, let it not be in the terms of railing and contumely. The Apostles Peter and Jude appear to carry the prohibition of this to the utmost limit, when they introduce the case of "Michael the archangel," when contending with Satan himself, not daring to "bring against him a railing accusation," but saying, "The Lord rebuke thee!"

In the second place: We owe to the government of our country, *all requisite support:*—verses 6, 7. "For this cause pay ye tribute also; for they are God's ministers, attending continually upon this very thing. Render therefore unto all their dues; tribute to whom tribute is due, custom to whom custom."—With this other parts of scripture are in harmony:—Thus "Render, therefore, unto Cæsar, the things which are Cæsar's; and unto God, the things which are God's."—"Of whom do the kings of the earth take custom or tribute? of their own children, or of strangers? Peter saith unto him, Of strangers. Jesus saith unto him, Then are the children free. Notwithstanding, lest we should offend them, go thou to the sea, and cast a hook, and take up the fish that first

---

* Rom. xiii. 7; 1 Pet. ii. 17; Eccl. x. 20.

cometh up; and when thou hast opened his mouth, thou shalt find a piece of money; that take, and give unto them for me and thee."*

It is, without doubt, the duty of rulers, as "ministers of God" to their people "for good," to make the taxes they require as light as is consistent with the real exigencies of the state; and to be righteous, disinterested, and economical, in the expenditure of the public money; especially in times of prevailing difficulty and distress in the community over which Providence has called them to preside. It is their duty, likewise, to lay on these necessary burdens, with as much equality as possible of proportional pressure, according to the various ranks and conditions of their subjects:—and, with whatever inconsiderate confidence some may speak, this must be a matter of no very easy adjustment; nay, in a country, such as ours, where the variety of circumstances and contending interests is so endless, a matter of superlative difficulty.

As to *our* duty, my brethren, who are the *subjects* of civil government, one thing must at once be evident to you; that it cannot be the province of each individual to judge for himself what taxes he is to pay and what to decline. It has been very truly observed, that "the *precept* to pay taxes should be considered by Christians as a blessing. Had not the precept been given expressly, conscientious men might have thought it necessary to know first how the money was to be applied, and to refuse, wherever they disapproved of the expenditure. This would have given occasion to endless trouble and contention. But now, in consequence of the express precept, all occasion of scruple or uneasiness is removed: and as, of old, Christians were permitted to buy whatever was sold in the shambles, asking no questions for conscience' sake; so now, whatever is imposed as a tax, it is our duty simply to pay, and to owe no man any thing, but to love one another."†
This, at the same time, is not to be understood as at all pre-

---

* Matt. xxii. 21; xvii. 25—27.
† The Duty of Christians to Civil Government:—A Sermon preached in Lady Glenorchy's Chapel, Edinburgh, on 29th November, 1798. By Greville Ewing.

cluding the lawful use, on particular occasions, of our right of remonstrance, when any proposed or existing impost appears either to be inconsistent with constitutional principles, or to fall with a disproportionate and inequitable pressure on some one class of the community.

In making such payments for the support, and according to the requisitions of government, a Christian, who is properly influenced by a sense of divine authority, will exercise the very same conscientiousness as in discharging his private debts. He will consider the one to be *due*, as much as the other, and hold the obligation sacred. Alas! that this view of the matter should be so little prevalent in practice! How many are there, and professing Christians too, who would be exceedingly shocked by any thing approaching to dishonesty or fraud in their mercantile transactions; who would spurn from them the slightest imputation against the honour of their dealings, with a frown of indignant scorn,—whose consciences are wonderfully easy, and unembarrassed with scruples, in all that relates to the pecuniary claims of government; who, with little if any hesitation, dispense with the fulfilment of these, on grounds which would not stand for a single instant before any other description of obligation;—nay, who even study the arts of evasion, give scope to their inventive ingenuity, and smile with conscious self-complacency at the prudence and cleverness of its devices; and reckon any thing fair, when the object is merely to defraud government, to gull a revenue-officer, or, as it is vulgarly termed, to cheat the king. —I cannot enlarge on this subject, further than to say, "These things ought not so to be;" and to add, with the earnestness of entreaty, and with the authority of the divine word on my side, "Let it not be so among *you*." Consider ye your taxes as *debts;*—and let there be no illegal and underhand arts, and no mean Jesuitical casuistry employed, to evade or to reduce their payment.

I may add, on the subject of the *support* due to government,—although I can do no more than mention it,—that in particular cases of emergency, it may become not only warrantable, but an incumbent duty, either for repelling foreign invasion, or for maintaining internal peace, to take up arms on behalf of lawful authority, and of our national liberties. Without this, in such emergencies, the magistrate, in a highly important sense, a sense involving the very existence of our country, might "bear the sword in vain."

In the third place: we owe to the government of our country, *obedience to its requirements;* subjection both to the established laws of the land, and to the occasional mandates of the higher powers.

On this part of the subject, there is one obvious restriction, which is applicable to all human requirements whatever. When the authority of men interferes with the authority of God; when the orders of the one contravene the positive commands of the other;—we cannot, we dare not, hesitate. We must take up the apostolic principle, and firmly abide by it:—"We ought to obey God rather than men:"— "Whether it be right in the sight of God, to hearken unto you more than unto God, judge ye." This is so self-evident that I stop not to illustrate or to establish it. Even in the refusal, however, there may be, and there ought to be, nothing of the spirit of resistance. There may, and there ought to be, the utmost respect and deference displayed towards the constituted authorities, in readily obeying every summons, in answering modestly to their charges and inquiries, in stating our case, and in pleading our cause. But if all will not avail to procure a dispensation for our consciences, we must submit to suffer, were it even unto death, rather than do what our God forbids, or abstain from doing what our God requires to be done. Noble exemplifications of resolute adherence to this principle will immediately present themselves to every mind familiar with the records of sacred history:—and not the least illustrious of these in the annals of our own beloved land.

With this exception, we are to be "subject to the higher powers" in all things. As individual Christians, living under the government of earthly rulers, I do not think there can be established any other scriptural limitation of the command to "be subject," than the one which has now been specified.

—The Scriptures, it ought to be remembered, were not written for the learned alone, but for ordinary men, for multitudes who are not at all versant in the "wisdom of this world," or in the history and the politics of nations. Every view, therefore, by which the right understanding and performance of any duty is made to depend on the possession of knowledge not within the reach of all, must be evidently and strongly objectionable. Now of this nature all limitations appear to be, excepting the one I have mentioned of the opposition of human orders to the commands of God.

For example:—Is it alleged, that we are bound only by the *just and reasonable* demands or enactments of our rulers? —It is perfectly true, that demands and enactments which do not partake of this character are wrong, and ought not to be made. But, who are to be the judges? Who are to draw the lines? The idea that every individual is to determine for himself what is just and reasonable, and what the contrary, cannot be admitted for a single moment by any man in his sober senses. The supposition puts an end at once to all subordination, and destroys the very *possibility* of government.

Again:—Is it said, we are under obligation to obedience, only as far as the proceedings and requirements of our governors are *constitutional?*—Here we are immediately met by the same difficulty. The matter is beyond the reach of by far the larger proportion of ordinary Christians. It would be necessary, on this hypothesis, that before a Christian could ascertain his duty as a subject of civil rule, he should be a profound politician; that he should maturely study the balance of power in the British Constitution, and be familiar with the limits of prerogative belonging respectively to King, Lords, and Commons. This surely will never do. Statesmen and politicians are perpetually differing, and differing widely, about what is constitutional, and what is not;—what is, and what is not, an encroachment of one branch of the government on the prerogatives of another.—How, then, can we ever think of making this a standard of duty, to men, who, from their situation, must, in most cases, be profoundly ignorant of the whole matter? Ground so uncertain, on which he must be incessantly halting, and hesitating, and vacillating, and frequently at an entire stand, and much more likely, if he acts at all, to act wrong than right,—will never do to be the rule of a Christian's conduct.

Let not these observations be foolishly and falsely interpreted, as implying that we are bound to *approve in our judgments*, of *every measure* of the existing government. No, my brethren. There is no attempt to impose any such shackles on your understandings. The thing is impracticable; and, were it practicable, would be most pernicious to the interests of British freedom. Abuses of official trust may occur, which are obvious and flagrant, and which, even on moral grounds, we cannot but in conscience condemn; and there may be many measures which, on principles of national expediency, apart from considerations of morality, we cannot approve as politically good. Pardon me, however, if I offer a hint or two as to the principles by which, on such matters, your judgments ought to be directed.—Considering the immense difficulty of managing the extensive and complicated affairs of a mighty empire, the Christian who has learned "not to think of himself more highly than he ought to think, but to think soberly," will surely feel the propriety of exercising his judgment with self-diffident caution, and, as far as he possibly can, of applying, both to men and measures, that charity which "thinketh no evil." He will beware of being on either side a violent political partizan; and, as too generally happens, both in and out of parliament, of approving without discrimination the proposals and proceedings of one set of men, and condemning as indiscriminately those of another;—of giving all his charity to the one side, and all his suspicion and antipathy to the opposite. Considering, at the same time, the strength of the propensity existing in our nature to the abuse of power, I freely admit the desirableness in a country, for the security of its liberties and privileges, that knowledge be diffusively circulated, and that the subjects be vigilantly though reasonably observant of the measures of public men. The control of public opinion is often of most salutary influence in the prevention of the encroachments of arbitrary rule.

Two things, however, have many a time surprised me not a little, in the conduct and language of Christians on such subjects:—

The first is, the easy confidence and decision with which they often speak of the proceedings of the government of the country. They seem as if they felt no sort of difficulty in the matter; as if all, both in principle and in practice, were as simple as a lesson in the alphabet. They decide for and against the measures of their rulers, with the same kind of perfect facility and readiness with which they commend or chide the behaviour of their own children.—Now, surely, there can be nothing more preposterous than this. Have you never, my friends, experienced any difficulties in your own private concerns?—in the conduct of your little businesses?—in the management and economy of your families? —in settling disputes amongst your children, or your neighbours?—in the affairs of your friendly societies? Have you never had to deliberate yourselves, and to ask the advice of others, and after all, found a good deal of hesitation in making up your minds, in these petty transactions? Be reasonable, then, my brethren. Consider for a moment, what the clashing interests must be of sixteen or seventeen millions of people; and how vast the difficulty of consulting and providing for them all. Think of the impossibility of adopting and executing almost a single purpose, that will not, in some point or other, be felt as a grievance. Think too of the numerous contending interests of foreign powers, and of the difficulty of adjusting these to mutual and universal satisfaction. Recollect, also, that your rulers are not, any more than yourselves, endowed with prescience. They cannot control future events. They cannot ascertain and overrule the providential purposes of Him, who "worketh all things after the counsel of his own will;"—who saith, "My counsel shall stand, and I will do all my pleasure;"—and under whose mysterious, unseen superintendence, events often run counter to the fairest and most apparently reasonable calculations.—

Are your own little plans and purposes never frustrated by unforeseen occurrences? And if designs are thus blasted, in the forming of which you had little or nothing to think of beyond yourselves; is no allowance to be made for the occasional disappointment and failure of schemes, the maturing of which has required their framers to take into their calculations a large proportion, perhaps, of the known world? Eager politicians may smile in contempt at all this. I cannot help it. I speak to my fellow-christians, from whom I expect moderation and candour.

A second thing, at which I have often wondered, is,—that Christians, in regard to their rulers, expect from *human nature* so much more than their knowledge of it, derived from the Bible and from their own experience, can warrant them to look for. It is no uncommon thing to hear men tracing all existing evils in society to human institutions;—to governments, and their administrators. That this should be done by persons whose views of human nature have not been formed from the Divine account of it, and from a spiritual knowledge of themselves, is no matter of wonder. But that Christians should be thus thoughtless, is surprising indeed. Surely they, who know the extent and inveteracy of human corruption, and who feel and mourn over its unholy tendencies in their own bosoms, should be sufficiently aware, that, whatever mischiefs may arise from defects or abuses in the governments of nations, the sad source of evil lies much deeper than in the influence of any human institutions. And is it not strange too, that, with this knowledge and this experience, Christians should have so little allowance to make for the failures and errors of their rulers?—as little sometimes, as if it were entirely forgotten that they are partakers of the common frailty and the common corruption of mankind. Is it at all fair to expect that they should be entirely free of propensities and passions that are common to the whole race? "*To err, is human,*" is a saying of proverbial authority. Are rulers alone, then, to be omniscient and infallible? To acknowledge and correct an error is one of the highest efforts of human wisdom and of human virtue.

Have you never yourselves been sensible of the reluctance of your proud nature to own a mistake or a fault?—and of the strength of the propensity to excuse, to palliate, and even to maintain and persist in it? I do not say that this is right. It is very far wrong. But neither surely is it right, to forget that your rulers are possessors of the same fallen nature with yourselves. Are you entitled, think you, my brethren, with the experience you have of the perverseness of your own hearts, to marvel, that "the higher powers" should at times discover the same slowness to admit an error, or even, as may happen, the same pertinacity in vindicating and persevering in it? You find it a trial of principle to confess a fault to an individual,—a friend,—in private. Must it not be a much severer trial, to make the confession in the face of a whole nation,—nay, of Europe, and of the world? I say again, I am far from excusing the conduct or the principle that produces it. All I mean is, that in the verdicts you pronounce on your rulers, you should remember that they are men; and that you should not therefore marvel so mightily at that occurring in *their* conduct, which your knowledge of your own hearts makes you sensible the same circumstances might probably produce in *your own.* "Judge not, that ye be not judged: for with what judgment ye judge ye shall be judged; and with what measure ye mete, it shall be measured to you again."* They are not in general the men whose own principles and conduct will bear the closest scrutiny, who are most inclined to be severe and censorious in their judgments of others, whether in public or in private life.

Further:—whilst the duty of submission does not at all imply our approving of everything done by the government of the country, nor prohibit our expressing the disapprobation we may feel, in a dignified and respectful manner, to the government itself, agreeably to the constitutional privileges of British subjects;—neither is it, by any means, inconsistent with our employing all lawful methods of avoid-

---

* Matt. vii. 1, 2.

ing personal evil, by pleading our just and sacred rights, either as members of the community, or as holding particular situations in it. I might illustrate this remark by a variety of examples, especially from the inspired history and writings of the Apostle Paul. I must pass over these, however, and proceed to my fourth and last particular on this head of discourse.

4. We owe to "the powers that be" *prayer to God for them.**
—Whatever is the duty of one man is the duty of every man. It is the duty of all, not merely to be subject, but to be subject on Christian principles; "not only (ver. 5) for wrath, but also for conscience' sake:"—that is, not only from fear of the wrath and the sword of the civil magistrate, but from higher and purer considerations,—from regard to the authority and the glory of the Supreme Ruler,—or, as Peter expresses it in the passage read from his first Epistle, "for the Lord's sake." So it is the duty of all to pray;— to pray on the ground which Christianity prescribes;—to pray in faith, and in the name of Jesus, as the atoning Saviour, and the only medium of acceptable worship. It is to believers in Jesus,—to Christians,—that both Paul and Peter address these apostolic admonitions and commands. Let me, therefore, earnestly entreat such to think of the importance attached in the Scriptures to their offering up their prayers to God *in a right spirit.* We are taught to pray for the spiritual interests of our rulers,—for their salvation by Jesus Christ;— the highest blessing we can ever ask even for the most exalted of our race. We ought to implore also the blessing of the universal Sovereign upon them in the discharge of their official duties; that, with divinely bestowed qualifications, they may rule in wisdom, justice, and humanity; and that, on all occasions, and especially in trying emergencies, they may be "men who have understanding of the times, to know what ought to be done."† But in fulfilling this Christian duty, O remember the apostolic admonition, "I will, therefore, that men pray everywhere, lifting up *holy hands, with-*

---

* 1 Tim. ii. 1—4, as already quoted.   † 1 Chron. xii. 32.

out wrath and doubting:" and the charge of the Apostle's Master, "When ye stand praying, *forgive, if ye have aught against any;* that your heavenly Father may also forgive you."* If there are feelings cherished in the Christian's heart of ill-will and rancour towards the government of his country, how can he, in such a state of mind, offer up his devotions acceptably to God? They are not the prayers of love; and the God of love cannot be pleased with them. No, my brethren: be assured that nothing of the gall and wormwood of human passions, towards whomsoever these passions are cherished, can ascend before God with the sweet and fragrant incense of the blessed Redeemer's merits and intercession. Prayer offered in such a temper of mind is closely allied to "blessing with the mouth, and cursing inwardly:"—and the heart of every child of God will tremble at the thought of being, even for a moment, in such a state of unsanctified feeling as would exclude his petitions from the acceptance of his heavenly Father.

II. I now proceed to notice THE CONSIDERATIONS BY WHICH THESE DUTIES ARE ENFORCED.

In the first place: *Civil government is an ordinance of God:*—"Let every soul be subject unto the higher powers; for there is no power but of God; the powers that be are ordained of God. Whosoever, therefore, resisteth the power, resisteth the ordinance of God:"—"he is the minister of God to thee for good:"—"they are God's ministers, attending continually upon this very thing."†

Peter, it is true, speaks of submission to "every *ordinance of man:*"—literally, to *every human creation;*‡ the expression being taken from the phraseology of Greece and Rome, where magistrates were spoken of as *created;* a mode of speech in use also amongst ourselves. But the phrase is in perfect consistency with government being at the same time an "ordinance of God,"—a *divine institute:*—and this consideration, indeed, is included, along with others, in the

---

* 1 Tim. ii. 8; Mark xi. 25.   † Verses 1, 2, 4, 6.
‡ Πάση ανθρωπίνη κτίσει.

particular form of admonition, of command, of entreaty, which Peter himself employs,—"*for the Lord's sake.*"

I waive at present any discussion, as to the abstract principle on which the right of human governments to exercise judicial restraint, and to inflict punishments, should be considered as resting:—some conceiving that it has its ground in views of obvious *utility;* and others, in the *transference into the hands of the public of the right of personal resentment and retaliation.* The first I am inclined to believe the true ground. It seems to be recognised by the Apostle, in the view which he gives of the ends and the benefits of government. Even when he speaks of the magistrate as "*a revenger*, to execute wrath upon him that doeth evil;" it is evidently *on behalf of God* that he represents him as sustaining this character:—of God, whom he had just described as reserving the right of vengeance to himself,—"Vengeance is mine, I will repay, saith the Lord;"*—and the evil avenged is not merely personal injury between man and man, but misdemeanour and crime in general, as they affect the safety and well-being of society.

In the passage immediately before us, the statement is first made *universally,*—" there is no power but of God:"—and it is then applied to *the government existing* at the time,—" the powers that be are ordained of God."

When it is affirmed, without qualification, that "there is no power but of God;" it cannot be meant, that particular rulers are, in every instance, immediately nominated and appointed of God. This was never the case except in Israel; and even there, only on particular occasions. But, it is the divine pleasure, manifested by the obvious, manifold, and valuable advantages resulting from it, as well as by the course of His providence, and the express intimations of His Spirit in His holy word, that government should exist in human society;—and at the same time, his providence exercises a constant superintendence over the nations; "ruling in the kingdom of men, and giving it to whomsoever he will."

---

* Rom. xii. 19.

The Scriptures pronounce no decisions on the comparative merits of different forms of civil polity. Few things are more dangerous or involve a greater perversion of the Bible from its proper and legitimate purpose than to introduce it, as an authoritative umpire, to decide between the contending claims of the various descriptions of government to human adoption, and especially to settle any one of them, to the exclusion of the rest, on the basis of a divine sanction. Our subjection is not made to depend on any such decisions; nor is the duty at all affected by the particular theoretical views which we may respectively entertain upon the subject. It is to the existing government, whatever it may be, of the country in which we live, that our submission is required:—"There is *no power* but of God:"—"Submit yourselves to *every ordinance of man*, for the Lord's sake."—Neither is it the Christian's business to trouble himself with what may often be matter of difficult discovery, and of doubtful disputation,—the legitimacy of the titles of existing princes, and reigning dynasties. It can never be that our submission should rest on the settlement of questions of this description —questions of legitimate right, or of the manner in which sovereigns may have been raised, whether remotely or recently, to the throne. How vain to think of suspending on a matter that may frequently be of delicate investigation and difficult decision, the duty of persons, of whom the large proportion are necessarily incapable of forming any judgment respecting it. You may tell a poor man that his allegiance is not due to a usurper. But this usurper, for aught he knows, may have succeeded to another usurper, or to a race of rulers whose succession commenced in usurpation. The imperial government of Rome might itself perhaps have been traced to such an origin:—which, if the duty were grounded on such considerations, would have annulled it in regard to the Romans who are here addressed. But nothing of the kind is hinted. The subjection inculcated is subjection to the then existing government, to the rulers then in actual possession. "There is no power but of God."

This should lead us to observe also, that subjection is due

to rulers irrespectively of their religious character. It appears to have been a favourite notion with the Jews, and to have been adopted by Gentile converts, that they were not under obligation to yield subjection to heathen rulers, who were the supporters of idolatry; that, in becoming subjects of the kingdom of Christ, they were loosed from their allegiance to such governors. The Apostle in this passage firmly and decidedly opposes an idea so dangerous and destructive to the order of existing society. If rulers indeed required any thing of them incompatible with their obedience to the will of Christ, they were to suffer unto death rather than do it. But the general duty of submission is enjoined on them, enjoined on "every soul," in regard to the rulers who were at the time in power.—And the same reasoning, it may be observed, which proves the sinfulness of refusing allegiance then to a heathen ruler, seems, with equal if not with stronger force, to inculpate those amongst ourselves who, from what we conceive a mistaken principle of conscience, refuse subjection to any other than a covenanted king. The Christian, according to this passage, has simply to do with "*the powers that be.*"

Under this designation, I have taken for granted, and it is very evident, the Apostle refers to the then existing government of Rome;—and by Peter the duty is extended to the subordinate provincial jurisdictions:—"whether it be to the king as supreme, or unto governors, as unto those that are sent by him, for the punishment of evil-doers, and for the praise of them that do well." Where there is any thing that is not to our mind, that thwarts inclination, that prevents the heart from going immediately and fully along with the precept, we are prone to seek, and ingenious to devise, excuses and palliations. The believers at Rome and in its provinces, might be disposed to say, Does the motive you suggest apply to *our* case? Are we to consider the present Roman government as included in the affirmation that "there is no power but of God?"—Yes, say both the Apostles, our exhortation is *to you:*—"the powers that be," the existing powers, under whom you now live, "are ordained of God."

—" Submit yourselves" both to the imperial and the provincial authorities, "for the Lord's sake."—This prevented, or silenced, all evasive objections, and settled their minds on the authority of God.

From the doctrine, that "there is no power but of God," and that "the existing powers were ordained of God," the Apostle Paul immediately deduces the obvious but alarming conclusion, "*Whosoever, therefore, resisteth the power, resisteth the ordinance of God; and they that resist shall receive to themselves condemnation.*" The meaning of this cannot be, that every act of every government, however iniquitous and oppressive, derives, from the mere circumstance of its being an act of Government, the sanction of divine authority. Far from our minds be a thought so foolish and so impious. The very description given of the design of Government, which will be noticed immediately, contains in it a tacit injunction on rulers, as to the principles by which they ought to regulate their official conduct, and the ends at which they should habitually and conscientiously aim.—The conclusion, therefore, must be understood *generally:*—that, government being an ordinance of God, and His will that we should be subject being so plainly and peremptorily declared; in resisting, we oppose not merely human authority, but divine.—Servants are commanded to be "subject to their masters, with all fear; not only to the good and gentle, *but also to the froward:*"—but this does not imply, that the capricious orders and oppressive rigour and harshness of froward masters, were pleasing to God, whose command to masters is, to "render to their servants that which is just and equal, knowing that they also have a Master in heaven, and that there is no respect of persons with him."

" They that resist," it is said, " shall receive to themselves *condemnation.*"—I am satisfied, that this refers, not to the sentence of the civil magistrate, but to the judgment of God. It is of divine authority, as requiring subjection, and prohibiting resistance, that the Apostle is speaking. It is that authority he is adducing to enforce the duty; and it is as a violation of that authority that the "condemnation" is incurred.

In the second place: The duty of subjection is further enforced, from *the beneficial design and tendency of civil government;—the important advantages arising from it to mankind:* —"Rulers are not a terror to *good works*, but to *the evil;"*— "he is the minister of God to thee *for good:"*—"they are God's ministers, *attending continually upon this very thing."** Thus also in Peter: "Submit yourselves to every ordinance of man, for the Lord's sake; whether it be to the king as supreme, or unto governors, as unto them that are sent by him, *for the punishment of evil doers, and for the praise of them that do well."*

Magistrates are nowhere, in the New Testament, directly addressed. In such passages, however, as those before us, their duties, or at least the great general principles by which their conduct should be guided, are most explicitly laid before them. It seems very evident, at the same time, that it was not the intention of the sacred writers to describe the character of any particular governments, or individual rulers, but to point out the beneficial tendency and effect of government in general:—namely, the protection of the good and peaceable members of society, and the restraint and punishment of the lawless and disobedient. This is the design of government, and this its general effect. It is the will of God, that the unprincipled should be kept in awe by the threatenings of the law, and that they should be punished when that restraint proves insufficient and is broken through. The laws themselves, the threatenings annexed to their violation, and the execution of these threatenings in punishment, are all designed to protect the persons, properties, and private rights of individuals from the injustice, cupidity, and violence of those whom conscience and the fear of God do not restrain from wronging others for their own real or fancied advantage. The description, accordingly, is not taken from any abstract theoretical view of what have been termed "the rights of man;" but from that which constitutes the leading and avowed end of every existing government;

---

* Verses 3, 4, 6.

and which, under every government, is, in a greater or less degree, realized. It is not only the theoretical principle, but it is the general practice of governments to punish crimes, not virtues, to protect and avenge the innocent and injured, and "execute wrath upon him that doeth evil;" thus far at least, to be "a terror to evil-doers, and a praise to them that do well,"—although under some there may be enjoyed a comparatively small portion of that civil liberty which we, in divine providence, possess in so abundant a measure. And it is on this view of the leading and general features of all governments, that the Apostle founds his reasonings and commands.—We have no experience, either suffered or recorded, of the effects that would ensue from the total absence of every kind of government,—from a state of entire lawlessness, insubordination, self-will, and anarchy:—but we cannot doubt, that the experience of such a state of things would serve, by the power of contrast, strongly to illustrate and establish the Apostle's argument.

Decidedly in confirmation of this view of the case, is the matter of fact, before alluded to, that both Paul and Peter employ the very consideration now under notice, for enforcing the commands of God on the subjects of the Imperial Despot—NERO: for he it was who then wore the purple at Rome. This fact effectually prevents us from evading, by our own abridgments and limiting qualifications, the obligation of the *general precept*. That the sacred writers intended their precepts for the present observance of the Christians to whom they wrote, will not surely admit of a moment's question. It were the perfection of absurdity, to suppose, that they delivered commands, in terms most explicit, unequivocal, and solemn, which were not applicable to the circumstances of those whom they addressed. And if the commands were intended for *their* obedience, then it follows, that the various motives by which that obedience is enforced, did, in the judgment of the inspired apostles, exist in *their case*.

Even under that government, accordingly, the protection of laws was experienced by those who "did that which was good." Paul himself, on various occasions, felt the advantage of being a subject of it. He was secured by it from open and violent assault, and from insidious and malignant treachery, and plots of way-laying and assassination; as well as enabled, when necessary, to take the high ground of appeal from inferior and provincial judicatories to the supreme imperial authority.

It is worse, indeed, than *absurdity*, to suppose the Apostle Paul not to speak of the Roman government existing at the time:—it approaches at least to *impiety*. Paul, let us remember, writes under the influence of the Spirit of God. There is, therefore, we may be assured, no "fleshly wisdom," no pitiful, shifting, evasive artifice of argument. We must not suppose him to say, what his words, on the supposition in question, would plainly amount to;—"It is your duty, my brethren, to be subject to civil government. But it is only to governments, remember, that answer, in the degree in which all governments ought, to the following description. You will at once be sensible, that this is far from being the case with the government under which you are now placed. It is far, therefore, from being my intention to inculcate subjection to *it*. It is rather your duty to resist a government, which answers so ill the ends of its institution."—Had Paul meant this, he would have said it in plain terms:—nay, he who can imagine the Spirit of truth, by whose direction he wrote, to have used such duplicity and mental reservation, is much more than unworthy of being reasoned with.

It has sometimes been alleged, that this Epistle was written in the early part of Nero's reign, previously to the commencement of his course of inhuman and oppressive administration: and consequently, as the allegation has been intended to insinuate, that the submission enjoined to his government then, might not be due to it afterwards. The supposition implied in this is, that Paul would not have written in the same terms, had he happened to write a few years later; a supposition, which only proves, what appears in many other ways, the strength of the propensity to make the Bible speak our own peculiar and favourite sentiments.

Laying other considerations apart, it is sufficient for its refutation to observe, that the Spirit of God in *Peter* is the same with the Spirit of God in *Paul;* and yet the language of Peter, at a time eight or nine years at least posterior to the date of the Epistle to the Romans, and when no room for any such evasive pretext could possibly exist, is the very same with that of Paul.

I do not feel myself called upon, either by the passages of Scripture on which the preceding observations are founded, or by any existing circumstances, to enter at all into abstract discussion of what have been termed the *rights of nations*, in their collective capacity;—when the sense of an entire people may be considered as thoroughly ascertained;—when the principles of justice and humanity are violated; the constitution and laws set aside and trampled upon; the ends of government perverted and lost; and civil and religious liberty extinguished in a course of iniquitous and ruthless oppression.—Civil government is the "ordinance of God;" and an attempt to live without it would be an attempt to contravene a divine intention, and to subsist and prosper independently of a divine appointment. Particular institutions and forms of civil polity, though, like everything else, under the regulating control of an over-ruling Providence, are the "*ordinance of man:*" and from this the general inference seems hardly capable of a question, that *man may alter them.*— But not only do discussions of this nature touch on a variety of delicate points, both in our own history, in the abstract principles of government, and in the various modifications of these principles under different constitutions and forms of social order;—they are, besides, totally uncalled for. And it is a sad thing when Christians, in the examination of such portions of the divine word, suffer themselves to be led away from the plain and unequivocal intimations of their individual duty, to speculate and debate about points of abstract disquisition, and political metaphysics.—Taking these passages in their simple and obvious meaning, I put it to any Christian, as an individual, subject to the dictates of his Master's will, whether he can find any other limit to the obedience which his Master demands of him to his civil rulers, than the one that has been laid down in the preceding part of this discourse.—I may just add one word applicable to my brethren and to myself in our religious capacity. As dissenters from the Established Church, we avow our disapprobation not of it only, but of every attempt to incorporate the kingdom of Christ with the kingdom of this world, as being inconsistent with its nature, and destructive of its genuine interests. It becomes us, in these circumstances, to show by our conduct as subjects that such dissent does not at all (as has at times been foolishly and artfully insinuated and even openly said) involve in the remotest degree the charge of disaffection to the civil government of the country. Let it ever be our desire, by setting an example of peaceable and patriotic loyalty, to live down this false reproach.—It is the Church and not the State that views dissenters with a jealous eye: and many a time have dissenters had cause to be thankful, that it was the State and not the Church that had the power to persecute.

The charge of sedition has been a common one in every country from the beginning till now, against such as presumed to differ from the established faith. It was brought against Jesus himself.* The manner in which he repels the insinuation that his claiming the character of a king involved opposition to the Roman government is deserving of special notice. It is not by denying his character and claim; but by explaining its nature.† So we, my brethren, are not to seek to escape the charge of sedition by any means inconsistent with subjection to our divine King, but by making it manifest that our views of his kingdom, as "not of this world," are in perfect consistency with the steadiest loyalty to earthly governments. Such loyalty, indeed, is one of the laws of this King to His subjects while they are living in the world. But while we may at times be perplexed by the conflicting claims of earthly governments and those of our divine Lord, our subjection to Him must be perfect and unhesitating.

* John xix. 12.   † John xviii. 33—37.

His is a reign in which all is righteousness and wisdom and love. There is righteousness and wisdom and love in every one of the laws which he enacts for the conduct of his subjects, and in every step of his own sovereign administration. We are bound to obey the one and to submit to the other; and both may be done with equal confidence. There is no danger to be feared either from obedience or from submission. In obeying we can never do what is wrong, in submitting we can never suffer ultimate injury.

And in conclusion, amidst many things that press for notice, allow me to select one, as the most important, and the most suitable to this place.—I might warn you against all unconstitutional and unchristian violence of conduct and intemperance of speech in seeking the attainment of particular measures, however desirable; and against expecting too much from them when they come to be attained,—as if they were to be a *panacea*, or universal cure, for all existing and all possible ills:—such violence and intemperance being not only wrong in themselves but the surest means of frustrating your own ends; and such utopian expectations tending only to ensure the fretfulness of disappointment. In a Government constituted like our own, in which there are three distinct powers combined and balanced on certain adjusted principles, should it so happen that on any particular measure, those powers, the royal, the aristocratic, and the popular, are divided in judgment,—it cannot of course be regarded as opposition to the Government if we judge and express the judgment in favour of the one or the two powers with which we agree, each of the three being as legitimate a part of the Government as the others. These are the very circumstances in which the expression of popular opinion, or the general sense of the country, is especially called for. But still, since, according to the constitution, it is necessary that the three powers agree before any measure can become the law of the land,—there is need for temperance and caution; lest by any sudden ebullition of popular and hasty zeal in behalf of any one measure, however desirable and however promising it may be deemed, there should be the breaking down of a system, which, in the theory of its construction, has been the object of so much admiration and eulogy, and which, with occasional impediments and difficulties, and evils inseparable from everything human, has for so many ages been found in practice to work so well. We may find occasion to lament over the desolation of the goodly fabric, when it is too late to repair the ill-advised precipitancy:—and the more especially, if the measure for whose sake the blow has been struck should not be found productive of the full amount of benefit which the public mind, with all its sanguine tendencies, is ever prone to anticipate. Be firm, be legitimate, be persevering in the use you make of your constitutional privileges:—but beware of violence. Be it yours, as subjects of the Lord Jesus, to employ your influence in repressing every tendency towards it.

That *Christians*, — that any followers of the Prince of peace, — whatever speculative principles in politics they may hold,—(and with these we pretend not to interfere, unless they are such as show themselves in practical disobedience to the express commands of God)—that any of *them* should be found taking part in measures of insurrection, and violence, and bloodshed:—away with the lamentable inconsistency!—" Tell it not in Gath; publish it not in the streets of Ashkelon, lest the daughters of the uncircumcised triumph." Instead of fulfilling the design of the precepts we have been considering—"that with well-doing ye may put to silence the ignorance of foolish men,"—this would be opening the mouths of adversaries to blaspheme;—giving occasion to those who desire occasion, to traduce your principles, and to revile the "worthy name by which ye are called,"—Let Christians, then,—let subjects of that kingdom which is "not of this world," shun all such participation. Let them say of such machinations and proceedings, with unqualified reprobation:—" Simeon and Levi are brethren; instruments of cruelty are in their habitation:—My soul, come not thou into their secret; unto their assembly, mine honour, be not thou united."

But the topic to which I would for a few moments longer

solicit your attention, is—*the tendency of vehement political feeling and discussion, in reference to your spiritual interests.*

These, my brethren, are of all your interests incomparably the highest;—highest in the estimation of God, of angels, of saints in heaven and saints on earth,—and of your own spiritually enlightened minds. These too are the interests over which we who hold the pastoral charge are especially called to watch, "as those that must give account." These are the interests, which the word and ordinances of God, and all external religious institutions, are intended to promote, and from the promotion of which they derive all their value. These are the interests which the Divine Spirit is given to maintain; the advancement of which forms the regulating principle of the whole procedure of God's providence towards his people; and in subserviency to which every chastisement is inflicted, and every temporal blessing given or withheld. To these, therefore, every thing else should be held inferior; and whatever bears towards them an injurious aspect should be deprecated and renounced. The prejudicial influence of drinking deeply into the spirit of politics, might be demonstrated from the nature of the thing. But I would rather make my appeal to the abundant experience of past and present times; to what some have felt, and what many more have witnessed. By the eagerness of political controversy, the mind is preoccupied, and the affections pre-engaged; and spiritual things are in danger of losing their place and their relish. Party politics become the only agreeable and effectual stimulant to the appetite for information. The blessed word of God gives place to the keen and high-seasoned productions of political pamphleteers. These become the lively oracles; while the former lose their quickening energy; are read to quiet the conscience, rather than for pleasure or for profit; and are either hurried over with impatience, or yawned over with listless, unimpressed vacancy. The time that should be devoted to the Bible, to meditation and prayer, and to family instruction, devotion, and spiritual converse, is given to books, and thoughts, and company, such as too often leave both the soul and the family alike neglected. You are well aware, how much the spirit of political vehemence has mingled itself, both in former and in present times, with the spirit of irreligion, and of virulent infidelity;—to what an unhappy degree the two have been blended together: so that it is impossible for any one to take a public and active part in the measures of the former, without awfully exposing himself to the distressing associations, and the perilous contagion of the latter. Passions, too, are frequently engendered by party politics, such as are in themselves opposite to the dictates of the word of God, and at the same time, as might be expected, directly tend to hinder its reception, and counteract its general influence. "Wherefore," says the Apostle Peter, "laying aside all malice, and all guile, and hypocrisies, and envies, and all evil-speakings; as new-born babes, desire the sincere milk of the word, that ye may grow thereby:—if so be ye have tasted that the Lord is gracious."* It matters not in what manner such evil tempers and passions are produced and maintained, or against whom and what descriptions of persons they are directed and cherished;—their declared tendency,—a tendency confirmed by much woful experience, is to "choke the word, and render it unfruitful."

If, therefore, beloved brethren, you regard the best interests of your own souls, of your families, and of the church of God, you will beware of suffering your minds to be too much engrossed by the speculations, pursuits, and controversies of worldly politics; and if you are conscious of a peculiar predilection for them, you will be proportionably jealous of its indulgence. Are the chains that bind your spirits to the earth,—the anxieties and businesses, the hopes and pleasures of a present life,—not sufficiently strong, that you must forge for yourselves new and voluntary fetters? Is there not enough of unavoidable entanglement to impede you in your Christian course, that, instead of "laying aside every weight," you should load yourselves with additional encumbrances? Is there not, in the ordinary atmosphere of the world, a sufficiency of heavy vapours, to damp the wings of

---

* 1 Pet. ii. 1, 2.

faith and love, and repress your heavenward flight, that you must surround yourselves with denser, and fouler, and more oppressive exhalations?—I do not forget that you are men, and Britons, as well as Christians;—members of a civil community, as well as of the communion of saints; and that you have an interest in the affairs of the one, as well as in those of the other. But your having a connexion with time, as well as with eternity, will not justify your "looking at the things that are seen and temporal," to the forgetfulness and neglect of "those which are unseen and eternal." Nay, whatever would draw away your minds from the latter, secularize your spirits, and chain your affections to the world, you must, if you feel as Christians, view with suspicion and dread. O beware, then, of such an eagerness about the politics of the kingdoms of this world, as would prove detrimental to the interests of "that kingdom of God" which is "within you." I speak not at present of one side of politics more than of another. Which side soever you espouse, if you are violent partizans, your souls are in danger; and it is my duty, with affectionate fidelity, to warn you;—to point to the many wrecks of Christian profession,—wrecks of "faith and a good conscience," with which the stormy sea of politics is strewed; and to say, "Be not high-minded, but fear."

"I am persuaded better things of you, my brethren, and things that accompany salvation, though I thus speak." You are alive to the authority of the divine word; and to the irresistible claims of "the mercies of God" bestowed upon you by the Gospel. It is *by these mercies* that the Apostle Paul enforces, with affectionate entreaty, the duties I have been endeavouring to lay before you, as well as all the other duties, personal and social, of the Christian life.*—"Thou, then, O man of God, flee these things; and follow after righteousness, godliness, faith, love, patience, meekness:— fight the good fight of faith, lay hold on eternal life:"— "Grieve not the Holy Spirit of God, whereby ye are sealed unto the day of redemption. Let all bitterness, and wrath,

* Rom. xii. 1, &c.

and anger, and clamour, and evil-speaking, be put away from you, with all malice:"—" Finally, brethren, whatsoever things are true, whatsoever things are honest, whatsoever things are just, whatsoever things are pure, whatsoever things are lovely, whatsoever things are of good report;—if there be any virtue, and if there be any praise, think on these things;—do these things: and the God of peace shall be with you.*

And let the careless sons of earth consider the transitory nature of all the governments of this world, and the value of a liberty higher in its nature, and more permanent in its duration than any, however highly and justly extolled, that can be enjoyed by any nation under heaven—the "liberty with which Christ makes his people free." O seek the blessings of the kingdom of grace here, that you may find your place in the kingdom of glory hereafter.†

* 1 Tim. vi. 11, 12: Eph. iv. 30, 31: Phil. iv. 8, 9.
† This Discourse is more than once quoted by Dr. John Brown in his elaborate work, entitled "THE LAW OF CHRIST RESPECTING CIVIL OBEDIENCE."

LECTURE LX.

ROMANS XIII. 8—14.

"Owe no man any thing, but to love one another: for he that loveth another hath fulfilled the law. For this, Thou shalt not commit adultery, Thou shalt not kill, Thou shalt not steal, Thou shalt not bear false witness, Thou shalt not covet; and if there be any other commandment, it is briefly comprehended in this saying, namely, Thou shalt love thy neighbour as thyself. Love worketh no ill to his neighbour: therefore love is the fulfilling of the law. And that, knowing the time, that now it is high time to awake out of sleep: for now is our salvation nearer than when we believed. The night is far spent, the day is at hand: let us therefore cast off the works of darkness, and let us put on the armour of light. Let us walk honestly, as in the day; not in rioting and drunkenness, not in chambering and wantonness, not in strife and envying: but put ye on the Lord Jesus Christ, and make not provision for the flesh, to fulfil the lusts thereof."

THE precept in the preceding verse, enjoining Christians to "render fear to whom fear was due, and honour to whom honour," we considered, from the connexion in which it stands, as having a special reference to civil rulers. It may be understood, however, with a more comprehensive range of application. It may include *all superiors.* There is "honour" due by the law of God, as well as by the dictates of nature, to parents.—"Honour thy father and mother" is "the first commandment with promise;" and one of the most sacred of all duties.* There is "honour" due also from servants to their earthly masters; to whom they are enjoined to be subject "with all fear."† The precept too may in-

---

* Prov. xxx. 17.   † 1 Pet. ii. 18; and compare 1 Tim. vi. 1.

clude the respect due from believers to those who are over them in the Lord, and whom they are elsewhere enjoined to "esteem very highly in love."*

If in this comprehensive acceptation of the terms, we "render to all their dues," we shall be found to have exhausted the import of the general precept in the eighth verse. If we "render to all their dues," we shall of course be found "*owing no man any thing.*" This language is quite too narrowly interpreted, when it is viewed in relation to mere pecuniary obligations. It includes obligations of all kinds;—whatever, in the various relations of life, whether permanent or incidental and temporary, is *due* to others. The spirit of the precept is, that we should endeavour so to discharge all our obligations as to leave no claim lying unfulfilled. That this has a direct and strong application to pecuniary claims, there can be no doubt.† That the precept goes the length of prohibiting Christians from ever contracting debt, in any degree, in any circumstances, or for any even the shortest time, would be a rigidness of interpretation such as would place it, in many situations, beyond the possibility of compliance. It would be inconvenient in almost any state of society; and in a commercial country would be incompatible with the free and uninterrupted intercourse of business. But let me not be mistaken. This is one of those admissions which, while we are obliged to make them, multitudes are in danger of abusing,—stretching them far beyond their legitimate limits, and taking, under the covert of the liberty which they allow, a license to indulge in the most unwarrantable risks and speculations, by which others as well as themselves and their families are many a time involved in loss and ruin. It is fearful to think of the extent to which this practice has been carried. It ought to be laid down as a principle for Christian conduct, that no debt should in any case be contracted, beyond a man's present or his regular and sure means of discharging; and in general, the maxim ought to be,—a maxim

---

* 1 Thess. v. 12, 13: 1 Tim. v. 17, 18. † Prov. iii. 27, 28.

not merely approved in theory but faithfully applied in practice,—*the less the better*. All that *can* be avoided *ought* to be avoided; inasmuch as no man knows by what unanticipated turns in providence he may be disabled from discharging his obligations. And as to any man's voluntarily and with his eyes open incurring debts which he has not—I do not say the honest *purpose*, for that is by no means enough—but which he has not the fair and reasonable *prospect* of being able at the stipulated time to discharge,—while it is a disgrace to the mercantile honour of the men of the world, is a much deeper disgrace to the profession of Christian principle. Sanguine honesty, though so often pleaded, is by no means a sufficient justification of it. Let the golden rule be uniformly applied.

There is *one* debt that is here represented as being *always due*. It is the debt of *love*. This is true both of the peculiar love we owe to fellow-christians, and of the general benevolence which comprehends in its obligations all our fellowmen. This, my brethren, is an account that is always open. It is not like a bill of a fixed amount and drawn at a certain date, which can be at once discharged, and there is an end of it. The claims of love are never filled up. The moment one bill is retired, another is presented; or rather, as I have already said, it is a constantly open and reciprocal account; and it should be the aim of all, as far as lieth in them, that in the form of mutual benefit and requital, it may stand always at a balance. We are taught by the language of the Apostle to regard love as *a debt*,—all its claims, according to the law of God, to be held sacred, and faithfully and cheerfully discharged. Hence it follows—"*For he that loveth another hath fulfilled the law.*" I need not say, surely, that here, as the love spoken of is the love due to fellowmen, the law of which love is the fulfilment is the law *as it respects* our fellow-men. The maxim, taken in an insulated and unconnected form, might be considered still more comprehensively. "*Love* is the fulfilling of the law" in regard to God as well as to men. All the duties which we owe to God are included in love to God; as all the duties which we owe to men are included in love to men. We have reason, indeed, to believe that the maxim, "he that loveth another hath fulfilled the law," holds true throughout the universe; that love is "heaven's first law,"—the sum of moral rectitude through the whole intelligent creation. Angels are "ministering spirits, sent forth to minister for them who shall be heirs of salvation;" and in all their visits of mercy, and secret influences of kindness of which they are the messengers and the agents in our world, what is their law but *love*? And are we not sensible, when we contemplate them in the relation which they bear to us as the active ambassadors of divine goodness, that, if we could obtain such a discernment of these invisible friends, and were capable of any actual reciprocation of intercourse with them, love would be the practical principle of such intercourse? and love, we may be assured, is the bond of union amongst the pure and holy members of that spiritual community. They love God, and they love one another.

In all such statements as the one before us, love to God is presupposed. It is the *first* principle, apart from which the other cannot exist and operate acceptably to Him, and as required by His law. The two go together; but the one takes precedence of the other, and is required in order to its exercise. They are not two precepts of which we may choose the one and practically implement its obligations, while we disregard the other. They *must* not, they *can* not be separated. In the estimate of the supreme Judge they never are. He who loves not men loves not God; and he who loves not God loves not men on the principles which the Law of God requires.

Had the Apostle been speaking of the duties of the first table of the Law, he would doubtless have summed them up in the former of the two principles,—love to *God;* but his subject being more immediately the duties which men ought by the second table to render to each other, he sums them up in the latter, love to *man*.

Perfect love to our neighbour would infallibly produce a perfect discharge of all the practical duties which the Law enjoins towards him: and this practical discharge will necessarily bear an exact proportion to the degree in which it exists:—verses 9, 10. "For this, Thou shalt not commit adultery, Thou shalt not kill, Thou shalt not steal, Thou shalt not bear false witness, Thou shalt not covet; and if there be any other commandment, it is briefly comprehended in this saying namely, Thou shalt love thy neighbour as thyself. Love worketh no ill to his neighbour: therefore love is the fulfilling of the law."

We are not called upon, of course, by the introduction of this enumeration of precepts here, to enter into the discussion and illustration of each of them. The position with which we have to do—and it is a position which does not require argument to establish it, for it does not admit of controversy, —is, that they are all summed up in LOVE—"briefly comprehended in this saying, "THOU SHALT LOVE THY NEIGHBOUR AS THYSELF."

It is self-evident, that each of these—adultery, murder, theft, false witness, and covetousness, is a wrong—a wrong either in act or in feeling; and equally self-evident, that every wrong is a violation of love; and that love, in proportion as it operates, will restrain from the doing of it. It is in the very nature of love to desire and to seek the good of its object. We cannot form the conception of any state of mind that can be called love, of which this is not true. Every kind and degree of *ill* is contrary to the spirit of love. The Apostle makes his statement in a *negative* form—"love *worketh no ill* to his neighbour." But in this he does no more than is done in the precepts of the law which he quotes. They are all in the same form—all negative. But according to the true spirit of these precepts, they *require* as well as *forbid*. And in the very phrase, "love *worketh no ill* to his neighbour," there is included the *withholding of no good* which it is in our power to do for the objects of our love. For in the high-toned spirit of divine requirements, to *withhold good* from him who needs it and to whom it is in our power to do it, is regarded as *doing evil*. It is evil to withhold *a debt;* and as love itself is a debt, all the good which it is in the power of love to do is a debt. This will the more strikingly appear from considering the practical counterparts of the precept of love—namely, "All things whatsoever ye would that men should do to you, do ye even so them: for this is the law and the prophets."* The law, "Thou shalt love thy neighbour as thyself," enjoins the inward principle, to which that God looks whose it is to "search the hearts;" and the precept "Whatsoever ye would that men should do to you, do ye even so them," enjoins the conduct which that principle will always produce. According to this law, there are *debts* of benevolence as well as debts of justice. They are both due; the payment of them alike incumbent. We are commanded "to love our neighbour *as ourselves.*" Now, we never willingly wrong and hurt ourselves. "No man ever yet hated his own flesh; but nourisheth and cherisheth it." We must never do to another what we should deprecate being done to ourselves, nor withhold from another what we should ourselves desire in his circumstances. And if you put the question, "Who is my neighbour," I have a *divine* answer: an answer from the lips of Jesus himself in the parable of the good Samaritan.† Fellow-men are your "neighbours;" enemies are your "neighbours;" all who in any way come within the reach of your benevolent influence are your "neighbours."

As to fellow-christians, the love that "worketh no ill" but is solicitous to do good, is reciprocally due amongst them on grounds additional to the general ones that support the obligations of man to man. Theirs is a peculiar love. It is what I may term the *natural affection* of the *new man*—the principle that unites all the members of the spiritual family of God:—a love, of which we can only at present say—If the love that connects man with man requires of its subjects that they "do to others as they would that others should do to them"—*how much more* the love which unites those who are "all one in Christ Jesus"—redeemed by the same blood, regenerated by the same Spirit, children of the same Father in Christ Jesus,

---

* Matt. vii. 12.   † Luke x. 30—37.

subjects of the same Lord, and heirs of the same inheritance! Love is the law of Christ as well as of Moses;—but "the grace and the truth that have come by Jesus Christ" have imparted to this love a peculiarity of power and tenderness, and a force of obligation, beyond whatever before existed, exhibiting it under new aspects, and enforcing it by new motives.

The connexion of all this with what follows is not at first view very apparent:—ver. 11. "And that, knowing the time, that now it is high time to awake out of sleep; for now is our salvation nearer than when we believed." It seems, however, to be this—for the words "*And that,*" evidently intimate a connexion; and a connexion according to which that which follows is considered as enforcing with peculiar emphasis the necessity of what he had just inculcated:—it seems, I say, to be this. He was about to rouse them to vigilance and to diligence. Now of all the active practical duties of the Christian life, the love of which he had been speaking is the grand operative principle. He felt, therefore, a special necessity for enforcing upon them the cultivation and exercise of this principle, when he regarded it in this light, and connected this with the shortness of the time which this principle might have for the active fulfilment of its benevolent purposes. In exciting them to the avoidance of practical evils and to the pursuit of practical virtues, he naturally connects his admonition with the recommendation of that principle which he had represented as "the fulfilling of the law."

By "*the time,*" some understand the near prospect of the overthrow of the Jewish state, as holding out another prospect, that of "*deliverance*" from Jewish persecution. But this can hardly be the meaning. The event supposed to be anticipated, though it deprived the Jews of their political power, and so put an end to legalized persecution, did not "slay the enmity" of their hearts against the Gospel, or prevent their stirring up in various places, as they had been accustomed to do, the opposition of the Gentiles. For, if you read the history of the Acts, you will find, that a large portion of the persecuting fury of the Jews was not what emanated from the seat of power in Jerusalem, but what vented itself in other places, when they were in a state of dispersion among the Gentiles; that it was the rage rather of individual malignity, than of public political animosity. Besides, the cessation of the political power of the Jews would be the abridgment of persecution only from a single source, and that source by no means the one which at Rome there was most reason to dread. To speak of their "*salvation*" as "nearer than when they believed" on account of an event which was still forty years distant, and the deliverance effected by which was to be only limited and partial,—when persecutions incomparably more violent and ferocious than any which Jewish power had ever been able to inflict were near at hand, from a power of demon cruelty and malice in the very city where they dwelt—when the bloody Nero, in the fourth year of whose reign the Epistle was written, was so soon about to satiate his sanguinary ferocity, and screen himself from popular vengeance, by the immolation, under a false charge, of hecatombs of innocent victims, in every form of torture which the ingenuity of hell could suggest to him:—this, I say, appears altogether unnatural.

The Apostle appears, in this passage at least, and perhaps in some others which certain commentators are fond of applying to the destruction of Jerusalem,—rather to have in his eye a truth of universal and immediate interest—*the rapid flight of time towards eternity.* This is viewed in a peculiar light with relation to believers, and in this light is urged upon them as an incitement to diligence in all the means of subduing sin and advancing holiness in themselves, and of promoting the present and final well-being of others. The *general* motive is that which Solomon long ago presented —" Whatsoever thy hand findeth to do, do it with thy might; for there is no work, nor device, nor knowledge, nor wisdom, in the grave, whither thou goest."*

Believers are ever in danger, and especially when, in peace

* Eccles. ix. 10.

and security, the blandishments of the world lull them to repose, of slumbering and sleeping; of falling into a state of listlessness and lethargy in the divine life; and of inactive sloth in the prosecution of the great ends of their being; of relaxing their efforts—of becoming "weary in well-doing." The admonition was meant to wake the dormant energies of any that had lapsed into this state, and to quicken to increased activity even the wakefulness of others.

But the motive suggested is not the *mere shortness of time*. There is also the peculiar view which the believer has of its termination—its termination, that is, to himself:—"Now is our *salvation* nearer than when we believed." When a sinner believes in Christ, he comes into a state of present salvation. But still sin remains in him; and still he sojourns in a valley of tears. His full salvation from sin and from sorrow is still future; and it is effected by that very event which to men in general, and to himself naturally, is the object of dread. *Death is his salvation.* It gives him complete emancipation; breaks every remaining thread of the cords of sin, and sets him for ever free. The very "king of terrors" is his conductor to the possession of immortal and fearless joys. He "departs, and is with Christ, which is far better." How cheering a view this to the believer's spirit! What should be its effect?—Surely the renewed contemplation of it should wake him from sleep, and its steady anticipation should keep him awake.

The prospect of this salvation drawing "nearer" should stimulate to persevering activity in present duty, under the influence of faith and hope, as the only way in which the final attainment of it can be secured. The hope of "glory and honour and immortality" arises solely from the death and resurrection of the Son of God; but it is by a "patient continuance in well-doing" that it must be sought.* Further, although the judgment-day should be long after the period of the believer's own departure,—yet death is the close of his time of trial as a servant of Christ, the one Master of his

* 2 Cor. v. 6—9; and so does Peter, 2 Pet. i. 5—11.

people; and to him it is the time of settlement—the time when he may be justly regarded as "giving an account of his stewardship." How solemn ought this view of the close of life ever to be felt by him! His Master charges him— "Occupy till I come." He comes, in as far as the period of service is concerned and the certainty of decision, at the hour of death. This each believer should feel, and wake to vigilance and activity, that when summoned hence, he may be found doing his Master's will, and may "give his account with joy and not with grief."* Still further:—from the happy and glorious nature of the prospect, it ought to operate with the more powerfully stimulating influence, in proportion as the attainment of it was *near*. The competitor in the Olympic race would press forward with renewed alacrity when he approached the goal. As the coveted laurel was more in his eye and nearer to his grasp, he would spring toward it with the more eager and elastic bound.†

The nature of the salvation, too, as a salvation *from sin* —its excellence consisting mainly in this,—ought to have, and when duly considered cannot fail to have, an influence corresponding with the admonitions of this passage. The hope of *such* a salvation must be miserably inconsistent with all intemperate and impure indulgences.—It cannot fail to excite those who are truly enjoying it, instead of "making provision for the flesh to fulfil the lusts thereof," to mortify and to crucify it,—to "strive against sin," and to follow that holiness, the perfection of which is the object of hope.‡

Verse 12. "The night is far spent, the day is at hand: let us therefore cast off the works of darkness, and let us put on the armour of light." This verse affords an example of the different and seemingly opposite senses in which the same figure may be used. *Life* is sometimes *the day*—and *death* the *night*.§ This is quite natural when life is regarded as the period of action, and the silence and darkness of the

---

* Luke xii. 35—38. † Comp. Phil. iii. 13, 14.
‡ 1 John iii. 1—3. § John ix. 4.

grave as the cessation of all activity. But life may not only be contrasted with death and the grave, but with the life to come—the life of heavenly light and purity and joy: and then it becomes appropriately "the night," being a time of *comparative* darkness, both as to knowledge, and holiness, and happiness. These are the three things signified by light; and their opposites, ignorance, impurity, and misery by darkness. When the day of eternity dawns, the darkness, in all the three senses, shall for ever pass away. It shall be a day of perfect light, of light without an obscuring cloud, and of which the Sun shall never go down. Of that eternal day the dawn was at hand; and they are exhorted to live a life consistent with their high and holy and blessed anticipations. Believers are already saved from the darkness of their native ignorance and pollution: and on *this* ground they are admonished to beware of courses inconsistent with their present spiritual character:—" For ye were sometimes darkness, but now are ye light in the Lord: walk as children of light: (for the fruit of the Spirit is in all goodness and righteousness and truth;) proving what is acceptable unto the Lord. And have no fellowship with the unfruitful works of darkness, but rather reprove them."*—*Here* they are exhorted on the ground of the perfect purity they had in prospect as the object of their believing hope. They who knew the only true God and Jesus Christ whom he had sent, and who were rejoicing in the anticipation of the perfection of that knowledge, must "no longer fashion themselves according to the former lusts in their ignorance." The heirs of light must not walk in darkness. The heirs of purity must not live in sin.— "Let us cast off the works of darkness"—throwing them from us with resolute renunciation; and "let us put on the armour of light." The armour of light is that which is provided for "the children of light." Knowledge, holiness, and happiness are themselves admirably efficient armour against all the enemies of our salvation. Knowledge fortifies the mind against the assaults of infidelity; holiness secures the heart

---

* Eph. v. 8—11.

against the inroads of temptation to sin; and the experience of the happiness of true religion deprives of their alluring and captivating influence the joys of the world, the pleasures of time and sense. There is an incessant warfare. The armour must never be put off, but the good fight of faith maintained till the end.*

Still following out the same general principle of the necessity of consistency, he adds in verse thirteenth, "Let us walk honestly, as in the day; not in rioting and drunkenness, not in chambering and wantonness, not in strife and envy." "*Honestly*" means not merely with integrity, but *honourably*—in the practice of all that is correct, and dignified, and becoming.† Their conduct was to be such as could "come to the light," such as neither sought nor required to court the darkness of concealment.—"*Not in rioting and drunkenness*"—not in the scenes of Bacchanalian revelry, common at the orgies of the god of wine,—nor in any of the more private excesses of intemperance:—"*not in chambering and wantonness;*" in any of those impure and obscene rites that were practised in the service and worship of the Paphian goddess, nor in the indulgence, in any form, of lascivious and unchaste desires:—"*not in strife and envying,*" the natural attendants and consequences of drunkenness and revellings and the jealousies of passion, and in themselves, on whatever occasions indulged, incompatible with the true Christian character—contrary to the influence of the Gospel of peace, and to the example of the Lord Jesus.

Verse 14. "But put ye on the Lord Jesus Christ, and make not provision for the flesh, to fulfil the lusts thereof." "*For the flesh;*" for the corrupt desires of fallen nature—the evil propensities of the old man, they were to "*make no provision,*"—a phrase in which "more is meant than meets the ear." It means, not merely that we are not actually, directly, positively to provide for their gratification—that were little:—but that, as they are ever rising with their demands for indulgence, and seeking the ascendency over

---

* Comp. Eph. vi. 10—18.   † εὐσχημόνως.

better principles, they must be opposed and suppressed,—their motions watched with all vigilance; their assaults on the spiritual principles of our souls resisted with all the energy of uncompromising resolution, and with all the earnestness of prayer for the "strength of the grace that is in Christ Jesus." We must not tamper with them. We must not listen to their insinuations. We must give no quarter to those lusts that "war against the soul." By every act of persuasion they will seek an opening by which to force their way into the citadel of our hearts. But they must not be admitted—not one of them; for if one makes good its entrance, a host may follow: if one gets a little wilful indulgence, there will be no end to its solicitations. "They that are Christ's have crucified the flesh with the affections and lusts."

In opposition to all provision for the flesh, stands the comprehensive precept—"PUT YE ON THE LORD JESUS CHRIST." There is great fulness of meaning in this expression. It occurs repeatedly in Paul's writings. It comprehends every thing excellent—every grace, every virtue. They had already "put on Christ."[*] The exhortation, therefore, implies a progressive increase in the holy influence of his doctrine apparent in them as the avowed professors of it; a growing likeness to him in all the divine beauties of his character; the bearing and exhibition of his image—the image of purity and peace. To *"put on Christ"* is, under the influence of the same Spirit, to be distinguished by the same devotion to God and benevolence to men which in His character appeared in all their sinless perfection,—the same submission and the same unreserved obedience to the divine will, the same meekness and lowliness united with the same lofty and unswerving resolution in all that is good; the same unbending integrity and truth; the same self-denial; the same zeal for the glory of God; the same condescension; the same self-sacrificing love; the same sympathizing tenderness; in a word, all the lovely graces which His character exempli-

---

[*] Gal. iii. 27.

fied, which His word inculcates, and which it is the work of His Spirit to produce.—How glorious, how beautiful the garb, when Christ is thus put on; when believers appear in the robe of righteousness and the garment of salvation! How glorious a Church—a collective body of those who have thus put on Christ! O let it be our desire, that the world around us may see more and more in us of this lovely resemblance to Him who is "fairer than the children of men!" How glorious will the Church be at last, when every one of its members shall have *fully* put on Christ—shall be perfectly "like him, seeing him as he is;" when He shall "present it to himself a glorious church, not having spot, or wrinkle, or any such thing;" when, in consequence of every one of His redeemed people bearing His perfect likeness, He shall be "glorified in his saints, and admired in all them that believe!"

Let all who name the name of Christ be impressed with the vanity of professing to be His while they appear, in regard to character, in the garb of this world! Let them remember, that there is no such thing as "putting on" Christ's justifying righteousness, without being at the same time invested with personal conformity to Him! that there is no obtaining an interest in Him as a justifying Saviour, without being at the same time transformed into His image.

And O! let careless sinners remember, that now it is high time for *them* to awake out of sleep. Instead of their salvation, their destruction is "nearer." How different your prospect from that of the believer in Christ! Death, not life,—perdition, not deliverance, is before you. Believers are accustomed to sing of their salvation, with the transport of humble joy—

"On all the wings of time it flies,
 Each moment brings it near;
Then welcome each declining day,
 And each revolving year."

Must we sing the same of your perdition? Ah! that is no subject for song. It is with a heavy heart that we see each moment passing over you laden with a curse;—each day declining, and each year revolving and bearing you on to eternity, and that eternity unprovided for!—the summer again past, the winter again ended, and you not saved!—your *day* far spent, your *night* at hand; and what a night! a night that shall never know a returning dawn,—the night of "the blackness of darkness for ever!" "What meanest thou, O sleeper?" when wilt thou shake off this infatuated listlessness that is ruining thy soul? when wilt thou awake from thy day-dreams of delusion and folly? "Yet a little sleep, a little slumber, a little folding of the hands to sleep: so shall thy poverty come as one that travelleth; and thy want as an armed man:"—poverty and want the most fearful—destitution for eternity. They shall come "as one that travelleth"—but not "as a wayfaring man to tarry for a night;" they shall quarter upon thee for ever. They shall come "as an armed man," assailing thy distracted spirit with a force which thou canst not resist; not to rob thee of the treasures and comforts of a passing day, but to strip thee bare, and leave thee helpless for a never-ending existence. O! "could I speak with the tongues of men and of angels," I would use all the terms of earthly and of heavenly persuasion to prevail with thee to rouse thyself to serious reflection, and "to-day, while it is called to-day," not to harden thy heart! . Methinks I hear the Redeemer of sinners, while he sheds over thy perishing soul the tears of pitying tenderness, saying to thee, "If thou hadst known, even thou, at least in this thy day, the things which belong unto thy peace!" but he does not yet add, "now they are hid from thine eyes!"— No: blessed be God! they are *not yet* hid from thine eyes. —We have set before thee anew life and death, blessing and cursing:—O choose the life, that thy soul may live!— for how soon they *may* be hid from thine eyes, *thou* knowest not, and no one amongst us can tell thee!

LECTURE LXI.

ROMANS XIV. 1—6.

"Him that is weak in the faith receive ye, but not to doubtful disputations. For one believeth that he may eat all things: another, who is weak, eateth herbs. Let not him that eateth despise him that eateth not; and let not him which eateth not judge him that eateth: for God hath received him. Who art thou that judgest another man's servant? to his own master he standeth or falleth; yea, he shall be holden up: for God is able to make him stand. One man esteemeth one day above another; another esteemeth every day alike. Let every man be fully persuaded in his own mind. He that regardeth the day, regardeth it unto the Lord; and he that regardeth not the day, to the Lord he doth not regard it. He that eateth, eateth to the Lord, for he giveth God thanks; and he that eateth not, to the Lord he eateth not, and giveth God thanks."

THERE are two parties, or two descriptions of persons, referred to in this chapter, to each of which monitory directions are addressed in regard to the feelings to be cherished and the conduct to be pursued toward the other. In order to our rightly understanding these directions, as well as the general lessons of the chapter, and the points in which they affect ourselves, it becomes indispensably necessary that we have accurate conceptions, as far as we can attain to them, respecting the situation and principles of those respectively counselled.

The subject of difference between the two parties is evidently a part of the Mosaic law. Two topics are specified— the distinction between clean and unclean meats, that is, meats which, according to that law, might be eaten and meats which were prohibited, as ceremonially polluting the eater and unfitting him for the instituted services of divine worship under the ancient dispensation, and subjecting him to punishment:—and the distinction between the various festivals or holy days appointed for Israelitish observance and the other ordinary days of the year:—verse *second*, "For one believeth that he may eat all things: another, who is weak, eateth herbs:"—and verse *fifth*, "One man esteemeth one day above another; another esteemeth every day alike. Let every man be fully persuaded in his own mind."

The first of the two classes of believers appears to have consisted of Jewish converts, who did not as yet feel their consciences released from the obligation of observing the rites of the ancient ceremonial, but still conceived that ceremonial to be binding upon them, not clearly discerning its fulfilment and repeal under the Gospel. The second was composed of two descriptions of individuals—first, of Gentile believers, who were under no obligation to such observances; and, secondly, of those converts from amongst the Jews, who were persuaded of their liberty, and disposed to use it, regarding the ritual of the ancient dispensation as having answered its temporary end, and, if not formally and by express revelation, yet virtually and in conformity to ancient prophetic intimations, having been done away in Christ.

With regard to Gentile converts, the first and largest portion of this class, there could be no dispute. Their case had been discussed and decided. By a decree which had in it all the decisiveness of apostolic authority, their freedom had been affirmed and chartered. The Holy Ghost had dictated the declaration of their liberty:—"The apostles, and elders, and brethren, send greeting unto the brethren which are of the Gentiles in Antioch, and Syria, and Cilicia: Forasmuch as we have heard, that certain which went out from us have troubled you with words, subverting your souls, saying, Ye must be circumcised, and keep the law; to whom we gave no such commandment: it seemed good unto us, being assembled with one accord, to send chosen men unto you with our beloved Barnabas and Paul; men that have hazarded their lives for the name of our Lord Jesus Christ. We have sent therefore Judas and Silas, who shall also tell you the same things by mouth. For it seemed good to THE HOLY GHOST, and to us, to lay upon you no greater burden than these necessary things; that ye abstain from meats offered to idols, and from blood, and from things strangled, and from fornication: from which if ye keep yourselves, ye shall do well." "And as they went through the cities, they delivered them the decrees for to keep, that were ordained of the apostles and elders which were at Jerusalem. And so were the churches established in the faith, and increased in number daily."*

The Gentiles, then, were at full liberty. Nay, more. For them to have submitted to the imposition of this yoke, in compliance with the dogmas and requisitions of the Judaizing teachers, who taught the doctrine that had caused the appeal to the Apostles, and produced the decision we have just adverted to,—would have been a renunciation of the grace of the Gospel and of the benefits and blessings which it bestows:—"Stand fast therefore in the liberty wherewith Christ hath made us free, and be not entangled again with the yoke of bondage. Behold, I Paul say unto you, that if ye be circumcised, Christ shall profit you nothing. For I testify again to every man that is circumcised, that he is a debtor to do the whole law. Christ is become of no effect unto you, whosoever of you are justified by the law; ye are fallen from grace. For we through the Spirit wait for the hope of righteousness by faith."† According to this statement, their submitting to circumcision implied their seeking to be justified by the Law; in which case, they forfeited salvation both by the Law and by the Gospel. For the Gospel being a scheme of *grace*, they necessarily renounced its offers in having at all recourse to the Law, or to any other ground of dependence, in whole or in part, than the mercy which it revealed through the cross;—and in having recourse at all to the Law, they became debtors to do *the whole*,—a perfect fulfilment of all that it required being the only ground of justification which the Law did or could propose;—and this being, in regard to crea-

---

* Acts xv. 23—29; xvi. 4, 5; see also xxi. 25. † Gal. v. 1—5.

tures that had already sinned, and were indeed by nature in a state of contrariety to its very principles, an utter impossibility, they of course shut themselves out from salvation in either way.

With regard to the *Jewish* converts of that period, it is the opinion of some, that they *were* still under the obligation of the ceremonial law; that there being as yet no explicit repeal of that law actually published, it did continue still in force,—the same authority with that which had enacted it, in an equally express form, being requisite to release from subjection to it:—and they conceive that the Epistle to the Hebrews contained such repeal; so that, till the time of the publication of that part of the inspired records, the practical discontinuance of the observance of Mosaic institutes was, on the part of any who ventured upon it, an unauthorized and self-assumed liberty.—As this is a point of some little interest and importance, let us try if we can discover what the New Testament, independently of that Epistle, seems to teach us. I would observe, then, in regard to this hypothesis:—

1. That it affords no explanation of the distinction made in this chapter and elsewhere, between "the *weak*" and "the *strong;*" that it furnishes, in fact, no ground whatever on which such a distinction could rest. That the *strong* did actually proceed upon the principle of their being at liberty to abstain from the observance of the Jewish ceremonial, is too obvious to stand in need of proof. But it is equally clear, that there could have been no *weakness* in even the strictest and most punctilious adherence to divine institutes, on the supposition of these institutes still remaining unabrogated, and in all the authority which they ever possessed. To have represented such adherence as weakness, would evidently have been impiety and presumption. The continued observance would, on this supposition, have been as imperative a duty as ever:—and there never can be weakness in obedience to God. How incongruous, how shocking, to imagine an inspired Apostle complimenting with the designation of *strong* those who had strength of mind enough to

set aside divine authority, and act upon the unauthorized and unsanctioned dictates of their own wisdom! There is nothing at all resembling this in the whole word of God. But—

2. You perceive that the Apostle Paul—himself a Jew—classes himself amongst the strong:—" *We* then that are strong ought to bear the infirmities of the weak, and not to please ourselves:"* and he teaches us wherein his strength consisted, " I know, and am persuaded by the Lord Jesus, that there is nothing unclean of itself: but to him that esteemeth anything to be unclean, to him it is unclean."† There can be nothing clearer to me, from this explicit declaration, than that Paul felt his own liberty. And this is corroborated by the spirit of the whole context. How, then, stood the case with the Apostle? The only conclusion to which I can come is this—that he felt himself at liberty in the matter to suit his conduct to circumstances:—that is, that he *was not imperatively obliged to conform,* and that neither was he *imperatively obliged to abstain.* This may seem rather a loose position. But the *first* question is—does it accord with facts? or is there any other supposition that accords better with them and more satisfactorily explains them?

That it was this Apostle's *general practice* to conform to the ritual of the Mosaic law, we learn from what is recorded in the Acts:—" Thou seest, brother, how many thousands of Jews there are which believe; and they are all zealous of the law: and they are informed of thee, that thou teachest all the Jews which are among the Gentiles to forsake Moses, saying that they ought not to circumcise their children, neither to walk after the customs. What is it therefore? the multitude must needs come together: for they will hear that thou art come. Do therefore this that we say to thee: We have four men which have a vow on them; them take, and purify thyself with them, and be at charges with them, that they may shave their heads: and all may know that those things, whereof they were informed concerning thee, are

---

* Chap. xv. 1. † Chap. xiv. 14.

nothing; but that thou thyself also walkest orderly, and keepest the law. Then Paul took the men, and the next day purifying himself with them entered into the temple, to signify the accomplishment of the days of purification, until that an offering should be offered for every one of them."* No man who has any right impressions of the firmness and consistent integrity of Paul's character, can allow himself for a moment to suppose, that there was any *chicane* in this—or any attempt to impose upon the minds of the Jewish converts in Jerusalem a false impression of the fact. To suppose this, indeed, is to suppose a combination to deceive— James and the elders suggesting the deception, and Paul acquiescing and acting upon it. There were two things with which Paul was, it seems, charged—his neglecting the Law himself, and his teaching all the Jews among the Gentiles to do the same. These accusations were generally credited by the myriads of Jewish converts in Jerusalem and Judea; and the belief of them had exasperated their spirits with the keenest indignation against him. The object in view, in the proposal made to the Apostle, was to undeceive the multitude; to satisfy them, that is, that the charges were false,— that *both* of them were false,—that he not only did *not* inculcate upon the Jews who were among the Gentiles the duty of forsaking Moses, but that "he himself walked orderly and kept the law." But if the fact was actually otherwise, if it was as rumour had said and as the people had credited, then his acting the part proposed was not *un*deceiving but *deceiving* them:—it was a mean and dastardly imposition— a *ruse* to escape danger altogether unworthy the honest and intrepid spirit of the Apostle of the Gentiles,—a littleness of subterfuge which would sink him from the lofty elevation which he so justly holds in our esteem. He showed himself at all times above the petty arts of dissimulation. Mark how he behaved to a fellow-Apostle when that Apostle acted a part inferior in the amount of dissembling to what this would have been—"When Peter was come to Antioch, I

* Acts xxi. 20—24, 26.

withstood him to the face, because he was to be blamed. For, before that certain came from James, he did eat with the Gentiles: but, when they were come, he withdrew, and separated himself, fearing them which were of the circumcision. And the other Jews dissembled likewise with him; insomuch that Barnabas also was carried away with their dissimulation. But when I saw that they walked not uprightly, according to the truth of the gospel, I said unto Peter before them all, If thou, being a Jew, livest after the manner of Gentiles, and not as do the Jews, why compellest thou the Gentiles to live as do the Jews?"* This was like himself. Peter's dissimulation was the effect of *fear*—the "fear of man," which so often "bringeth a snare." And although we dare not pronounce it impossible that a similar fear might overcome Paul also, yet it is very unlikely that after having acted so decided and bold a part at Antioch in opposition to simulation, he should have conformed to this simulation at Jerusalem, and have there proceeded on the principles of a timid and temporizing and truthless policy. We conclude, therefore, that in regard to his general conduct, the fact was as the step proposed to him, and which he adopted, was intended to intimate.

The question then comes to be, assuming the fact that his general practice was to keep the law,—*What was his reason for so doing?* Was it because he considered and felt it still unrepealed, and obligatory in all its extent upon his conscience?—We have already referred, in proof of the negative of this, to verse fourteenth of this chapter.

You may now compare with this the reason for his circumcising Timothy:—"Then came he to Derbe and Lystra: and, behold, a certain disciple was there, named Timotheus, the son of a certain woman, which was a Jewess, and believed; but his father was a Greek: which was well reported of by the brethren that were at Lystra and Iconium. Him would Paul have to go forth with him; and took and circumcised him because of the Jews which were in those quar-

* Gal. ii. 11—14.

ters: for they knew all that his father was a Greek."* This clearly intimates, that but for the particular cause assigned, he would not have considered it as at all incumbent. Add to this *the ground* on which he withstood and blamed Peter. It was not his "living after the manner of Gentiles and not as did the Jews," which was contrary to the prescriptions of the Mosaic ritual; but his inconsistency and dissimulation afterwards.† This appears to me incapable of explanation on any other ground than that the Apostle felt himself at liberty to observe or to refrain from observing according to his situation, and the influence which he saw his conduct was likely to have on the success or hindrance of his ministry. Had the law of Moses been still in full force, it could have been no matter of option with him how he should act. He could have had no choice—but *being* a Jew, he must, at all times and in all places, have acted as a Jew. There are various passages also, in Epistles written long before the date of that to the Hebrews, from which, more or less explicitly, the same thing appears.‡

I recur again for a moment to the case of *Peter;* with the view of observing that we have in it not only an indication of Paul's mind, but of Peter's also. We learn from it the fact that this Apostle himself, the Apostle of the circumcision, felt himself at liberty to "*live as did the Gentiles*"—that, as far as he himself was concerned, he could do this without any scruple of conscience, and that it was only when the presence of other Jews, who felt not the same freedom but were still "zealous of the law," constrained him, that he deemed it incumbent upon him to act otherwise. The same appears to have been the case with Paul. There were very few places, in the circuit of his extensive travels, where he did not meet with his countrymen; and this affected his general practice, as, for their sakes he conformed to the law,

---

* Acts xvi. 1—3.
† See also as decisively strong his representation of the principle by which he regulated his conduct—1 Cor. ix. 19—22.
‡ See Eph. ii. 15: Col. ii. 13, 14: Gal. iii. 23—25.

or, as he expresses it, "became as a Jew:"—but this was not from any obligation of the law upon his conscience.

There is a passage in the first Epistle to the Corinthians which has been adduced as containing apostolic authority and even injunction, for a converted Jew not giving up but continuing to maintain the observance of the law:—"But as God hath distributed to every man, as the Lord hath called every one, so let him walk: and so ordain I in all churches. Is any man called being circumcised? let him not become uncircumcised: is any called in uncircumcision? let him not be circumcised."* It should be laid down, however, as a principle of criticism, that, when a passage is evidently susceptible of two interpretations, that should be preferred which is most in harmony with *other* passages. All the passages which have been quoted appear to me clearly to intimate that *this* must not be understood as a positive injunction, but only as an intimation that in order to the harmonious communion of Jewish and Gentile believers, no change on either side was necessary. And this accords with the entire tenor of the New Testament. The observance of the Law by the Jewish converts, was not prohibited, and not obligatory. It was allowed to remain, in accommodation to Jewish prejudices, with which the Lord always appears dealing very gently, enlightening by degrees, and by this gradual illumination and the constraining events of His providence, gradually subduing and clearing them away. The fulfilment of the law in the work of Jesus was progressively explained and understood, and in a short time the very means of its observance were entirely removed. Whether this divine forbearance extended beyond the period of the publication of the Epistle to the Hebrews, which contains so full and distinct an explanation of the purposes and temporary duration of the Law, I am not prepared to say. We have not, I presume, sufficient grounds on which to rest an affirmation either for or against the supposition. The gradual removal and final extinction of the Jewish polity appears to be the

---

* 1 Cor. vii. 17, 18.

idea conveyed by the Apostle's expression:—"In that he saith, A new covenant, he hath made the first old. Now that which decayeth and waxeth old is ready to vanish away."*

To infer from the state of things which thus for a time existed after the Law had found its fulfilment in Christ and had been virtually set aside—a state of things which only proceeded on the principle of divine lenity and forbearance towards old and long-established attachments to divine institutions—institutions which, as they prefigured the Gospel were of course in perfect harmony with its truths,—a state of things, in short, which seems to have been an exemplification of our Lord's maxim figuratively and parabolically delivered—"No man putteth new wine into old bottles; else the new wine doth burst the bottles, and the wine is spilled, and the bottles will be marred: but new wine must be put into new bottles,"—to infer, I say, from the temporary existence of this state of things, curious and anomalous as it may seem, that the Jewish ceremonial is not abrogated but only suspended, and that it is to be re-instituted in all its extent amongst the Jews on their restoration, —is to fly in the face of the whole tenor of divine revelation respecting the relation of the two dispensations, and especially of the clear and explicit statement of the Epistle to the Hebrews.

The Apostle addresses himself to "*the strong;*" or rather, I should perhaps say, to the body of believers constituting the church, of whom probably the greater part were Gentiles, and so required, as well as the more enlightened Jewish converts, to be admonished as to their treatment of such as could not clearly discern their liberty and privilege as "freemen of Christ," and still continued in the observance of the rites of Moses. He addresses himself to those whose views of the truth as it "is in Jesus" were distinct and comprehensive— embracing its various bearings and connexions—and more especially the relation of the two dispensations to each other;

* Heb. viii. 13.

that of Moses as preparatory and introductory to that of Christ, and intended to pass away when it had answered its end—the "shadow of good things to come." The Gentile believers understood that they now possessed *the substance* of that dispensation of shadows, and perceived that it would be a reversing of the divine order of things, and an opposing and frustrating of the very purposes of God, for them to go back to the "weak and beggarly elements"—an act of disobedience, and a most ungrateful requital for the liberty wherewith Christ had made them free. And the "strong" amongst the Jewish believers felt themselves by a right understanding of the same thing,—the temporary and preparatory nature of the former dispensation,—released from the yoke, and no longer under any obligation of conscience to keep up the observance of those institutions which had found their fulfilment in Christ and his finished work. The particulars specified we shall notice more fully afterwards. In the meantime observe the injunction he addresses to "the strong" in regard to the weak:—verse 1. "Him that is weak in the faith receive ye, but not to doubtful disputations."

Those, observe, whom they are enjoined to "receive" are persons "*in the faith*"—believers in Christ. To "*receive*" them is, to acknowledge them as brethren, and manifest the cordial esteem and love due to such:—to welcome them to all the intimacy of Christian intercourse, and to the fellowship of the Church of God.

The "weakness," consisting in the want of clear and comprehensive views of the truth, might arise from different *causes.* It might arise from natural imbecility of mind; which was no crime, some minds being constituted with more ample and vigorous powers than others, capable of taking in a wider range of vision, and of forming their judgments with greater promptitude and decision; seeing their ground more clearly, and resting upon it with greater steadfastness. Or it might be owing with some, from being noviciates in the knowledge of divine truth, partially instructed, and not yet discerning its various relations, and the connexion and unity of the divine dispensations; so that they did not feel their consciences released from the one dispensation, because they did not fully discern its cessation in the other.

It might exist also in various *degrees.* From the want of a distinct and enlarged view of the *principle* of the case as affecting the entire introductory dispensation, they might feel their liberty in some points but not in all. There were points in which the fulfilment of the typical import of the ancient ceremonial in Christ might be more apparent than it was in others. They might, for example, readily perceive, as being obvious and striking, the fulfilment of the *sacrificial* rites in the sacrifice of Christ; while they did not so readily discern the abolition of the law respecting matters of which the typical import and temporary design were not so manifest—as in the instance here specified of different clean and unclean meats. In this particular, "the strong" "believed that they might *eat all things*"—that is, that the distinction, authoritatively instituted under the Law, was at an end.* The "weak" still adhered to the distinction; and they did rightly—their conscience not being clear of the obligation, from their not discerning the cessation of the authority. Under the influence of this timidity, and apprehensiveness of conscience, they even went beyond the law, being represented here as restricting themselves, if not entirely, yet in a great degree to the " eating of herbs." Why so? it may naturally be asked. There were many kinds of animal food permitted to the Jews as "clean" by the same law that prohibited the "*unclean.*" It is said, however, to have been the practice of many Jews, residing among the Gentiles in various parts of the world, to abstain from animal food entirely, in order to secure themselves against all the ceremonial pollutions which such food might possibly contract when not killed and prepared in the Jewish manner. What was sold in heathen shambles might, moreover, have been previously "offered in sacrifice to idols." As so, to avoid the possibility of even unwittingly defiling themselves, they thought it safest to abstain from animal food altogether.

* Comp. 1 Tim. iv. 4, 5.

The general principles on which "the strong" and "the weak," both in this point and on others, are admonished reciprocally to conduct themselves, we must leave for consideration in another Lecture.

The only remark I shall offer at present—leaving the practical application of the principles of the passage till we have more fully considered them—is, the information which even this first part of the counsel and admonition of the Apostle—"him that is weak in the faith receive ye"—affords as to the true nature of a church of Christ. It ought to be composed of those, and of those only, who are "*in the faith.*" This must be a first principle; and it ought to be a self-evident one. A church of Christ is a society of believers in Christ,—of those who have obtained the "precious faith" of his Gospel. There can be no substitute for this in the qualifications for membership. Nothing can supply its place. Rank, riches, talents, and endowments of the first order; nay, the best of mere worldly characters in business and in the intercourse of life, are not to be regarded, if the faith of Christ, and true godliness be wanting. The church that acts steadily on this principle will enjoy the blessing of the Lord. He will smile on the spiritual community, how obscure soever its members may be in worldly position, and will "lift upon them the light of his countenance." Let every church remember that in "receiving" any others than those who are "in the faith," they not only dishonour Christ and mar at once the beauty and the prosperity of his church, but essentially injure the souls of those whom they thus admit. They settle them in their delusions, and so far aid in conducting them to the grave "with a lie in their right hand."

But we have here another principle—that in every church there ought to be room made *for the weakest who are in the faith.* If they give evidence of knowing "the truth as it is in Jesus,"—if they profess the faith of the Gospel with lowliness and sincerity, with self-abasing conscious unworthiness, a simple-hearted reliance on mercy, and an humble and earnest desire to learn more of Christ and to love him and live to him,—their "weakness," whether arising from deficiency in the vigour of mental powers, or from their being but "babes in Christ," must never be a bar in their way. A church of Christ, while it must not "bear them who are *evil*," is bound by the will and example of Him who would not "break the bruised reed," to bear them that are "*weak*," —to "receive" them—to encourage and cherish them, and to show a tender respect to the scruples of conscience which the "weakness" may engender.

Finally, let all remember that it is only by "being in the faith," that they can have any connexion not only with the society of the people of God in church fellowship on earth, but with Christ himself and "the church of the first-born in heaven." The faith is indeed "precious" that is the bond of such a union—a union which, begun in time, and partially experienced in the happiness arising from it on earth, shall be perfected on high, and endure, in "fulness of joy," for ever and ever. Yes: in the day that shall determine the final destinies of men, and that shall discover on what different principles the estimates of true honour and true happiness are formed on the part of God and on that of His sinful creatures, the poorest believer in Christ will be the envy of the wealthiest and the greatest of the sons of earth; and the *weakest* believer in Christ the envy of the most splendid genius that ever Heaven endowed, and that ever drew by the display of its transcendent powers the applause of an admiring world. The least in the kingdom of heaven shall be greater than he!

LECTURE LXII.

ROMANS XIV. 1—6.

(SECOND DISCOURSE.)

I WISH to extend the application of the principles formerly laid down, in refutation of an argument which has been drawn from the passage before us, and its parallels, against the obligation of the Christian Sabbath.—I regret not having taken more particular notice of this argument when we had the subject of the Sabbath under consideration, as its due proportion of weight might have been more easily and correctly ascertained had it appeared in connexion with the other parts of the reasoning, which we cannot now of course go over again.*

The argument I refer to, it need hardly be said, is founded upon the language of verse fifth:—"One man esteemeth one day above another; another esteemeth every day alike. Let every man be fully persuaded in his own mind."

It has been argued thus:—" If we adopt the modern supposition, that there was a Christian law then in force which required the sanctification of a weekly portion of time to God's exclusive service, the propriety of the Apostle's counsel" (of mutual forbearance, namely) "must necessarily appear very questionable. If the observance of the first or of any other day of the week had at that time been enjoined as a

---

* The Author seems here to refer to a Series of Discourses on the Sabbath which were subsequently published. I do not, however, find any discussion of this passage.—ED.

Christian duty, the law must have been regarded by all to have been of indispensable obligation. Were we to suppose, therefore, that the observance of a weekly Sabbath had actually been commanded, we should be greatly at a loss to conceive how Paul could, in that case, have been warranted in affirming, that 'he that regardeth not the day, to the Lord he doth not regard it.' It is surely inconceivable that any Christian, whether of Jewish or Gentile extraction, could possibly have manifested his allegiance to Christ, by not regarding the observance of any one day, and 'esteeming every day alike' holy, if the observance of a certain day as more holy than others, had formed a part of the things which Christ had commanded."

In reply to this, it may be observed—1. That with respect to the passage before us, there is no evidence that the *Sabbath* was included in the Apostle's representation at all. For—

First: The statement and the whole reasoning have reference to observances distinctly and properly Jewish. The previous question, therefore, comes in the way, whether the Sabbath *was* such an institution. I formerly endeavoured to show you that it was not; but that it was instituted for mankind at the creation of the world.—If there was any force or conclusiveness in that argument, then the Sabbath was *not* an institution of the temporary Jewish ceremonial merely, and was not, therefore, among the things that "vanished away," when it came to a close.

Secondly: The terms, it is true, are universal, and without qualification. Every one, however, is aware that in writing with regard to a matter of controversy well known by those to whom we write, such unqualified terms are always to be understood according to the extent of the subject in dispute.— Suppose, for instance, in any particular Christian society a controversy were known to exist respecting the propriety of observing certain days that have been of long standing in the Romish and Anglican churches; a person in writing to that society might use in regard to its different members the language before us, and speak to them of one man among them "esteeming one day above another," while "another esteemed every day alike,"—without the least risk of being misunderstood as if he had any reference to the Christian Sabbath. No one would think of such a thing; but simply of the days respecting which the difference existed.—So in the present case. The difference was about days of Jewish observance; and therefore, I repeat, the previous question would naturally demand settlement, Was the Sabbath properly and exclusively one of these?

Thirdly: The language cannot be understood absolutely —with *no* qualification: for in that case it would follow, that there was *no day whatever* which any of them were under obligation to appropriate, in whole or in part, to any religious services at all—to observe differently from any other.—Now, let us try this in application both to the *seventh* and to the *first* day of the week.

As to the *former*—the writer whose argument I am considering, holds the continued obligation of the seventh day Sabbath upon Jewish believers, regarded as members of the Jewish commonwealth, till the final overthrow of the whole civil as well as ecclesiastical polity of the nation. It is true he grants that the ceremonial of Judaism (of which he affirms the Sabbath to have been a part) was virtually set aside by the coming and work of Christ; but he conceives it to have remained in actual force, in a political view, on all the subjects of the Jewish government. Now it is quite obvious, that, on whatever ground it was binding, if it *did* continue obligatory, there could be nothing optional as to its observance. It would not, on his own principles, be left to the mere persuasion of every man's own mind whether he should observe it, and the Sabbath as a part of it or not. There is a perfect inconsistency between continued obligation and optional observance.

Then with regard to "the *first* day of the week"—it is clear that if the reference in the passage be to *it*, the Apostle's language leaves all at perfect liberty, whether to make any difference between it and other days or not. It will be vain to say, that *by agreement of the church*, although not by any divine authority, its stated meetings for worship were held on that day: for the very terms of the passage contradict the idea of any such agreement. Whatever be the subject, nothing can be plainer than that it is a subject about which there was a difference actually existing. If, therefore, there be any reference to the first day at all, then the members of the church were not agreed as to whether that day should differ in any respect from other days. From which it would follow, that here was a church that had no fixed observance of social worship,—no times at which the members were under any obligation whatever to attend, but all in confusion—every one left to do that which was "right in his own eyes." Whether such a state of things be consistent with the character of that God who is not the Author of confusion but of order, I leave you to judge.—The passage, therefore, having reference to *Jewish days*, bears not at all upon "the *first* day of the week," and does not in the least invalidate the fact of its observance, as it confessedly had no place among the days respecting which the dispute existed. And if it has no bearing *against* the observance of the first day, it leaves the reasonings *for* it from other sources in full force.

2. As regards other passages, Gal. iv. 9—11 is appealed to:—"But now, after that ye have known God, or rather are known of God, how turn ye again to the weak and beggarly elements, whereunto ye desire again to be in bondage? Ye observe days, and months, and times, and years. I am afraid of you, lest I have bestowed upon you labour in vain." But there is no certain reference here to the Sabbath. The reference is to times and seasons of Jewish observance: and the burden of proof that the Sabbath is included in the passage rests with those who choose to affirm that it is.—The only remaining passage is Coloss. ii. 16, 17. "Let no man therefore judge you in meat, or in drink, or in respect of an holiday, or of the new-moon, or of the sabbath-days; which are a shadow of things to come: but the body is of Christ." I have no wish to evade the force of the objection by denying the reference of the

"*sabbath days*" to the seventh day rest. I admit it. The sole question, then, comes to be whether the seventh day rest was entirely Jewish, and so, as a part of the Jewish ritual, entirely set aside? or, whether it was designed that under the New Christian dispensation there should be a transference of the sabbatical observance from the *seventh to the first* day of the week. In the former case, the dispute was, whether *any day at all* should be held sacred to the worship of God. In the latter, the matter of difference was confined to the question of the continued obligation of the *seventh* day; the other being understood and in regular practice. Now—

3. Although it may be, we think, demonstrated that the Sabbath was an original and universal, not a peculiarly Jewish, institution, yet it *was* enjoined upon the Israelites, and enjoined upon them by additional motives peculiar to themselves; and on this account the continued observance of that particular day might be insisted on as part of the Mosaic institutes to Israel. And we need have no timid hesitation, therefore, in admitting that the Apostle refers to the seventh day, in the light in which it was contended for by the adherents of the law:—because, if the original and universal Sabbath was transferred to "the first day of the week" in commemoration and honour of the finished work of redemption, then it could only be *as a part of the Jewish law* that the retention of the seventh day was contended for. And this view of the case, it may be observed, suits well with the Apostle's argument, and at the same time avoids the difficulty formerly mentioned, as to there being *no day at all* on which they were at one, as to the duty of in any way observing it religiously, or spending it in any respect differently from other days.

4. While the supposition of the first day of the week being the day on which the social worship of the apostolic churches was observed (of which there can be no reasonable doubt) fairly reconciles every difficulty, leaving the sole dispute, so far as the Sabbath is concerned, about the seventh day as part of the Mosaic institutes—we may observe lastly

that the whole state of things was at that time *anomalous*, If there was any transference, it has been alleged, of the Sabbatical rest to the first day of the week, then in the Christian church the *seventh* could not have been continued in observance. But why? Is there anything more singular in the continued observance of the seventh day, for a time, on the part of the Jewish converts, *along with* a celebration of the first, than there is in the union of other Jewish observances with the Christian worship. They had circumcision still, but submitted at the same time to baptism. They observed the passover, as well as the Lord's supper. They attended the temple service as well as that of the Christian assemblies. There is nothing more strange in their attending to the Jewish Sabbath, and celebrating the Christian, than in any of these other apparent inconsistencies. As the Jewish believers continuing to celebrate the passover does not in the least degree invalidate the obligation of the Lord's supper in the Christian church; neither does their continuing for a time the observance of the seventh day, interfere at all with the obligation of the first.

I have thought it right to take a view of this argument, although it is not immediately connected with the general scope of the passage. To the illustration of *that* we now return.

We have seen that "the strong" are admonished to "*receive the weak;*" which, beyond all reasonable question, includes, chiefly, though not solely receiving and owning them as brethren in the fellowship of the church of Christ,—holding communion with them as fellow-disciples of the Lord Jesus. The spirit in which this was to be done is added—"*but not to doubtful disputations.*" This is not to be understood as implying that the matter in dispute between "the strong" and "the weak" was *to himself* a point in which there was doubt. There was none. His mind was quite settled about it—"I know, and am persuaded by the Lord Jesus, that there is nothing unclean of itself."* The words

* Verse 14.

might be rendered, "but *not to disputatious reasonings.*"* These were to be avoided. The case was one in which it was better that each conscience should be left to itself. It had been found, it would appear, that the subject could not be discussed with calmness and mutual goodwill. It "gendered strifes;" and these strifes were destructive of the spirit of mutual love, and consequently of all the benefits of Christian fellowship,—which is a fellowship of love, and can yield its beneficial results only in proportion as this sacred principle is cultivated and maintained in exercise. There will be edification just to the extent in which there is love and unity and peace:—" Where envying and strife are, there is confusion and every evil work." " Love edifieth;" and whatever mars love mars the beauty, the harmony, the comfort, the growth, and the vigour of the body of Christ. Their duty, therefore, was the same as that enjoined on the believers at Ephesus:—" I therefore, the prisoner of the Lord, beseech you, that ye walk worthy of the vocation wherewith ye are called. With all lowliness and meekness, with long-suffering, forbearing one another in love; endeavouring to keep the unity of the Spirit in the bond of peace."†

While these tempers were to be studied by *both* parties in the church, there were at the same time dispositions peculiar to each; and to each an exhortation is adduced:— verse 3. " Let not him that eateth despise him that eateth not; and let not him which eateth not judge him that eateth: for God hath received him." " The strong " were in danger of *scorn*,—"the weak" of *uncharitableness*. The strong, considering their brethren as weak-minded, silly people, bigoted, and foolishly scrupulous, and blind to the simplest and most obvious truths, were in hazard of the evil against which the Apostle before admonishes—" I say, through the grace given unto me, to every man that is among you, not

---

* διακρίσεις διαλογισμῶν. The margin of the English Version has "*not to judge his doubtful thoughts.*" Another rendering is, "*not with a view to discernments of thoughts;*" another, "*not to the deciding of doubts.*" They all present much the same idea.—ED.

† Eph. iv. 1—3.

to think of himself more highly than he ought to think:"* for there cannot be indulged a lofty opinion of ourselves, without a corresponding contempt of others. They were thus in danger of getting fretted and irritated, and of failing in the allowance which it was their duty to make for scrupulous consciences. The Apostle cautions them against this spirit. But he does not *take a side.* He deals impartially. He admonishes both parties according to their respective characters and peculiar tendencies. He addresses "the weak" as well as "the strong." He warns them to beware of judging others by themselves—of making their own consciences the standard for other men's; concluding that their brethren who did not feel themselves under obligation to act as they did must be deficient in regard to the will of God. This would have been a harsh and unfair inference. He counsels them to guard against it, and reminds them in effect that the liberty of the strong was not to be judged by the consciences of the weak.†

He assigns a substantial reason—"*For God hath received him.*" We know this in regard to Gentiles from direct divine intimations both in word and by significant action.‡ With regard to the Jews who were strong, and whose conduct is the chief subject of the discussion—God had also received *them.* Their conduct was in harmony with the divine intention in the ancient rites, which were truly, acccording to the principle on which they acted, set aside by the death of Christ. Jehovah received the spiritual offerings of "the strong" presented in His spiritual temple, and dispensed with their observance of the old ceremonial, not at all requiring it of those whom His enlightening Spirit had taught its temporary nature, its fulfilment, and its consequent abolition.

There can be no stronger reason, surely, presented to the mind of a believer, than *the example of God.* It was irresistible. They could not but feel,—and neither can we but feel, how presumptuous the thought is of making that a bar to

---

* Chap. xii. 3.   † 1 Cor. x. 29; Matt. vii. 1.
‡ Acts x. 44; xi. 17; and chap. xv.

fellowship with any man, which the Holy One does not make a hinderance to communion with Himself.

"Who art thou," continues the Apostle (ver. 4), "that judgest another man's servant?"* The *judging* here is the judging of others to condemnation for doing that which their divine Master has not prohibited, or for failing to do that which he has not commanded. Such judging evidently implies the prescription of rules and principles of conduct to those who belong to another master, and visiting them with censure because they do not adopt and follow them. It was setting themselves above Christ. It was usurping His prerogative. This was remarkably the case with the conduct of those Jews who were for imposing the Mosaic yoke upon the Gentiles. This was in opposition to the will and appointment of the divine Master. Independently altogether of their subjection to that yoke "God had received them." The sentiment is the same as in the language of James:—" Speak not evil one of another, brethren. He that speaketh evil of his brother, and judgeth his brother, speaketh evil of the law, and judgeth the law: but if thou judge the law, thou art not a doer of the law, but a judge. There is one lawgiver, who is able to save and to destroy: who art thou that judgest another?"† This is not our province. We, as well as our brethren, and equally with them, are subjects of the Law. We must not set up for judges and denouncers of its sentences; far less as critics on the provisions of the Law itself,—condemning for what it does not contain.

It is a most solemn and interesting truth which follows—" *To his own master he standeth or falleth.*" This Master is the Lord Jesus Christ.‡ It is with *Him* we have all to do. To Him we must render our final account. His decisions are irreversible. They fix the doom of every soul for eternity. Our appearance before HIM should be our chief solicitude. Thus it was with this conscientious Apostle him-

---

* Better simply—*the servant of another.*—ED.
† James iv. 11, 12.   ‡ Matt xxiii. 10.

self:—" But with me it is a very small thing that I should be judged of you, or of man's judgment; yea, I judge not mine own self: for I am conscious to myself of nothing;* yet am I not hereby justified: but he that judgeth me is the Lord."†

In the present case—"*he shall be holden up,*‡ for God is able to make him stand." It is evident that, in this verse, "the *weak*" are addressed. They "*judge;*" "the strong" "*despise.*" The weak pronounced sentence severely against the strong, as acting presumptuously and in contravention of divine statutes. But the presumption was their own. While they condemned, God the righteous Judge would justify. The "holding up" and "making to stand" appears to have special reference to the final judgment—agreeable to the ordinary phraseology of Scripture.§ And the expression "God is able to make him stand," seems to be spoken of the divine *authority:*—"There is one lawgiver, who is able to save and to destroy: who art thou that judgest another?"‖ It is a very serious thing to form and to pronounce judgments against others in opposition to the judgment of God. In order to our avoiding this, it is of first-rate importance for us to study well the principles of the divine procedure as they are taught and exemplified in the divine word. And while we do so, let us bear in mind that our chief purpose should be, not to apply the principles to the judgment of others, but rather to the examination and correction of ourselves. With ourselves we can hardly be too severe or rigid in scrutiny and in judgment:—and even when our judgment is favourable, it should be with a consciousness of the deceitfulness of our own hearts, and a reservation to the judgment of the Lord.

The same principle is then further applied to *the days of*

---

* οὐδὲν γὰρ ἐμαυτῷ σύνοιδα. † 1 Cor. iv. 3, 4.
‡ *made to stand, σταθήσεται.*—ED.
§ Psal. i. 5. Others maintain that the reference is not to the day of judgment, but that he speaks of standing *here* in the true fellowship of the church in spite of censure.—ED.
‖ Jam. iv. 12.

Jewish observance—verse 5. "One man esteemeth one day above another; another esteemeth every day alike. Let every man be fully persuaded in his own mind."—The description of the two classes of persons here is too simple to require illustration;—one class feeling their consciences still bound to the celebration of these days, and the other satisfied of their release from the obligation by the fulfilment of their typical import in Christ. The great general principle laid down is—"*Let every man be fully persuaded in his own mind.*" It is the principle, on the subject under discussion, of mutual confidence and forbearance, in following out every one the dictates of his own conscience, with sincere and earnest desires to know the mind of the Lord. The inquiry of Saul of Tarsus at his conversion is the simple and earnest inquiry of every convert—"Lord, what wilt THOU have me to do?"* This is the authority by which each conscience was to be imperatively bound; and it was of necessity that it should feel the obligation according to its discernment of the command or will. Nothing can be clearer than that, with regard to the observances of the Jewish law, the Apostle treats it as a matter to be regulated by the conscience of each,—a matter neither enjoined on the one hand nor prohibited and pronounced sinful on the other, but still *permitted* in condescension to existing prejudice. "The weak" and "the strong" were each to seek a full persuasion of duty, and in the exercise of mutual charity as to the motives by which they were respectively influenced, they were mutually to bear with each other.

Verse 6. "He that regardeth the day, regardeth it unto the Lord; and he that regardeth not the day, to the Lord he doth not regard it. He that eateth, eateth to the Lord, for he giveth God thanks; and he that eateth not, to the Lord he eateth not, and giveth God thanks." The plain meaning of this is, that every one of them was to regard his brother as acting under the influence of a conscientious subjection to the will of their common Lord, though they did not see

---

* Acts ix. 6.

that will as yet in the same light.—" He that regardeth the day, regardeth it *unto the Lord*"—that is, he acts under the conviction that the Lord requires it of him, not discerning his release from the obligation of the ancient statutes. And on the other hand, "he who observeth *not* the day, to the Lord he doth not regard it," that is, the Gentile under the full conviction that the Lord required of *him* no such subjection, and the enlightened Jew in the persuasion that the Lord Jesus, by fulfilling the Law, had released him from the obligation of its ceremonial observances, these having served their temporary typical purpose, and being set aside. In like manner—"he that eateth, *eateth to the Lord*,"—that is, he eateth with the sanction of the Lord's permission in his conscience, being satisfied of the cessation of the ancient distinctions of meats, which formerly had bound his conscience. In token of this, he "*giveth God thanks,*" expressing his gratitude for the food and for the liberty to use it.*—" And he who eateth *not*, to the Lord he eateth not, and giveth God thanks." The scrupulous brother acted under the influence of the same principle, not satisfied that the Lord had given him liberty—and he expressed the principle in the same way; thanking God for having provided *other* food for him, which he can use without offence to his conscience,—even were it herbs. This abstinence was to be viewed as a sign of *conscientiousness;* the principle which in each was to be esteemed by the other; each being satisfied that the other, with the convictions which he entertained, would be guilty of a violation of subjection to the will of the common Master, were he to act in any other way than he did; that in either case, the action which by the different parties respectively might be regarded as outwardly right, would when done by the members of the opposite party be inwardly wrong—right in *act*, but wrong in *principle*. This is sufficiently obvious; and it will appear more fully in illustrating the subsequent discussions. It is equally clear that the entire system of forbearance recommended proceeds on the assump-

---

* Comp. 1 Tim. iv. 4, 5; with 1 Cor. x. 29, 30.

tion of the mutual persuasion of one another's conscientiousness. Without this mutual charitable admission of *sincerity* on both sides, forbearance must of course have been out of the question; as each must have viewed the other as wilful and presumptuous transgressors. If any one on either side had appeared wilfully opposing and disregarding the acknowledged authority of Christ, the case had been essentially different. To all who thus presume to set at nought any part of his will, Jesus says, "Why call ye me Lord, Lord, and do not the things which I say?" "Not every one that saith unto me, Lord, Lord, shall enter into the kingdom of heaven; but he that doeth the will of my Father which is in heaven."*

* Luke vi. 46: Matth. vii. 21.

LECTURE LXIII.

ROMANS XIV. 7—13.

" For none of us liveth to himself, and no man dieth to himself. For whether we live, we live unto the Lord; and whether we die, we die unto the Lord: whether we live, therefore, or die, we are the Lord's. For to this end Christ both died, and rose, and revived, that he might be Lord both of the dead and living. But why dost thou judge thy brother? or why dost thou set at nought thy brother? for we shall all stand before the judgment-seat of Christ. For it is written, As I live, saith the Lord, every knee shall bow to me, and every tongue shall confess to God. So then every one of us shall give account of himself to God. Let us not therefore judge one another any more: but judge this rather, that no man put a stumblingblock, or an occasion to fall, in his brother's way."

In the close of last lecture we had occasion to remark, that the ground of mutual forbearance between "the weak" and "the strong" in this passage is the mutual conviction of conscientiousness in each other's views and practices. On no other ground could it possibly be recommended. Jesus Christ is the only Lord of the conscience, to whom each individual of his subjects and servants is directly and solely responsible; and for one to act according to the conscience of another, in opposition to his own, is *in principle* to be the "servant of men;" even supposing the act itself to be in conformity with the laws of the kingdom. Each of the two parties was obeying THE LORD, and was to be so regarded by the other, when they were following, respectively, the convictions of their own minds respecting the will of their common Master.*

The "*full persuasion*" spoken of, is the persuasion that the

* Verses 4, 5, 6.

course which each pursues is consistent with the will of Christ. Then, in connexion with this, there follows, in verse seventh, a general description of the great principle of the Christian character—" For none of us liveth to himself, and no man dieth to himself."

The expression "*no man*" in verse seventh is not to be understood of *men* in general. It is literally "*no one*," and the words "*of us*" are to be understood as in the first clause of the verse: "None, or no one of us liveth to himself, and none, or no one of us dieth to himself." It is of Christians, of believers, the Apostle speaks. There is a sense in which all men, and all creatures, live *to* or *for* the Lord; all being subject to His control, and all rendered subservient to His purposes and His glory. But the language before us is evidently descriptive, not of the mere use that the Lord makes of creatures in effecting His own ends, but of *the principles and intentions of the agents.*

Here is the extent of Christian devotedness. He *lives* not to himself, but to the Lord:—he *dies* not to himself, but to the Lord.

1. His LIFE is the Lord's. This implies, in the first place, that he lives not according to *his own will*, but according to the *will of the Lord.* This is his only rule. His sole question is, " What wilt thou have me to do?" His own wisdom and his own inclination are entirely relinquished, and his mind and conscience, with all simplicity, subjected to the dictation of his Lord. No principle is of more importance than this complete surrender of the conscience to the authority of Christ. Here, in His own word, is the standard; and by this standard every true and faithful subject of Christ is desirous undeviatingly to abide. Tell him anything that is of a nature congenial to his own inclination, as that which it is best to do, the very circumstance of its being so will make him jealous of himself. The moment he sees that, although congenial to his own will, it accords not with that of his Master, his answer is—No: I LIVE NOT TO MYSELF.*

* Comp. John x. 2—5; xiv. 15, 21—24.

It implies, further, that, in his conduct, he *seeks not his own glory*, but the glory of *his Lord*. Such was the principle, in an eminent degree, of Paul himself. This is the prominent idea in his remarkable words, " To ME TO LIVE IS CHRIST." He lived but for his Lord. The advancement of the honour of His name was the very end of his being. His " soul would have chosen strangling and death rather than life," if his life was not to bring glory to his Master. And thus it is, though in very various degrees, with all the true subjects of the Redeemer. His glory they make the grand aim of their lives. Life they reckon lost—its chief end unattained, when it is spent without successful effort for the advancement of that glory.

2. Christians DIE to the Lord. This first of all implies, that their lives are at His disposal; and that the time and all the circumstances of their deaths are ordered by Him with a view to his own glory.—And this is what His people desire —to die such a death, at such a time, and in such circumstances, as shall be most conducive to the honour of His name. Amongst various modes of death, many may be disposed to choose which they would prefer. The believer has no choice but one—that which will be most for his Master's glory. To His pleasure he leaves it, delighted with the thought of his death as well as his life being rendered conducive to such an end. He does not consider life at his own disposal. He knows that he cannot lengthen it at his pleasure; neither does he feel himself at liberty to shorten it. He waits the Lord's time; he submits to the Lord's appointment,—his only solicitude that whether he suffer death for the cause of the Lord or not, he may be enabled to bear a dying testimony to His grace, and by resignation to His will, and the manifestation of the influence of His gospel, in imparting peace and hope in the season of nature's direst extremity, to recommend to others the choice of His salvation, and bring credit to His name.—It implies a readiness, should the Lord see fit to call him to the sacrifice, to relinquish cheerfully life itself for His sake. Such readiness the Lord requires of

all his followers: They must be in spirit *martyrs*—" If any man come to me, and hate not his father, and mother, and wife, and children, and brethren, and sisters, yea, and his own life also, he cannot be my disciple."* And the sentiments and feelings involved in the description before us are finely exemplified by Paul himself when he says—" For I know that this shall turn to my salvation through your prayer, and the supply of the Spirit of Jesus Christ, according to my earnest expectation and my hope, that in nothing I shall be ashamed, but that with all boldness, as always, so now also Christ shall be magnified in my body, whether it be by life, or by death. For to me to live is Christ, and to die is gain. But if I live in the flesh, this is the fruit of my labour: yet what I shall choose I wot not. For I am in a strait betwixt two, having a desire to depart, and to be with Christ, which is far better."† And the language of unshrinking self-devotion in which he addressed the elders of Ephesus is in the full spirit of the passage before us,—the language of one who felt that his life and his death were altogether the Lord's— " And now, behold, I go bound in the spirit unto Jerusalem, not knowing the things that shall befall me there: save that the Holy Ghost witnesseth in every city, saying that bonds and afflictions abide me. But none of these things move me, neither count I my life dear unto myself, so that I might finish my course with joy, and the ministry which I have received of the Lord Jesus, to testify the gospel of the grace of God."‡

Thus he was the Lord's whether in life or in death— the Lord's by sovereign right of possession, the purchase of His own most precious blood; and the Lord's by voluntary self-consecration, given up unreservedly, soul, body, and spirit, to His service and to the advancement of His glory. And such should be the character of every believer. Of every one of them the language should in spirit be that of David's friends when they joined him in the wilderness—" Thine are we, O Jesus, and on thy side, thou son of David;" or that

* Luke xiv. 26. † Phil. i. 19—23. ‡ Acts xx. 22—24.

of Peter, although not with self-confidence in which *he* uttered it—" I am ready to go with thee to prison and to death!"

And when death comes, in whatever way, and at whatever time, it does not sever the believer from his living Lord. It breaks not his connexion with him. No. The connexion is spiritual and eternal. Death only perfects it. It introduces the believer to the presence of Him whom his soul loves. He is still "the Lord's;" the Lord's by the same indefeasible right of property; the Lord's, in the sinless perfection of principle and of service; the Lord's, to glorify and enjoy Him for ever. There is an immediate connexion between the eighth verse and the ninth—" Whether we live therefore, or die, we are the Lord's. *For* to this end Christ both died, and rose, and revived, that he might be Lord *both of the dead and living."*

1. He *is* "Lord both of the dead and living." The two classes of subjects mentioned form one community.* The *dead* are the dead *in Christ.* We may learn the extent of his lordship over them from what he himself says— "As touching the resurrection of the dead, have ye not read that which was spoken unto you by God, saying, I am the God of Abraham, and the God of Isaac, and the God of Jacob? God is not the God of the dead, but of the living."† Their souls, when they part from the body, which is their earthly prison, do not pass into a state of torpor and insensibility; nor even into an intermediate state of mere safe custody and assurance of future joy; they are received into His presence, where they are "made perfect"—like Him, and with Him. They are a more advanced class of subjects, freed from all the defilements of sin and all the encumbrances of mortality, serving Him, though in ways necessarily out of the sphere of our conceptions, "day and night in his temple." And *their bodies*—they "rest in hope;" they "sleep in Jesus." They are not forgotten,—any more than the body of Jesus himself was forgotten, when it lay in the grave.

* Heb. xii. 23. † Matth. xxii. 31, 32.

He himself trusted in the divine care of both his soul and body: "For thou wilt not leave my soul in hell; neither wilt thou suffer thine Holy One to see corruption. Thou wilt shew me the path of life: in thy presence is fulness of joy; at thy right hand there are pleasures for evermore."[*] And now that this expectation has been fulfilled—now that he is in possession of the joy that was set before him—and "all power in heaven and on earth" committed into his hands, He will exercise that power, and give proof of his lordship by the raising up of their dead bodies from the corruption of the tomb: "This is the Father's will which hath sent me, that of all which he hath given me I should lose nothing, but should raise it up at the last day."[†]

"*The living*" are all the saints on earth in successive generations—the "general assembly and church of the firstborn whose names are written in heaven," though they themselves are not yet there,—as distinguished from "the spirits of just men made perfect." They include especially those who shall be "alive at his coming." Thus, He is Lord of all who died in the faith and hope of his first coming; Lord of all who have since lived and died in the faith; Lord of all the saints now on the earth; and, prospectively, Lord of all who shall arise in future generations, as the trophies of his grace—of the seed that shall serve him and be "counted to him for a generation while sun and moon endure."

There is no doubt a more extensive view of his lordship. He is "Lord of all" in regard to his dominion over the world and over the universe so far as it stands connected with this portion or province of it. But in this passage the Apostle appears to me to speak in a special manner of his lordship over his redeemed people.

2. We have here the way in which he arrived at this dignity—"To this end Christ both died, and rose, and revived."[‡] i. He *died* that he might be Lord. Without dying he would not have had a people over whom to reign. He re-

---
[*] Psal. xvi. 10, 11. [†] John vi. 39: Phil. iii. 21.
[‡] It is right to notice that the reading now almost universally regarded as genuine is εἰς τοῦτο γὰρ Χριστὸς ἀπέθανεν καὶ ἔζησεν.—Ed.

deemed them from the spiritual power of another master by his death, and obtained right to them as his own. They are a purchased people.* His cross laid the foundation of his throne — his supreme lordship being the reward of his death. He "made himself of no reputation, and took upon him the form of a servant, and was made in the likeness of men: and being found in fashion as a man, he humbled himself, and became obedient unto death, even the death of the cross. Wherefore God also hath highly exalted him, and given him a name which is above every name: that at the name of Jesus every knee should bow, of things in heaven, and things in earth, and things under the earth; and that every tongue should confess that Jesus Christ is Lord, to the glory of God the Father."† Hence he himself founds his petition for glory on his *finished work:*—" I have glorified thee on the earth: I have finished the work which thou gavest me to do. And now, O Father, glorify thou me with thine own self with the glory which I had with thee before the world was."‡ He suffered with a view to this glory as the stipulated result—"*For the joy that was set before him,* he endured the cross, despising the shame, and is set down at the right hand of the throne of God.§"

ii. He "*rose again,*" that he might be Lord. His death being necessary to his having a people, his resurrection was equally necessary to his reigning over them. For this end He was raised up that he might reign: "God raised him from the dead, and set him at his own right hand in the heavenly places, far above all principality, and power, and might, and dominion, and every name that is named, not only in this world, but also in that which is to come." "For David is not ascended into the heavens; but he saith himself, The Lord said unto my Lord, Sit thou on my right hand, until I make thy foes thy footstool. Therefore let all the house of Israel know assuredly, that God hath made that same Jesus, whom ye have crucified, both Lord and Christ."‖

* Acts xx. 28: 1 Pet. i. 18; with chap. ii. 9.
† Phil. ii. 5—11.   ‡ John xvii. 4, 5.   § Heb. xii. 2.
‖ Eph. i. 19—21: Acts ii. 30—36.

—iii. He *revived*—he lived again; that is, he entered at his rising on a new and endless life not to return to corruption.* The phrase seems to have this meaning, as distinguished from his "*rising again.*" "He lives to reign;" and he shall live and reign, till all the purposes of his mediatorial government shall have been perfectly accomplished:—"Then cometh the end, when he shall have delivered up the kingdom to God, even the Father; when he shall have put down all rule, and all authority and power. For he must reign, till he hath put all enemies under his feet.†

In verse tenth, it is obvious, "the weak" and "the strong" are respectively addressed—the first question being to the former, the second to the latter: this appears from the nature of the thing, and from the language of verse third.

"Why dost thou"—*the weak*—"judge thy brother?" condemning him uncharitably and censoriously for his liberty: —"And why dost thou"—*the strong*—"set at nought thy brother?" holding him in contempt for his conscientious scruples. One consideration is adduced to both, to enforce the admonition contained in each of these questions. It is a solemn one—one which neither party, if under the influence of right principles at all, could treat with indifference or lightness. It is the prospect of judgment. And here, as in other places, *Christ* is the Judge.‡

In connexion with this we must remark that the Scriptures affirm *God alone to be Judge.*§ We may safely affirm indeed, that none else *can be* Judge but God. No Being but one possessed of divine perfections can be competent to the work. To be the Judge is not to be a mere *announcer of the sentences.* *This* might be done by a creature—by any creature. But to be Judge is to be the investigator of the cases, and the framer of the decisions. We have been charged with presumption for affirming that none but God

---

* Rom. vi. 9: Acts xiii. 34. † 1 Cor. xv. 24, 25.
‡ See his own assurance of this—John v. 22, 23, 27, and that of the Apostles, who deliver it as a part of their expressly commissioned message to men—Acts x. 42.
§ Psal. l. 6: Eccl. xii. 14, &c.

can do this. But we must repeat the presumption and affirm anew—the whole tenor of the Bible, as well as the dictates of common sense, bearing us out in the affirmation, that no qualifications are competent to such a work but *omniscience* and *omnipotence*. The perfect and unerring discrimination of all the endless diversities and shades of character amongst the countless millions of mankind from the beginning to the end of time, together with the universal, irresistible, and irreversible decision and infliction of the dooms pronounced—are beyond any knowledge and any power but those of Deity. But Christ is to do this. Therefore Christ is God. This is strikingly confirmed by the quotation which immediately follows:—"For it is written, As I live, saith the Lord, every knee shall bow to me, and every tongue shall confess to God. So then every one of us shall give account of himself to God." It is evident that the same person is throughout the passage indiscriminately denominated *Lord*, and *Christ*, and *God*.

In the prophet Isaiah, from which the first passage is quoted, the connexion with the preceding and following context evinces most conclusively the reference of the words to Him who is "Jehovah our righteousness."*

It should be observed, that, although the designation rendered *Lord* in the New Testament is not always equivalent to *Jehovah*, yet that it certainly is so in those passages in which it is used as the translation of Jehovah in quotations from the Old. It is so put in verse eleventh. There is a difference, therefore, in the meaning of *Lord* in this verse and in those which precede. In the preceding verses it refers to the *Mediatorial lordship* of Jesus; in this verse it signifies *Jehovah*, the incommunicable Name of the one true God. And this is here applied to Christ.

There is a twofold difference between the words in Isaiah and in Paul:—

1. The one says, "*By myself have I sworn*"—the other, "*As I live.*" It is surely needless to dwell on a distinction

---

* Isa. xlv. 22—25; comp. with 1 Cor. i. 30, 31.

in which there is no real difference. The sense is essentially the same. In both, Jehovah swears *by himself.*

2. In the one we have "every tongue shall *swear*," in the other "every tongue shall *confess* to God." It appears to me that the true principle of harmony here is to be found in the allusion contained in the words to the forms of judicial process amongst men. Those who appear at the tribunal give their depositions upon oath. If, therefore, there is an allusion to the emitting of solemn declarations, to "*swear*" to God and to "*confess*" to God will amount to the same thing. It is in either case the making of a solemn deposition as to a judge. This view of the case receives confirmation from the explanatory terms which follow in the twelfth verse— "So then, every one of us shall *give account of himself* to God."

The general idea in the *quotation* as here applied is—that in standing before the judgment-seat of Christ, his authority will be owned. This is equally signified by the two expressions—"bowing the knee"—and "swearing" or "confessing with the tongue." The acts involve an acknowledgment of supremacy. This acknowledgment shall be made by all— either with cheerful joy and delight, or with the reluctance of enmity and despair. "*Every* knee shall bow, *every* tongue shall confess."*

The assurance is a very solemn one—"Every one of us shall give account of himself to God." O that this were felt as it ought to be felt! "*Every one* of us!" Let it be brought home to the conscience of each individual. Let each one say with serious anticipation—"*I* must give account of myself to God!" How blessed the results could men only be prevailed upon to give this prospect a serious thought. But there is no getting them to think. They do not like it. They cannot bear it. It interferes with their present indulgences; and the very art of their present enjoyment,—the very secret of their present pleasures,—lies

---

* Comp. Phil. ii. 9—11. where the various expressions of the Apostle are more comprehensive than the *living and the dead* in the passage before us:—but they of course include them.

in the exclusion of such thoughts! O infatuated indulgences! O unworthy pleasures! that cannot be enjoyed but in the banishment of God, and in the exclusion of all such reflection as might lead to the avoidance of eternal ruin and the attainment of everlasting life!—But here the prospect is held out in a special manner to the *people of God:*—whence, as well as from many other passages and considerations, you may see how unscriptural is the idea of those millenarians, who deny the judgment of the righteous altogether, alleging that it is to be confined to *the wicked.* Every description of the judgment assures us of the contrary.*

The prospect should teach the followers of Christ *two* lessons:—1. To *judge themselves.*†—It behoves us, in the view of our coming account, to be "jealous over ourselves;" to scrutinize our conduct—not in the action merely, but in the motive and principle. We should see to it, that conscience be well-informed, and then, that we implicitly and fully follow its dictates—"abhorring that which is evil," and "cleaving to that which is good"—confessing and forsaking whereinsoever we are conscious of wrong, and persevering in the face of all temptations in what is right. It is *of ourselves*, not of others, that we are to give account; and of ourselves, not in comparison with others, but in comparison with the will of the Lord, and our opportunities of knowing it. We do well, therefore, to "prove our own work," in the prospect of appearing before Him who "searcheth"—and who shall *then* especially "search the hearts and try the reins of the children of men."

2. We are taught *not to judge others.*—And this brings us at once to verse thirteenth, "Let us not judge one another any more." They are condemned and reproved for the past, and admonished for the future.—We are not lords of the conscience; and the right to judge the consciences of our brethren is not ours. It is "to God" that we are to "give account," not to one another. How appalling should the

* Matt. xxv. 31—33: 2 Cor. v. 10.
† Gal. vi. 4; 2 Cor. xiii. 5; 1 Cor. xi. 31.

thought be to us, that we may be judging in opposition to Christ; despising what He despises not; condemning what He condemns not; pronouncing sentence, in our minds, or with our lips, *against* those whom He has received! Let us imitate Paul himself as he describes the principle on which he acted and admonishes others to act:—" With me it is a very small thing that I should be judged of you, or of man's judgment: yea, I judge not mine own self. For I am conscious to myself of nothing; yet am I not hereby justified: but he that judgeth me is the Lord."* This corresponds in the spirit of it with what follows here—" But judge this rather." *Determine:* let this be the subject of *self-judgment:* let this be your fixed principle, in prospect of the judgment of the Lord—" that no one put a stumblingblock or an occasion to fall in his brother's way."

A brother may *stumble* without *falling.* But we are to beware of everything that might even be the means of *stumbling* another,—of putting another to the hazard of a fall—of shaking the resolution of the weakest conscience—" It is good neither to eat flesh, nor to drink wine, nor anything whereby thy brother stumbleth, or is offended, or is made weak."†

The general duty of mutual care one for another is often inculcated:—" Look not every man on his own things, but every man also on the things of others. Let this mind be in you, which was also in Christ Jesus." "Let no man seek his own, but every man another's wealth."‡ And the care should especially be exercised for spiritual good:—" Let us consider one another, to provoke unto love, and to good works."§ The conduct forbidden in the verse before us is the very opposite of this. It is being *the occasion of sin* to our brethren; for this is evidently meant by *falling.* This is the import of an oft-recurring word in our English version of the New Testament—*offend.* It signifies to *cause to sin,* including whatever in our con-

---

* 1 Cor. iv. 1—4. † Verse 21.
‡ Phil. ii. 4, 5; 1 Cor. x. 24. § Heb. x. 24.

duct may have this *tendency*, even although not actually producing the effect. We may throw a stumblingblock in another's way, although he does not fall over it or even stumble at it and wound or endanger himself. That God gives him grace to shun it is no palliation of our sin. To be guilty of this *lightly* is at utter variance with the spirit of the Gospel. We are to be very tenderly cautious lest we even inadvertently be chargeable with it. The admonitions of Christ himself on the subject are in such terms as should make us tremble at the thought of it:—"Whoso shall offend one of these little ones which believe in me, it were better for him that a millstone were hanged about his neck, and that he were drowned in the depth of the sea."*

It is true, we may by our conduct be "an offence" to others, without criminality. Whatever is the occasion to men of stumbling is an offence. But it does not necessarily imply *sin* in that which causes offence. The sin may be in the dispositions of those who stumble. *Christ* is an offence. Men "stumble at that stumbling-stone:"—but there is no evil in Christ: his very sinless excellence is the occasion of the offence. Men "stumble *at the word*, being disobedient:"—but there is no sin in the word—the offence is taken at its perfect and uncompromising opposition to sin. So we may, by a strict adherence to the dictates of conscience and the directions of the divine word, be the occasion of exciting improper feelings, of irritation and pride, and opposition and persecution, for which *not we* but those who take the offence are to blame. They may sin against God and sin against us, because we *will not sin*—will not do as they wish.—But the conduct here condemned, as the whole of the subsequent context will fully show, is untender dealing with the consciences of "the weak," and presumptuous judgment of the consciences of "the strong." In either case, but especially in the former, we may cause to sin. We may both excite passions at variance with the love which the Gospel exemplifies and produces, and we may tempt to conduct that is not in

* Matt. xviii. 6; see also Mark ix. 41, 42.

harmony with a straightforward adherence to the dictates of conscience in our brethren.

We cannot go further without anticipating the illustration of what follows. Neither can we enter into the general application of the principles of the passage, till we come forward to the beginning of the next chapter.

In the meantime, however, in the prospect of that appearance to be made by every one of us before the judgment-seat of Christ,—let me put to all who name his name, who profess to be his subjects, the solemn question—Are you acting up to the spirited description of the Christian character in these verses? are you *living to the Lord?* Is His will your rule? His glory your end? His grace your motive? The question is one not of mere name and general undistinguishing profession;—it is one of principle and practice. It is not whether you are calling him "Lord, Lord," but whether you are "doing the things which he says." Is the surrender which you have made of yourselves unreserved? Is your *heart* His?—is your *life* His? Will your subjection to Him abide the test, I do not say of the vague, undefined, nominal, worldly Christianity of the day—but of the descriptions of true Christianity in the word of God? O remember, this will be the test which He himself will apply when you appear at His tribunal. It will not be enough to have passed under the name of Christian—in order to your acceptance there, you must have been a Christian "in deed and in truth." Be not satisfied, then, with the name. Apply the only test—and apply it *now*. Do you say to Jesus, with an entire surrender of yourselves to him,

> "May I be thine in life and death,
> And thine for evermore?"

O forget not his own words—"If any man shall be ashamed of me and of my words, of him shall the Son of man be ashamed, when he shall come in his own glory, and in his Father's, and of the holy angels." If you are not Christ's in life, you cannot be Christ's in death, nor Christ's in the judgment.

Let *Christless* sinners be persuaded to consider what is before them. The Judge at whose bar they are to stand is the very Saviour whom they are despising. You *must* appear there: you must "give account of yourselves" to Him. O how will you bear to stand before Him? How will you abide the penetrating and searching look of those "eyes that are as a flame of fire?" Those eyes were once closed in death for sinners. They are now open on all your ways;— they see every hidden recess of your hearts. They now look upon you with the melting of pity, and with the imploring expression, " Ye will not come unto me, that ye might have life." Turn not—O turn not away from this look of beseeching earnestness. You will not be able to shun His look on the throne of judgment. "Every eye shall see him"— riveted by terror or by love. And He to whom you now refuse submission will say—" As for those mine enemies, which would not that I should reign over them, bring hither, and slay them before me."

LECTURE LXIV.

ROMANS XIV. 14—23.

"I know, and am persuaded by the Lord Jesus, that there is nothing unclean of itself: but to him that esteemeth any thing to be unclean, to him it is unclean. But if thy brother be grieved with thy meat, now walkest thou not charitably. Destroy not him with thy meat for whom Christ died. Let not then your good be evil spoken of: for the kingdom of God is not meat and drink; but righteousness, and peace, and joy in the Holy Ghost. For he that in these things serveth Christ is acceptable to God, and approved of men. Let us therefore follow after the things which make for peace, and things wherewith one may edify another. For meat destroy not the work of God. All things indeed are pure; but it is evil for that man who eateth with offence. It is good neither to eat flesh, nor to drink wine, nor any thing whereby thy brother stumbleth, or is offended, or is made weak. Hast thou faith? have it to thyself before God. Happy is he that condemneth not himself in that thing which he alloweth. And he that doubteth is damned if he eat, because he eateth not of faith: for whatsoever is not of faith is sin."

IN the preceding verse, in the form of reproof for the past and admonition for the future, and on the ground of the account to be rendered of their principles and conduct at the judgment-seat of Christ, the Apostle had inculcated an important general duty: "Let us not therefore judge one another any more: but judge this rather, that no man put a stumbling-block, or an occasion to fall, in his brother's way."

He proceeds here to apply this general precept to the particular case: and he speaks with no uncertainty or hesitation. He expresses his "knowledge" and full "persuasion,"—as a principle on which he felt himself at perfect liberty to act, without the slightest demurring of conscience—that there was "nothing unclean of itself."

By this phrase "unclean *of itself,*" he cannot mean merely that the distinction did not lie in the *nature of the thing.* The distinction between "clean" and "unclean" animals *in sacrifice* seems to have existed from the beginning.* This was a distinction made by Jehovah himself when sacrificial rites were instituted. Whether, when the grant of animal food was made to man, the distinction between "clean" and "unclean" which afterwards had place among the Jews was introduced, is a matter of uncertainty. But whether it was or not, there does not appear the smallest ground for believing that it would ever have suggested itself independently of a divine interdict. That men would have discovered, and have acted upon the discovery, that different kinds of food were more and less agreeable and wholesome, is true. But the distinction between "clean" and "unclean" meats proceeds on considerations, whatever they might be, independent of this, or, if in some instances connected with it, not uniformly so. It is obvious that the Apostle's "knowledge" and "persuasion" that the distinction rested not in the nature of the thing would have been nothing at all to the purpose. If God had made the distinction, it was enough. If it still had the sanction of divine authority, no man could be at liberty to dispense with it. The *ground* or *reason* of the law was not the question. The sole inquiry was whether the law, of the existence of which there could be no doubt, was still in force. The distinction had originated, not in the nature of things but in the sovereign will of God. The expression "*of itself,*" therefore, does not mean independently of God's appointment, but independently of the conscientious convictions of His people. Accordingly, he does not say, that although there is nothing "unclean *of itself,*" the will of God has made certain kinds of food "unclean;" but that the uncleanness now depended on the state of mind of the eater—"there is nothing unclean of itself, *but to him that esteemeth any thing*

---

* Gen. viii. 20.

to be unclean, to him it is unclean." A Jew under the old economy could not have spoken thus. The distinction did not then depend at all on any convictions of his mind, on any views of nature or of duty which he might entertain: —it was a matter of explicit divine prescription. The meaning evidently is, that *now* the case was different; that the difference, whence soever arising of old, no longer existed. And, accordingly, in verse twentieth there is a still more unqualified statement of the doing away of the distinction, "*All* things are pure"—or "*clean.*" The duty or the sin now arose, not from any actually existing and obligatory statute, but from the state of the individual's convictions in regard to statutes that had been formerly in force. If any man with the conviction in his conscience that the statute was *not* repealed, should eat of meats which by that statute had been pronounced "unclean," he sinned:—for *to him* they still *were* "unclean." No one was to act against the convictions of his own mind. For such a man to eat would obviously, in the principle of it, be a violation of the divine law, that law still maintaining its authority in his conscience. *More of this on verse twentieth.*

The Apostle's "knowledge" and "persuasion" were "*by the Lord Jesus.*" They rested, that is, *on the authority* of the Lord Jesus:—they were in accordance with the views which he had obtained, and that by revelation, of the nature of the work of Christ and the principles of His kingdom. It amounts to this, that under the New Testament dispensation, the dispensation introduced and established by the Lord Jesus, the distinction in question was done away. There can be no doubt, that his conviction was based on the same authority with *all* that he states as the mind and will of his divine Master.*

The statements of the Lord Jesus during his life, in introducing the spiritual principles of His kingdom, are in harmony with the Apostle's views: "Do ye not perceive, that whatsoever thing from without entereth into the man,

---

* Comp. 1 Cor. xi. 23; xiv. 37 &c.

it cannot defile him; because it entereth not into the heart, but into the belly, and goeth out into the draught, purging all meats? And he said, That which cometh out of the man, that defileth the man. For from within, out of the heart of men, proceed evil thoughts, adulteries, fornications, murders, thefts, covetousness, wickedness, deceit, lasciviousness, an evil eye, blasphemy, pride, foolishness: all these evil things come from within, and defile the man."* I do not mean that our Lord is to be understood as setting aside the Law: but he shows the folly of those who, without adverting to the design of ceremonial distinctions, trusted in their freedom from legal defilements while they were chargeable with such moral pollutions as he here enumerates. While the grand design of the vision of Peter on his being sent for by Cornelius was to do away the distinction between Jew and Gentile, which had even been carried beyond the limits of the Law's prescriptions to an unwarranted and superstitious excess, the effect of spiritual pride rather than of commendable self-jealousy,—the nature of the emblem by which, in the vision, the cessation of this distinction was indicated, conveyed, at the same time, a lesson of the abolition of the difference between "clean" and "unclean" meats.†

The fifteenth verse is evidently addressed to "*the strong:*" —"But if thy brother be grieved with thy meat, now walkest thou not charitably. Destroy not him with thy meat for whom Christ died." The word "*grieved*" does not signify merely his being displeased or annoyed—but his conscience being wounded and tempted, and his mind thus shaken, perplexed and harassed. It may include also the grief arising in any case from his being led to imitate, and so to bring guilt on his spirit—sorrow for the sin, whether in act or only in wish. If "the strong" used their liberty so as to produce any such effects; if they were thus regardless of the scruples of "the weak," glorying over them, showing off their freedom and superiority to prejudice, in contempt of the scruples of their brethren;—they walked not—that is, did

* Mark vii. 18—23.   † See Acts x. 9—16.

not conduct themselves "*charitably,*" or "*according to love.*"*
Christ their common Master's "new commandment" was to
be one of the great badges and distinctive marks of disciple-
ship. "By this shall all men know that ye are my disciples,
if ye have love one to another."† This love is the perfect
bond of Christianity.‡ This love seeks the salvation of its
objects. But the conduct reprobated, having the very opposite tendency, is the most flagrant violation of the law of
love:—"*Destroy not him with thy meat for whom Christ
died.*"

I should lead you quite away from the spirit and scope
of the passage, were I to enter here into doctrinal discussion as to general and particular redemption, or the extent of the atonement made by Christ's death. Here one
is supposed liable to be destroyed, or to perish, "*for whom
Christ died.*"§ I feel very independent of any imputa-
tions of Arminianism, or of any other *ism*, so long as I
have the word of God with me. It should be our only
object, without any partiality for one *ism* more than another, to ascertain what that word teaches. That there is
a sense in which it is true that Christ died *for all men*, I
dare not hesitate to admit, on the simple ground that *the
Bible says it;* and says it in terms of which the meaning
cannot be otherwise explained without unwarrantable sup-
plements or unnatural straining. There are other passages
in which the design of Christ's death is as evidently restricted
to the elect—to those who believe. Both classes of passages
declare truth; and the principle of harmony between them
seems to be that the atonement was a general remedy with a
particular application,—that its sufficiency was universal, its
purposed efficiency limited; that for the great ends of God's
moral government it was general, and formed the ground of

---

* κάτα ἀγάπην. It may be worth noticing, that in most if not all the places where αγαπη is rendered *charity* in our Authorized Version, it is rendered *love* in the older English translations of Wycliffe, Tyndale, and Cranmer. Why our translators altered to *charity* does not appear.—Ed.
† John xiii. 35. ‡ Col. iii. 14. § See also 1 Cor. viii. 11.

the general offers and invitations of the Gospel, while in the special designs of grace it was particular,—its particularity appearing in its sovereign application. On any other principle than this, I feel myself embarrassed by the opposing passages: while this principle harmonizes both. If I am asked, Are you then an advocate of *particular* redemption, or of *general* redemption? I answer, These are mere phrases of scholastic divinity, which, in our inquiries into the meaning of God's word, had better be laid aside as only fettering the mind:—and the reply to the question will depend entirely on an explanation of the phrases. In the sense usually attached to them by their respective adherents, I would say I am *neither*—in the sense which I have just been explaining, I would say I am *both*.

But the spirit of the passage before us is independent of such distinctions. Every one is spoken of, in the New Testament, as a "brother for whom Christ died," even in the more particular sense of the purpose of God's electing love to make his death savingly effectual, who bears the profession of the Gospel, so long as he adheres to that profession, and does not throw it off either by open disavowal or practical inconsistency. And the spirit of the admonition in the verse—"*Destroy not the work of God*," evidently is, Act not in opposition to the design and tendency of the death of Christ. The design and tendency are *salvation:* but to tempt to sin, to be the occasion of committing it, has the very opposite tendency—the tendency to *destruction*. The grace of God may prevent the effect from taking place; but he who does what tends to it is guilty of the evil warned against. And nothing could be better fitted to impress the conviction of an unworthy selfishness, of which they had good cause to be ashamed, than thus setting in contrast the mere gratification of appetite, or, it may be, of the spirit of independence, with the perdition of a soul, and of the soul of one of whom they had reason to believe he was a brother in Christ, an object of His love, a subject of His grace, an heir of His glory. It is the solemn thought of contravening the purpose of God,—of opposing the design of the death of

Christ,—of endangering and ruining one who ought to be the object of special interest and love,—it is this that is held out as a motive to tenderness and caution in dealing with the consciences of others. And it is the *tendency*, not the actual result, that constitutes the criminality. Thus it was in the case of Peter, when he received so severe a rebuke from his Master:—" Get thee behind me, Satan; thou art an offence unto me; for thou savourest not the things that be of God, but those that be of men."* Peter was an "*offence*,"—not merely in exciting *displeasure;* but in as much as, had Jesus acted upon the principle which Peter would have had him to adopt, the consequence must have been the abandonment of the work that was given him to do. He would have spared himself the drinking of his bitter cup; but it must have been at the expense of God's glory and the world's salvation.

An additional motive is suggested in verse sixteenth, "*Let not then your good be evil spoken of.*" The liberty of "the strong," the Apostle admits, was good:—the Christian profession of both parties was good. But the abuse of their liberty,—the uncharitable and disdainful indulgence of it, not only caused it to be " evil spoken of" by those who differed from them :— the heart-burnings and jealousies and contentions to which this gave rise, one party despising the other for their weakness, and the other condemning them in return for their presumption and neglect of divine institutions, or acting against their consciences by conforming to what others did, without conviction:—these things caused their good profession to be "evil spoken of." The world saw not in this the true spirit of Christ. Instead of being led to say, " Behold how these Christians love one another!" they were led to the very opposite reflections—"See how they bite and devour one another! And these are the disciples of the meek and lowly Jesus! Behold the gentleness of Christ! How good and how pleasant, is it for brethren to dwell together in unity!"—Thus their conduct would expose the cause of

---

* Matt. xvi. 23.

Christ to serious and to ironical reproach; while, instead of glorying together in the cross of Christ, and bearing one another's burdens in fulfilment of his law of love, they gloried in their respective differences and cherished mutual ill-will by disputatious reasonings. Instead of this, their conduct should have been in accordance with his admonition to the Philippians:—"Do all things without murmurings and disputings; that ye may be blameless and harmless, the sons of God, without rebuke, in the midst of a crooked and perverse nation, among whom ye shine as lights in the world; holding forth the word of life; that I may rejoice in the day of Christ, that I have not run in vain, neither laboured in vain."*

The exhortation is enforced by the view given in the next verse of the nature of the Gospel kingdom:—"For the kingdom of God is not meat and drink; but righteousness, and peace, and joy in the Holy Ghost."—The "*kingdom of God*" is the New Testament dispensation—the reign of grace—the spiritual kingdom, of which the glorified Saviour is the living and reigning Head, and of which the subjects are all who are "born again,"—who are, as he himself expresses it, "of the truth."†

"It is not *meat and drink.*" This is the *negative* view of its character. The expression is brief but full of meaning. It is taken from the particular subject in hand. The Apostle would have said the very same of any external observances of the ancient ritual. The spirit of the expression identifies with that of some more extended contrasts between the new dispensation and that of Moses which occur in other passages.‡ Such passages, however, are by no means to be understood as if under the old covenant there was nothing spiritual, either in requisition or in fact, in the character of the worshippers—nothing but external service. Many believed in the Messiah to come, and served God acceptably, "in spirit

---

* Phil. ii. 14—16.
† See John xviii. 36, 37. Of this kingdom the general nature or genius is *internal*—Luke xvii. 20, 21.
‡ As in Heb. ix. 9—14.

and in truth." That God who "is a Spirit" *always* "sought such to worship him." But still it was comparatively a carnal and worldly dispensation. Spiritual truths were wrapt up in outward symbols. All its institutions served only "as an example and shadow of heavenly things." The kingdom to which it was introductory is on the contrary characterised here as "*righteousness, and peace, and joy in the Holy Ghost.*"—You will at once perceive from the eighteenth verse that these are characteristics of the *subjects* of this kingdom. The grand design of the Gospel is to form a people for God, to show forth His praise, not by the strict observance of a merely outward ritual, by the "tithing of mint and anise and cummin," by abstinence from "meats and drinks," by the scrupulous celebration of "days and months and times and years" dedicated to acts of external service, but by the cultivation and display of the principles of righteousness and the spirit of peace and joy.

"*Righteousness*" here is general conformity to the will of God, which, under the influence of "faith working by love," appears in every one who believes the Gospel.* The entire New Testament, in all its practical injunctions, and all its delineations of Christian character, might be quoted to show that there is no subjection to Christ and no interest in the blessings of his kingdom, without personal righteousness.†

With righteousness is associated "*peace.*" God is "the God of peace;" Christ is "the Prince of peace;" the Gospel is "the Gospel of peace;" the "fruit of the Spirit is peace." It seems to be not so much the *blessing* of peace as the *spirit* of peace that is here intended,—not the peace that is inwardly enjoyed through faith in the blood of Christ, but peace as a disposition of the mind, manifested in the outward conduct; though the two indeed are very closely connected. This spirit of peace is very often enjoined as an essential

---

* See Luke i. 74, 75; words which celebrate the commencement of the approaching reign of heaven, and strikingly describe its characteristic nature—1 Peter ii. 24.

† Matt. v. 20.

part of the influence of the Gospel and of the character of all who believe it.*

"*Joy in the Holy Ghost*" is the joy which the Holy Ghost produces and sustains; and He produces and sustains it by the truth.† It is joy in God; joy in Christ,—in all that he is and in all the offices which he sustains;—joy in hope; joy in the exercise of those holy affections which the Spirit inspires; joy in the ways of God, and in the possession of the Spirit as the earnest of the promised inheritance, the pledge of life eternal. This joy is a duty, as well as a privilege, being one of the ways in which the nature of the Gospel evinces itself. It will appear in a cheerful serenity of temper; a sunshine in the soul of him who enjoys it; not, however, confined to his own breast, but diffusing its cheering influence on all around him.

These three things, taken comprehensively, include the sum of what is required for human character and human happiness:—verse 18. "For he that in these things serveth Christ is acceptable to God, and approved of men."—"*He that in these things*"—in the principles and practice of righteousness, and in the spirit of peace and joy—"*serveth Christ.*" He is LORD. This shows the true nature of Christian obedience. It is the service of Christ: and the principle of service to him as our *Lord* is love to him as our Saviour.— By the voice from the excellent glory, both at his baptism and on the holy mount, Jehovah testified of Jesus, "This is my beloved Son, in whom I am well-pleased." When Jesus was on earth he said, "If any man serve me, him will my Father honour."‡ He who said, "Hear ye HIM," takes delight in the service that is rendered to Christ. He who, from faith and love, serves Christ is "*acceptable to God:*" and no service but what is rendered to Christ, or to God in his name, is or can be "acceptable."

But how is it added—"*and approved of men?*" We at

---

* Eph. iv. 1—3, 31, 32, is only a specimen of many passages of like import. The two, righteousness and peace, are connected—Jam. iii. 13—18.

† 1 Thess. i. 6; Rom. xv. 13.   ‡ John xii. 26.

once understand how such service should command the approbation and conciliate the favour of fellow-believers. But is the saying to be confined to *them?* I should think *not.* The principles of the Gospel may be held in dislike and contempt by the world; and yet there are lights in which the consistent display of the practical influence of those principles cannot but commend itself to general approval and admiration. The service of Christ includes all the practical virtues that render a man an estimable and useful member of society. It comprehends "whatsoever things are true, whatsoever things are honest, whatsoever things are just, whatsoever things are pure, whatsoever things are lovely, whatsoever things are of good report."* The man who lives thus is esteemed by the world *in spite* of the obnoxious principles from which the effects arise. There is moreover in a *consistent* character what commands the approbation of all who witness it. The world are very good judges of such consistency. The contrary they may flatter with their lips, but they inwardly despise and condemn it. He who, in righteousness and peace and joy, serveth Christ, is one who will stand the test of his profession;—and whatever is acceptable to God is what ought to be "approved of men." And men often do secretly approve of what they neither praise with their lips nor follow in their lives.

The practical use of all this we have in verse nineteenth: " Let us therefore follow after the things which make for peace, and things wherewith one may *edify* another." "*Edification*" signifies growth in all the principles, affections, and holy habits of the spiritual life. All the institutions of social as well as of personal religion are designed for this end. "Peace" and "edification" are inseparably connected, and will always be found proportionate to each other. Edification can be promoted only in proportion as peace is maintained. This is the only soil in which the virtues of the Christian life are ever seen to flourish. Hence we are solemnly enjoined to "*follow after* the things which make for

* Phil. iv. 8.

peace, and things wherewith one may edify another"—to make it a matter of serious consideration, and of studious, earnest, unceasing endeavour. We go not, perhaps, too far when we say that there is nothing which Christians should not be willing to sacrifice for "peace and edification," short of "a good conscience." "Seek peace, then, and pursue it:" "Edify one another in love."

The spirit of the *twentieth* verse is precisely the same as that of the *fifteenth:*—" For meat destroy not the work of God. All things indeed are pure; but it is evil for that man who eateth with offence."—" *The work of God*" is evidently what God by his Spirit has effected in the hearts and lives of sinners—which constitute them in Scripture phraseology " God's workmanship."* The spirit of this, then, is— Put the gratification of what you eat and drink in comparison with tempting, ensnaring, and endangering the soul of a fellow-christian—placing his salvation in jeopardy,—depriving him of that final blessedness for which "God hath wrought him," by inducing him to "make shipwreck of a good conscience!" The man who hesitates for an instant between the two parts of such an alternative most assuredly gives evidence that he "has not the spirit of Christ," and is "none of his."

"All things are pure" or clean; "but it is evil to eat *with offence;*" that is, as before explained, when the use of our liberty is a stumbling-block to "the weak,"—an "occasion to fall" in the way of any of our brethren. "It is *evil,*" because it is contrary to love.† It is evil, because disregard of another's conscience is in fact disregard of the sacred principle of subjection to God; and is thus a making light of divine authority.

The converse of this is in verse twenty-first:—" It is good neither to eat flesh, nor to drink wine, nor anything whereby thy brother stumbleth, or is offended, or is made weak." This is an important principle. If in anything our own consciences are bound by divine authority—then we must on no

---

* Eph. ii. 10; Isa. xliii. 21. † Ver. 15.

account, for the sake of others, either do what God forbids, or abstain from doing what God enjoins. The maxim before us relates to things which are not obligatory; which we feel we are at liberty to do, but which we are not bound to do; which we are at liberty to abstain from but not forbidden to do; things in which there is a *may* but not a *must*. We are not in such cases to mind only ourselves. We are to pay tender regard to the consciences of others. We are chargeable with sin, if we either do what we *may* abstain from, or abstain from what we may do, when the doing or the abstaining will throw a temptation in the way of a single conscience. If our brother "*stumbleth or is offended*"—that is, tempted or caused to sin; or is "*made weak*"—his mind shaken and unhinged; his faith and resolution enfeebled, and an opportunity thus given to the adversary to lead him captive:—in these circumstances, we must deny ourselves for our brethren's sake.*

The same spirit is inculcated in verse *twenty-second:*— "Hast thou faith? have it to thyself before God. Happy is he that condemneth not himself in that thing which he alloweth." "Hast thou *faith?*" It is very evident that *faith* here does not mean the faith of the Gospel, but *the conviction of the authority of God in the particular case*. It is the "persuasion" in verse fifth. He speaks of some as "*weak* in the faith." Hast thou faith? may signify Hast thou that strength of faith that enables thee to see thy liberty from the yoke of bondage? It is the conviction of this liberty that is evidently meant. And of this the Apostle says—"*Have it to thyself before God.*" This does not mean keep your sentiments entirely to yourselves; say nothing about them; let them be between yourselves and God:—a favourite sentiment with multitudes who dislike religion; who cannot endure to hear about it; and who are ever insisting upon the propriety of every man's keeping his religion to himself, as a thing with which his neighbours have nothing to do. I need hardly say that this is not a sentiment of Paul's. The import of the

---

* See for the same principle 1 Cor. viii. 13; x. 23—33.

words before us is—in regard to the faith or persuasion of liberty—" Hold it with respect to thyself* before God." The preceding exhortation is not an exhortation to give it up:— it is, to use it, but to use it *in love*—to use it, that is, on all occasions to the glory of God, when it can be done without offence or stumbling to others. " Hold it *as to thyself*"—but do not seek to impose it or to force it on others—nor condemn those who cannot see as you see. " Happy is he that *condemneth not himself* in that thing which he alloweth:"— whose *conscience is fully satisfied* in that which he alloweth ; who has no misgivings, but who, with an enlightened mind, feels his ground firm: for even the secret suspicions of conscience as well as its more decided reproaches are exquisitely painful. Either this is the meaning—or Happy is he who, while he is sensible of his liberty as a valuable privilege, " condemneth not himself "—has no charge of conscience against himself for the uncharitable, contemptuous, and improper use of it. It is the happiness of a clear, well-informed, simple, unembarrassed conscience—such as Paul himself describes:—" For our rejoicing is this, the testimony of our conscience, that in simplicity and godly sincerity, not with fleshly wisdom, but by the grace of God, we have had our conversation in the world, and more abundantly to you-ward."†

That the former of the two interpretations given of the twenty-second verse is the true one, is likely from verse *twenty-third*, where the state of mind opposite to that of clear and full conviction is introduced—" But he that *doubteth* "—more properly, " he that maketh a difference "‡—who still holds the distinction—or who is not clear in his conscience as to his freedom from it—" is condemned if he eat:" and the reason is—" he eateth not of faith ;" and then this is generalized into a principle of conduct—a law of the kingdom—" for *whatsoever is not of faith is sin.*"

" *Faith* " here has the same import as before. They greatly mistake who suppose the Apostle to mean that the *faith of*

---

* κάτα σεαυτὸν ἴχι.   † 2 Cor. i. 12.   ‡ ἰδιακρινόμενος.

the gospel must be the principle of all that is acceptable to God—of all right obedience. When I say they mistake, I do not mean that they adopt a false sentiment, but that they misapprehend the import of this passage. The sentiment may be true;* but it is not the sentiment of this verse. The faith in this maxim is *a conviction of the will of God:*— and the maxim is, that whatever proceeds not from this conviction "is sin." So that it is not enough that we refrain from doing a thing when we are convinced that it is *not* the will of God; we must refrain unless we are convinced that it *is*. Even uncertainty or suspicion is a sufficient reason for refraining. Let us never treat conscience with lightness,— never trifle with the will of God. Let us inquire after that will, that we may know it; let us not act *till* we know it; and *whenever* we do know it, let us act. We may apply the maxim to all cases in which there is room for hesitation, in which we feel "*not quite sure.*" We may, in many cases, be tempted by others into a step or into a course in which *they* see no harm; but if we do not see *our own* way clear, we must by no means comply. It is wrong, very wrong on their part to attempt to persuade us.

But does the converse of the maxim hold? If whatsoever is *not* of faith is sin; does it follow, that whatsoever *is* of faith is duty? That were a very false and perilous conclusion indeed—unsettling the law of God and the principles of duty, and leaving all to be determined by every man's private opinions. This would be to justify the most enormous evils —even all the evils that have arisen from an ill-informed and misguided conscience. Christ says to his disciples:— "They shall put you out of the synagogues: yea, the time cometh, that whosoever killeth you will think that he doeth God service."† And Paul, in consistency with this statement, says of himself:—" I verily thought that I ought to do many things contrary to the name of Jesus of Nazareth."‡ But did this justify him? No: he *ought* to have known better. And when he attained true self-knowledge he per-

---

* Heb. xi. 6; Gal. v. 6, &c.   † John xvi. 2.   ‡ Acts xxvi. 9.

ceived and owned his sin—even that pride and worldliness of heart that had withstood and resisted the truth. He felt that the principles by which he had been actuated were such as, instead of vindicating, constituted him the " chief of sinners." It would be fearful in the extreme to invert the maxim, and justify whatever any man under the influence of a mind misguided by a deceitful and wicked heart might fancy to be duty or to be lawful. Even the testimony of the believer's conscience to his integrity, and innocence of charges brought against him, is no infallible proof of such innocence. Our first duty, then, is to have conscience well-informed from the word of God, and never in any case to anticipate, far less to violate, its decisions.

LECTURE LXV.

ROMANS XV. 1—7.

"We then that are strong ought to bear the infirmities of the weak, and not to please ourselves. Let every one of us please his neighbour for his good to edification. For even Christ pleased not himself; but, as it is written, The reproaches of them that reproached thee fell on me. For whatsoever things were written aforetime were written for our learning; that we, through patience and comfort of the scriptures, might have hope. Now the God of patience and consolation grant you to be like-minded one toward another according to Christ Jesus; that ye may with one mind and one mouth glorify God, even the Father of our Lord Jesus Christ. Wherefore receive ye one another, as Christ also received us, to the glory of God."

THIS is a continuation of the same subject, of which the discussion commenced at the beginning of the preceding chapter. In the first verse, an inference is drawn from something that had gone before—"We, *then*, that are strong ought to bear the infirmities of the weak, and not to please ourselves." This conclusion seems to be deduced especially from what the Apostle had said respecting the serious consequences which might result from "offending the weak"—from tempting them by our conduct to violate the dictates of their consciences, and so to endanger their souls.*

To "*bear* the infirmities of the weak," is opposed to "setting them at nought,"—treating them with harshness, and pride, and supercilious disregard. It means to deal gently with their scruples, holding themselves in affectionate esteem, as conscientious although feeble-minded, and offering even

* Chap. xiv. 15, 20—23.

their prejudices, as we may reckon them, no unnecessary violence; living with them in peace and love, in the fellowship of the Gospel.—Opposed to "bearing *their infirmities*" is "*pleasing ourselves.*" To please ourselves is to act according to our own views of things, our own inclinations, without consideration of the consequences to others. It is to gratify our selfish principles—our pride, for example, of superior discernment and strength of mind; which would tempt us to say disdainfully, Let them do as they will, we will follow our own course—Who would heed such weakness? This is often a strong temptation. Of few things are we more apt to be proud than of our superior discernment. We like vastly to show it off; and there is nothing, we know, that serves that end so effectually as setting it in practical contrast with the weakness of others.—Or in such a case as that chiefly dwelt upon in the context, "the strong" might "please themselves" by preferring the gratification of their own appetites to accommodation to the conscientious scruples of their weak-minded brethren. "Why," say they, "should we be debarred the use of any description of food we like, when we are satisfied ourselves that there is no difference, merely to please the whims of those who do not see so far as we do? we will take our own way, and eat what we choose." That such a motive might operate, sensual and unworthy as it was, the language cited from the preceding chapter is sufficient to show.*—Or, further, we may "please ourselves" by consulting simply our own convenience; doing what suits us at the time, without regard to what others may think or feel, or be tempted to do,—saying, It is our own conscience and not that of another that is to regulate our conduct. We don't interfere with other people's consciences, and they have no right to interfere with ours; why should we be cramped and put to inconvenience in this way?

The general principle is, that selfishness ought to be repressed; that even in regard to things which in our own view are lawful and right,—in cases wherein our refraining

---

* Chap. xiv. 20, 21, with which compare 1 Cor. viii. 13.

violates no obligation of duty, and our acting would prove injurious to others,—self-denial is to be exercised, and self-will and self-indulgence laid under control.—Instead of making self-pleasing our end (v. 2), "Let every one of us please his neighbour for his good to edification." It is quite evident, that there are limits to the principle of pleasing our neighbour, as well as to that of pleasing ourselves: and indeed the limits are suggested by the very expression here used—"*for his good to edification.*"

There is, first, the limit of *sin in ourselves.* When we are convinced that He who is the acknowledged Lord of the conscience *requires* us to do a thing—then it would be sin in us to decline or abstain from the doing of it. No consideration of other consciences can release our own from any positive obligation. We must neither do what Christ forbids, nor refrain from doing what Christ enjoins, for any consideration whatever. There is nothing that can set aside the express requisitions of His will.

There is, secondly, the limit of *sin in them.* While we must not commit the one, neither must we encourage the other. The case in question was not one of sin. It was neither sin in "the weak" to maintain the distinctions of meats nor was it sin in "the strong" to abstain from eating what they were convinced it was lawful for them to partake. Had there been sin on either the one side or the other, the case would have been entirely altered. Though "the strong" are commanded to "bear the *infirmities* of the weak," they could never be commanded to bear their *sins*—to treat with indulgence their transgressions of the divine will. Pleasing their neighbour *in sin* would have been anything but "*for his good to edification.*" "The strong" would have been reprehensible in acting such a part as would have tempted "the weak" to sin by violating the dictates of their own consciences; or such a part as would have engendered the exercise in their bosoms of unchristian tempers and feelings toward "the strong." This is the spirit of the whole preceding chapter.*

---

* It is expressed briefly—1 Cor. x. 32, 33, which is in harmony with

"For his good to edification" means—for his good, for *his* edification, and for *general edification*.* The principle laid down was, in its personal application in particular cases, for the good and edification of the individual:—the principle, considered *at large*, was in its effects conducive to the general good—the general edification of the Church of Christ. There could be no edification without love; and there could be no love without mutual forbearance—in the exercise of humble-mindedness.

We have next a high example, even the highest of all, adduced, for our imitation:—verse 3. "For even Christ pleased not himself; but, as it is written, The reproaches of them that reproached thee fell on me." The words are quoted from Psalm lxix. 9, "For the zeal of thine house hath eaten me up; and the reproaches of them that reproached thee are fallen upon me." That the psalm refers to Christ this quotation shows.†

Jesus "*pleased not himself.*" Mark his frequent words— "I can of mine own self do nothing: as I hear I judge; and my judgment is just; because I seek not mine own will, but the will of the Father which hath sent me:"—"For I came down from heaven, not to do mine own will, but the will of him that sent me."‡ It was in executing the will of the Father that sent him that the words quoted were verified,— that he endured the contradiction of sinners against himself. The revilers of God reviled *him*. It was in *God's* service and for *God's* glory that he "endured reproach"—reproach that "broke his heart:" and it was for *our* salvation. In both respects, he "pleased not himself." Had Christ "pleased himself"—had he acted on the principle of a selfish regard to his own happiness, he never had left the bosom of the Father and the independent blessedness of his own eternity, and taken

---

the general principle laid down by the Apostle for his own conduct— 1 Cor. ix. 19—23.
* *Bonum*, genus, *edificatio*, species.—*Bengel.*—ED.
† Compare John ii. 17. Also compare verse 4 with John xv. 25; verse 21 with Matt. xxvii. 34 and John xix. 29.
‡ John v. 30; vi. 38.

upon him our nature, and "humbled himself, and become obedient unto death, even the death of the cross." His example is, in this very particular, held up to our special imitation—" Look not every man on his own things, but every man also on the things of others. Let this mind be in you, which was also in Christ Jesus."* Such is the spirit we are called to imitate—such the example we are called to copy. And the force of the motive lies in the obligation under which this disinterested and wonderful conduct of the divine Redeemer has laid us. When the Apostle says, " For even Christ pleased not himself; but, as it is written, The reproaches of them that reproached thee fell on me," he says what could not fail to tell instantly and persuasively on the heart and conscience of every believer in his name. The mention of *His* example was fitted to cover with the blushes of shame all who were conscious to themselves of any feeling approaching to high-mindedness and disregard of others. Those who "pleased themselves" acted on a principle the very opposite of that by which their divine Lord was influenced in what he had done for *them*. Had He acted toward them on the self-regarding principle by which they were disposed to regulate their behaviour to their fellow-believers, they themselves must have perished. Nothing, therefore, could be fitted more effectually to bring down the disdainful loftiness of those who were inclined to set at nought their brethren:—they were not in this "walking worthy of the Lord." They were not imitating Him. They were not giving evidence of their having his Spirit. They were grievously dishonouring Him, and preferring themselves not only to their fellow-christians, but to Him. Besides, those whom they were thus despising were included with themselves in the end of Christ's death—the joint objects of His love, the joint subjects of His grace, for whom, as well as for *them*, He endured reproach, and submitted to all his sufferings. In *this* view, the motive becomes nearly akin to that in the preceding chapter:—" If thy brother be grieved with thy meat,

* Phil. ii. 4—8.

now walkest thou not charitably. Destroy not him with thy meat for whom Christ died."*

Verse *fourth* seems, in its connexion, as if suggested by the prophetic language just quoted from the sixty-ninth psalm,—"*For* whatsoever things were written aforetime were written for our learning; that we, through patience and comfort of the scriptures, might have hope." All that the prophets testified concerning "the sufferings of Christ and the glory that should follow"—(and to Him they all gave witness, so that "the testimony of Jesus is the spirit of prophecy") was written, not only to animate the hopes of the people of God before the fulness of time; but also for the "*learning*," or spiritual instruction and edification, of those who should come after; inasmuch as it is by a comparison of the predictions with their corresponding events, that our faith is confirmed in the truth of the Gospel, and our hopes sustained as to the fulfilment of all that yet remains in promise. And few things are more edifying than comparing the events connected with the birth and life, the miracles and doctrines; the sufferings, death, resurrection and ascension of Jesus and the "prophecies that went before" concerning him. But the sentiment is a general one. Paul applies it to particular Israelitish institutes, deriving from them practical principles of permanent application:—"Say I these things as a man? or saith not the law the same also. For it is written in the law of Moses, Thou shalt not muzzle the mouth of the ox that treadeth out the corn. Doth God take care for oxen? Or saith he it altogether for our sakes? For our sakes, no doubt, this is written: that he that ploweth should plow in hope; and that he that thresheth in hope should be partaker of his hope."† He applies it also to the details of the history of Israel and of God's dealings with them in the wilderness:—"Now all these things happened unto them for ensamples: and they are written for our admonition, upon whom the ends of the world are come."‡ In various instances, in the Epistle to the Galatians, he derives

---

* Chap. xiv. 15.　　† 1 Cor. ix. 8—10.　　‡ 1 Cor. x. 11.

both illustration and argument from the incidents of the Old Testament revelation:—and he lays down the general principle as to the whole of that revelation (for it is of *it* he there speaks) when he says, "All scripture is given by inspiration of God, and is profitable for doctrine, for reproof, for correction, for instruction in righteousness: that the man of God may be perfect, throughly furnished unto all good works."*

And the end of all the "learning" we thence derive is, —"*that we through patience and comfort of the Scriptures might have hope.*" The "patience and comfort of the Scriptures" can mean nothing else than "the patience and comfort" which the Scriptures impart and maintain; or which are practically exemplified in their records for our encouragement:—that we might "*have* hope"—that is, that we might retain it in exercise unto the end;—that animated by "patience" and "consolation" derived from the Holy Scriptures we might "hold fast our confidence" till we obtain the "great recompense of reward." Both the doctrines, and the examples of Scripture are fitted to produce this effect. It is on the faith of its doctrines that our hope rests; and by the recorded instances of the power of faith and hope our spirits are quickened, and our souls encouraged to perseverance.

We have the example of *Christ himself* in *this* particular also—"Let us run with patience the race that is set before us, looking unto Jesus the author and finisher of our faith; who for the joy that was set before him endured the cross, despising the shame, and is set down at the right hand of the throne of God. For consider him that endured such contradiction of sinners against himself, lest ye be wearied and faint in your minds."† And the things "written aforetime" contain numerous intimations of this part of his character, which is so beautifully exemplified in the facts of his life on earth.

There are many bonds of union among the people of

* 2 Tim. iii. 16, 17. † Heb. xii. 1—4.

God.* One of these—one which existed then, and which has ever since existed, though not always in the same degree, is *fellowship in suffering;* and there is no time when the union of love and sympathy is so valuable and necessary as a time of common trial. Nothing, therefore, could be more natural than the manner in which the Apostle introduces "patience" and "comfort" and "hope" in connexion with exhortations to love and concord, and in which he presents his prayer for the prevalence of such love and concord amongst them—verse 5. "Now the God of patience and consolation grant you to be like-minded one toward another, according to Christ Jesus."

"*The God of patience and consolation.*" This is one amongst many brief but delightful descriptions of the divine Being,—descriptions which convey to the soul the richest encouragement. The very reading of the words—the very repeating of them in the ear of the afflicted—has a soothing power over the heart. He is "the God of *patience*," as being himself infinitely distinguished by the exercise of long-suffering and forbearance—"The Lord, The Lord God, merciful and gracious, longsuffering, and abundant in goodness and truth."† The whole history of the dealings of Jehovah with Israel forms a comment on this part of His character. Nay, what is His daily conduct towards our fallen world at large but a continued unceasing miracle of long-suffering kindness? He thus exemplifies the "patience" He inculcates. By the influence of the Spirit, He produces and maintains the grace in the hearts of His people. And as this must be the sense in which he is here called the "*God of consolation,*" it is probably in the same sense that he is called the "God of patience." He is himself the Comforter of his children—the Author of all the inward peace which their souls enjoy. He gives in his word the sources and means of comfort; and he opens the heart to their influence. His truths are full of comfort; and his Spirit brings them home in their refreshing and invigorating effi-

---

* Comp. Eph. iv. 1—3.   † Exod. xxxiv. 6: also Psal. ciii. 8, 9.

cacy. When gospel times and gospel discoveries are predicted of old, they are introduced with—"Comfort ye, comfort ye my people, saith your God."* "Sing, O heavens; and be joyful, O earth; and break forth into singing, O mountains: for the Lord hath comforted his people, and will have mercy upon his afflicted."† "The Spirit of the Lord God is upon me; because the Lord hath anointed me to preach good tidings unto the meek; he hath sent me to bind up the broken-hearted, to proclaim liberty to the captives, and the opening of the prison to them that are bound; to proclaim the acceptable year of the Lord, and the day of vengeance of our God; to comfort all that mourn; to appoint unto them that mourn in Zion, to give unto them beauty for ashes, the oil of joy for mourning, the garment of praise for the spirit of heaviness."‡ God is the God of "patience" by his being the God of "consolation;" for it is the communication of the "consolation" that inspires and maintains the patience. And he is the God of both patience and consolation, as being the Author of those Scriptures from which they are both derived; and the Giver of the Spirit by which the Scriptures are opened and applied in their saving and gladdening energy. The same character is given of God by this Apostle as the result not of inspiration only but of his own personal experience:—"Blessed be God, even the Father of our Lord Jesus Christ, the Father of mercies, and the God of all comfort; who comforteth us in all our tribulation, that we may be able to comfort them which are in any trouble by the comfort wherewith we ourselves are comforted of God. For as the sufferings of Christ abound in us, so our consolation also aboundeth by Christ."§

God, the "God of patience and consolation," is the Author of *every* gracious disposition. Hence the Apostle's petition in verse fifth—"Now the God of patience and consolation grant you to be like-minded one toward another according to Christ Jesus." If "*like-minded*" were to be under-

---

* Isa. xl. 1.   † Isa. xlix. 13.   ‡ Isa. lxi. 1—3.
§ 2 Cor. i. 3—7.

stood as meaning *one in sentiment*, the Apostle must then be interpreted as intimating his desire that God might enlarge the minds and strengthen the faith of "the weak," so that they might "see eye to eye" with himself and others to whom it had been given to recognize the doing away in Christ of the ancient typical and temporary ceremonial. But the expression refers more to *affection* than to sentiment. The whole discussion shows this. It proceeds on the supposition of both retaining their respective views, and following their respective practices, but feeling and acting towards one another on the principles of mutual forbearance and love: each attending to the duty enjoined upon them respectively.*

"*According to Christ Jesus:*"—that is, according to his *example;* for he is the pattern of forbearance and love: according to his *will*—which is the law of love: and according to the *influence of his truth*—which is the revelation of love. The faith of that truth fills the soul with a spirit of lowly humility and tender affection. These feelings are a part of "the fruits of the Spirit." They come from God. They are produced by a due impression of the importance of of the "one faith." *The truth*—the "truth as it is in Jesus," was the bond of union amongst these disciples,—both "the weak" and "the strong." They ought to have felt that this bond was much more powerful in uniting them, than any diversity in their conscientious views and practices on minor points was in keeping them asunder. And the same remark applies still to the points in which believers differ. If they felt as they ought, not the trivial nature of these—for they may in their place be far from trivial; and nothing, indeed, which our divine Master has thought it worth *His* while to make known or to enjoin, can his people ever be warranted in regarding as not worth their while to attend to:—but if they felt as they ought the greatly superior importance of the truth in which they agree, and which constitutes the real bond of their union; the very existence of differences would render the

* Chap. xiv. 3, &c.

power of that truth in knitting their hearts together in love the more strikingly apparent. We may estimate the power of moral principles as we estimate the amount of forces in mechanics. If there are two forces, one uniting and the other divellent, the power of the uniting is rendered the more conspicuous by its overcoming the divellent:—and the greater the number and amount of forces that are overcome, the more striking is the superiority of that which, in spite of them all, holds the objects together. Thus, if Christians were sufficiently sensible of the paramount grandeur and importance of *the one uniting truth*, their very differences might be made to contribute to the glory of that truth, by manifesting the more impressively its binding and conciliating influence. I do not say they would *think nothing* of their differences; for this would be inconsistent with the very principle I am now illustrating—forasmuch as, if they thought nothing of them, the truth would have no resistance from that quarter to overcome:—but while they give the points in which they differ their due weight, they would feel the truth overpowering them all, and show to the world, that notwithstanding those differences, they still felt themselves "all one in Christ Jesus."

This unity of heart and spirit, the Apostle next teaches them, was necessary to unity of *worship*—verse 6. "That we may with one mind and one mouth glorify God, even the Father of our Lord Jesus Christ." As the "Father of our Lord Jesus Christ," He is *our* Father.* The relation in which he is thus presented to us, is the only one in which, as guilty creatures, we can acceptably serve Him. In this character He is worshipped in the "assemblies of his saints." Regard to Him as our common Father in Christ Jesus constitutes us brethren to one another—members together of one family. All animosity and strife are inconsistent with this union, and serve to mar, to undermine, and to destroy it. This was sadly the case in the Corinthian church. It was divided into parties, under various leaders—so that, in-

* John xx. 17.

stead of all saying "I am of Christ," they forgot their union in their difference, and one said, "I am of Paul, and I of Apollos, and I of Cephas, and I of Christ." But not this verse only—other parts of Scripture also teach us, that we cannot present to God acceptable worship, while we are under the influence of an unforgiving and bitter spirit—the spirit of animosity and variance.*

When we worship God, we appear as one; and if, under this appearance, we are not in reality one in heart, the appearance is hypocritical, which the God of truth cannot regard with complacency. "There is *one body*"—and in glorifying God, this "one body" should have "*one mind and one mouth*." There should be such unity of sentiment and feeling, that what one utters will be expressive of what all feel;—there being a spiritual sympathy among the united members of the body of Christ. And surely, my brethren, nothing can more impressively teach us the necessity of pure communion in the churches. When this is not attended to, how can there ever be a manifestation of the lovely scene supposed in this verse?—How can there be a "glorifying of God, even the Father of our Lord Jesus Christ with *one mind and one mouth*," when those who are received into fellowship who are not believers in Christ, have no spiritual relation to those that are his, and must be strangers to the sympathy of sentiment and feeling which is the very soul of the social worship of the churches? Where there *is* unity of mind and heart, it will impart freedom and fervour to social devotion. He who is the mouth of the assembly in addressing the divine throne, will then enjoy the delightful consciousness that he is uttering, in adoration and thanksgiving, and confession, and humiliation and petition, not what he himself feels only, but what finds a responding sensibility in every bosom around him. When he says, "Our Father, who art in heaven," he feels that he is addressing God as one of a family, all whose members experience common wants, common affections, and common desires. The contrary—the

---

* See Matt. vi. 12; v. 23, 24; xviii. 19, 20, &c.

impression, or even the suspicion, that those with whom he seems to plead, are without the "spiritual understanding" and the spiritual sensibility of God's children, cannot fail to have a most disheartening, deadening, freezing influence upon his soul. It is the union of kindred spirits that is the animation, the zest and relish of all social worship—of all the "fellowship of the saints."

Hence the Apostle adds—in order that they might realize the pleasure and the profit of social religion, and at the same time set before the world an exhibition of loveliness:—verse 7. "Wherefore receive ye one another, as Christ also received us, to the glory of God."

There ought to be no room for questions supposed as to the meaning of the command to "*receive* one another." It can be nothing less than cordially welcoming one another, not only in private intercourse but in public Christian communion—the communion of the Church. It is in the last degree unreasonable to suppose anything less than this intended, in such a connexion. There were to be no divisions, no heart-burnings, no alienating and unbrotherly schisms amongst them, on account of the differences subsisting in sentiment and practice which are the subjects of the whole discussion. They were "one in Christ Jesus." If they acknowledged one another's relation to Him, there could not be on earth a grosser inconsistency than to refuse the recognition of their relation to each other. The expression used shows the extent of the communion included in "receiving one another"—"*as Christ also hath received us.*" It must be evident, that when the Apostle uses the pronoun *us* here, he does not mean himself and others *in distinction from* the two parties he is addressing. He comprehends under it the parties themselves—both of them alike—and associates himself with them. In this lies the charm and force of the appeal. Christ had received both parties alike. If they admitted this, how could they act on the principle of excluding one another? If it is incongruous for those who are Christ's to appear as one in Christian communion with those who are *not* Christ's; is it less incongruous for those who are his to be holding one another at a distance, and appearing as distinct, when in reality, and whether they are openly recognizing the union or not, they *are one?* I am utterly at a loss to conceive of any scriptural principle on which I can refuse to hold fellowship in "the communion of saints,"—in every form of that communion, private and public—with one of whom I have reason to believe that Christ has received him, and with whom, consequently, I expect, in Christ's presence, to hold the higher and holier communion of eternity. This seems to be the most incongruous of all incongruities—the most anomalous of all anomalies. The principles or grounds on which the believers here addressed were to receive one another have been already illustrated. They are the principles of charity and conscientious forbearance—each party giving the other credit for being influenced by the same regard to divine authority.

Their so receiving one another was—as their common reception by Christ was—"*to the glory of God.*" In the reception of sinners by Christ, God is glorified. So testifies the Saviour himself:—" Father, the hour is come; glorify thy Son, that thy Son also may glorify thee: as thou hast given him power over all flesh, that he should give eternal life to as many as thou hast given him."* And this accords with the general testimony of Scripture.† If God was thus glorified in their being received by Christ, they dishonoured God in refusing to "receive one another"—in not owning those whom Christ had received. On the other hand, their "receiving one another" was glorifying to God as being in harmony with His own mind. It could not but be dishonouring to Him, when they showed a mind so presumptuously contrary to His, as to keep aloof from those whom He received and acknowledged. The manifestation, too, of the principles of love and unity was to the glory of God; these being the principles of His gospel, and in accordance with its design. They glorified Him by unanimity in their worship—the fervour of united thanksgiving and prayer;

* John xvii. 1, 2. † Isa. lxi. 3; Eph. i. 6, 12.

and by harmonious co-operation in the efforts of combined zeal. Union also tends to promote fruitfulness; and *this* is to the glory of God. "Herein," says Jesus, "is my Father glorified, that ye bear much fruit; so shall ye be my disciples." "And this I pray," says Paul, "that your love may abound yet more and more in knowledge and in all judgment: that ye may approve things that are excellent; that ye may be sincere, and without offence, till the day of Christ; being filled with the fruits of righteousness, which are by Jesus Christ, unto the glory and praise of God."* That the social union of love and mutual excitement tends to promote the productiveness of God's people in the fruits of righteousness all experience testifies. "As iron sharpeneth iron; so a man sharpeneth the countenance of his friend." The exercises of social religion keep alive the spirit and energy of devotion; and by mutual admonition and exhortation, believers "consider one another to provoke unto love and to good works."

* John xv. 8; Phil. i. 9—11.

LECTURE LXVI.

Romans xv. 8—13.

"Now I say, that Jesus Christ was a minister of the circumcision for the truth of God, to confirm the promises made unto the fathers: and that the Gentiles might glorify God for his mercy; as it is written, For this cause I will confess to thee among the Gentiles, and sing unto thy name. And again he saith, Rejoice, ye Gentiles, with his people. And again, Praise the Lord, all ye Gentiles; and laud him, all ye people. And again Esaias saith, There shall be a root of Jesse, and he that shall rise to reign over the Gentiles; in him shall the Gentiles trust. Now the God of hope fill you with all joy and peace in believing, that ye may abound in hope, through the power of the Holy Ghost."

IN this passage, the Apostle is evidently pursuing the same end as in the verses preceding. In the seventh verse, he had summed up his admonitions to the two parties whom he had been addressing—"*the weak*" and "*the strong*"—"Wherefore receive ye one another, as Christ also received us, to the glory of God." The latter of these two parties included in it of course the converted Gentiles, who were authoritatively absolved from conformity to the Jewish ceremonial. Hence the jealousy of those Jewish believers who did not clearly see the cessation of that ceremonial in the coming and work of Christ, was apt to extend to these Gentiles; from whom they might imagine their *non-conforming* brethren of the seed of Abraham derived encouragement in what was in their eyes a presumptuous laxity. The Apostle's object, therefore, from verse eighth to verse thirteenth, is to conciliate all parties—at once to show the Gentiles how much they ought to respect the Jewish brethren; and to convince the Jews that their own

Scriptures gave them no ground on which to "despise" the Gentiles. Both the one and the other, as he had just before stated, had been "received" by Jesus Christ, the Great Head of both the Jewish and the Christian Church,—the Churches, indeed, being but one, under different dispensations, the one introductory and comparatively carnal, the other more spiritual, and permanent. The admission of the Gentiles and their incorporation with the Jews, on an equal footing in the Church of God, in the period of the Messiah's reign, was in harmony with the plain prophetic intimations of the Old Testament Scriptures.

Verse 8. "Now* I say that Jesus Christ was a minister of the circumcision for the truth of God, to confirm the promises made unto the fathers." Under the designation of a "*minister*," or servant of Jehovah, the Messiah had been spoken of in prophecy, especially in that noted passage of Isaiah, in which Jehovah appears pointing Him out to special notice, as, beyond all that had gone before or were to follow, meriting the title;—the paramount dignity of the servant, and the nature and importance of the work he was commissioned to do, being the grounds of his peculiar honour.†

This minister of God was "*of the circumcision;*" and the phrase implies that the service which he had to perform was, in the respect which the verse specifies, for the Jewish people—namely, to "fulfil the promises made to the fathers." Three things, therefore, appear to be signified by this:—

1. He was himself *a Jew*. He was, by his real mother and his reputed father, of the seed of Abraham, of the tribe of Judah, and of the royal house of David. This was one of the peculiar honours of that people, and is introduced by Paul as the last and highest in his enumeration of them.‡

2. He was commissioned and sent, in the first instance, and in a special manner, *to the Jews*. Many passages both

---

* The reading now accepted on the very strongest evidence is γαρ, *for* instead of δε. It fully harmonizes with the view here taken of the connexion, and indeed strengthens it.—ED.

† Isa. xlii. 1—4.   ‡ See chap. ix. 3—5.

in the Old and New Testament Scriptures,* clearly intimate a divinely appointed precedence to the Jewish people in the blessings of the covenant—the new and everlasting covenant—that was to be ratified by the blood of Messiah's atoning sacrifice. For—

3. The "promises" which Jesus fulfilled or "confirmed," were the promises made to the *Jewish* fathers, and were contained in that covenant of which circumcision was the sign and seal. He was "a minister of the circumcision *for the truth of God*"—that is, to make good by his ministry all that the God of Abraham, Isaac, and Jacob had spoken in the form of promise to these great progenitors of the people of Israel. It is clear from the Apostle's representation here, that these were *covenant* promises, to be fulfilled to the Jewish people apart from and independent of the calling of the Gentiles into a participation with them; for he states the one separately from and subsequently to the other—"*And that* the Gentiles might glorify God for his mercy; as it is written, For this cause I will confess to thee among the Gentiles, and sing unto thy name." What, then, could these "promises" mean? We cannot suppose the reference to be to the promise of the earthly inheritance: for, instead of their being, at the coming of Christ, confirmed in the possession of it, they were actually, and by heavy judgments, ejected from it. The reference must be to blessings of a higher order—even to all that was included in the all-gracious and comprehensive assurance, " I will be a God to thee, and to thy seed after thee." That in this assurance the promise of the *eternal* inheritance was contained is expressly affirmed:—"By faith Abraham, when he was called to go out into a place which he should after receive for an inheritance, obeyed; and he went out, not knowing whither he went. By faith he sojourned in the land of promise, as in a strange country, dwelling in tabernacles with Isaac and Jacob, the heirs with him of the same promise: for he looked for a city which hath foundations, whose

---

* See Deut. xviii. 15 compared with Acts iii. 22—26; Matt. x. 5, 6; Rom. i. 16; Acts xiii. 46, 47; Jer. xxxi. 31, &c.

builder and maker is God." "These all died in faith, not having received the promises, but having seen them afar off, and were persuaded of them, and embraced them, and confessed that they were strangers and pilgrims on the earth. For they that say such things declare plainly that they seek a country. And truly, if they had been mindful of that country from whence they came out, they might have had opportunity to have returned: but now they desire a better country, that is, an heavenly: wherefore God is not ashamed to be called their God; for he hath prepared for them a city."* The promises of the covenant comprehended all "spiritual blessings" here, and "everlasting life" hereafter. The latter appears in the passages just cited; and the former in the very terms of the new covenant represented as to be made in "the latter days" with the "House of Israel and the House of Judah:" "But this shall be the covenant that I will make with the house of Israel; after those days, saith the Lord; I will put my law in their inward parts, and write it in their hearts; and will be their God, and they shall be my people."†

The rite of circumcision signified the coming of Christ from the "loins of Abraham," and was the sign and seal of that "covenant of promise," which the Apostle represents as "confirmed before of God in Christ," and as entirely independent of the Law, or Sinai covenant, which was "four hundred and thirty years after it:"—and of the promise of that covenant he accordingly represents the Gentiles as becoming heirs in virtue of their faith in Christ. "And this I say, that the covenant that was confirmed before of God in Christ, the law, which was four hundred and thirty years after, cannot disannul, that it should make the promise of none effect. For if the inheritance be of the law, it is no more of promise: but God gave it to Abraham by promise. And if ye be Christ's, then are ye Abraham's seed, and heirs according to the promise."‡

The truth of God was manifested in the coming and min-

* Heb. xi. 8—10, 13—16.   † Jer. xxxi. 31—33.
‡ Gal. iii. 17, 18, 29.

istry of Jesus, inasmuch as the divine covenant was then ratified in all the fulness of spiritual and eternal import in its "exceeding great and precious promises;" in which promises, the texts formerly quoted show, there was a special and primary regard to the people of Israel, the natural offspring of "the fathers" to whom they were made:—but a regard, though primary, not *exclusive*. Hence it follows here—Verse 9. "And* that the Gentiles might glorify God for his mercy; as it is written, For this cause I will confess to thee among the Gentiles, and sing unto thy name." So far from the Gentiles being excluded, they were expressly comprehended in "the promises made to the fathers."† It was thus the avowed purpose of God that for the "mercy" revealed in the mission and work of THE CHRIST the Gentiles as well as the Jews should have reason to "*glorify God.*" The Gospel is the revelation of God's mercy; and the mercy was designed for both Jew and Gentile—for mankind, considered as sustaining the common character of *sinners*. This is clearly and impressively set forth in the words of Peter to the assembly at Jerusalem on the appeal from Antioch:—"Men and brethren, ye know how that a good while ago God made choice among us, that the Gentiles by my mouth should hear the word of the gospel, and believe. And God, which knoweth the hearts, bare them witness, giving them the Holy Ghost, even as he did unto us; and put no difference between us and them, purifying their hearts by faith. Now therefore why tempt ye God, to put a yoke upon the neck of the disciples, which neither our fathers nor we were able to bear? But we believe that, through the grace of the Lord Jesus Christ, we shall be saved even as they."‡ It was a part

---

* Some object to thus subordinating (as in the English version) this clause to the εἰς τὸ of the clause preceding; but we venture to think on insufficient grounds. The structure of the sentence does not forbid it; and it suits the sense, as the author here shows. Alford renders—"*But* (I say) *that the Gentiles glorified God,*" &c.; and adds, "or should glorify God. Winer takes it as a perfect, and co-ordinate with γιγενῆσθαι. I would regard it as the historic aorist, and understand 'each man at his conversion.'"—ED.

† Gen. xii. 3; xxii. 18.   ‡ Acts xv. 7—11.

of the original purpose of God that the participation of the Gentiles in the blessings of the covenant should be *immediate and free*—independent of all subjection to the previous system of Judaism and all incorporation with the Jews as a community. " He made known unto me the mystery that the Gentiles should be fellow-heirs, and of the same body, and partakers of his promise in Christ by the gospel."* And when this promise *is* partaken, God is to be " glorified." It is ground of praise to Him from all who share in it. His glory is the grand end of the whole scheme of mediation; and Jews and Gentiles shall for ever unite in glorifying God " for His mercy:" and all who have learned to glorify God for it now anticipate with joy their joining the everlasting song above.

The Apostle's object being here with believing Jews—he quotes passages to his purpose from their own Scriptures, and such as they were accustomed to interpret of the reign of the Messiah, though in ignorance of its true nature.

1. Psalm xviii. 49. "Therefore will I give thanks unto thee, O Lord, among the heathen, and sing praises unto thy name." The fiftieth verse is applied by the Jews themselves to Messiah: and the preceding verses are very strikingly applicable—much more unqualifiedly than ever they were to the typical David—"Thou hast delivered me from the strivings of the people; and thou hast made me the head of the heathen: a people whom I have not known shall serve me. As soon as they hear of me, they shall obey me: the strangers shall submit themselves unto me. The strangers shall fade away, and be afraid out of their close places. The Lord liveth; and blessed be my Rock; and let the God of my salvation be exalted. We may interpret the forty-ninth verse, then, here quoted, as Messiah's praise to Jehovah for this part of the fruits of his mediation—the "travail of his soul;"—a praise in which he is conceived to be joined by the favoured partakers of the blessing.

2. Deut. xxxii. 43. " Rejoice, O ye nations, with his peo-

* Eph. iii. 3, 6.

ple; for he will avenge the blood of his servants, and will render vengeance to his adversaries, and will be merciful unto his land, and to his people." The Apostle here teaches us to give a large interpretation to these words of the inspired Lawgiver of Israel. In the regard which Jehovah should show to His people Israel, the nations of the Gentiles should have reason for rejoicing:—and the grand manifestation of His regard was to be in the fulfilment of the "promises made unto the fathers;" to the final accomplishment of which their whole previous history was introductory and preparatory—all bringing on "the fulness of time." And to this, perhaps, in a special manner, the latter part of the verse may be considered as referring—" He will be merciful to his land and to his people." The Gentiles should glorify God, as sharing this mercy.

3. Psalm cxvii. 1. "O praise the Lord, all ye nations; praise him, all ye people." This praise too is "on account of his mercy"—verse 2. "For his merciful kindness is great toward us: and the truth of the Lord endureth for ever." This verse indeed shows the reference of the psalm to be to Gospel times; when, in the work of Christ, "mercy and truth were to meet together," and divine faithfulness to be manifested in the fulfilment of the promises of divine grace. The "*us*" means the Jewish people, the ancient church of God; and the Gentiles are called to praise and laud the name of Jehovah for His "mercy and truth" to the house of Jacob, because it was His purpose that they should all be blessed in the promised seed.*

4. Isa. xi. 10. "And in that day there shall be a root of Jesse, which shall stand for an ensign of the people; to it shall the Gentiles seek: and his rest shall be glorious." All the four passages are given by the Apostle as they stand in the Septuagint version; and they all agree with the Hebrew and with our own translation but this last. Quotations are given sometimes in exact coincidence with the Hebrew; sometimes precisely from the Greek; and occasionally not

* This corresponds with the prayer of Psalm lxvii. 1, 2.

in perfect verbal agreement with either. When made by the inspired writers of the New Testament, we are sure that in every instance the sense, or mind of the Spirit, is truly given. The same meaning may be expressed in somewhat varying words. If the Spirit of God chooses either mode of expression, *we* are then sure that either is right. But this is not a warrant for *us* to alter the phraseology in which those "holy men of God," who wrote "as they were moved by the Holy Ghost," have expressed the truth of God. Not that we must never presume to put the truth into any other language than that which has actually been used; but we must never presume to demand of others the acceptance of our phraseology as infallibly the counterpart of that which the Spirit has employed.

In the present instance the harmony of import, amid slight verbal difference, is sufficiently apparent. Read the verse as in Isaiah and as here. "*An ensign*" is always in Scripture the figure for that around which men gather, and which they obediently follow. It conveys the idea of power and guidance, and authority. It is the same general idea that is conveyed by "he that shall rise to rule over the Gentiles." In his royal authority he sets up his "Ensign," to which the nations flock, and round which they rally in token of their subjection.

There is no material difference between "trusting (or *hoping**) in him," and "seeking to him." Whether we consider "seeking to him" as signifying their abandoning their ancient false and deceitful oracles, and having recourse to Him for instruction in the mind of God, or repairing to Him as their royal "leader and commander," bowing to his authority and placing themselves under his direction and rule. This is just the expression and exercise of *trust*. They "shall trust in Him," both as a prophet, a priest, and a king; and shall "seek to him" in all these official characters for the peculiar benefits of each.

The truth of God was as deeply implicated in the case of

---

* ἰλπιοῦσιν.

the Gentiles as in that of the Jews. Had the Gentiles been left destitute, there would have been a failure of His word, as really as if the "mercy to Abraham," and "the truth to Jacob, which he had sworn unto the fathers from the days of old," had failed of accomplishment to Israel.

Addressing the believing Jews and Gentiles together, the Apostle then, in terms the most fitted to conciliate and unite both in mutual good feeling, expresses his fervent desires for the divine goodness to them all—verse 13. "Now the God of hope fill you with all joy and peace in believing, that ye may abound in hope, through the power of the Holy Ghost." He loved them all; and desired their common good. Their differences pained and distressed him, as they marred their own social comfort and spiritual prosperity, and were materially injurious to the cause of the Gospel. In thus expressing himself in behalf of both, he exemplified the spirit which it was their duty to cherish towards each other.

"The God *of hope.*" The designation is taken from the last word of the preceding quotation—"In him shall the Gentiles *hope.*" The word is the same. How delightful to us sinners, guilty and polluted, weak and wretched, that the God whom we have offended has revealed himself under such a designation. He might have confined all his discoveries of himself to righteousness and vengeance, and so have appeared in our eyes in no other relation than the God of terror and despair. How far otherwise has He dealt with us! He is "the God of peace," the "God of patience and consolation," "the God of all grace," "the God of hope," "the God of salvation;" and these, with every other encouraging designation, he has as "the God and Father of our Lord Jesus Christ."

He is "the God of hope," as being the original Author of hope to guilty man by the revelation and promise of a Saviour. He first appeared in this character in the very outset of the history of our apostate world, when he said, "I will put enmity between thee and the woman, and between thy seed and her seed: it shall bruise thy head, and thou shalt bruise his heel."* For a long time, in a subsequent period, after the call of Abraham, he was known in this character to the Jews only, the revelation of His promised mercy through a Mediator being almost entirely confined to that people. There were many hints, however, and more than hints, intimations sufficiently plain, had the Jews been disposed to understand them, that it was not always to be so; that it was His purpose to make himself known to the Gentiles also in the same character. It is in this view of His character and relation to sinners, that "the only begotten Son who is in the bosom of the Father hath declared him." Viewed out of Christ, His character, to a creature conscious of guilt, must engender despair.

And God, the God of light and love, is not only "the God of hope," as revealing hope to the lost in the blessed scheme of his Son's mediation; He is also the *author* of hope in the bosoms of such creatures by the influences of his Holy Spirit, through the truth concerning his Son. He is, indeed, the author not of this grace alone, but of all the rest. They are all connected with each other. They appear so in the very terms of this verse—"The God of *hope* fill you with all *joy* and *peace*, in *believing*." Here, therefore, he appears as the author of faith, and hope, and joy, and peace. Faith itself is "the gift of God:"—that is, He so enlightens the mind by His Spirit, as to give a spiritual discovery of the excellence and glory of the doctrine of the cross; by which spiritual discernment the enlightened sinner receives it as the truth of God. From this faith of the testimony of God concerning his Son, and of the "exceeding great and precious promises" founded upon it—arise "peace and joy" in the soul of the believing sinner; peace of conscience through the blood of atonement; a delightful sense of pardon and reconciliation with God through Jesus Christ; and that tranquil satisfied serenity of mind which arises from confidence in the God of grace, as at the same time the God of providence, ordering the whole of His providential administration

* Gen. iii. 15.

with a view to the ends of His grace and mercy. This peace is nearly akin to joy. Joy indeed may be regarded as just the peace in a higher degree. The very thought of a state of "peace with God," and of a solid and satisfactory ground on which it is possessed, is itself enough to inspire the heart with joy;—yes, even with "joy unspeakable and full of glory:"—joy in Christ Jesus, in the dignity of his person, the perfection of his righteousness, the preciousness and divine acceptance of his atonement, the triumph of his resurrection, the prevalence of his intercession, the perpetuity of his love;—joy in God, as "the God of peace," the Father, the friend, and the portion, of all who come to him in the name of His Son;—joy in the present possession of spiritual blessings, and in anticipation of all that the divine promises, which are "yea and amen in Christ," give the hope of enjoying in a future and better world. These kindred feelings of "peace and joy" are the native results of the faith of the Gospel. They arise from its very nature. It is fitted to impart them:—nay more, it is *designed* to impart them. The enjoyment of them by the believing sinner is the very purpose of God in sending to that sinner the message of his Gospel. The Gospel is "good tidings of great joy." Why are the tidings sent us, but that believing them we may have the "joy and peace" which they are in their very nature fitted to give. There must be some mistake when any one professes to believe the Gospel, and derives from it no peace, no joy. There must be a misunderstanding of the import of the message, or a deficiency in the simplicity and the entireness of its acceptance. We have various instances in the New Testament of peace and joy as the immediate effects of the understanding and belief of the Gospel message.[*] And in many passages this state of mind is inculcated on believers, as at once their privilege and their duty; their *privilege*, if they would live up to the measure of enjoyment designed by the God of all grace in the message of mercy to sinners through his Son; and their *duty*, if

---

[*] Acts ii. 46, 47.; viii. 39.; xvi. 34.

they would set before the world a just and inviting, and not an unfair and repulsive view of the truth which they profess to have received.*

The Apostle's prayer is not only that they might *have* this "joy and peace"—but that they might have it *abundantly* —in the largest measure in which their hearts could hold it:—"The God of hope *fill* you with *all* joy and peace in believing, that ye may *abound* in hope, through the power of the Holy Ghost." "*All* joy and peace," is a form of expression peculiar to this Apostle, and indicates the greatest degree of the thing of which he happens to speak.— There is, however, a connexion to be noticed between the two parts of the verse. "That ye may abound in hope" is not a mere repetition of the same thing in other words as "The God of hope fill you with all joy and peace in believing." But the one is represented as *arising out of* the other: "The God of hope fill you with all peace and joy in believing, *that ye may* abound in hope." How is this? One should rather expect an inversion of the statement: "The God of hope make you to abound in hope through the power of the Holy Ghost, that ye may be filled with joy and peace." And there would be a natural and important meaning in this. "Good hope" does impart joy; and the measure of the joy is proportioned to the nature and the stability of the hope—its object and its ground. But this is not the sentiment here. Here, the experience of the influence of the Gospel in imparting to the soul a peace and joy unfelt before—such as nothing else can yield—which are perceived and felt to be in full accordance, in the source of them, with every attribute of the divine character, and with every demand of God's law—a peace and joy of which the grounds bear the fullest examination, and which the soul is delightfully sensible it can fully share without the slightest misgiving from any one point in the nature or the government of the God with whom it has to do:—this experience is part of what may be called the *experimental evidence* of the truth; and, when taken in

* Phil. iv. 4: Rom. v. 1—5, 11: John xiv. 27; xvi. 33, &c.

connexion with the power of the truth in purifying the heart from the pollution, and freeing it from the love and the power of sin, is a species of proof perfectly reasonable in its nature, and one which, existing in the consciousness of the renewed sinner himself, cannot by any sophistry be taken from him. From this experimental evidence, therefore, his hope receives confirmation; and the more he has of this "witness in himself," the more abundant will his hope become.*

"*The power of the Holy Ghost*" is the immediate agent in producing and maintaining the divine life in the soul, in all its various principles and affections. It is the Spirit's regenerating energy that quickens the soul, when "dead in trespasses and sins," inspiring it with holy love, and animating it with the joy of hope, which it feels to be its strength, for duty, for temptation, for adversity. All is the effect of His mighty and gracious operation. Let us not, amidst our gratitude for the love of the Father, and for the grace and mediation of the Son, forget or under-rate what we owe to the influence of the Spirit. It is his to testify of Christ—both in the word, and in the minds and hearts of sinners—opening their understandings to a spiritual apprehension of the truth, and bowing their spirits to a glad and grateful acceptance of the mercy revealed in it, and cleansing the soul from pollution for a temple of the living God.

Let me now remark, in conclusion—

1. That there is often among believers too little of this decidedly happy influence of the truths and hopes of the Gospel. In running down the doctrine that assurance is of the essence of faith,—that perfect undoubting confidence is indispensable to any one being really a believer in Christ,—there is often a mournful tendency to be satisfied in an opposite extreme. There is a resting in a state of doubt and fear, and of, at the best, a trembling hope that hardly dares to flatter itself with safety. Because convinced that assurance is not of the essence of faith, many associate the idea of it with pre-

---

* Comp. chap. v. 4.

sumption, and almost fear to think of it, as if the very approach to it were heretical. This is not at all as it ought to be. Let us not be afraid of *a word*. The "full assurance of faith," and "the full assurance of hope," are New Testament phrases. They must have their meaning; and believers ought to enjoy what corresponds to them. There is certainly nothing heretical in being "filled with all joy and peace in believing, that we may abound in hope, through the power of the Holy Ghost." And yet this is a state of mind, which, though expressed in other terms, amounts to much the same thing. But while we exhort believers to seek and to cherish this happy state of confidence towards God as that which the New Testament represents as their legitimate privilege; the same inspired record never allows them to forget that their joy must be a holy joy, their hope a hope that sanctifies; and the more the joy and the hope abound, the more should their influence appear in the abundance of holy practice. If we walk in the comfort of the Holy Ghost, let us see to it that this be invariably associated with our walking in the fear of the Lord.*

2. Since we owe so much to the Holy Spirit; since He alone is our regenerator, and sanctifier, and guide, and strengthener, and comforter; since it is by His commissioned power that we are "filled with joy and peace in believing," and are sustained by the animating energy of the good hope through grace, let us cherish the gratitude we owe to this divine agent, and not forget the solemn admonition of this Apostle:—"Grieve not the Holy Spirit of God, whereby ye are sealed unto the day of redemption."† Let every temper, every desire, every word, every action, be carefully shunned by us, that is contrary to his will and to his influence,—that is abhorrent to his nature, and dishonouring to his name. While you seek that He may dwell in you,—seek to cast out everything from your heart of which the presence is inconsistent with his residence there, and might provoke him to forsake the dwelling-place:—"Cleanse yourselves

* Heb. xii. 14.; 1 John iii. 2, 3, &c. † Eph. iv. 30.

from all filthiness of the flesh and spirit, perfecting holiness in the fear of God."

3. Let us praise God together because in the Gospel he appears, not as "the God of the Jews only but also of the Gentiles." Let us, with one heart and one soul, "glorify God for his mercy;"—and let this be associated also with practical duty. Let us cultivate suitable feelings both towards Jews and Gentiles, and let these feelings not be inoperative; not slumbering in our bosoms, but lively and busily active. Let us never indulge contempt towards the Jews, the seed of Abraham, God's friend. "Jesus Christ," let us not forget, was himself "of the circumcision," and in a primary and special sense, "a minister of the circumcision." He assumed our nature amongst the seed of David; and his first commission was to the "lost sheep of the house of Israel." These guilty outcasts are still regarded with purposes of mercy. They are not finally cast off. Jesus Christ will yet more abundantly and strikingly show himself the "minister of the circumcision." The designs of his mediation in regard to them are far from being completed. "The deliverer shall yet come to Zion, and shall turn away ungodliness from Jacob." Let us seek to hasten this consummation; and let us aim at "the fulness of the Gentiles." The predictions of this passage have been fulfilled in part; they still wait their more full accomplishment. Let our prayer be—and let the sincerity of it be shown in action and in liberality—" God be merciful unto us, and bless us; and cause his face to shine upon us. That thy way may be known upon earth, thy saving health among all nations. Let the people praise thee, O God; let all the people praise thee. O let the nations be glad and sing for joy: for thou shalt judge the people righteously, and govern the nations upon earth. Let the people praise thee, O God; let all the people praise thee. Then shall the earth yield her increase; and God, even our own God, shall bless us. God shall bless us; and all the ends of the earth shall fear him."*

* Psa. lxvii.

LECTURE LXVII.

ROMANS xv. 14—21.

"And I myself also am persuaded of you, my brethren, that ye also are full of goodness, filled with all knowledge, able also to admonish one another. Nevertheless, brethren, I have written the more boldly unto you in some sort, as putting you in mind, because of the grace that is given to me of God, that I should be the minister of Jesus Christ to the Gentiles, ministering the gospel of God, that the offering up of the Gentiles might be acceptable, being sanctified by the Holy Ghost. I have therefore whereof I may glory through Jesus Christ in those things which pertain to God. For I will not dare to speak of any of those things which Christ hath not wrought by me, to make the Gentiles obedient, by word and deed, through mighty signs and wonders, by the power of the Spirit of God; so that from Jerusalem, and round about unto Illyricum, I have fully preached the gospel of Christ. Yea, so have I strived to preach the gospel, not where Christ was named, lest I should build upon another man's foundation: but as it is written, To whom he was not spoken of, they shall see: and they that have not heard shall understand."

THE Apostle wrote with authority. What he wrote was not properly his own, but the dictate of the Spirit of Christ. But we have many occasions for observing that divine inspiration did not interfere with human feeling in its conscious possessor. The play of all the legitimate sensibilities of the heart continues, on the very subjects the matter of which is suggested by the Holy Spirit. The admonitions which Paul had, in the preceding chapter and the beginning of this, addressed to the believers at Rome, were divinely suggested and divinely expressed. They had in them the full sanction of heaven. But in writing them, the Apostle felt a rising apprehension lest they should be regarded as severe, or as implying a too unfavourable estimate of the character of the church. This delicacy of feeling was not in itself improper. There was nothing in it, therefore, of which it was needful that the divine Spirit should restrain the utterance. Nay, the utterance of it, by its conciliatory influence, might have the beneficial effect of recommending to a suitable regard and practical compliance, in spirit and in conduct, the reproofs and counsels that had been administered. The Holy Spirit, therefore, interferes not with the breathings of affectionate feeling,—the feeling itself being in harmony with His own gracious influence; and, in its expression, not running beyond the line of truth.—The language of the first two verses here is closely akin to that addressed to the Hebrews:—"But, beloved, we are persuaded better things of you, and things that accompany salvation, though we thus speak. For God is not unrighteous, to forget your work and labour of love, which ye have shewed toward his name, in that ye have ministered to the saints, and do minister."* It amounts to a declaration of confidence, resting on his knowledge of their character as a church, that his admonitions would be duly weighed and practically followed. The preceding admonitions may have been addressed to them in the way of *prevention*, on the ground of their probable need of them, from the tendency of circumstances to produce the evils against which they are directed. Or,—on the more likely supposition that, to a certain extent, the evils actually existed, the "persuasion" expressed in verse fourteenth may be interpreted *generally*—implying that, although individuals might have discovered deficiency in the virtues commended, yet *as a collective body* the character given of them was deserved.†

"*Goodness*" has here the sense, as in other occurrences of the same word, of a mild, kindly, benevolent disposition.‡ Such was, in the Apostle's estimation, their general temper and state of mind, and he had the conviction that they would be ready, under the influence of this

---

* Heb. vi. 9, 10. † Comp. chap. i. 8; xvi. 19.
‡ Comp. Matt. xx. 15: Gal. v. 22: Rom. v. 7.

temper, to listen to and bear his admonitions; while, in compliance with them, they would cherish this temper towards one another "with all lowliness and meekness, with long-suffering, forbearing one another in love."*

"*All* knowledge" signifies, according to the usage of this writer, enlarged acquaintance with the mind and will of God —with the great principles of the Gospel scheme, and with the duties arising out of them and to which they contained the motives. It is "knowledge" not merely of a speculative kind, but that which arises from "spiritual discernment." "*Filled* with all knowledge," seems to refer to their having received it from Him "in whom are hid all the treasures of wisdom and knowledge," and who imparts it to the mind by the illuminating influence of his Spirit.† Their ability to "*admonish one another*" consisted in both the "goodness" and the "knowledge." The word for "admonishing"‡ is a general one, referring to the regulation of the mind and conduct, by instruction, direction, warning, and reproof. This is a duty which daily lies upon believers in church fellowship in all their associations and intercourse in life.§ To the right fulfilment of this duty, I have said, both "knowledge" and "goodness" are requisite. The one is needful for the *matter* of admonition, and the other for the *manner* of it. It is not sufficient that the matter be right. The sentiments we utter may be sound, the practice we inculcate correct, and our reproofs well-merited; but if they are not administered in the spirit of "goodness," they cannot prove effectual. Both the head and the heart must be right. And in Paul's own admonitions we have the union of both happily exemplified. He blends admonition with commendation. While he reproves what is wrong, he does not overlook what is right. There is a severity that hardly knows how to commend; and there is a softness that cannot bring itself to censure. Both are extremes. We should win a way for reproof to the heart by duly commending what is laudable; we should

---

* Eph. iv. 2. † 1 Cor. ii. 14. ‡ *νουθεσία*.
§ Heb. iii. 12, 13.

prevent commendation from operating with the mischief of flattery by faithfully reproving what is reprehensible.

Verse 15. "Nevertheless, brethren, I have written the more boldly unto you in some sort, as putting you in mind, because of the grace that is given to me of God." The phrase "*in some sort*,"* which is here connected with the preceding part of the verse, it is not easy exactly to understand. It seems hardly natural to make the Apostle say that he wrote to them *in some degree* the more boldly, because of the grace given to him of God; seeing *all* his boldness, and boldness of the most undaunted kind, and boldness which required no apology, arose from that grace,—the grace of Him who had "counted him faithful, putting him into the ministry." The phrase has been rendered "*in this part*"— meaning in this portion of his Epistle. But this is not in harmony with the ordinary signification of the adverbial phrase (for such it is) of which the established meaning is "in part,"—"to a certain degree." It appears to me, that it may with propriety be connected with the subsequent rather than with the antecedent clause, and be thus rendered —"partly as putting you in mind." This is in fine agreement with the spirit of the passage. He would not be understood as entirely inculcating what was new, but reminding them of principles and duties with which they were previously acquainted. This is like the terms used by Peter:— "Wherefore I will not be negligent to put you always in remembrance of these things, though ye know them, and be established in the present truth. Yea, I think it meet, as long as I am in this tabernacle, to stir you up by putting you in remembrance; knowing that shortly I must put off this my tabernacle, even as our Lord Jesus Christ hath shewed me. Moreover I will endeavour that ye may be able after my decease to have these things always in remembrance."†

Perhaps, however, although it is unnatural to connect the phrase with the ministry with which he was graciously intrusted, considered generally, yet it may with propriety be

---

* ἀπὸ μέρους.   † 2 Pet. i. 12—15; also iii. 1.

associated with the *specialty* in that ministry,—namely, its being in a peculiar manner "*to the Gentiles*,"—which he mentions in verse sixteenth. The meaning will then be, that he was in part emboldened to speak freely to them by the consideration that he was addressing a Gentile church —a church, that is, in a Gentile community, and consisting chiefly of Gentile converts; which brought it in a special manner within the terms of his commission. I am not sure but this, after all, may be the most natural and easy interpretation.—The believing Romans stood in need (and *we* stand in need as well as they) to be put in mind of what they knew; to have both truths and duties brought afresh before their view, impressed on their memories, and urged on their attention and practice. Our hearts are deceitful; and a deceitful heart makes a treacherous memory. We need "line upon line, precept upon precept." There are varieties in the powers of memory; but it is to be feared that in many instances the memory gets blame that is due to the heart. ·

"*The grace that was given to him of God*," which he mentions in the end of this verse as inspiring him with boldness, is the favour bestowed upon him which he immediately specifies—"that I should be the minister of Jesus Christ for the Gentiles."* He had the boldness of authority, as a commissioned ambassador of heaven—as an Apostle of Jesus Christ, to whom belonged officially "the care of all the churches;"—the Apostolic diocese being the whole extent of the Church of Christ. And he had this boldness especially towards *them* as the "Apostle of the Gentiles."

The terms here translated "*minister*" and "*ministering*," are different from each other; and they are both different from that which is usually rendered *minister* or *servant*. Both terms here are taken from the *priestly office*† and its peculiar functions. And this accords with the figurative light in which he represents the nature of his service in reference to

---

* Comp. chap. i. 5; xii. 3.
† The one is λειτουργον; the other ιερουργοῦντα.—ED.

the Gentiles. He exercised a sacred function, as the ministering servant of Jesus Christ the common Master of all who were engaged in "*ministering the Gospel of God,*" or the glad tidings of salvation which God had commissioned them, in the name of Christ, to proclaim. And what was the end of this his sacred sacerdotal ministry?—"That the offering up," or sacrificial oblation "of the Gentiles might be acceptable, being sanctified by the Holy Ghost." The converted Gentiles are thus represented as brought to God by the agency of the Apostle, and consecrated to His service. In the figure, the Apostle appears as the officiating priest in this great spiritual oblation. The idea is grand and interesting. It is an extension of the one contained in the first verse of the twelfth chapter, with these differences, that in the latter passage, each individual is the offering and each individual the priest that presents it,—in the passage before us, the sacrifice consists of a large number, and, instead of each presenting himself, the instrument of their conversion presents the whole. It is like one of those occasions, recorded in the Old Testament history, when hundreds and thousands of victims were presented and immolated, as one grand sacrificial act of homage.* In the passage quoted from the twelfth chapter, the sacrifice which each individual presents is designated " a *holy* sacrifice, *acceptable* unto God." You will observe the same connexion of ideas in the verse before us :—"that the offering up of the Gentiles might be *acceptable*, being *sanctified* by the Holy Ghost." The acceptableness of the offering in both cases is connected with its holiness.

The ancient sacrifices were accepted, when presented to God according to the prescribed order;—and of this order one of the leading particulars was their being *without blemish;*" a requisite which in its full import typified that "Lamb of God without blemish and without spot," which in the fulness of time was to "take away the sins of the world."

---

* The same kind of figure is employed by the prophet Isaiah, in chap. lxvi. 20.

The salt also which was invariably to be used in sacrifice was an emblem of purity and incorruption; and the washing of the victims with water had the same general significance; all rendering them the more appropriate emblems of the spotlessly holy Saviour. But while this unblemished perfection was designed to be in the first instance a type of the absolute sinlessness of the great atoning sacrifice; it adumbrated also the necessary holiness of all persons and things employed in the service of the holy God. And in regard to *persons*, this holiness of course consisted in moral purification from the pollutions of sin. This, accordingly, is here especially meant by being "*sanctified by the Holy Ghost.*"

Some, I am aware, would interpret this phrase of the descent of the Holy Spirit on the first Gentile converts; or of his miraculous influences bestowed on converted Gentiles on any other occasion—as implying God's setting them apart to himself on the same footing as he had done the Jews. But this is to deprive the words of their most obvious and most important signification. They clearly mean the nature or character of the sacrifice, as that which gave it its acceptableness to God. It is true that *sanctified* primarily means *set apart:* but when it is applied to a moral agent, it should be remembered, that as the setting apart of any inanimate or irrational creature consisted in its being duly purified according to the prescriptions of the ceremonial law; so the setting apart of such an agent consists in his being purified after his kind—purified in the principles of his moral agency,—brought under the influence of holy affections and desires, and thus fitted for the service of Him who "is light, and in whom there is no darkness at all." Under the spiritual dispensation of the Gospel, it was nothing merely external that the Apostle meant, when he spoke of the "offering up of the Gentiles." It is the presenting to God of those "who are renewed in the spirit of their minds,"—washed from their pollution—"salted with fire"—"saved by the washing of regeneration and renewing of the Holy Ghost." No man in presenting himself, and no minister in presenting his converts, offers an "acceptable" sacrifice, unless the essence of the character has been thus changed; unless enmity has given place to love,—pollution to holiness,—the heart of stone to the heart of flesh—the principles of "the old man" to those of "the new."

When the Apostle adds in verse 17. "I have, therefore, whereof I may glory through Jesus Christ," (or matter of glorying in Christ Jesus,) "in those things which" (as to the things that) "pertain to God"*—we must not understand it as the language of boasting *in himself.* The sequel will show this. It was ever far from him. He at times "magnifies his office;" but never himself. Of himself he always speaks in terms of self abasement and conscious unworthiness; or when, by the malignity of his slanderous adversaries, he is constrained to stand upon the defensive, and to set forth his claims in what might be construed into the language of self-glorying, he writes with reluctance, with hesitation and shame, and incessant apology. There is all the dignity of conscious truth with all the modesty of conscious obligation to grace: "If I must needs glory, I will glory of the things which concern mine infirmities." "Of myself I will not glory, but in mine infirmities. I am become a fool in glorying; ye have compelled me: for I ought to have been commended of you: for in nothing am I behind the very chiefest apostles, though I be nothing."†

The same is the spirit here. It is of his office, and of this office as bestowed by the Lord, and of his success in the discharge of its duties, that he glories. But still his "matter of glorying" is not in himself, but "*in Christ Jesus.*" He owed to Jesus Christ—and he owns the obligation—both the office and his support and success in it. "*As to the things that pertain to God.*"—The phrase is one in excellent keeping with the general representation of his office in the preceding verses; and has immediate relation to the functions of the sacred office to which he there makes allusion.‡

The Apostle was honoured with signal success in his ministry among the Gentiles. He was the chief instrument

---

* Ἔχω οὖν καύχησιν ἐν Χριστῷ Ἰησοῦ τὰ πρὸς Θεόν.
† 2 Cor. xi. 30; xii. 5, 11. ‡ Comp. Heb. v. 1.

of their early ingathering. But when he gloried in this, he both remembered that he was *only an instrument*, and also that there were *other instruments*. Hence he says— verse 18. "For I will not dare to speak of any of those things which Christ hath not wrought by me, to make the Gentiles obedient, by word and deed."

The meaning is *first*, That he would not speak of anything that "*Christ* had not wrought by him"—as if there were any such thing—anything of which he was himself the efficient doer. All that he had done Christ had wrought *by* him: he was the mere instrument, Christ the mighty agent. He would not "*dare*"—he would not be so profanely and vainly presumptuous, as to pretend to anything of his own. If the Gentiles had been converted, it was Christ's doing. All the power of evidence, and all the power of converting influence were from Him, or, which is the same thing, from God through Him.*

It means farther, that he would not boast of anything of which *others* had been the instruments. Of what Christ had wrought by others, he would not in any one iota take to himself, directly or indirectly, the credit.† He had too much *piety* to do the former:—he had too much *honour* and *integrity* to do the latter. Let us imitate him in both. Of all the good we are enabled and honoured to accomplish let us unreservedly give the entire glory where it is due—even to that Lord with whom is "the residue of the Spirit," and without whom we can do nothing. The more unreservedly—the greater the simplicity of heart with which we decline the glory ourselves and ascribe it to Him, the more will He be pleased to bless and prosper our otherwise fruitless endeavours; for he hath said—"Him that honoureth me I will honour." And never let us be so ungenerous, so unjust, so pitiful, as to appropriate to ourselves the smallest portion of the credit or the honour that belongs to others—to invest our brows with laurels which are not our own! On the contrary, if aught is, by mistake, imputed to us which others

---

* 1 Cor. iii. 5—7.　　† Ver. 20; and 2 Cor. x. 15, 16.

have done, let us correct the error, and give every one without the slightest stirrings of envy, but with sincere delight, all that is his due.

The object of his ministry is indirectly stated—"to make the Gentiles obedient"—or "for the subjection of the Gentiles:"—that is, to bring them into a state of willing subjection to the Redeemer's spiritual reign. This is the subjection to which it was the end of Paul's ministry to bring the Gentiles. It was "to open their eyes, and to turn them from darkness to light, and from the power of Satan unto God, that they may receive forgiveness of sins, and inheritance among them which are sanctified."*

The expression "*in word and deed*" seems most usually to be connected with the subjection of the Gentiles, and considered as descriptive of the extent of that subjection in *profession* and *conduct*. I am disposed rather to agree with those who connect it otherwise, and consider it as expressing in part the *means* by which the subjection of the Gentiles is effected: —" I will not dare to speak of any of those things which Christ hath not wrought by me, to make the Gentiles obedient, by word and deed; by the energy of signs and wonders, by the power of the Holy Ghost:"—"*By word:*" that is, by the public proclamation of the truth and private conversation with such as fell in his way; by the doctrine which he taught, and his manner of teaching it:—"*By deed:*" by his labours and his sufferings in the cause in which he was engaged; and the manner in which he had been enabled to act and to suffer. These were what we may call *ordinary* means; the means connected with the instrument. Then follow, verse nineteenth, the *extraordinary* or divine—"Through mighty signs and wonders, by the power of the Spirit of God."

1. "By mighty signs and wonders"—literally, "by the energy of signs and wonders."† "*Signs*" expresses the true *nature* and design of a miracle. It is a sign from heaven— a sign of the divine mission of the prophet at whose word it is performed, and of the divine authority of the doctrine with

---

* See Acts xxvi. 18; See also Eph. ii. 12, 13, 16.

† ἐν δυνάμει σημείων καὶ τεράτων.

the declaration of which it was associated. "*Wonders*" is also a designation of the same description of events,—of miracles namely;—a designation derived from their first effect upon the minds of those who witness them—the astonishment which they excite. Events that are in harmony with the ordinary course of nature, with what is under our eye from day to day, excite no surprise, nay, pass often altogether unnoticed. But a miracle is a temporary suspension or inversion of this course; and is meant, by the wonder which it inspires, to lead to such attention and inquiry as may issue in full conviction of truth. The effect is stated with great simplicity by Nicodemus—" Rabbi, we know that thou art a teacher come from God: for no man can do these miracles that thou doest, except God be with him."* Of this effect of a miracle we have a fine exemplification in the case of the lame man who received healing at the hand of Peter and John—" The people saw him walking and praising God: and they knew that it was he which sat for alms at the Beautiful gate of the temple: and they were filled with wonder and amazement at that which had happened unto him. And as the lame man which was healed held Peter and John, all the people ran together unto them in the porch that is called Solomon's, greatly wondering."† This is "the power of signs and wonders"—which appears to mean here, not so much the might by which they were effected, as their operation upon men's mind, their power to awaken attention and produce conviction.

"*The power of the Holy Ghost*"‡ is by some understood of the apostolic power of conferring his various supernatural gifts; and by others of those gifts themselves, which in different enumerations are distinguished from miracles, the latter being done by the apostles, the former conveyed by them to others.§ I am inclined to think that here the

---

* John iii. 2. † Acts iii. 9—11.
‡ The author seems to have adopted the reading ἁγίου for θεοῦ; which is better sustained, though some read simply πνεύματος, which is according to codex B.—ED.
§ See Heb. ii. 4.

phrase means those gracious influences of the Holy Spirit which were necessary to the saving efficacy of external evidences and means of conversion. There were multitudes who, both in our Lord's own days, and afterwards, saw all the numberless signs wrought by himself and his apostles, without the effect following of such conviction of the truth as appeared in conversion of heart and profession of Christ's name. So far from producing this effect, they served in proportion to their amount of striking evidence, to stir up into the more bitter opposition the deep-seated enmity of the heart. While, therefore, miraculous works were in their nature conclusive proofs of divine authority, and calculated and intended to work conviction (else why were they wrought?) yet something more was necessary; it was in many cases made impressively apparent, that there was no kind and no amount of external evidence sufficient to overcome this enmity. God made manifest the truth of his own declaration,—"not by might, nor by power, but my Spirit, saith the Lord of Hosts;" a declaration which may be fairly applied, not merely to *human* might, but to the outward displays of the power of God himself.

There is a climax in this enumeration of *the means* by which, through the instrumentality of Paul, Christ wrought in subjecting the Gentiles—"by word and deed, by the energy of signs and wonders, *by the power of the Spirit of God.*"* The powerful operation of the Spirit was apparent, not only in the effects resulting from the Gospel when preached, but in the amount of labour in which the instrument of the good was sustained:—"*so that from Jerusalem, and round about unto Illyricum, I have fully preached the gospel of Christ.*" Illyricum lay beyond Macedonia, on the north-east coast of the Adriatic gulf, or gulf of Venice. Paul had laboured in Arabia, Syria, Asia, Greece, Macedonia, Illyricum, and in the adjacent islands. His ministry had embraced a very wide and long circuit. It is about twelve or thirteen hundred miles in a straight line; and, when taken

* Comp. 1 Thess. i. 5.

in all its width and windings, with all its cities and towns, and populous districts and islands, the extent of it strikingly shows the indefatigable zeal of this Apostle—his determination to spend and be spent for Christ. O for a larger portion of this spirit among all the ministers of the cross both at home and abroad!—a more entire, unreserved, and laborious devotedness to the work of the gospel! He did the work effectually. "I have *fully* preached the gospel of Christ:"—I have filled the whole of that vast extent of country with the light of divine truth—not passing hastily and in each place doing a little—with the view of having the larger space of which to boast as gone over in his missionary travels:—but "making full proof" everywhere "of his ministry;" visiting some places more than once; in some protracting his stay for months and years, in places where, as he expresses it, "a wide door and effectual was opened to him, and there were many adversaries,"—and where, from his head-quarters, he had a large surrounding region to traverse. And wherever he went, he was not satisfied with delivering a portion of truth, but declared everywhere, "the whole counsel of God." Of his labours and sufferings in this extent of missionary field, he himself gives us a brief enumeration; and we know it to be but partial when he says—"Are they ministers of Christ? (I speak as a fool,) I am more: in labours more abundant, in stripes above measure, in prisons more frequent, in deaths oft. Of the Jews five times received I forty stripes save one. Thrice was I beaten with rods, once was I stoned, thrice I suffered shipwreck, a night and a day I have been in the deep; in journeyings often, in perils of waters, in perils of robbers, in perils by mine own countrymen, in perils by the heathen, in perils in the city, in perils in the wilderness, in perils in the sea, in perils among false brethren; in weariness and painfulness, in watchings often, in hunger and thirst, in fastings often, in cold and nakedness. Besides those things that are without, that which cometh upon me daily, the care of all the churches."*

* 2 Cor. xi. 23—28.

There was one principle by which Paul's labours were remarkably distinguished, which he states in verses 20, 21, "Yea, so have I strived to preach the gospel, not where Christ was named, lest I should build upon another man's foundation: but as it is written, To whom he was not spoken of, they shall see: and they that have not heard shall understand." His supreme desire—his sacred ambition, was to break up new ground. This was not from love of ease; for it was beyond question the most difficult and the most dangerous work. In acting thus, he was influenced, we may presume, by *two* considerations.—The first is founded in our Lord's declaration, "I say unto you, that likewise joy shall be in heaven over one sinner that repenteth, more than over ninety and nine just persons, which need no repentance."* The addition of new spiritual children to the family of God is a ground of livelier joy than the continued life and health of those already born; the increase of the Redeemer's kingdom by the accession of new subjects, than the steadfast loyalty of the old; the planting of new jewels in his royal crown than the undiminished brilliancy of those already sparkling there. This made it more desirable to plant than to water, to convert than to edify. He planted, and left others to water; a "master-builder," he "laid the foundation," and left it to others to rear the superstructure; he brought in the waste land, "the desolate heritages," and left others to keep it in cultivation.—Then, secondly, the Apostle's special commission was, to carry the Gospel to the Gentile nations—to bear through the world to men of every "kindred, and tongue, and people, and nation." This indeed was the apostolic commission as given to all of them:—"GO YE INTO ALL THE WORLD, AND PREACH THE GOSPEL TO EVERY CREATURE."† Paul, therefore, acted up to this commission—as a messenger to the nations. And there is surely a peculiar pleasure in being the first messenger of good tidings. Every man of sensibility shrinks from being the bearer of news that are to give pain—the news of disaster and distress and hopelessness.

* Luke xv. 7.   † Matt. xxviii. 19; Mark xvi. 15. 16.

But to be the first to proclaim tidings of joy is one of the most delightful offices to which he can be called. And if this be true with regard to tidings that relate only to the interests of this world, O what ought to be the delight of the spiritual mind to be the first announcer of news such as the Gospel brings—the news of a reconciled God, and of a free and full and everlasting salvation! It was a joyous embassy to the angels of light, the children of God's purity and love, when to the shepherds of Bethlehem they were sent from heaven with the message of divine mercy—" Fear not: for, behold, I bring you good tidings of great joy, which shall be to all people;" and when they joined in the anthem of praise, with the transport of piety and benevolence, " Glory to God in the highest, and on earth peace, good will toward men."—Similar must be the feelings, though mingled with many fears and uncertainties, of a first missionary in a heathen land. The stronger his faith of the message with which he comes, and his confidence for success in the promises of that God whose message it is, will be the absence of fear, and the predominance of joy and hope, and I may add, too, the likelihood of success.—The Apostle Paul, instead of being disheartened by the false accusations, and spiteful opposition of his many adversaries, was only the more animated to make "full proof of his ministry,"—to act up, as far as possible, to the extent of his commission. He began, as he himself assures us, instantly on his receiving the truth, with all the ardour that continued to the end to distinguish him,—" When it pleased God, who separated me from my mother's womb, and called me by his grace, to reveal his Son in me, that I might preach him among the heathen; immediately I conferred not with flesh and blood: neither went I up to Jerusalem to them which were apostles before me; but I went into Arabia, and returned again unto Damascus."*

The meaning of "*building upon another man's foundation*" is sufficiently plain, especially from what was formerly said of its conformity with other parts of his writings. And so

* Gal. i. 15—17.

is the application of the words of Isaiah in verse twenty-first—"To whom he was not spoken of, they shall see: and they that have not heard shall understand."*

In drawing to a close, I call upon you to imitate the great Apostle of the Gentiles—

1. In his *zeal:* his zeal in spirit and in practice for the glory of Christ and the salvation of men. Let every Christian imitate it in the station assigned him, and by the means that are legitimately in his power. There is not a Christian on earth that has not, in some degree, the opportunity of doing good—some sphere of usefulness. Let every one be diligent in filling up the sphere allotted to him. What objects of interest are those I have mentioned! Every believer's bosom must glow with ardent desire to honour his Saviour—and that Saviour *is* honoured in the salvation of souls. And O what an object to save souls from death!†

2. In his *humility.* He ascribes all that he had done to Christ. *He* had qualified him *for* his work; he had blessed him *in* it. His office, his knowledge, his power, his ability for labour and hardship, and the efficacy of his ministry—all were from Christ:—" For I am the least of the apostles, that am not meet to be called an apostle, because I persecuted the church of God. But by the grace of God I am what I am: and his grace which was bestowed upon me was not in vain; but I laboured more abundantly than they all: yet not I, but the grace of God which was with me."‡ It is the work of Christ by his Spirit to make men willingly obedient—not ours. All his servants should look to him for the blessing, without which their labours will be vain.

3. In his *generosity.* He disdains to be indebted for any part of his honour to others. Rather would he part with his own to others, than take that of others to himself. Rather would he pluck the laurel from his own brow and place it on another's, than pluck a single leaf from the brow of another for himself.

---

* The words are from chap. lii. 15, as they stand in the Septuagint version.

† Jam. v. 20; Matt. xvi. 26.   ‡ 1 Cor. xv. 9, 10.

LECTURE LXVIII.

ROMANS XV. 22—33.

"For which cause also I have been much hindered from coming to you. But now having no more place in these parts, and having a great desire these many years to come unto you; whensoever I take my journey into Spain, I will come to you: for I trust to see you in my journey, and to be brought on my way thitherward by you, if first I be somewhat filled with your company. But now I go unto Jerusalem to minister unto the saints. For it hath pleased them of Macedonia and Achaia to make a certain contribution for the poor saints which are at Jerusalem. It hath pleased them verily; and their debtors they are. For if the Gentiles have been made partakers of their spiritual things, their duty is also to minister unto them in carnal things. When therefore I have performed this, and have sealed to them this fruit, I will come by you into Spain. And I am sure that, when I come unto you, I shall come in the fulness of the blessing of the gospel of Christ. Now, I beseech you, brethren, for the Lord Jesus Christ's sake, and for the love of the Spirit, that ye strive together with me in your prayers to God for me; that I may be delivered from them that do not believe in Judea; and that my service which I have for Jerusalem may be accepted of the saints; that I may come unto you with joy by the will of God, and may with you be refreshed. Now the God of peace be with you all. Amen."

THE Apostle had mentioned in the beginning of his letter the desire which he had long cherished to visit Rome.* He here repeats the same assurance. The cause which had prevented him from accomplishing his desire was, the principle by which he was influenced in regard to his apostolic labours, mentioned in the preceding verses; his eagerness, namely, to break up fresh ground—to occupy fields on which others had not preceded him.† In fulfilment of this purpose, he

* Chap. i. 9—13. † Verses 20 21.

was now busy in Achaia, and wherever he could find an entrance for the Gospel. New openings having presented themselves in succession, for a long period, "in these parts"—Macedonia, Achaia, and the surrounding districts, —he had been detained from gratifying his wish to see Rome—a wish which we find him expressing at Ephesus, before his second visit to Europe.* The occasion on which this wish was expressed is strikingly indicative of the indefatigable zeal and enlarged spirit of this servant of God. While there remained a spot of inhabited earth within his reach, which had not been visited by the Gospel, he could not be satisfied. On the principle of preaching "where Christ was not yet known," it is likely he would not even have thought of Rome, had there been no "*region beyond*" into which he might be the first to carry the lamp of truth. How desirous soever of seeing the Christians there, of enjoying their company, and even of adding amongst them by his ministry some additional trophies to the Saviour's grace, he yet longed to enlighten what was still in darkness, and to bear the tidings of mercy to those whose ears had not heard "the joyful sound."—Accordingly, you observe, that even Rome, the metropolis of the world, is not here his *primary* object. It is only secondary and by the way. He had filled all the region whence he wrote with the proclamation of the Gospel; so that, on looking round him, he saw no portion of it remaining where there was an immediate call for his further ministrations. And now, to what new quarter does he look? To Rome? No; but to SPAIN,—and to Rome as lying in his way. He would "make his journey into Spain," and take Italy in passing thither:—" for," says he, "I trust to see you in my journey, and to be brought on my way thitherward by you, if first I be somewhat filled with your company."

Here is, first, *open honesty*. He does not pretend that Rome was the immediate, far less the sole object of his proposed journey. He does not say—I come for the sake of seeing you at Rome; and, as I shall then be so far on my

---

* Acts xix. 21.

way to Spain, I may take the opportunity of advancing a little further and penetrating into that country. He does not, for the sake of ingratiating himself, make more of the believers at Rome than the truth of the case warranted. There is often, my brethren, in our intercourse and correspondence, great danger of a kind of insincerity arising from such a cause as I have hinted at. We wish to impress those to whom we speak or write with their holding a prominent place in our regards; and we tacitly leave them, by an indirect mode of expression, to think, if we do not even in words directly assure them, that we have come, or purpose coming, *to see them*, when the real object of our visit to the place is different, and our seeing them, however truly gratifying to us, is only an incidental enjoyment. There is too much of this kind of hypocritical courtesy even amongst Christians. Better were it, if "simplicity and godly sincerity" had in all our conduct and conversation a more decided sway. When we cannot be courteous but at the expense of truth, it is better to say nothing at all. Many a glozing lie has been covered by a too courtly civility.

We have further, *real affection, accompanied with genuine politeness*—the politeness of honest feeling. It appears here in *two ways:* First, in his confidence in their kindness to himself. He does not hesitate in expressing his assurance that they would help him forward on his proposed journey beyond them:—"for I trust to see you in my journey, and to be brought on my way thitherward by you." His being "*brought on his way*" means his being conducted, and supplied with what might be needful for the journey.* This unaffected confidence is always one of the marks of true friendship and affection. Whenever we feel it necessary to make many apologies for presuming to request or to expect a favour, it is a proof that between us and the person we address such friendly confidence does not exist. There is, however, a *tact* and propriety in such matters. There

---

* Such convoys were a common way of manifesting regard, Acts xvii. 15; xxi. 5.

are persons who have a knack of availing themselves of the very slightest acquaintance for taxing others with trouble and even expense on their account, in a way that is quite unbecoming and presumptuous. To those whose overweening self-sufficiency prevents this sense of propriety, there is no imparting it. Their obtrusive forwardness and unreasonable expectations are irksome and tormenting to a mind of sensibility that knows not how to bring itself to refuse what yet it sees and feels to be a violation of all decorum. But still, where there is true friendship, there will be mutual freedom, and the fullest confidence that it will be a pleasure to our friend to serve and to help us.—Paul had friends at Rome—many whom he personally knew, and some probably to whom he could have said as he does to Philemon—"Albeit I do not say to thee how thou owest unto me even thine own self besides;"* and with regard to them all, he confided in their friendly regard to himself as an Apostle of Christ, and in the interest they felt about the cause in which he was engaged. This is a ground of confidence, on which ministers of the Gospel may often have to presume in prosecuting their work. Even from those of whom they have no personal knowledge, or with whom they are not at all on habits of intimacy, they may look for attention and aid *for the sake of their cause.* This was the principle by which Gaius was influenced, and which the Apostle John so highly commends.†

His affection further appears in the pleasure with which he anticipates their company, and his desire to be with them for as long a time as his ulterior objects and engagements would permit—"if first I be somewhat filled with your company." "*Filled:*" that is, satisfied. But he does not speak of being *fully* satisfied, or even simply of being satisfied with their company: he speaks in the terms of heartfelt love, and yet of the most unexceptionable courtesy—"if first I be *somewhat* filled." He knew he might not have it in his power to stay so long as his inclination might dictate;

---

* Philem. verse 19.   † 3 John 5—8.

but he hoped to be able to spend *some short time* with them. In many cases, there is little pleasure, and less profit, in merely seeing individuals for an hour or for a day. If they are strangers, you cannot know them in that time; and it is not till you come in some measure to know them that you can have the truest enjoyment of their society, or derive from their conversation the pleasure and the profit it might yield. The most valuable characteristics are frequently those which it requires considerable time to elicit. The superficial are soonest known, because there is least to know. You are speedily at the bottom; but when there, you find but little that is of any worth. If on the other hand they are well-known friends, there is the pain of parting uncompensated by the profit of meeting. The fondness of true friendship always produces a lingering reluctance to part: but *duty* ought to dictate against inclination. When an important object demands our presence and attention elsewhere, however fascinating and even however improving the company of friends we love may be, it must not be allowed to detain us; nor should we, in such cases, attempt to detain those whom we might even like to keep permanently, lest we should subject them, for the sake of a temporary gratification, to the distress of self-reflection afterwards, when duty is found to have been delayed till a precious opportunity of good perhaps has been lost. There are few things more pleasing than to meet, in different places, with Christian friends, whose conversation and intercourse are refreshing and edifying, and with some of whom you feel that you could settle for an indefinite period. Wherever there is *Christianity*—the common faith and hope of the Gospel—there is ground for affectionate attachment. You feel it even for those whose faces you have not "seen in the flesh;" and you feel it especially, wherever you come in contact with those whose dispositions and deportment show them to be truly the "excellent of the earth." Thus at least it *ought* always to be; and when the mutual affection and unwillingness to part is not at all experienced, there must, on the one side, or on the other, or on both, be some grievous defect. Wherever there is the faith of the Gospel, there should be the love of the Gospel,—the love that unites in the bonds of friendship and of brotherhood all who believe it. Yet true it is that you sometimes find the faith of the Gospel in union with features of character that are not amiable; and that, painful to your own minds as it may be, you feel it impossible to experience the complacency of affection. There is a coldness of temperament, or there is an ill-natured censoriousness, or an obtrusive and self-sufficient forwardness, or a distant reserve, or a something else, you may hardly be able to tell what, that makes you very soon "filled with the company" of such, and quite well-pleased to be out of it. You think you have met with such characters. Have you ever thought of asking yourselves whether the fault has not been *your own?* Those who are themselves in the fault are sometimes the readiest to complain. Let us all for ourselves cultivate those dispositions, and display them in the intercourse of life, which will attach others to us, and render our company the object not of aversion but of desire.

Again:—While Paul's designs were formed according to inclination, guided by considerations relative to the great objects of his official life, they were formed in the spirit of *dependence on God*. He had learned by experience that all his plans for the future were subject to an overruling will superior to his own. When he says, even in this passage, "I *trust* to see you in my journey, and to be brought on my way thitherward by you, if first I be somewhat filled with your company," it was not with him a mere unmeaning utterance. His trust rested somewhere; and who that knows anything of Paul can doubt where? The language as used by *him*, was equivalent to—*If God will.* His purposes were sometimes frustrated, or were accomplished in ways and by means very different from what he anticipated. Sometimes the direct command of the Spirit interdicted them.* Sometimes by visions he was carried where he had not at the time intended.† Sometimes remarkable turns in

---

* Acts xvi. 6, 7. † Acts xvi. 9, 10.

providence introduced the greatest and most unexpected changes. Thus it was in the present instance as to his visit to Rome:—" I must see Rome," said he:—" I will come by you into Spain—I trust to see you." And he *did* see Rome. But it was in another way than he thought of. He went thither as "a prisoner in bonds." It was the way in which it pleased the Lord to send him: and he himself found that it contributed to the benefit of his cause.* Let us, in all our schemes, while we trust in God for their fulfilment, trust *with submission,* leaving everything in His hands as the infinitely wise. *We* know not what is best;—and what seems best in our eyes may be far from appearing so in His. We know not what a day may bring forth: "He knows the end from the beginning." Whether the Apostle ever made out his projected visit to Spain is a matter of entire uncertainty. There is no evidence whatever of his having been there:† and as from what he says in verse twentieth, the probability is that Spain was yet an unevangelized country, there seems no foundation for what is called the " Legend of St. James," according to which that Apostle had been by this time fifteen years in Spain, and according to the views of ecclesiastical polity held by those, whosoever they were, to whom the unauthentic legend is imputable, had instituted there various bishoprics.

But Paul had something else in hand, which, at all events, must first be done: verse 25. "But now I go unto Jerusalem to minister unto the saints." This "*ministering to the saints,*" refers to the fulfilment of a trust reposed in him by the Gentile churches, which he had been visiting, in relation to the poor in "the churches of Judea."‡ " For it hath pleased them of Macedonia and Achaia to make a certain contribution for the poor saints which are at Jerusalem. It hath pleased them verily; and their

---

* See Phil. i. 12—14.

† This would seem rather strong a statement. The point is still much disputed.—ED.

‡ For the *time,* see Acts xx. 1—3; and for the *purpose,* Acts xxiv. 17. Thus, accordingly, he explains his words in the verses which follow.

debtors they are. For if the Gentiles have been made partakers of their spiritual things, their duty is also to minister unto them in carnal things." From the general complexion of other passages on the same subject, as well as from the fact of the different churches through extensive districts concurring at one time in the same object, there can be little doubt that the contribution was made at the Apostle's suggestion. He was desirous to have this general expression of the good-will of the Gentile believers to their brethren in Judea, with the view of mitigating and doing away the jealousy that subsisted between these two great sections, if we may so denominate them, of the Christian church. This was like the man;—seeking the amalgamation of all parties, and the entire removal of everything that marred the uniting influence of the "love of the Spirit" among those who, whether Jew or Gentile, were "all one in Christ Jesus." And the manner in which he here alludes to it is equally like him. A man of self-display would have found room for the intimation of the proposal for such a collection having come from himself. Not so with the Apostle. He keeps himself out of view. Even if he had mentioned his own suggestion and influence, what he says would have been perfectly true, "*It hath pleased them.*" Even although a project may not be of our own originating, yet the instant the hint of it is given, we may catch at it, and take it up with hearty good-will, it may with equal propriety be said that "it pleases us" to do it. But there is something very amiable in the Apostle keeping his own part in the matter out of sight, that so the churches themselves might have the greater credit in it.

The Epistle to the Romans is thus shown to have been written after these collections had been made, and before they were taken to Jerusalem. And from the references to the collections in the second Epistle to the Corinthians, and indeed in the first also, it is evident that these two Epistles were written previously to this.*

---

* Comp. 1 Cor. xvi. 1—4: 2 Cor. viii. 1—4; ix. 1—4.

While, on the one hand, this contribution was a "freewill offering," there was a sense at the same time in which it was but the payment of a debt—"It hath pleased them verily, *and their debtors they are.*" There was first the willing mind—the disposition of a cheerful giver to "sow bountifully." Yet there was the obligation of justice as well as of generosity lying upon them. The contribution was a thing, it is true, which the Jewish brethren could not demand. Yet, considering the benefits which through their instrumentality the Gentiles had obtained, they might have had reason for thinking there was an absence of right feeling, if when those who had been the instruments of imparting such benefits stood, in any way, in need of their aid, they had, instead of volunteering it instantly, withheld it even when the granting of it was proposed to them.

The ground of the obligation is simply and forcibly stated —"*For if the Gentiles have been made partakers of their spiritual things, their duty is also to minister unto them in carnal things.*" Why are the discoveries and blessings of the Gospel called "*their* spiritual things?" Not merely, I apprehend, from their having actually been participated first by the Jews, but from the fact of the Jews having, from the beginning, been the chosen depositaries of the oracles of God, and of the knowledge and the blessings of His covenant; and from the covenant itself being ever represented as primarily *theirs.** In this way "salvation was of the Jews;" and its truths and blessings came from them to the Gentiles, having been throughout in the purposes and intimations and actual procedure of God "*to the Jew first.*" The Gentiles were deeply indebted to the zeal and benevolence of the Apostles and other preachers of the Cross; who were Jews, and by much suffering and self-denial had communicated the tidings of salvation, with all the blessings thence arising in possession and in hope. The obligation, therefore, on every principle of justice and generosity, was manifest—"If the Gentiles have been made partakers of their spiritual things, their

* Chap. ix. 4, 5.

duty is also to minister unto them in carnal things." The recompense, or rather the expression of gratitude, was infinitely beneath the amount of obligation, taking the estimate from the comparative value of "carnal" and "spiritual" things —things temporal and things eternal. The words of Paul on another occasion might in their full spirit and emphasis be applied here:—" If we have sown unto you spiritual things, is it a great thing if we shall reap your carnal things?"* My brethren, the obligation remains. *We* are still their debtors. We have all our knowledge from the Jews, from whom it was *first* imparted to the Gentiles; and from the "lively oracles," both of the Old and New Testaments, which were written by "holy men of God" among that people. Whenever, therefore, any appeal is made to us on behalf of the Jews, whether for their temporal or their spiritual good, we ought to feel the emotions of gratitude and the sacredness of the obligation to comply with its claims. I confess, I am not so sure about appeals made in behalf of *churches of Christian Israelites* amongst ourselves; because I can see no scriptural ground for converted Israelites not incorporating themselves with the churches of the Gentiles among whom they dwell: but the general obligation of gratitude and justice to the Jewish people should lead us, with all liberality and with all zeal, " to do them good as we have opportunity." And the principle of this applies in every case in which we may stand indebted to individuals as instruments of conveying the grace of God and the blessings of His salvation to our souls. For I have further to remark, that gratitude to God, as the supreme Author of salvation, does not at all preclude the exercise of gratitude to the human instruments into whose hearts and into whose power He puts it to convey its blessings to us,—and who, in doing this, may themselves be influenced by motives of the purest benevolence. .

The communication of this *love-token* to the saints in Judea was Paul's *first* object:—verse 28. " When therefore I have performed this, and have sealed to them this fruit, I

---

* 1 Cor. ix. 11.

will come by you into Spain." The collection was the *fruit* of Christian love.* And are we not taught by the simple figure that liberality is produced by Christian faith and love as naturally and spontaneously as the fruit is produced by the tree? There is no true principle that is not productive.† There is no faith, unless there be the "work of faith,"—no love, unless there be "the labour of love,"—no hope, unless there be "the patience of hope,"—no possession of the Spirit, unless there be "the fruits of the Spirit." "Either make the tree good, and his fruit good; or else make the tree corrupt, and his fruit corrupt: for the tree is known by his fruit."‡

" When I have *sealed to them* this fruit"—that is, when I have safely delivered, and so secured its appropriation to its purpose; a seal being used for security. When this had been done, he would follow out his purpose as to Rome and Spain :— and it was his delight to anticipate his visit—for he trusted that the divine Spirit and blessing would be with him when he came —verse 29. "And I am sure that, when I come unto you, I shall come in the fulness of the blessing of the gospel of Christ." He knew that they would pray for him, that when he did come his visit might be for the good of the church and for the glory of God, and he had a firm and cheerful confidence that a gracious answer would be vouchsafed both to their prayers for this and to his own. He *knew* it on this general ground, that this was something according to God's will, and which would therefore without fail be granted;— and he knew it from the gracious promise of his Master's presence with His servants, which would be for no other purpose than to bless them and to make them a blessing.§ He knew it, moreover, from his own past experience in the service of Christ. He had all along hitherto experienced the divine blessing attendant upon his labours, so that he could say, "Thanks be unto God who always causeth us to triumph in Christ, and maketh manifest the savour of his knowledge by us in every place."

---

* Compare 2 Cor. ix. 10; Phil. iv. 17.   † 1 John iii. 16—18.
‡ Matt. xii. 33.   § Matt. xxviii. 20.

To come "*in the fulness of the blessing of the gospel of Christ*" has been explained as of the same import as coming "with a full and abundant blessing attending my ministerial and evangelical labours." But there appears to be more in the phrase than this. "The fulness of the blessing of the gospel of Christ" is the fulness of spiritual blessing which the Gospel reveals, and is designed by the faith of it to communicate:—not mere supernatural gifts, as some would interpret the words. These are hardly to be reckoned as a part of the blessing of the Gospel. They were rather evidences of the truth and divine authority of the Gospel by which the blessing came. The gifts of tongues, of healing, of prophecy, and others, were very far from "the fulness of the blessing of the Gospel." Whatever good of a direct kind arose from them, their *in*direct was their highest use. They were signs of divine truth. The truth itself contained and communicated the blessing. It is the blessing of present salvation—of peace, and joy, and hope, and love, and all the spiritual affections, and general holiness, with the happiness thence arising:—it is all that is contained in the subject of the Apostle's thanksgiving:—" Blessed be the God and Father of our Lord Jesus Christ, who hath blessed us with all spiritual blessings in heavenly places in Christ."* By his coming, all the holy principles and affections engendered by the Gospel would be abundantly increased, and all the joys of God's salvation more largely and richly experienced by them and by himself. He did anticipate the imparting to them of "spiritual gifts"—but all these were in subordination and subserviency to the increase of grace and of "meetness for the inheritance of the saints in light:"—and while there may be an immediate reference to the edification of the church, there may also be included an abundant blessing by means of the Gospel to others, in order to its increase.†

What were the means by which all this was to be brought about?—verses 30—32. "Now, I beseech you, brethren, for the Lord Jesus Christ's sake, and for the love of the Spirit,

---

* Eph. i. 3. † Chap. i. 13.

that ye strive together with me in your prayers to God for me; that I may be delivered from them that do not believe in Judea; and that my service which I have for Jerusalem may be accepted of the saints; that I may come unto you with joy by the will of God, and may with you be refreshed."

He speaks here with *great earnestness*. The thirtieth verse contains the very strongest pleas which it is possible to use with fellow-christians. He beseeches them " for the Lord Jesus Christ's sake." The plea involves an appeal to all the obligations under which the "love that passeth knowledge" had laid them. It brings before their minds the grace of Him who "though he was rich, yet for our sakes became poor." What heart that felt its obligations to the Saviour could resist such an appeal? And yet the appeal is stronger than in our version it appears. Our translators have, by a simple inadvertence probably, left out the word our —" by *our* Lord Jesus Christ."* This adds force to the appeal, bringing before them his and their union in Christ.†

To this he adds "*the love of the Spirit.*" The designation is capable of different senses. It may mean the love manifested by the Spirit in the part which He takes in effecting the salvation of sinners; His work being as essential to salvation as the work of Christ, and as much the result of free self-moving compassion. And whatever was the case with Christians *then*, it is to be feared that Christians now-a-days are far from being duly impressed with their obligations to "the love of the Spirit." They think mainly of the love of the Father and the Son. And yet, when believers reflect how much they owe to the Spirit in the commencement, and progress, and consummation of the divine life, ought not this appeal to be equally powerful with the other?—But "the love of the Spirit" may signify that love which is the fruit of the Spirit,—which the Spirit inspires and maintains. The appeal will then be to the love in whose bonds believers, as members of the redeemed family of God, are united: the mutual reciprocal attachment by which they were knit to each

---

* Διὰ τοῦ κυρίου ἡμῶν Ἰησοῦ Χριστοῦ. † Comp 1 Cor. i. 2.

other,—he to them and they to him; just as men frequently adjure one another by the strength and tenderness of their mutual friendships. It is thus equivalent to saying—" As you love the Saviour and would show your regard for Him; as you are grateful for the grace of the Spirit, and would give evidence of your being under the influence of the love He inspires—' I beseech you, brethren, that ye strive together with me in your prayers to God for me.' "

He seeks their personal and their social prayers; their earnest, importunate, persevering prayers; prayers in which they should " *strive* " for an answer in his behalf,— saying like the wrestling patriarch, " We will not let thee go except thou bless thy servant:" and he seeks their prayers to accompany and second his own. He prayed for himself— and he desired their prayers for him; knowing the assurance of his Master—" Verily I say unto you, if two of you shall agree on earth as touching anything that they shall ask, it shall be done for them of my Father which is in heaven."

The points to which he wished their petitions to be directed are indicated in the following verses:—

1. "*That he might be delivered from them that did not believe in Judea.*" There was in the bosoms of his unbelieving countrymen a special hostility to Paul, on three grounds—his having been at first so virulent and so active an assistant of their own cause in opposing the Gospel, and his having passed, like a turncoat as they would call him, from the one side to the other, and become so signally zealous a promoter of "the faith" which once he destroyed; his being in a peculiar manner "the Apostle of the Gentiles;" and the report which falsely prevailed concerning him that he inculcated upon the Jews that were among the Gentiles the entire abandonment of circumcision and the Mosaic law. —The event showed that his fears were far from groundless. He anticipated evil, and he found it.* His own prayers and his urgent request for theirs proceed on the knowledge that "the Lord could make the wrath of man to praise him: and

---

* Acts xx. 21—24.

restrain the remainder thereof;" that He who had sent out his servants as "sheep among wolves," could preserve them from falling a prey to their teeth. It was a sense of the value of his life to the cause of Christ, not the mere natural love of life itself, that made him thus urgent. Mark his language to the Philippians—" For me to live is Christ, and to die is gain. But if I live in the flesh, this is the fruit of my labour: yet what I shall choose I wot not. For I am in a strait betwixt two, having a desire to depart, and to be with Christ, which is far better: nevertheless to abide in the flesh is more needful for you.

2. "*That his service which he had for Jerusalem might be accepted of the saints.*" It was a fruit of love; and he was solicitous that, given in love, it might be received in love; that thus it might have the desired and important effect of smoothing down discordant feelings, of conciliating the affections of the Jewish to the Gentile believers, and so knitting them more closely in the bonds of a cordial union, as "all one in Christ Jesus."* If their prayers were mercifully answered in these two points, it would contribute to—

3. The *third* object for which he wished their prayers: "*That he might come unto them with joy by the will of God, and might with them be refreshed.*" Here is the distinct recognition in words of the principle before adverted to. All depended on "the will of God." The "*refeshing*" which he anticipated was a spiritual exhilaration and strengthening of the principles and affections of the divine life in the soul:—joy and consolation from the mutual interchange of sentiment and feeling, than which there are few things either more pleasant or more profitable for Christians in pursuing their journey to the celestial country; and the increase of all the Christian graces—of "faith working by love"—of "fortitude, and knowledge, and temperance, and patience, and godliness, and brotherly kindness, and charity."

Before proceeding to the more personal part of his letter, the Apostle closes this part by giving utterance, as he was

* See 2 Cor. ix. 11—14.

wont to do, (and with him all such expressions came from the heart,) to his desire that they might enjoy the presence and blessing of God—that God who had revealed himself as "reconciling the world unto himself by Jesus Christ"—as at peace through him with our guilty race, and who was the author by his Spirit of the blessed sense of peace with himself in the believing soul, and of the spirit of peace amongst His people:—Now the God of peace be with you all. Amen!"

1. There is much to imitate in Paul's character. We noticed different points on the former passage. We now remark his *unselfishness*. How anxiously concerned he is about these collections for others!—and how careless and indifferent as to any temporal provision for himself!* How much is here of the spirit of his divine Master! He was delighted with the thought of a supply to the wants of the poor; and the cementing of the hearts of the saints in holy and affectionate union was to him a source of the purest joy. Thus let it be with us. Let us "remember the poor;" and, above all things, for Christ's sake, for his people's sake, for the world's sake, let us "seek and pray for the peace of Jerusalem." And from the approved and recorded example of the churches of Macedonia and Achaia, let us learn the duty and study the practice of liberality—of liberality for the saints of God, the members of the "household of faith." We are stewards for God; and everything, whether temporal or spiritual, by the bestowment of which He has put it in our power to be of service to others, has constituted us debtors to our fellow-christians, and our fellow-men, upon the great principle of the divine example, and of the royal Law.

2. Observe the value set by Paul on the prayers of the brethren, and from this too learn to pray for ourselves, and to pray one for another;—especially in times and circumstances of difficulty and danger; and more especially still for lives of eminent usefulness in the church and in the world when they are exposed to peril. The Lord, it is true,

---

* Acts xx. 33—35; 2 Cor. xii. 14, 15.

is never at a loss for instruments to promote His cause;—and we may often form very false notions of what is best for its advancement. He has shown us that He could do without Paul and without all the Apostles: and many a time has He taken away servants of high eminence at the very time when their life seemed most desirable and necessary. It is still, however, our duty to pray for the lives of such, though always with the reservation—"Not as we will, but as THOU wilt." But if "the effectual fervent prayer of one righteous man availeth much," what power must there be in the united prayers of a church of Christ!—Prayer may be answered, though not in the way we might be expecting. If the *end* for which we pray be good, our prayers are truly and effectually answered, when the Lord ensures that end, although it should be by other *means* than those for which we petitioned. When Paul was seized by the Jews at Jerusalem, part of the prayers which he here solicits seemed as if forgotten: yet this was the appointed means of bringing him to Rome, in circumstances which, however seemingly untoward, "turned out," as we have seen, "to the furtherance of the Gospel;"—and if he was hindered from going to Spain, God would say to him as he did to David—"It was well that it was in thy heart;" while he would order matters otherwise, but better, we may be assured, than Paul had projected. If Spain was favoured at that early period with the pure Gospel of peace and spiritual freedom, how sad has been the change! How dense the cloud of darkness over that land of superstition and idolatry and spiritual delusion and bondage! Let it be our prayer that *there*, and wherever the same fearful system of Antichristian error prevails, the simple principles of the Gospel and of the spiritual kingdom of the Redeemer may be introduced and prosper. The Gospel will never achieve its final triumphs in the world, till cleared of all its impurities, and freed from all its trammels, it sets out, as it did at first, with its own divine energies and resources, "conquering and to conquer."

LECTURE LXIX.

ROMANS XVI. 1—15.

"I commend unto you Phebe our sister, which is a servant of the church which is at Cenchrea: that ye receive her in the Lord, as becometh saints, and that ye assist her in whatsoever business she hath need of you: for she hath been a succourer of many, and of myself also. Greet Priscilla and Aquila my helpers in Christ Jesus; who have for my life laid down their own necks: unto whom not only I give thanks, but also all the churches of the Gentiles. Likewise greet the church that is in their house. Salute my well-beloved Epenetus, who is the first-fruits of Achaia unto Christ. Greet Mary, who bestowed much labour on us. Salute Andronicus and Junia, my kinsmen, and my fellow-prisoners, who are of note among the apostles, who also were in Christ before me. Greet Amplias, my beloved in the Lord. Salute Urbane, our helper in Christ, and Stachys my beloved. Salute Apelles, approved in Christ. Salute them which are of Aristobulus' household. Salute Herodion my kinsman. Greet them that be of the household of Narcissus, which are in the Lord. Salute Tryphena and Tryphosa, who labour in the Lord. Salute the beloved Persis, which laboured much in the Lord. Salute Rufus, chosen in the Lord, and his mother and mine. Salute Asyncritus, Phlegon, Hermas, Patrobas, Hermes, and the brethren which are with them. Salute Philologus, and Julia, Nereus, and his sister, and Olympas, and all the saints which are with them."

THE Apostle, agreeably to his ordinary practice, closes his letter with a variety of personal salutations, or as we might express it, affectionate Christian remembrances. The Epistle is in the outset addressed to all the believers in Rome.* Yet in this chapter individuals and families are selected as the objects of special regard. The names of those individuals are chiefly Grecian; and they seem to have been persons

* Chap. i. 7.

whom Paul, (who before this had not been at Rome,) had met with in his travels elsewhere, and who had subsequently either returned to Rome in consequence of the cessation of the Emperor Claudius's edict of banishment, or had gone for the first time to settle there.

From this general fact we learn two lessons:—1. The general love with which we regard the disciples of Jesus, is not inconsistent with those special attachments which arise either from peculiarities of character or from particular circumstances. The idea of universal, and still more of equal, intimacy among all the members of numerous churches (and such, to a very great degree, the primitive churches frequently were) is as absurd in theory as it would be injurious in practice. It could not be maintained without a sacrifice both of the retirement of private life, and of the liberty which every man must have of selecting those bosom friends or intimate companions, to whom he is drawn by similarity of disposition and character, or from whose society he finds that he derives the largest amount of spiritual benefit and enjoyment; and it would infallibly lead to a system of unceasing interchange of visitation, such as would materially interfere with all domestic and relative duties; with the engagements of life, and the sobriety and stayedness of the Christian character —a scene of "busy idleness" and unprofitable gossip, such as cannot be too strongly deprecated. Private intimacies must of necessity be select and mutually voluntary. Even amongst "the twelve" we find Jesus himself had a disciple whom he loved, and who, with one or two others, was evidently admitted to a closer and more constant intimacy than the rest. And in almost all Paul's Epistles he distinguishes individuals with a speciality of remembrance which shows that while all were the objects of his Christian love, he was not insensible either to the peculiar attractions of individual character or to the influence of uniting circumstances.—2. The Apostle was not afraid of exciting feelings of envy and jealousy by thus specifying individual objects of his kind regards. Love should be the uniting bond amongst all the members of a Christian church; and this love should be practical in regard to *all;*

each attending, as far as in him lies, to the interests, both temporal and spiritual, of the rest, and no one presuming to say of any other—"Am I my brother's keeper?" In this way the general power of that love which holds together all the members of the body should be kept in action; while all, at the same time, without any feeling of coolness, or of grudging and discontent, are allowed the exercise of their freedom in the selection of their more immediate and intimate friendships, companionships, and domestic intercommunions. Let us now attend more particularly to the passage before us:—verses 1, 2. "I commend unto you Phebe our sister, which is a servant of the church which is at Cenchrea; that ye receive her in the Lord, as becometh saints, and that ye assist her in whatsoever business she hath need of you: for she hath been a succourer of many, and of myself also." The Apostle wrote from Corinth, and sent his letter by the female messenger here named. Cenchrea was the seaport of Corinth—about nine miles from the city, on the Saronic gulph. There a Christian church had been formed; of which church Phebe was "*a servant.*" I have no doubt that this means an *official* servant; that she acted in the capacity of *deaconess*.* Paul recommends her both as a sister —or member of "the household of faith," the spiritual family of God, and as an office-bearer in the Cenchrean church.

You will ask me, perhaps, if there was a deaconess, or if there were deaconesses, in that church, why have we not deaconesses still? I answer this question by another—Why were there no deaconesses in the church at Jerusalem? "When the number of disciples was multiplied," we are told in the sixth chapter of the Acts, "there arose a murmuring of the Grecians against the Hebrews, because their widows were neglected in the daily ministration. Then the twelve called the multitude of the disciples unto them, and said, It is not reason that we should leave the word of God, and serve tables. Wherefore, brethren, look ye out among you seven men of honest report, full of the Holy Ghost and wisdom,

---

* So Alford and others.—ED.

whom we may appoint over this business."* In this instance, it is remarkable, the objects of attention more immediately in view were *females—widows.* Yet no females are appointed to office. From what could this difference between the Judean and the Grecian and Asiatic churches originate? We find it readily in the difference in the state of manners in the different countries? In Greece, and still more in Asia, the freedom of intercourse between the sexes was under restrictions; and it was necessary, to avoid reproach among the disciples, that these restrictions should not unnecessarily be broken through. In these circumstances, the same kind of necessity which gave origin to the office gave occasion to this peculiarity of it—its administration in part by females, who could at all times have free access to the sisterhood of the churches that required their attendance and aid. You will from this be sensible, that it is *the office* that is the divine institution; and that where *men* are in circumstances to fulfil its duties, their appointment is a satisfactory conformity to the rule and example of the Apostles; and that in circumstances of a different description, it would be more than justifiable, it would be a duty to conform to the Grecian and Asiatic custom, which has evidently the sanction of the same authority.

Paul enjoins the believers at Rome to "*receive Phebe in the Lord.*" They were to receive her, that is, as belonging to Christ, —one of his true spiritual disciples. It is the same disposition of mind with that which the Lord himself commends, and promises to reward.† They were to receive her to the fellowship of the church, to friendly intercourse, to needful accommodation. Thus, the Apostle taught them, and teaches us, "*it becometh saints.*" It becomes them to "receive one another," not with cold reserve and distant formality, with worldly ceremony and hollow-hearted politeness, but with the open sincerity and warmth of love, as members of the same family,—all alike "sons and daughters of the Lord Almighty." The relation between them is ever the same; and when

* Acts vi. 1—3. † Mark ix. 41.

strangers come amongst us from a distance, we do well to bear in mind the admonition—"Let brotherly love continue. Be not forgetful to entertain strangers: for thereby some have entertained angels unawares."*

The reception was not to be confined to kind words; there were to be kind deeds too:—"And assist her in whatsoever business she hath need of you." Phebe seems to have gone to Rome on some business of her own, of the nature of which it would be foolish and silly to conjecture. They were to show their kindness by forwarding for her the object of her journey. Such, in similar cases, is our duty. It is the duty of ordinary friendship, and much more should it be felt the duty of Christian love.—There is a special reason assigned in the case before us for their practical regard:—"for she hath been a *succourer* of many, and of myself also." The word is by some rendered *patroness*. It means one who *stands forward* for the help of another.† It is unnatural to consider this as relating to the discharge of her *official* functions. In this view the aid would have been, not so much hers as the church's; and it is very unlikely that such aid should either have come to the Apostle and his fellow-labourers through *her* hands, or, if it had, should have been so warmly commended by him as if it had been her own.—She was probably a woman of substance, who had in this way a good deal in her power. There were such godly women in our Lord's time—"women which had been healed of evil spirits and infirmities, Mary called Magdalene, out of whom went seven devils, and Joanna, the wife of Chuza, Herod's steward, and Susanna, and many others, which ministered unto him of their substance."‡ The record is to their perpetual honour. To what higher or better purpose could they apply any portion of their wealth, than in contributing to *His* relief, who, "though rich, yet for our sakes became poor;" and whose voluntary poverty was such that he could say, "Foxes have holes, and the birds of the air have nests, but the Son of man hath not where to lay his head?"—We know that there

---

* Heb. xiii. 1, 2.   † προστάτις.   ‡ Luke viii. 2, 3.

were, in various places, women of rank and property brought under the saving power of the truth.*—Phebe was neither ashamed nor reluctant to "take upon her the fellowship of the ministering to the saints." She felt it an honour to be a "servant of the church for Jesus' sake;" and in ministering of her own private substance for the support and comfort of the servants and brethren of Christ, she remembered Him who said, "Verily I say unto you, inasmuch as ye have done it unto one of the least of these my brethren, ye have done it unto me."

Learn, and act upon the two lessons, which this case immediately suggests. The first is, that "the least of all and servant of all" is truly the greatest in the kingdom of Christ. The disciple that is humblest and does most good has the highest dignity. And lest the poor should think this bears hard on them, having so little in their power, we remind them of the maxim, "If there be first a willing mind, it is accepted according to that a man hath, and not according to that he hath not;" and of the Lord's verdict on the poor widow who contributed her two mites to the offerings of the sanctuary, "Verily I say unto you, That this poor widow hath cast more in than all they which have cast into the treasury."—The other lesson is, that those who have "succoured" others in need have themselves a peculiar claim to be "succoured." The benevolence of Phebe had not, it is true, been bestowed upon the members of the church at Rome; but it had been bestowed on members of the same spiritual family elsewhere; and especially it had been conferred on one whom, from his office, his known character and his eminent usefulness, they could not but hold in high estimation. It would be the extreme of injustice and ingratitude, if those who have laid themselves out for the benefit of others should, when standing in need of aid, be neglected.

Verses 3—5. "Greet Priscilla and Aquila my helpers in Christ Jesus; (who have for my life laid down their own necks: unto whom not only I give thanks, but also all the

---

* Acts xvii. 12, and 4.

churches of the Gentiles.) Likewise greet the church that is in their house. Salute my well-beloved Epenctus, who is the first-fruits of Achaia unto Christ." "*Greet*" and "*salute*" are only different renderings of the same original word.* It expresses here, evidently, his best wishes—his affectionate Christian regards. The first mentioned—"*Priscilla and Aquila*"—are mention d with fervent gratitude and high honour. We learn from the opening verses of the eighteenth chapter of the Acts that this excellent pair had left Rome in consequence of the decree before referred to; and had for the time settled at Corinth. There Paul first met them. They attached themselves to him, and accompanied him to Ephesus, in which place they were eminently useful. They afterwards returned to Rome, and were there when this Epistle was written; though they appear afterwards to have returned again to Ephesus, as they were there when Paul wrote his second Epistle to Timothy.†—Paul here acknowledges them as his "*helpers in Christ Jesus.*" Though an Apostle of Christ, occupying the very highest station of authority and honour in the church, he does not despise others; he does not speak lightly of their labours, and dwell with exclusive complacency upon his own. He gratefully owns the help which, in his apostolic work, he had received from these humble individuals.—Here, too, learn a lesson; never to *over*value our own doings, and to *under*value the doings of others; never to cover others by interposing ourselves, but humbly, generously, and thankfully, to give to every one his due meed of commendation and praise.

Other women are mentioned (verses 6, 12) as well as *Priscilla*. There is no need for supposing that the labours thus acknowledged were in any of the cases *official*. Paul and his fellow-labourers experienced no little of the kindness of these godly women towards themselves personally; and they might have many private opportunities and means of usefulness in assisting the progress of the cause of Christ, as well as in visiting the destitute, instructing the ignorant,

---

* ἀσπάσασθε, lit. *embrace*.—ED.   † 2 Tim. iv. 19.

accommodating the servants of God, and otherwise helping them on in their labours. And all such benevolent attentions and services, performed for Christ's sake, come under the general denomination of "*labouring in the Lord;*" all being done in his name, for his sake, from the principles of his Gospel in the mind, and love to him in the heart.—All in their respective spheres should thus labour, in every way that the Lord puts in their power, that is consistent with a due attention to domestic and relative duties, and with that unobtrusive modesty which is one of the principal ornaments and recommendations of the female character,—the "meek and quiet spirit," which is "in the sight of God of great price." The labours of these godly women, we may be assured, were not inconsistent with any principle of the female character, or any duties of female life; else the Apostle would not have honoured them with his commendation: and, wherever there is a union of female energy and female sensibility and modesty, we shall rejoice to see them imitated.

We return to Aquila and Priscilla—"*who have*," says the Apostle, "*for my life laid down their own necks.*" In the form of expression there is an allusion to persons condemned to be beheaded voluntarily laying their necks upon the block. The obvious meaning is, that these two zealous and devoted saints, in their attachment to Christ, and to his servant for his sake, had exposed themselves to the imminent jeopardy of their own lives for the protection and preservation of the Apostle's. On what occasion this took place, or what were the particular circumstances of the case, we know not. The Acts of the Apostles being only memoirs, and these but brief, contains no mention of it. It is supposed to have happened on the occasion recorded in the eighteenth chapter, the twelfth and following verses, when, under the government of the deputy of Achaia, Gallio, the Jews "made insurrection against Paul," eagerly seeking his destruction. To cover from danger so precious a life, they had come boldly forward, and exposed themselves to the risk of popular fury by taking his part, or otherwise exposing their own lives to hazard in his defence.

In this, these disciples set an example of a love formed upon the pattern of Christ's. Their conduct was especially illustrative of the words, "Peradventure for a good man some would even dare to die."* Paul came fully up to the description of character for whom some might even be disposed not to "hazard" merely but to sacrifice life. It was not from personal attachment alone, though that doubtless was strong, but from regard to the interests of the church and of the cause of God that they thus showed their self-devotion. They therefore acted up to the Saviour's requisition of the spirit of martyrdom in all his disciples.† And the Apostle himself had many a time exemplified the same disinterested spirit. He "died daily;" being perpetually in peril of his life. He was willing, from his affection for the churches, to sacrifice his life in their cause:—"Yea, and if I be offered upon the sacrifice and service of your faith, I joy, and rejoice with you all."‡ In recollecting their disinterested boldness, Paul himself expresses his gratitude—"*unto whom I give thanks;*" and he unites with himself in the expression of it "*all the churches of the Gentiles.*" Paul was in a special manner the Apostle of the Gentiles. They were thankful for the preservation of their own Apostle. Aquilas and Priscilla were Jews; and there was the greater ground for thankfulness to them on the part of the Gentiles. My brethren, *we* have cause to join in the grateful acknowledgments. All the churches of God to the end of time lie under a debt of gratitude to those who, under God, saved such a life at the risk of their own. The cutting of it short would have robbed them of a large portion of most valuable inspired instruction—even of a large portion of the Apostle's invaluable writings. Do not you feel the obligation? Does not your love to Paul inspire you with love to such as thus interposed in his behalf? and to that God, who put it by His grace into their hearts?—What is the best way to testify our gratitude? Not by merely praising them; far less, at this distance of time, by rearing any

---

* Rom. v. 7.   † Luke xiv. 26.   ‡ Phil. ii. 17.

monument to their memory. Let us imitate their generous, disinterested love. The requisition has not been erased from the statute-book of the kingdom—"A new commandment I give unto you, That ye love one another; as I have loved you, that ye also love one another;" "Hereby perceive we the love of God, because he laid down his life for us: and we ought to lay down our lives for the brethren."* There they stand, as binding as ever. Do we love Christ, then, more than life? Do we love his Gospel more than life? Do we love his servants, do we love his people, more than life? Do we hold ourselves in readiness to make the sacrifice, were we in providence called to it? We are not placed in circumstances where tumults and insurrections expose the lives of God's servants or of fellow-disciples to hazard. We should, therefore, bring our love to other tests. Let us judge of what we should do with our *lives* from what we actually do with our *property*. The same divine Redeemer who says, —"If any man come to me, and hate not his father and mother, and wife, and children, and brethren, and sisters, yea, and his own life also, he cannot be my disciple;" † says also—"So likewise, whosoever he be of you that forsaketh not all that he hath, he cannot be my disciple:"‡—and the same inspired Apostle who says—"Hereby perceive we the love of God, because he laid down his life for us: and we ought to lay down our lives for the brethren;"§— "adds, "But whoso hath this world's good, and seeth his brother have need, and shutteth up his bowels of compassion from him, how dwelleth the love of God in him?"|| Let us see to it, then, that our love both to Christ and to his people be practical—"not in word nor in tongue, but in deed and in truth." Let us be thankful that the sacrifice of life and the abandonment of all that we have are not practically called for at our hands by the violence of persecution; but let us beware of flattering ourselves that we have a love which would abide this test, if, with abundant means to relieve our needy brethren, to protect them from injustice and oppres-

---

* John xiii. 34: 1 John iii. 16.   † Luke xiv. 26.
‡ Verse 33.   § 1 John iii. 16. || 1 John iii. 17.

sion, or to promote the cause of God, we keep our hand close upon the pittance of our substance that is required for such purposes; or, fond of luxurious ease, will not bestir ourselves in any active and self-denying efforts for their attainment. It is in vain we profess to give thanks to Aquila and Priscilla, or to any of the voluntary martyrs of Christ, if we do not testify our admiration by imbibing the spirit and principles of their character, and imitating their zeal.

Along with his salutations to themselves, he salutes also "*the church in their house.*" The same expression occurs repeatedly in other Epistles: and from this and the phrases in other parts of the chapter,* some have inferred that there were various distinct *churches* properly so called, that is, Christian societies with their appropriate bishops and deacons at that time in Rome. I will not absolutely affirm the contrary: but the considerations in opposition to it are such as I cannot easily get over. Observe the address in the beginning of the Epistle—"To all that be in Rome, beloved of God, called to be saints: Grace to you and peace from God our Father, and the Lord Jesus Christ." Thus the letter is addressed to all the believers in Rome, and yet, upon the hypothesis, there were various churches in the place, of which the one to which the Apostle here writes is desired to salute the rest. We are at no loss to conceive how a collective body, thus addressed, may be requested to present special regards to individuals and domestic circles themselves belonging to it, but marked in the writer's mind by special circumstances. This is a very different thing from all the believers in Rome being comprehended in the address of the letter, and yet the whole body desired to salute other and distinct churches. This may be further illustrated from comparing 1 Cor. xvi. 19. "The churches of Asia salute you. Aquila and Priscilla salute you much in the Lord, with the church that is in their house." This was written *from Ephesus*,† but in Ephesus there was but one church.‡ Also from Col. iv. 15, 16. "Salute the brethren which are in

---

* Verses 14, 15.   † Verse 8.   ‡ Acts xx. 17: Rev. ii. 1.

Laodicea, and Nymphas, and the church which is in his house. And when this epistle is read among you, cause that it be read also in the church of the Laodiceans; and that ye likewise read the epistle from Laodicea." In this passage, the church in the house of Nymphas is mentioned, at the very same time that the church of the Laodiceans is spoken of as *one*.

It appears to me from these instances, that the Apostle uses the word church in a less strict and proper acceptation, as meaning a religious household, of which all the members were Christians, constituting a little worshipping assembly. The church in the house of Aquila and Priscilla at Ephesus was in all likelihood the same as the church in their house at Rome—that is, the worshipping family and friends of these "excellent of the earth." O what a happy state of things, when the families of God's people are thus little churches—worshipping companies of the "general assembly and church of the first-born who are written in heaven!"—united in the double bonds of nature and of grace—one in Christ Jesus—and heirs together of his heavenly kingdom!

"*Epenetus*," the Apostle's well-beloved, is here spoken of as the "*first-fruits of Achaia unto Christ.*"* But Paul says elsewhere, "Ye know the house of Stephanas, that it is the first-fruits of Achaia, and that they have addicted themselves to the ministry of the saints." Some have concluded from this, that Epenetus belonged to the household of Stephanas, and that he was perhaps the first convert of the family. There is a various reading, however, which almost all the principal critics prefer as having the preponderance of authorities in its favour—namely, "the first-fruits of *Asia;*"—and if this reading is, as we think it ought to be, adopted—then by Asia we are to understand not Asia generally, nor even Asia Minor, but proconsular Asia, of which Ephesus was the capital city.

In verse seventh, *Junia* should probably be *Junias*—the brother, perhaps, of *Andronicus;* though some, retaining the

---

* 1 Cor. xvi. 15.

feminine termination, suppose it to be the wife or sister of that disciple. The whole phraseology is more favourable to the former supposition. He calls them his "kinsmen." The same word* is used to signify simply *Jews*.† But as other Jews are mentioned without any such epithet or designation, it probably expresses here some nearer connexion:—it would not otherwise have been distinctive even from the two he had already mentioned in verse third. They were on some occasion his fellow-prisoners for Christ's sake; but where or when we know not, and need not conjecture. Paul was in prisons frequently: and he here remembers himself and reminds them of the bond of sympathy by which, as fellow-sufferers, they were united. It was a recollection that endeared them to him, and he doubted not would awaken the same feeling in their bosoms of reciprocal attachment. He adds *two other* distinctions. They were "*of note among the Apostles;*" that is, they were held by the Apostles in high estimation for their zeal and their general excellence of Christian character. They were early converts, probably either of the original "hundred and twenty," or among the converts of Pentecost; and they were as highly respected and beloved as they were long known. How desirable, my brethren, the approbation and esteem of the good! and especially of those who are capable in an eminent degree of appreciating character. Such above all others were the Apostles of Christ. To stand high in their estimation was enviable eminence indeed.

The other of the two distinctions is—"*Who also were in Christ before me.*" What an interesting distinction this, when we recollect what were once the feelings of him who makes it! He was formerly, as the history, and as he himself tells us, "exceedingly mad against the disciples of Jesus, breathing out against them threatenings and slaughter:" and now he blushes to think of his long-continued opposition to His name and cause, and with the tear of penitential tenderness, envies those who "were in Christ before him!" Before, he had scorned and derided them; now he felt that

* συγγενεῖς. † Rom. ix. 3.

he had himself been the fool. These very disciples, it is possible, had prior to his conversion been among the objects of his direct personal hatred, hostility, and persecution; and they had since been in bonds together for Christ! How interesting, how tender the feeling awakened by such recollections! He would be anxious to make up, in present warmth of affection and interest in their well-being, for all the injury his virulence might before have done them. His own highest honour he now felt to consist in his connexion with Christ; and those who had preceded him in this connexion he regarded as preceding him in honour. He held them in estimation as older disciples than himself, who had been longer in spiritual union with the living Head of the church, and who had been longer in the service of this divine and blessed Master; whose infinite dignity made his service even in the lowest grade of it the truest glory. Let us learn to consider connexion with Christ as the best and most desirable of all distinctions,—incomparably preferable to connexion with the very highest of earthly dignitaries. To be one with HIM is to have "the honour that cometh from God," an honour that is not confined to time, but shall last

"When gems and monuments and crowns
Are moulder'd into dust."

Verses 8—10. "Greet Amplias my beloved in the Lord. Salute Urbane, our helper in Christ, and Stachys my beloved. Salute Apelles approved in Christ. Salute them which are of Aristobulus' household." Of Amplias, Urbanus (for so the name should be written) and Stachys, we know nothing but the names. Apelles was "*approved in Christ;*" one who had been tried and found faithful in the profession and work of Christ, by steady consistent perseverance in labour and in suffering for his sake.—Of Herodion in verse eleventh, we know merely his being in some relation of consanguinity to the Apostle—his "kinsman," like Andronicus and Junias. You will observe that *Aristobulus* and *Narcissus* are not themselves mentioned among those to whom the Apostle sends his salutation; but only those of their respective households who had embraced the faith of the Gospel. There is no evidence, therefore, that they themselves were Christians. They were possibly heads of families, but strangers to the power of the truth which members of their households had received. The converts in their families might, in that case, stand in need of especial notice and encouragement. There is something very affecting in seeing families embracing the truth and experiencing the power of divine grace, while the heads of them remain in a state of alienation from God. Such members of families should give themselves to earnest prayer for the spiritual life of their fathers or mothers, and use every means which affection guided by respect admits of, for preventing the fearful and agonizing result of a final and eternal separation. They were possibly persons of rank who had Christians among their domestics. Many indeed think that Narcissus was the freedman and favourite of the Emperor Claudius: for though before the date of this Epistle he was probably dead, yet the household might retain his name.*

Rufus was probably the same as the Rufus mentioned Mark xv. 21. Paul had met with his mother elsewhere, and experienced a great deal of parental kindness from the aged Christian. She had acted the part of a mother to him. Paul owns this kindness briefly, but tenderly and emphatically, by claiming the filial relation to her, "*his* mother, and *mine*"—his by blood,—mine by the tie of affection, engendered by her motherly care and attention. Such mothers in Israel are valuable; and nothing is more delightful than to see age extending a parental care to those members of the family of God that come within its reach,—seeking by all its motherly attentions the comfort and well-being of the servants and people of Christ.

Of those mentioned in verses fourteenth and fifteenth we know nothing but the names, and the one fact—a most inter-

* The members of these households might be in similar circumstances with those in Phil. iv. 22. [That the family of Narcissus retained his name after his death is also the idea entertained by Winer. Alford seems doubtful on the point.—ED.]

esting and unspeakably important one to them—of their being *Christians*—or, as the Apostle elsewhere says, "partakers of the benefit"—the benefit of the Gospel; a benefit, or rather an assemblage and accumulation of benefits, of incalculable preciousness, and of everlasting duration. To be in such a list as this, is to be in the roll of true honour and lasting fame. It may be little thought of in this world; but it will be envied in eternity. The humblest name in this list will stand higher in the world to come than that of the mightiest monarch that ever swayed a sceptre who lived and died without the grace of God. These names have come down to us in this imperishable memorial; and they shall go down to the close of time. That is little. Those who owned the names have enjoyed centuries of heavenly felicity and glory, if we may apply to the eternity on which they have entered the terms of the arithmetic of time. How many of the men who panted while they lived for a posthumous immortality of fame on earth, and whose names are emblazoned in the page of their country's history, and graven with a "pen of iron" on the sepulchral monument, now feel all the worthlessness of the meed of human honour and sigh in unavailing anguish over the infatuation that bartered the substantial realities of eternity for the cheap and perishable baubles of time. O my brethren, seek to have your names associated with those of the saints of God here enumerated, —among those whom an Apostle would have acknowledged as Christ's, and whom Christ will acknowledge as His own. These are the names of sterling worth. *Men* may despise them: *God* honours them. And whether is it better to be despised of men and honoured of God, or to have all the honour that men can bestow, and by God to be lightly esteemed? I know on which side your *judgments* answer this question, to whichsoever your hearts may be inclined. But I would entreat every hearer, with all earnestness to make his choice—to cast in his lot with the people of God. "Come with us, and we will do you good: for the Lord hath spoken good concerning Israel."

LECTURE LXX.

ROMANS XVI. 16—20.

"Salute one another with an holy kiss. The churches of Christ salute you. Now I beseech you, brethren, mark them which cause divisions and offences contrary to the doctrine which ye have learned; and avoid them. For they that are such serve not our Lord Jesus Christ, but their own belly; and by good words and fair speeches deceive the hearts of the simple. For your obedience is come abroad unto all men. I am glad therefore on your behalf: but yet I would have you wise unto that which is good, and simple concerning evil. And the God of peace shall bruise Satan under your feet shortly. The grace of our Lord Jesus Christ be with you. Amen."

HAVING enjoined his affectionate salutations to various individuals and Christian families in Rome, with whom he had more intimate acquaintance than with the rest of the believers there, the Apostle follows them with a command to the church generally respecting their intercourse with one another—"*Salute one another with an holy kiss.*" On this and similar expressions in other Epistles has been founded by some what they have been pleased to dignify with the designation of "*the ordinance* of salutation,"—"the ordinance of the holy kiss." I feel it very unnecessary to dwell on such a subject. One would have thought that the very connexion in which the words occur should have been enough to preclude the possibility of so groundless a conclusion. They stand in the midst of a number of salutations from the Apostle to different individuals. Did he mean by these, that they were to continue, statedly and permanently saluting Aquilas and Priscilla, and Epenetus and Mary, and Andronicus and Junias, and Tryphena and Tryphosa, and all the rest of them? I need not answer the question. Every one, in an instant, sees and feels the absurdity of the supposition. And yet there is just the same reason for assigning permanence to these and exalting them into stated observances, so long as the individuals lived, as for doing this in regard to the mutual salutation in the verse before us. Were I to allege, that what Paul means is, that on their receiving his letter, they should in the way mentioned express their mutual affection to each other and their common attachment to himself,—the injunction would be of a piece with the rest. To suppose more—anything like a stated public practice —is the extravagance of inferential interpretation; supposing the institution of an ordinance, without the slightest intimation, either in the form of precept or example, as to *when* or *how* it should be observed! There is no evidence even of *publicity:* and granting this Epistle to have been addressed to one church in its collective capacity, the inference drawn from this, that whatever is enjoined in these circumstances must be regarded as obligatory upon them *as a corporate body* when assembled together, is utterly unreasonable, and might be demonstrated to be so by other cases in which the absurdity is apparent. But I will not spend your time with such a subject—a subject which, according to the disposition of the speaker, might be placed in lights either ludicrous or seriously offensive.

A kiss on the cheek was then the prevailing mode of friendly salutation. This is one of the customs which vary in various countries; and in all cases in which there is nothing that is inconsistent with propriety or of evil tendency, it is custom that should, among Christians as well as others, regulate practice.

The Apostle admonishes them that in their salutations of each other they should bear in mind their Christian character and profession. Their salutation is called "a *holy kiss,*" and "a *kiss of love:*"—that is, it should be the expression not of mere common courtesy or even ordinary friendship; but they should salute each other *as saints,* with a pure fervent affection, for the truth's sake:—they should cherish the sentiments of mutual esteem and love; and in all their intercourse maintain, with propriety and dignity, the fondness which the common faith and hope of the Gospel engender. I have said with *propriety* and *dignity;* for there is a kind of intercourse sometimes to be found, in certain classes of professors, which may be styled the sentimentalism of Christian love; which exhausts the vocabulary of a simpering and fondling endearment, and whines itself away in languishing tones and looks and caresses, which is as disgusting as it is weak, and in danger of proving as pernicious as it is either weak or disgusting,

He sends them the salutations of the "*churches of Christ.*" In going from place to place, Paul had received in charge the expression of the affectionate interest of the different Christian societies in the welfare of the rest—to be communicated as he had opportunity.* Here he discharges a part of this commission. Although "the churches of Christ" were all independent one of another in their government and discipline, they were not unconnected and insulated. In those happy days of simplicity and love, to be a member of one church was to be a member of all. They were all united by a bond of common faith—all "one in Christ Jesus." And here we have one of the ways in which they recognized and expressed this unity. Such mutual remembrances were encouraging and animating. Paul understood human nature. He was well aware how ill we like to be forgotten; and how disheartening it is, both to individuals and to churches, to have the impression that there are none who take any interest in them. He knew what a thrill of social pleasure and excitement would be produced by the simple mention of other churches as having them in mind, and desiring their love to them. There ought to be more of this mutual remembrance among the churches still. When pastors go

---

* So *Bengel* "quibuscam fui c. xv. 26." Alford says, "The assurance is stated evidently on the Apostle's authority; speaking for the churches." Why *evidently?* The other seems quite as probable.— ED.

from one place to another, why should they not carry the brotherly salutations of their respective churches with them? —and why should there not, on special occasions, either of remarkable prosperity or of peculiar trial, be direct and special communications from church to church, both of congratulation and of condolence? The Congregational Union has had a happy influence in these respects upon the churches in our own fellowship: but there is still wanting some plan by which they may obtain a more intimate knowledge from time to time of each other's condition.

The Apostle had breathed the desire of his heart for their social peace and edification.* The counsel which here follows, in verse seventeenth, was necessary to their union and spiritual prosperity: "Now I beseech you, brethren, mark them which cause divisions and offences contrary to the doctrines which ye have learned; and avoid them." Who are spoken of?—and what is the treatment of them enjoined? "*Divisions*" are factions or parties in the church. "*Offences*" are properly stumbling-blocks or causes of sin; and they mean especially here that description of offences which occasioned the alienation of mutual love, and the consequent breaking down of the church into factions and parties. By the expression—"*contrary to the doctrine which ye have learned,*" the Apostle shows to what descriptions of persons he refers; even such as introduced, or endeavoured to introduce, doctrines or practices at variance with what had been taught by the commissioned ambassadors of Christ. They had learned the Gospel, and the constitution, ordinances, and laws of the church from inspired authority. What they had before received had now been confirmed by himself in this Epistle. It was their duty to try whatever others taught by what had been attested to be from God by "signs and wonders, and mighty deeds."† And respecting THE GOSPEL, which it was of chief importance for them to hold fast in its simplicity and purity, he writes to the Galatians—"I marvel that ye are so soon removed from him that called you into

---

* Chap. xv. 5, 6.   † 1 John iv. 1—6.

the grace of Christ unto another gospel: which is not another; but there be some that trouble you, and would pervert the gospel of Christ. But though we, or an angel from heaven, preach any other gospel unto you than that which we have preached unto you, let him be accursed." "I certify you, brethren, that the gospel which was preached of me is not after man. For I neither received it of man, neither was I taught it, but by the revelation of Jesus Christ."*

From the character here given of the persons to whom Paul refers, they seem to have been the same as those respecting whom he uses language of similar severity in other Epistles—those usually denominated *Judaizing teachers.* It is of them he speaks in the passage just quoted from the Epistle to the Galatians; as appears from comparing it with what he says of their doctrine as a subversion of the Gospel.† It was a heresy by which the churches were early and extensively infested:—the same about which the deputation was sent up from Antioch to Jerusalem, and on which the Apostles then delivered their inspired decision.‡ Not only was the doctrine taught subversive of the grace of the Gospel, but the principles and character of those who taught it were, it would seem, in a high degree reprehensible for selfishness, worldliness and sensuality. So they are represented here in the eighteenth verse:—"For they that are such serve not our Lord Jesus Christ, but their own belly."

They were influenced by a regard, not to the honour of Christ and the advancement of the interests of his cause, whatever they might in words pretend, but to their own temporal emolument and worldly advantage, and sensual indulgence. This corresponds with the character given of the same description of persons elsewhere:—"For there are many unruly and vain talkers and deceivers, specially they of the circumcision: whose mouths must be stopped; who subvert whole houses, teaching things which they ought not for filthy lucre's sake."§

---

* Gal. i. 6—9. with 11, 12. † Gal. v. 1—8.
‡ Acts xv. It is referred to in many parts of the Apostolic Epistles.
§ Tit. i. 10, 11; see also Gal. vi. 12—15; Phil. iii. 2 with 18, 19.

We have indicated in the same verse, the way in which they accomplished their selfish ends;—"*and by good words and fair speeches deceive the hearts of the simple.*" These expressions comprehend plausible reasonings, of which the sophistry may not at once be apparent; winning and insinuating modes of address; and fair but deceitful promises and assurances. The doctrines which they taught were very palatable to the pride and self-righteousness of the human heart, as well as to the love of the world and of sin; and their whole manner of recommending them was in consistency both with the nature of the doctrines themselves and with the principles by which they were influenced in teaching them. By such means, "they deceived the hearts of the *simple.*" The word means free from evil.* It is applied to *Christ* in its full amount of import—" For such an high priest became us, who is holy, *harmless,* undefiled, and separate from sinners."† But, while indicating freedom from evil generally, it means also freedom from *malice*—simple, artless, undesigning. This seems its import here. Such persons are usually unsuspicious:—guileless themselves, they are incredulous of evil principle in others; they are thus in danger of being easily imposed upon by the artful and disingenuous.‡

Those who "caused divisions" professed great interest in the welfare of such as they addressed, artfully insinuating that Paul was influenced by the desire to "make a gain of them," while this was in reality their own motive. This is one of the most successful ways of imposing on the " simple "—pretending great abhorrence of the very principles by which they who make the pretensions are themselves actuated. " The simple," says Solomon, "believeth every word." These artful men, therefore, discovered such, wherever they were to be found, in the churches; and by the means already de-

---

* ἀκάκος.   † Heb. vii. 26.
‡ The noun in this composite word signifies in Greek sometimes *wickedness* generally, and sometimes *maliciousness;* and the compound word itself has corresponding significations. See the LXX.—Job viii. 20; and Prov. i. 4.

scribed, succeeded in "drawing away disciples after them"—traducing the Apostle, and exalting themselves: "For such are false apostles, deceitful workers, transforming themselves into the apostles of Christ. And no marvel; for Satan himself is transformed into an angel of light. Therefore it is no great thing if his ministers also be transformed as the ministers of righteousness; whose end shall be according to their works."* Such testimonies may seem severe. But they are, we should recollect, the testimonies of the Spirit of God; and, with regard to Paul, his whole character, as indicated by his writings, should satisfy us, that they were "more in sorrow than in anger." He was indignant, indeed; but it was the indignation of grief that his usefulness as a servant of God should be impaired, and thus the glory of Christ and the good of souls prevented.

How were they to treat such men—artful perverters of the truth, and subverters of the minds of those who believed it? They are enjoined to "*mark*" and "*avoid* them." They were by no means to tolerate them; but to notice, that they might shun them. This cannot of course signify that they should abstain from other intercourse, and yet admit them to the fellowship of the church; but to refuse both the one and the other. "But now I have written unto you not to keep company, if any man that is called a brother be a fornicator, or covetous, or an idolater, or a railer, or a drunkard, or an extortioner; with such an one no not to eat." "Put away from among yourselves that wicked person." "A man that is an heretic, after the first and second admonition reject; knowing that he that is such is subverted, and sinneth, being condemned of himself." "A little leaven leaveneth the whole lump. I have confidence in you through the Lord, that ye will be none otherwise minded: but he that troubleth you shall bear his judgment, whosoever he be. And I, brethren, if I yet preach circumcision, why do I yet suffer persecution? then is the offence of the cross ceased. I would they were even cut off which trouble you."†

* 2 Cor. xi. 13—15.
† 1 Cor. v. 11 with ver. 13; Titus iii. 10, 11; Gal. v. 9—12.

And what was thus "written aforetime" was written "for our learning." We must act upon the same principles. We must not "bear them who are evil." And those are to be held by us among the evil who are not to be borne—tolerated, that is, and treated with forbearance,—who endeavour to introduce doctrines that are subversive of the Gospel, and seek to "turn away the disciples from the faith." There is a firm adherence to principle, for which the church of Ephesus, in its first which was its best state, is most particularly commended—"I know thy works, and thy labour, and thy patience, and how thou canst not bear them which are evil: and thou hast tried them which say they are apostles, and are not, and hast found them liars."* With some we may expose ourselves to the imputation of bigotry and narrow-mindedness, because we do not admit of the utmost latitude of free-thinking amongst us:—but "the truth as it is in Jesus" is the bond of our spiritual union. From this there must be no departure tolerated; such departure not only being destructive of the soul of the individual, but subversive of the very foundation on which the church is built, and dissolving the cement that holds it together.

The Apostle was the more solicitous on this head, because the church at Rome stood high in their character for faith and obedience; and he was earnestly desirous for their own sakes, and for the sake of the purity of the truth, the glory of Christ, and the general prosperity of His cause in the world, that they should keep up their character—verse 19. "For your obedience is come abroad unto all men.† I am glad therefore on your behalf: but yet I would have you wise unto that which is good, and simple concerning evil." The obedience, we thus learn, by which they were so eminently distinguished, was the obedience of faith,—springing from the faith of the gospel as its principle. Their belief of Christ's doctrine was manifested in their subjection to Christ's authority.

The Apostle Paul was distinguished by the warm interest

* Rev. ii. 2. † Comp. chap. i. 8.

he took in the concerns of "all the churches." This "came upon him daily." It was the joy of his heart to see or to hear of their prosperity; and it was his acutest sorrow to receive tidings of their discords or declensions. No one can read his Epistles without perceiving and feeling this to be a predominant part of his character. And it is a spirit in which we should all resemble him. It was not *official;* it was not peculiar to him as an Apostle. The cause of the churches is the cause of God and of truth; the cause of Christ and of human salvation. To be unconcerned about their state is a sad symptom of apathy about divine things in general. It should be *our* delight to hear of any of them being in a spiritually thriving condition, and our grief to hear of the contrary; and such feelings should excite us to do all that lies in our power to correct what is evil, to supply what is deficient, and to stimulate and promote what is right and good. Paul was "glad on their behalf." His joy for them was sincere and fervent; and led him, we may be sure, to "the throne of grace" in thanksgiving and praise. But still he admonishes and cautions them. They were not perfect; and they were not out of danger:—"But yet I would have you wise unto that which is good, and simple concerning evil." He was desirous that they might, instead of allowing their views and their character to become deteriorated by the intermixture of error and of sin, be more and more qualified to resist evil—to detect and to withstand the subtleties of error and of temptation. To be "*wise unto that which is good,*" is to have both a discerning mind and a right disposition of heart towards it—towards what is true in doctrine and right in practice. It is to be able to distinguish the good from the evil; to winnow the chaff from the wheat; and then to act in regard to the good as true wisdom dictates—holding it fast—the truth in faith —the right in conduct. Nothing is more desirable than the clear and discriminating discernment of truth and of duty; and nothing could be more contrary to wisdom than, when they are discerned, to disbelieve the one or disobey the other. Wisdom requires that truth be received, according to the evidence by which it is accompanied; and that duty be done in everything in which the will of God is ascertained. Neither truth nor duty are *wisely* treated otherwise. It is folly to disregard or to trifle with either the one or the other. To be "wise unto that which is good," implies also, being prudent, discreet, cautious, and steady; not easily moved away from one sentiment to another—not light and volatile, and "carried about with every wind of doctrine by the sleight of men, and cunning craftiness, whereby they lie in wait to deceive;" for these are attributes not of wisdom but of weakness and folly. Wisdom having ascertained truth, grasps it and retains it;—having determined duty, perseveres in doing it. It "buys the truth, and sells it not." Having found "the pearl of great price," it keeps it with a care proportioned to its high estimation of its value; and, having ascertained the path of duty, it is not *every* consideration—nay there is not *any* consideration that will tempt it to quit that path.

To be "*simple concerning evil*" may be illustrated by the primitive state of man, and his state after he sinned.* Our first parents before their fall, were, in the full amount of the expression, "simple concerning evil." Well had it been for them had they retained this simplicity. But the tempter would have them know the evil as well as the good. He succeeded in inspiring the desire; and the consequence was the introduction of "death and all our woe."—The word here rendered "*simple*" is not the same as in verse eighteenth. The word means literally *free from mixture*,†—the mixture, that is, of deceit and guile—which is in effect much the same as the former term. To be "simple concerning evil," is to have a happy ignorance of it in its principles and practices, and to have no desire of acquaintance with it or experience of it; not disposed to receive or even to tamper with it. This is a very different thing from the simplicity frequently mentioned and deprecated by Solomon. He admonishes those who are the victims of that simplicity to reflection and to wisdom—

* See Gen. iii. 5. † ἀκεραίους.

"How long, ye simple ones, will ye love simplicity? and the scorners delight in their scorning, and fools hate knowledge? Turn ye at my reproof."* "The prudent man foreseeth the evil, and hideth himself: but the simple pass on, and are punished." *That* simplicity is thoughtless folly: the simplicity before us is true wisdom. It is sincerity of heart towards God—a single desire to know and to do His will, and to have no connexion with evil—"no fellowship with the unfruitful works of darkness."†

There are some things which it is better not to know than to know by experience. It is better to be ignorant of the tendencies of a deadly poison, than to ascertain them by their deadly effects in our own persons. And what poison is to the body, error and sin are to the soul. The only use of knowing them is that we may shun them, and escape their mischievous and destructive consequences. There is a high-minded self-will that cannot brook restraint, that will not be withheld from trying for itself; that glories in its affected freedom; that loves the singularity of holding error, or of trying what can be said in its behalf,—making light of it; and that determines, with contumacious resistance of all authority and of all persuasion, to explore the secrets of evil, and taste for itself the tempting sweets of the cup of sin. But this is a fearfully perilous state of mind;—a state of mind against which I would affectionately warn my young hearers, who are in danger of being fascinated and led away by it—"Be ye wise unto that which is good, and simple concerning evil."

Verse 20. "And the God of peace shall bruise Satan under your feet shortly. The grace of our Lord Jesus Christ be with you. Amen."‡—He had been speaking of the false teachers. They were the ministers of Satan:—and the influence of his emissaries, as a part of the means by which he exerts his own power, may be included in the promise or assurance thus given.—"*Satan*" means an adver-

---
* Prov. i. 22, 23.
† We have the opposite of the character before us in Jer. iv. 22.
‡ The connexion here is similar to that in 2 Cor. xi. 13—15.

sary; and here, without question, it means the first and chief adversary of God and men; of whom and of whose power we read so much in the word of God. We are charged to *resist* him as an adversary.* We must resist both his direct temptations, and those which he presents by his emissaries, false teachers and wicked men. Our resistance is not hopeless—"*The God of peace shall bruise Satan under your feet shortly.*" In the character of the God of peace, Jehovah made his first appearance and his first promise to fallen man. It was a promise of destruction to his wicked and treacherous tempter.† *This* was fulfilled by the Son of God in the fulness of time, when he came to "destroy the works of the devil." He obtained the victory:—" Now is the judgment of this world: now shall the prince of this world be cast out. And I, if I be lifted up from the earth, will draw all men unto me." "Having spoiled principalities and powers, he made a show of them openly, triumphing over them in it."‡ Thus *Christ* overcame. The power of "the prince of this world" is broken, and doomed to final extinction. But he is still allowed to act as a tempter and an adversary to the church—"going about seeking whom he may devour." But *we* too shall overcome. We shall be "more than conquerors." He is already under Christ's feet; and in due time he shall be under ours. God, in the character of the "God of peace," who "brought again from the dead the great Shepherd of the sheep, through the blood of the everlasting covenant," will give us full and final triumph over this enemy of our soul's salvation. There seems an allusion in the words—"*shall bruise Satan*," to the terms of the first promise:—and in the phrase, "*under our feet*," to the ancient practice of conquerors putting their feet upon the necks of their vanquished foes.§—"*God*" will do this. We have no strength of our own in which to meet and to contend with our archadversary. But God, by communicated grace, will enable us successfully to withstand both his open assaults and his

---

* James iv. 7; 1 Peter v. 8, 9.   † Gen. iii. 15.
‡ John xii. 31, 32; Col. ii. 15.   § See Josh. x. 24.

secret wiles; so that we shall be brought safely and victoriously through, and introduced to that holy and happy place, into which no tempter, no adversary, no sin, no death, shall ever find admission. And, finally, the conquest shall be rendered complete, when "Death, the last enemy, shall be destroyed." "He who has the power of death, that is the devil," shall then be utterly discomfited; all the redeemed of the Lord being perfectly and for ever rescued from every remaining vestige of his power.

In order to their present safety and their future triumph, he adds—anticipating the usual close of his Epistles—" The grace of our Lord Jesus Christ be with you!" *"His grace"* is, in general, *his favour* in all its blessed fruits; the communications of his Spirit from the fulness which it hath pleased the Father should dwell in him; grace according to their day; "grace to help in time of need;" the grace of Him who hath said, "My grace is sufficient for thee; for my strength is made perfect in weakness."

Such passages have sometimes in our own days been urged against what has been stigmatized as the factious spirit of *dissent;* and weak people have been greatly alarmed in some instances by such application, and prevented from following out the dictates of conscience in regard to the will of God. I say *weak* people; for the difference between the two cases is so apparent that it can affect only such. The "doctrine which they had learned" is the doctrine of the Apostles. Now, suppose that either in what *they* taught respecting the truth of God, or the constitution of his kingdom, there have been grievous departures from them; in that case, what is duty? Does not the very principle of the passage require dissent by apostolic authority? inasmuch as, in such case, dissent from existing establishments is, or may at least be, return to the Apostles,—a restored conformity to the doctrine which they taught. There is no necessity that the spirit of dissent be the spirit of faction and division: it may be the spirit of simple conscientious adherence to the authority of Christ and his Apostles. And they who are ever characterizing dissenters as factious and schismatical, ought to recollect that they are themselves dissenters. They are separatists from what was formerly the established and dominant faith. What was the entire reformation, but dissent? and assuredly there is the same liberty, and may be the same conscientiousness in dissent *now* as in dissent *then*. This liberty exists, and this conscientiousness is a duty in *all* bodies. And it may be laid down as a principle, that whenever any difference respecting the mind of Christ comes to be viewed as of such importance that the conscience cannot have rest in conformity—*separation* is better than *schism*, that is, a division *from* the church than a division *in* it. But in all cases, let the spirit of conscientiousness be the spirit of peace and love.

Let the principle of our whole conduct in the church be, not a selfish regard to our own enjoyment or aggrandizement, but a pure and disinterested solicitude for the glory of Christ. Let our sole inquiry at all times be, not what will benefit ourselves, but what will please and honour Him. If we act on this principle, we shall seldom be at a loss for our course.*

Let us be more solicitous about deliverance from *sin* than about deliverance from suffering. While we seek to be "wise unto that which is good, and simple concerning evil," and "to resist the devil, that he may flee from us," let it be the joy of our hearts that all his temptations shall come to an end. It is not as an inflictor of evil—an executioner of a sentence of suffering, that we should chiefly fear his power and deprecate subjection to it; but as a tempter to sin. The chief recommendation of heaven to us should be, that it is a world WITHOUT SIN—a paradise of purity into which no tempter shall ever find an entrance, to effect an apostasy among its blessed inhabitants. He shall be shut up in his prison, not for a thousand years merely, but for eternity! Having these hopes, let us "purify ourselves even as Christ is pure"—let us "cleanse ourselves from all filthiness of the flesh and spirit, perfecting holiness in the fear of God."†

* See Phil. iii. 15, 16.   † 2 Cor. vii. 1.

LECTURE LXXI.

ROMANS XVI. 21—27.

"Timotheus my work-fellow, and Lucius, and Jason, and Sosipater, my kinsmen, salute you. I Tertius, who wrote this epistle, salute you in the Lord. Gaius mine host, and of the whole church, saluteth you. Erastus, the chamberlain of the city, saluteth you, and Quartus a brother. The grace of our Lord Jesus Christ be with you all. Amen. Now to him that is of power to stablish you according to my gospel, and the preaching of Jesus Christ, (according to the revelation of the mystery, which was kept secret since the world began, but now is made manifest, and by the scriptures of the prophets, according to the commandment of the everlasting God, made known to all nations for the obedience of faith;) to God only wise, be glory through Jesus Christ for ever. Amen."

THESE verses may be regarded as a kind of postscript to the Epistle, which appeared to close in the customary style at the twentieth verse. Even of these verses there is a portion, respecting the collocation of which in the Epistle eminent critics have conceived a misarrangement has crept in. On the authority of various ancient versions and manuscripts their more proper place has been thought to be the close of the fourteenth chapter. I refer to verses twenty-fifth to the twenty-seventh. It is not a matter of great moment in which connexion the words are inserted. It is their *place* only, not their *genuineness* that is questioned.* The doxology itself is quite in Paul's style; and the instruction to be derived from it is as profitable in this connexion, as a close

* The genuineness also of the doxology has been questioned, but on insufficient grounds. Its genuineness Alford justly regards as "*placed beyond all reasonable doubt.*"—ED.

to the whole Epistle, as in the other, where it would be the close only of one particular branch of it.

He first of all subjoins some additional salutations; or rather having sent his own salutations to various individuals, he fulfils the request of those who were with him by expressing *their* good wishes as well as his own for the church —verse 21. " Timotheus my work-fellow, and Lucius, and Jason, and Sosipater, my kinsmen, salute you." Timotheus is first introduced to our notice in the history as "a certain disciple" whom Paul met with on his visit to Derbe and Lystra.* From that time he became one of the most constant attendants on the Apostle, and one of the most assiduous and highly-esteemed of his " fellow-workmen," as he here denominates him. When he was not *with* Paul, he was left by him at different stations, to follow up the work he had begun, and superintend in those places the interests of the Gospel and of the churches:—and the two Epistles to Timothy are addressed to him while engaged at Ephesus in the duties of such superintendence. He was with the Apostle at Corinth when this letter to Rome was despatched.

Jason and Sosipater are also spoken of in the history; the former in the account given of the tumults at Thessalonica,† from which it appears that he had come prominently and intrepidly forward in the face of danger.‡ The latter is simply mentioned.§ The very place to which he belonged —*Berea*, gives us a favourable impression of his character, from the account we have of the reception there given to the Gospel.‖

Lucius was either Lucius of Cyrene, of whom mention is made in the opening of the thirteenth chapter of the Acts, or another of the same name who is not mentioned elsewhere. Some suppose Luke to be meant,—a Roman termination being given to his name.¶ The sole reason for this is

---

* Acts xvi. 1—3.   † Acts xvii.   ‡ Verses 5—9.
§ Acts xx. 4. [The identity of the two persons is strongly questioned by Alford; but he does not give any reason, unless it be the mention of the name of the father of Sopater.—ED.]
‖ Acts xvii. 11, 12.   ¶ Would it not be *Lucanus* in that case?—ED.

our knowing that Luke *was* a companion of Paul's journeyings and labours, as apparent from other Epistles, and from the style of some parts of the Acts.* It is necessarily but conjecture, and not worth more than a simple mention.

Verse 22. " I Tertius, who wrote this epistle, salute you in the Lord." Tertius is conjectured to have been the same as Silas—the former being as nearly as possible a translation of the latter name into Latin.† This too is of course uncertain; and founded in part on the fact of Silas also being Paul's companion in travel.

Whosoever he was, he acted as Paul's *amanuensis;* the Apostle writing in Greek, and finding the formation of the letters not familiar to his hand, or being subject to some infirmity in writing. It seems to have been his practice to use an amanuensis; and to add with his own hand his salutation, or, as we should express it, his signature. ‡ And when he acted otherwise, and wrote the entire Epistle himself, he speaks of it as an extraordinary thing—" Ye see how large a letter I have written unto you with mine own hand."§

Tertius appears to have availed himself of a pause in the Apostle's dictation, to insert his own affectionate salutation. ‖ He salutes them "*in the Lord;*" that is, as his brethren in Christ; united as members of God's spiritual family in Him.

Paul's using an amanuensis is a fact that, like some others, shows most clearly the principle that God does not needlessly employ miracle. He could have enabled his servant to write a known language with ease and rapidity, as well as to speak with fluency and correctness such as were *unknown*. But no miraculous aid, it appears, is imparted to supply this

---

* Acts xvi. 10—12.

† So F. Burmann and Lightfoot; from the mere resemblance of the consonants in the Hebrew word שלש, *three*, and the consonants in the name Silas. Silas, however, is much more likely another form of *Silvanus*. See Kitto's Bib. Cycl.—ED.

‡ 2 Thess. iii. 17.

§ Gal. vi. 11. [The Greek, however, is πηλίκοις γράμμασιν, lit. *with what sort of letters;* and many regard it as an apology for the bad writing with which he probably closed the letter.—ED.]

‖ "Tholuck notices this irregularity as a corroboration of the genuineness of the chapter."—ED.

deficiency:—and the case forms rather a curious contrast to that of certain modern pretenders, who tell us of their *writing* in unknown languages by a supernatural impulse carrying their hand along, independently of any volition or effort of theirs, with the rapidity of lightning!* This outstrips the Apostle quite. Yet I feel as if I had degraded him and his inspiration and supernatural gifts by so much as mentioning the two cases together. To dwell upon it would be insufferable.

If, as may be supposed, Tertius added his own name at what he thought the end, that Paul might subjoin the salutation,—it appears that other names suggested themselves to the Apostle's mind—verse 23. " Gaius mine host, and of the whole church, saluteth you. Erastus, the chamberlain of the city, saluteth you, and Quartus a brother."—There are two persons of the name of Gaius; one mentioned Acts xix. 29, and xx. 4; the other, 1 Cor. i. 14. As the Epistle to the Romans was written from Corinth, the latter appears to be the benevolent and hospitable individual here named. He was probably—we may say certainly—a man of some worldly substance; and he showed that he knew the proper use of it. He kept, in a manner, an open house, for all who at any time stood in need of his hospitable entertainment. This was the way in which his kindly and generous disposition discovered itself.

Let not the example be passed by without due notice, and, in all cases in which there is ability and opportunity, imitation. The conduct of Gaius or Caius is an exemplification of a principle.† We should beware of allowing a penurious disposition to shut our door against brethren, and especially strangers, of which last Paul says—" Be not forgetful to entertain strangers; for thereby some have entertained angels unawares."‡ And, although there is a great diversity in the peculiar situations of individuals and families, rendering the duty in question much less convenient to some than to others, yet we should take care that we do not avail our-

---

* Allusion manifestly to some of the followers of Irving.—ED.
† Chap. xii. 13; 1 Pet. iv. 9.   ‡ Heb. xiii. 2.

selves too far of the excuse of inconvenience—to which we ought on all occasions, when it is really required, cheerfully to put ourselves.

From the character and the name, this is in all probability the same Gaius to whom John addresses his third Epistle. It is a lovely pattern as there described for imitation:— "The elder unto the well-beloved Gaius, whom I love in the truth. Beloved, I wish above all things that thou mayest prosper and be in health, even as thy soul prospereth. For I rejoiced greatly when the brethren came and testified of the truth that is in thee, even as thou walkest in the truth. I have no greater joy than to hear that my children walk in truth. Beloved, thou doest faithfully whatsoever thou doest to the brethren, and to strangers; which have borne witness of thy charity before the church; whom if thou bring forward on their journey after a godly sort, thou shalt do well: because that for his name's sake they went forth, taking nothing of the Gentiles. We therefore ought to receive such, that we might be fellow-helpers to the truth."*

"Erastus, the chamberlain of the city, saluteth you, and Quartus a brother." There is an Erastus of whom we read in Acts xix. 22, 2 Tim. iv. 20. From his abiding at Corinth, we might be led to consider him as the person here mentioned as "*chamberlain*"—steward or treasurer of the city. There is, however, an obvious difficulty in this supposition. How could he accompany Paul, and minister to him and with him, and yet hold this public office in the city of Corinth? To remove the difficulty, some imagine him to have retained the title after he had retired from it; which, as you are aware, is not an unusual practice with ourselves. Others conceive that he might accompany Paul only for a time, and then, as the passage quoted expresses it, "*abide in Corinth.*" The only other supposition is, that they were two different persons of the same name. The point is not worth further discussion. We should end about where we began respecting it, and be little the wiser, could we settle

* 3 John 1—8.

it. From the verse before us, we learn, as we do also from various other parts of the New Testament, that there were persons of note and distinction, as well as those of inferior condition, who embraced the profession of the Gospel. The general fact indeed was as stated by the Apostle when he says, "Not many wise after the flesh, not many mighty, not many noble, are called."* God "chose the poor of this world, rich in faith, and heirs of the kingdom which he hath promised to them that love him." But there were exceptions; and, according to one or two passages, in some places not a few. If, when a Christian, he retained the office, the fact speaks highly in favour of the reputation in which he was held as a citizen, and of the exemplary and useful manner in which he discharged his official functions. The disciples of Jesus are still citizens and subjects of civil government, and members of society. It is their duty to do what lies in their power for the benefit of the community to which they belong: and if on any occasion, from confidence in their ability and integrity, their fellow-citizens call them to the occupation of any situation of power and authority and influence—if it be one of which the functions do not interfere with their Christian principles by requiring anything inconsistent with them,—it may not only be lawful, it may even become an imperative duty for them to accept the nomination. Whatever station we are called in providence to fill, let us see to it that our principles be not *hid;* that we never compromise them, or act the part of a trimming worldly policy. In every situation—and the more public and conspicuous so much the more imperative is the duty—"let our light so shine before men, that they may see our good works, and glorify our Father which is in heaven." There *is* danger, when Christians are placed in situations of worldly honour and influence, of their getting secularized, and amalgamating in too great a degree with the customs and manners of the men of the world with whom they associate and act. Sad is it when this is the case; for

* 1 Cor. i. 26.

it is alike injurious to the spiritual interests of the individual, and hurtful to his profession and to the cause of Christ. O for grace, according to our situation, and according to our day—that God in all things may be glorified!

Having repeated his benediction, the Apostle closes with ascriptions of glory to God:—"Now to him that is of power to stablish you according to my gospel, and the preaching of Jesus Christ, (according to the revelation of the mystery, which was kept secret since the world began, but now is made manifest, and by the scriptures of the prophets, according to the commandment of the everlasting God, made known to all nations for the obedience of faith;) to God only wise, be glory through Jesus Christ for ever. Amen."

This is more than a simple doxology. It brings before our minds views of God in Christ, which are in the highest degree interesting and encouraging.—"*To Him who is of power to stablish you.*" God is omnipotent. His power has been put forth and continues to be displayed in the natural world, in the creation and preservation and government of the universe. His power is pledged by promise in behalf of His people. This is one of the spheres of its operation—the keeping of his saints through faith unto salvation.* By this power—by the living energy of his Holy Spirit, He strengthens them against temptation and all their spiritual enemies; confirming them in the faith, love, hope, and obedience of the truth; sustaining them under all trials, fitting them for all duties, animating them with fortitude and vigour to resist the wicked one.† Power would be nothing without the disposition to use it in our behalf. Nothing can be more tantalizing than, when our hearts are set on any object, to be told of some one that he *can* do it for us *if he will*. Alas! what is the power without the will. In the passage before us, the will is assumed: or rather, perhaps, we may consider it as comprehended in the next clause—"*According to my gospel*"—that is, according to the good tidings with

---

* 1 Pet. i. 6.
† Comp. Isa. xl. 28—31; Psalm cxlvi. 5, 6; 1 Pet. v. 10, &c.

which, as an ambassador, he was intrusted:—"*and the preaching of Jesus Christ.*" The two are one.* Or the two expressions may mean, the glad tidings committed to him, and the preaching of Jesus Christ the great and glorious subject of it.†

To stablish them "according to this gospel," is, either to stablish them agreeably to the provisions and engagements of its "exceeding great and precious promises;" or to stablish them in a profession and character bearing conformity to it;—to prevent, on the one hand, their being "removed from the grace of Christ unto another gospel;" and, on the other, their being seduced from its holy influence to the practice of sin. These are the two leading articles, on the inseparable union of which Paul is ever insisting. No one is stablished by the power of God according to the Gospel, who is not alike stable in the belief, profession, and practice which the divine word enjoins. He departs from the faith who departs from the practice.

The "preaching of Jesus Christ" was "*in conformity to the revelation of the mystery, which was kept secret since the world began.*" That mystery had been fully and clearly revealed to Paul; and his official ministry in preaching was in perfect agreement with divine discoveries. The mystery in the present instance is the mystery of *the Gospel*—the great "mystery of godliness." A *mystery* in New Testament language means generally something that had been kept secret and is now revealed,—and which could only be made known by the Being who had kept it secret. The mystery of the Gospel had been "*kept secret since the world began,*" —for to the great bulk of mankind it had not been revealed *at all*, and to those few who were favoured with it, it was discovered very imperfectly and darkly—being all wrapped up in symbol and type, and requiring to be searched out as secrets are.‡

The sentence, in its different clauses, has been variously arranged: some translating—" but now and by the prophetic

---

* Heb. ii. 3, 4. † Gal. i. 11, 12, with 16; 1 Cor. ii. 2.
‡ 1 Cor. ii. 7, 9—12; Eph. i. 9, 10; iii. 2—9.

writings made manifest:" but the arrangement in the authorised version is more natural.

1. The Gospel mystery was made manifest in order to its being "*made known to all nations.*" Such was the extent of the apostolic commission.*

2. The end of its being made known was of course "*for the obedience of faith;*" in order, that is, to its being believed and obeyed in its divine design and influence,—producing obedience by the faith of it. A doctrine is obeyed when it is received into the mind and heart as the object of faith, and allowed to operate there according to its true nature, and to bring forth corresponding fruits in the life. The same phraseology we had before us in the beginning of the Epistle.†

3. The Jews had the prophetic writings: yet they continued in very gross and criminal ignorance for many ages as to the Messiah's character and kingdom and work. But now we have the commentary on the prophecies. The minds of the Apostles were fully enlightened as to their true meaning—the dark veil entirely taken away from their minds.‡ This, and the subsequent illumination of the Holy Spirit, enabled them to make known the Gospel "*by the writings of the prophets.*" To these accordingly they make frequent reference—always to Jews, and sometimes also to Gentiles. §

4. This gospel was to be published *with authority:* "according to *the commandment of the everlasting God*, made known to all nations for the obedience of faith."|| The commission given by Jesus Christ was sanctioned and ratified by the Father that sent him. Two things then are to be noticed here. First, that the proclamation of the Gospel is the fulfilment of an eternal divine purpose:—this seems implied in the designation—"*the everlasting God.*" He is from eternity the same—in nature, purpose and design; but he "keeps the times and the seasons in his own power." Secondly, that the Gospel comes with the full authority of God. It is

---

* Mark xvi. 15; Luke xxiv. 46, 47.
† Chap. i. 5. ‡ Luke xxiv. 44—48; and verses 25—27.
§ 1 Cor. xv. 1—4; Acts x. 43, &c. || Gal. i. 1; Luke xxiv. 49.

His word—declaring the method of His infinite wisdom for the extension of His mercy to the guilty. It has in it the same authority to man as a fallen and guilty creature, as His law had to man originally. The latter was the authoritative rule of life; the former is the authoritative rule of his recovery from his fallen state. The Gospel is accordingly called *a law*—the "law of faith"—the "law of liberty." It has the force and sanction of a law, being a divine institute for a special end. It is the " law of faith," as opposed to the law of works; being the law or institute of God, according to which sinners are to be justified and accepted, not on the ground of works of their own, but through faith in the mediatorial work of another:—and it is the "law of liberty," being the divinely appointed and authoritative way of giving the guilty their emancipation from the condemnation and from the power of sin, from the curse of the law which they had broken, and from the fears of death and hell. The rejection of this Gospel is an act of disobedience and of obstinate and unthankful rebellion.*

The next designation is also in this connexion peculiarly appropriate—" *To the only wise God.*" He alone is wise *in himself*—independently, essentially, infinitely; the concentration of all possible knowledge—the fountain of all the intelligence in the universe. This attribute of God is especially apparent in the Gospel. In it is the grand display of His wisdom; a wisdom that pursues the best ends by the best means—overcoming difficulties that seemed insurmountable, and reconciling contradictions that appeared incapable of reconciliation—causing " mercy and truth to meet together," and uniting the claims of justice and purity with the pleadings of love and grace. This showed a wisdom infinitely transcending that of man—accomplishing effects by means which men deemed " foolishness " the most worthy of himself and the most important to His creatures:—" To the intent that now, unto the principalities and powers in heavenly places, might be known by the church the manifold wisdom

---

* John iii. 18, 19.

of God."* These celestial intelligences know much of the varied manifestations of the divine wisdom:—but here, they not only see a *new variety* of its displays, but one incomparably more attractive and wonderful than all the rest. "These things the angels desire to look into." The scheme is fully developed in this very Epistle. It is truly divine; bearing the impress of Godhead upon it as distinctly as any one of the divine doings. God's skill and wisdom are conspicuous in all creation. They are not less conspicuous— they are even infinitely more so—in redemption. If we desire to have the most exalted views and the deepest and most reverential impressions of the "manifold wisdom of God," we must take the cross, and the work which the divine Redeemer finished there as our *study*—dwelling upon it in all its scriptural lights, and eliciting all its wonders. This will fill us with equal admiration and delight; fear, and love, and joy, and praise. We will then join the Apostle in saying from our inmost souls—"To God only wise, *be glory through Jesus Christ for ever. Amen.*"

Jesus Christ, while as God's "unspeakable gift" he is the *subject* of thanksgiving,—is, at the same time, the only *medium* of all acceptance, and worship, and praise. Through HIM Paul ever offers his praises to God; and teaches us to do the same. He expresses, with a heart overflowing with adoring gratitude, his desire that the manifestation of the divine perfections in the work of salvation might be seen by all flesh together, and might draw from every kindred and tongue and people and nation the hymn of fervent united homage;—that He might receive from this apostate world the glory due to his name for this manifestation of his wisdom and grace;—that praise might ascend to Him on this account to the end of time, and through eternity—beginning below and continuing above;—that men and angels might unite in the anthem of joyful adoration for ever and ever! His own soul gives glory to the God of salvation *for* and *through* Jesus Christ;—and the desires of his soul would only be

---

* Eph. iii. 10; see also 1 Cor. i. 22—24; ii. 6, 7.

satisfied when the vision of John should be realized—" And I beheld, and I heard the voice of many angels round about the throne, and the living creatures,* and the elders: and the number of them was ten thousand times ten thousand, and thousands of thousands; saying with a loud voice, Worthy is the Lamb that was slain to receive power, and riches, and wisdom, and strength, and honour, and glory, and blessing. And every creature which is in heaven, and on the earth, and under the earth, and such as are in the sea, and all that are in them, heard I saying, Blessing, and honour, and glory, and power, be unto him that sitteth upon the throne, and unto the Lamb for ever and ever."†

The Gospel is the manifestation to sinners of the love and mercy of God, in unison with His purity and righteousness. By the faith of it sinners find mercy in consistency with the claims of eternal justice. To all my hearers who have thus believed and found mercy—the *power* and the *wisdom* of the God of mercy, with whom through Jesus Christ they walk in reconciliation and peace, become the ground of confidence for the final attainment of all that is included in their salvation. This power must uphold them, this wisdom must guide them, if ever they are to reach the full enjoyment of eternal life. Let our trust, then, my brethren, be in " Him who is of power to stablish us," and who is " God only wise." Let our humble but confiding language be—" Surely in the Lord have I righteousness and strength;"—" Thou shalt guide me with thy counsel, and afterward receive me to glory." We have no power and no wisdom of our own; but in the God of our salvation we have an infinite supply; and, according to the Gospel and the preaching of Jesus Christ, the supply is free—" Ask, and ye shall receive, that your joy may be full." The power and the wisdom of God are pledged in promise to work out effectually the purposes of His love: but this is not to be done independently of the use, and the diligent use too, of means on our part. We are to " work out our own salvation with fear and trembling."‡

* ζῶα.—Ed.   † Rev. v. 11—13.   ‡ Phil. ii. 12, 13.

LECTURE LXXI.

Well may *we*, my brethren, give glory to God—"God only wise," and mighty, and merciful, for the discoveries and promises of the Gospel. The glory is all His own. It was the suggestion of His own love, the device of His own wisdom, the work of His own power. O! for what shall we give glory to God, if not for this! Our obligations are beyond being estimated. And while we give Him glory for His whole word, in which the mystery of His wisdom and grace is unfolded, shall we not, in closing our review of *this Epistle*, give glory to God for it. Paul himself says of the churches of Judea when they heard of his conversion—"They glorified God in me." We join with them in their thanksgiving. It has not, I trust, been without pleasure and profit that we have gone through this most important and interesting portion of the word of God; so full of clear and simple statements of Gospel truth; of reasonings so divinely plain and conclusive, although containing, at the same time, some of those "deep things of God" "which they that are unlearned and unstable wrest, as they do also the other scriptures, unto their own destruction;" and in connexion with these, of preceptive instructions and admonitions so admirably deduced from the discoveries of truth, and enforced by the motives which the truth contains; and still more, of exceeding great and precious promises, and prophetic intimations that animate the soul with the delight of anticipation and hope. We give glory to God for the conversion of Saul of Tarsus;—and, among other reasons, for those parts of the canon of inspired scripture, of which the Spirit of God was pleased to make him the medium of communication. These Epistles he wrote, as Peter expresses it, "according to the wisdom given unto him;" and that wisdom was from the "God only wise," to whom he here gives the glory. Let us see to it that of his writings, and of all the Scriptures, we make such a use as will promote our growth in grace and "make us meet to be partakers of the inheritance of the saints in light;" so that we may at last give in our account of this invaluable privilege with joy and not with grief!

My careless fellow-sinners, let me remind you that the

Gospel comes to you with authority. Every thing *must* that comes from God. It is not a scheme which you may or may not accept according to your own pleasure; which you are at liberty to receive or to refuse without any result as to your state and prospects. It comes to you "BY THE COMMANDMENT OF THE EVERLASTING GOD." If you trifle with it, it is at your peril:—you place your souls in jeopardy. If you persist in refusing it, you fix upon your souls all the accumulated guilt of a violated law, and add to that guilt the still deeper of rejected mercy; and you must thus perish with a double destruction. But the God of power and wisdom and purity and justice, is also "THE GOD OF ALL GRACE." He still waits to be gracious. It is only indeed in one way. He cannot be gracious to sinners otherwise than through the merits of his Son; because this is the only way that is honourable to himself. But in Christ Jesus, he stands ready to receive you; ready to pardon, to bless, and to save, the very chief of sinners:—"God was in Christ, reconciling the world unto himself, not imputing their trespasses unto them; and hath committed unto us the word of reconciliation. Now then we are ambassadors for Christ, as though God did beseech you by us: we pray you in Christ's stead, be ye reconciled to God. For he hath made him to be sin for us, who knew no sin; that we might be made the righteousness of God in him."*

* 2 Cor. v. 19—21.

www.ingramcontent.com/pod-product-compliance
Lightning Source LLC
Chambersburg PA
CBHW020309240426
43673CB00039B/755